Friday Night Lights

A Prayer for the City

A Prayer for the City

Buzz Bissinger

Photographs by Robert Clark

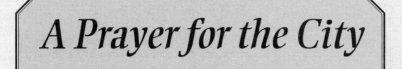 RANDOM HOUSE NEW YORK

AUTHOR'S NOTE

This is a work of nonfiction. All the names used are real. There has been no melding of characters, nor has there been any rearrangement of the chronology to heighten drama or suit the convenience of the author. Much of what appears in these pages was personally observed. Scenes I was not present for were reconstructed on the basis of interviews with the actual participants, correspondence, memos, and other documentation. There has been no guesswork.

LIBRARY OF CONGRESS CATALOGING-IN-PUBLICATION DATA
Bissinger, H. G.
A prayer for the city / Buzz Bissinger.
p.   cm.
Includes index.
ISBN 0-679-42198-X
1. Rendell, Edward G. (Edward Gene).   2. Philadelphia (Pa.)—Politics and government—1865– 3. Philadelphia (Pa.)—Social conditions.   4. Mayors—Pennsylvania—Philadelphia.   I. Title.
F158.54.R46B57   1997   974.8'11043'092—dc21   97-9637

Random House website address: www.randomhouse.com

Printed in the United States of America on acid-free paper
2   4   6   8   9   7   5   3
First Edition
Design by Tanya M. Pérez-Rock

To Mom and Dad,
two of the world's great city dwellers

Cohen: That was interesting. And totally useless.
Rendell: Like most meetings.
Cohen: No. Most meetings aren't interesting.

Preface

The seeds of this book came from many sources, but the first inspiration was a deep feeling of sorrow I did not know how to shake.

I was on my way to a newspaper assignment. I remember neither the precise route I took nor the particulars of what I was supposed to be covering, but I do remember what I saw that day in the city of Philadelphia: an assemblage of vacant houses and boarded-up windows and collapsed porches that seemed to stretch forever, one block bleeding into another without relief.

I knew little of urban policy and even less about urban planning. What I understood of the mechanics of cities came from books I admired—*Common Ground* by Anthony Lukas, *The Power Broker* by Robert Caro. The condition of what I saw was unimaginable, but I remember feeling overwhelmed by a sense of loss. Even amid the horror, delicate touches had somehow survived—an inscription over a doorway, molding around a window, a row of porches, a set of front steps.

Why had this happened?

This question kept returning, as did some other ones. Were these conditions somehow inevitable due to a process of progress and civilization in which older areas die so that new ones can grow? Or were they the result of something willful, a deliberate sacrifice? The delicate touches told me that whoever had built these blocks had not intended them for doom. Finally, there was the most nagging and difficult question of all:

Could anything be done?

The questions came and went until a May night in 1991. I was living in the Midwest, and fiddling with the radio, when I heard a scratchy report from a station in Philadelphia announcing that Edward G. Rendell had just won the Democratic nomination for mayor. I had known him when he had been the city's district attorney, and I had covered his failed campaign for mayor in 1987. When I heard of his victory, the questions that had been set aside percolated again.

I called David Cohen, Rendell's campaign manager. I told him about my desire to write a book about urban America in a way that was wholly different, not exclusively a book of history or a book of policy, but a book of heart and humor and humanity rooted in the present. Then I dropped the question: Would Rendell, if he won election the following November, consider letting me be at his side not just for a year, but for the political equivalent of a season in sports—a full four-year term in office?

I met with Rendell several months later. I had not seen him in three years, and in literally the same breath as he said "hello," he also said "yes." If he did become mayor, he would give me access to anywhere I wanted to go in the administration.

He ultimately won the election in a landslide. I was there in January 1992 on the eve of his inauguration, and there I stayed for the next four years, observing events from this remarkable vantage point. Cohen, who served as the mayor's chief of staff, opened his office to me. So, as promised, did the mayor. Aware of what happens when people learn that a journalist is in the room, how unvarnished truth turns into calculation, both men not only provided me with virtually unrestricted access but also went out of their way to make sure that my presence did not affect the agenda.

The mayor never once asked me what I was planning to write about, but he understood the major aims of my project—to create a vivid and unique portrait of a politician trying to save a city, and to create an equally vivid and unique portrait of the politics of self-interest that must be negotiated daily, almost hourly, to even attempt to act in the public interest. It didn't take four years, but closer to four hours, to learn that Ed Rendell was a complicated man of many hues. But it also became clear from the very beginning that he represented the very essence of what a politician should be in this country but almost never is, a man unafraid to be human.

That humanity was made all the more remarkable by what he inherited on that first Monday in January 1992. The literal second he became mayor, he found himself at the helm of a city utterly on the brink, so many hundreds of millions of dollars in debt that it could not pay its own bills. Almost simultaneously, he entered into negotiations with the municipal unions the likes of which had never been seen in the modern history of the American city, and sought givebacks and concessions so enormous it seemed almost lunatic to publicly talk of them.

Intertwined was the crisis of unabated job and population loss, and the crisis of public housing so nightmarish that even the president himself became aware of it, and the crisis of trying to create new jobs. For each and every day Rendell was mayor, he also had to grapple with the fate of the Navy Yard—the city's most fabled employer, builder of 119 of America's greatest ships over a span of nearly two centuries, and a place of spiritual presence in the psyche of the city. What eventually happened to the yard was something that no one, not even the mayor, could have possibly predicted.

As I did my research, I realized that this book, to attempt to be a full portrait of urban America, must extend beyond the walls of City Hall and the offices of the mayor and his chief of staff. As a result the book is interwoven with the lives of four different individuals who live in the city. I chose them because they provided vivid windows into the types of issues that affect city dwellers everywhere in the country—fear of crime, the plague of drugs, prohibitive taxes, loss of faith in the public schools, the disappearance of work through plant closure, the fissures of race. I also chose them because of their love for the place in which they lived.

This book is about one city in the United States. But it isn't hyperbole to say that it could have been written about virtually any major city in North America. No two cities are alike—each has its own character and identity and spirit—but in all of them, the struggle for survival and finding a place in the changing landscape of the country goes on without relief. During my research, thousands of documents found their way into a black file cabinet, but none was more disturbing than a study showing poverty rates for children in our cities: *69 percent* in New Orleans, *58 percent* in Cleveland, *49 percent* in Washington, *45 percent* in New York, *43 percent* in Houston, *41 percent* in Baltimore, *40 percent* in Los Angeles, *38 percent* in Philadelphia.

I still drive through the streets of Philadelphia and see the vacant homes and the slabs of metal where windows used to be. I see the swirls of trash and the piles of discarded tires. I can't help but think that here, in the United States, lies our own shameful holocaust. But then I drive through other streets and see beautiful row-house blocks. I see places that are crowded and energized and filled with people who are unique and vibrant. I can't help but think that here, in the United States, lies the very best definition of us.

This book may have been originally spawned from a feeling of loss, but it has its foundation in the strength of the human spirit. It seems strange that I spent so many years researching and writing about people who never once sat together in the same room. The mayor and his chief of staff could not have been more different from the four other people whose lives I also followed. Yet all were linked by resilience and hope and a refusal to succumb. In their own powerful way, they all understood why a city is worth saving and why it is worthwhile to live in one. Regardless of background or circumstance, each of them was heroic, each of them offering, in their daily acts of living and survival, a prayer for the city.

Contents

Prologue

I

Success followed success, and as he persuaded more and more people with the spontaneous symphony of his hands and the infectious rhythm of his voice to see a place that he saw, it became easier to believe that there was something wondrous about him, regardless of the patches of hair sprouting from his head like a failed English garden, not to mention the balled-up blue suits that looked as if they had been burrowed away in gym bags.

National story spawned national story, each one better than the last, stories so gushing that even his own press secretary, Kevin Feeley, seemed a little embarrassed. *The Wall Street Journal* basically started it with a front-page profile that Feeley described as a "blow job," and then the rest of the national media eventually followed like coins from a slot machine: *Forbes, Reader's Digest, U.S. News and World Report, Newsweek, The New York Times, New York Magazine, The Washington Post*. They all proclaimed him the miracle man who at Mach speed had reversed a seemingly irreversible spiral of decline and decay. The war was over, they so strongly implied in what they wrote. The impossible had become possible. A dying American city had been drawn back to life by the man Vice President Al Gore had ordained "America's mayor."

Ed Rendell read most of these clips. Sometimes he liked them because the accompanying pictures were big and showed him with an affable smile and more hair than he could take credit for in person, and he knew such a sight would make his eighty-four-year-old mother in New York happy. Sometimes he cringed over the effusion of them because it raised the bar of his success ever higher, and he knew that fellow mayors, while offering congratulations in public, would start sticking little pins into the ears and eyes of their voodoo dolls in private. Sometimes he obsessed over the three or four paragraphs out of two hundred that described him as impulsive, because he hated the idea that he was impulsive, and he hated having it pointed out, even though, of course, he was totally impulsive, and after five minutes with him it was impossible for *anyone* not to point it out, whether the visitor was nine or ninety. But he knew better than to pay a whole lot of attention to the cacophony of what was written.

He knew it that day in Washington when he went before the Senate Finance Committee to testify about the urgent need for urban enterprise zones to stimulate investment in America's depleted inner cities through the use of business tax credits. The senators sat at the front of the room in an elevated semicircle, a little bit weary, a little bit pleasant. Some actually seemed to care, but others listened to snippets of testimony and then, like the revolving door of a department store, just disappeared behind a back door altogether. If there was any urgency in Washington that day, it wasn't in the obligatory chill of this solemn room in the Dirksen Senate Office Building, with its cavernous ceilings and Wuthering Heights gloom. Senator Daniel Patrick Moynihan of New York was there, with that long, persnickety face that always seems on the verge of smelling something rotten, expounding on the historical precedents of enterprise zones like a precocious schoolboy. Senator Bill Bradley of New Jersey was there, looking sleepy and unfocused. Senator Bob Dole of Kansas was there, with that brow of perpetual brooding as heavy as a ship's anchor. So was Senator Lloyd Bentsen of Texas, with that silky twang of whiskey and smoke that sounds almost British. So was Senator John Breaux of Louisiana, who seemed as interested in his own territorial rights as he did in the tired tales of horror from the urban crypt, at one point giving his podium several sharp whacks so a photographer would stop leaning against it.

In his prior life as a district attorney, Rendell himself had been to Washington countless times, and he knew the routine: you came for a two-hour meeting; you were introduced; then everyone else in the room was introduced; then, in the thirty minutes that were left after the introductions, you spoke quickly and told the grizzled lions of the capital in five hundred words what was needed; then they spoke slowly and told you in ten thousand words what they thought was needed, until the two-hour meeting had suddenly become four hours, and then you went back home on the train as if the whole thing had been some vague dream. This event had seemed no different, particularly when Moynihan and another of those testifying, Housing and Urban Development Secretary Jack Kemp, got into a spirited argument, as if they were the only ones there, over where enterprise zones had first been used to promote investment, in the Philippines or in Puerto Rico.

"I wasted a half day of work so I could hear about the Philippines and Puerto Rico?" whispered Rendell to an aide as he waited his turn to testify, his leg pumping up and down so furiously that it looked as if he might become airborne at any second. At another point, as Kemp made reference to talmudic philosophy and talked with fevered gesticulations and finger-pointing about how the great entrepreneurship of the inner city had been pushed underground, Rendell whispered to the aide, *"I like Jack, but he's crazy."*

After about an hour, Rendell's turn to speak finally came. Forty-eight years old, he was neither intimidated nor nervous. Much of his life had been spent in the public eye, and while he was a devoted Democrat, his political philosophy reflected that of a man who simply said what he thought and what he felt regardless of how it came out. He sat on a red leather chair, his six-foot-tall body hunched over the table as if he had slightly miscalculated the distance between table and chair so he was leaning a bit more than he really needed to and might tip over altogether at any moment. He wore a gray suit, but because of the way clothing instantly rumpled around the large and rounded frame that he constantly fought to keep at 235 pounds, a pair of sweatpants and a sweatshirt would have fit him better. He gestured sharply with his hands as if he were trying to catch a fly. He spoke with a passion that reached just a notch below outrage, the exact passion that he used with nine-year-olds when they trudged into his office and sat there, first glum, then transfixed, as he described the vagaries of what it was he did for a living. His voice had a gravelly edge, phrases coming out of him in rat-a-tat bursts. He never stammered but apparently considered the idea of pausing between sentences a sign of unforgivable weakness.

He told the senators how his city—the city of Philadelphia—had lost $2 billion of its tax base over the past twenty years, after the city had raised various taxes nineteen times. He talked about the violence of the inner city, how simple disputes, disputes that in his teens had been settled with a punch thrown here and a punch thrown there, were now being settled with guns and knives and the inevitable end product of someone dying over nothing at all. He talked urgently, as if the words couldn't keep up with the fervor of his belief in them. He worked hard to make the members of the Senate Finance Committee believe that he wasn't looking for a taxpayer handout, a reversion to the wonder days of revenue sharing, when mayors could live out their edifice complexes, but that he was seeking a way, at minimal public expense, of bringing an obliterated portion of the American landscape back to life.

"We in the cities are very confused," said Rendell as he hunched forward. "We see a great deal of support—and we think it's meritorious—of aid to the Soviet people. But we are perplexed why you don't give a similar package to cities that are on the brink. We're also confused at how readily you found money for S and Ls, how readily you found money for Desert Storm." His words were sharp and unflinching, and they had an impact.

"We had no choice [on S and Ls]," countered Senator Bentsen, the chairman of the committee, with simmering indignation that made his fine whiskey twang go suddenly sharp and raspy, as if a piece of metal had gotten stuck in his throat.

"I submit we have no choice here," countered Rendell with equal indignation.

Some in the room, like Senator Donald Riegle of Michigan, actually seemed to be moved by what Rendell had to say. It clearly hit a chord with the senator, which wasn't surprising perhaps, given the misery of Detroit and the growing sense that at any time now it would become the first major American city to expire and go extinct. Unused sections of the city were so prevalent and considered so hopeless that one local politician would suggest putting a fence around them and mothballing them for good. The idea would result in public ridicule around the country, but the serious point remained that Detroit and other cities like it, so obsessed throughout their histories with growth and development and expansion, must start thinking about shrinkage and neighborhood consolidation if they were ever going to survive.

"What's happening here is that cities are being destroyed," said Riegle. "We have a war going on within our own country. We're going to end up with a *Clockwork Orange* society."

They were poignant words, but most of the senators looked on glumly, as if this were a blind date that wasn't going nearly as well as expected and they were just looking for an excuse to get home early—except when it came their turn to speak. Then the color flew back into their faces, and instead of leaning back in their huge-backed chairs in bored silence, they leaned forward in grand interrogator style and spoke with a kind of incision and eloquence that was admirable and a clear gift of the gods. But when the moment of attention passed, when the cameras pecked and clicked away at another face in the semicircle, they cocked their heads to the side, and they leaned back again in their chairs, and their eyes became glazed, and many just disappeared altogether behind the Bermuda Triangle of that back door, never to be seen or heard from again.

Realizing afterward that his impassioned pleas for help for the city had dissolved into the infinite netherworld of Washington rhetoric, Rendell had said angrily, "Where the fuck are they? Don't they understand they have no choice?" As he boarded the Metroliner to return to the city, he took his customary seat in the dining car so he could spread out his endless piles of work on the table in front of him. His face wound tightly in a grimace, he dipped into his briefcase and, like some bad magician's trick, pulled out one piece of paper after another after another—reports, invitations, summary memos of meetings, pleas for help from citizens who had run out of places to plead. But as the train spun by the rotting factories on the fringes of Washington and Baltimore and Wilmington, the work largely stayed untouched. Instead, the flash of panic eased, and Rendell mused aloud on the difference between him and his older brother, a corporate lawyer in Dallas: "He doesn't suffer fools gladly. My best, or maybe my worst, trait is that I do suffer fools gladly." He admitted that one of his great frustrations of being mayor was that his wife, Midge, kept dragging him to classical music concerts and operas. While he admitted to liking *Pagliacci* more than he ever could have imagined, he said that what he really dreamed about when he closed his eyes and listened to all that music was having a little earplug in his ear so he could listen to the Phillies without anybody knowing why he had such a broad smile on his face. He also talked about his own political aspirations, and with the events of the day still sharp, he said he had absolutely no interest in becoming a U.S. senator, although he could clearly see why some might be attracted to it. "It's an incredibly easy job," he said. "They don't do shit."

And then shortly after Wilmington, with eight hours of work under his belt and at least eight hours more to go, he fell asleep. Sitting in that little booth in the dining car with his eyes sweetly closed and his head gently drooped to the side, he looked like a little boy who suddenly, midsentence, had just run out of steam, and were it not for the gentle rousings of the conductor when the train reached the Thirtieth Street Station, the mayor of Philadelphia might well have ended up in Newark.

He knew not to believe his clippings on those days when so much of his time seemed taken up not by what was good for the city but by the push and pull of what black politicians wanted and what white politicians wanted and what black politicians would do to make life a living hell for the mayor if they didn't get what they wanted and what white politicians would do to make life a living hell for the mayor if they didn't get what they wanted—the cycle of threat and extortion that had become the purest extract of modern politics, prompting him to blurt out to a political colleague, "Everything that goes on is a power struggle between black politicians and white politicians, and it isn't because of what's for the good of the citizens. It's about who controls what project. I'm so fed up with this blackmail stuff that goes on I could just scream. I could just take a machine gun and shoot 'em all." Or as he put it on another occasion, offering his own twenty-five-words-or-less job description, "A good portion of my job is spent on my knees, sucking people off to keep them happy."

He knew it on the day the private line in his office began to ring repeatedly with emphatic and complicated complaints from citizens, which didn't make any sense until he discovered that the number had inadvertently been published in one of the local phone books. Or the time his vigorous effort to lobby members of the city council on behalf of a vote crucial to the future funding of the city's beleaguered school system was curtailed in midstream when one of them gasped in shock at the sight of a mouse running along one of the walls of his office. For most politicians, the presence of mice in the office might have been disconcerting. For Rendell, the rodents seemed to offer a certain comfort, symbolic of what it is like to be the mayor of an American city. "Don't worry," he said. "They almost never come out to the center of the room."

He knew not to believe his clippings the time he agreed to go up in a cherry picker with a rabbi to light a giant-sized menorah only to realize, as the cherry picker lifted them higher and higher, that the rabbi was wobbly, somewhat older than he had looked on the ground, and was wielding the blowtorch in such a way that it was becoming increasingly hard to ascertain just what was going to burst aglow with the spirit of Hanukkah, the mayor or the menorah. "The rabbi was sort of shaking a little bit. I was afraid he was going to slip, turn around, and set me on fire. Somewhere about sixty feet above, I said to myself, 'I have to stop doing this.' "

But most of all, he had known it on November nights such as this one— a silent race through the city where nothing he did could make any difference. Up until the shots rang out, the night had had a sweet placidity. His round of appearances—a reception for Red Bell beer over at the Katmandu down on the Delaware, a series of painless speeches before the American Red Cross and at the annual Stephen Girard Award dinner, a quick stop at the Legg Mason open-house celebration high atop the shiny gleam of a downtown skyscraper—meant that he might actually get home before the usual witching hour of 10:00 P.M.

But then, just around 6:00 P.M., came the crackle of gunfire on a West Philadelphia street and reports that two Philadelphia narcotics officers had been shot during an undercover drug deal. One of the officers had suffered a relatively minor graze wound in the hand. But the other, a three-year veteran of the force named Dathan Enoch, had been shot in the left side of the chest and rushed to Lankenau Hospital just outside the city limits. As Enoch underwent surgery, members of his family began to gather in a makeshift reception room. High-ranking members of the police department arrived. And so did several members of the mayor's office: David L. Cohen, the chief of staff, who, like Radar in *M*A*S*H,* had the ability to be in the right place well before anyone even knew there was a right place; and Anthony Buchanico, a police sergeant in charge of security for the mayor.

Rendell himself was en route. In the meantime, about twenty people awkwardly milled about, speaking to one another in small and hushed circles, biding the time with trivial talk and small talk that never rose above the trace of a whisper, eyeing the cookies and soft drinks that had been laid out on a long white table but reluctant to take anything because it would seem crass and uncaring, waiting for some glimmer to indicate that Enoch was not going to die. When unofficial word filtered into the room that he was going to make it, the relief was palpable—among the family members sitting around one of the tables in a silent knot, among the police officials who several months earlier had gathered outside a city church on a blue and windswept day to say good-bye to a fellow officer who had been killed in the line of duty during what should have been a routine traffic stop. There would also be relief for the mayor himself, who hated hospital scenes such as this in an almost pathological way, perhaps because they conflicted so terribly with his eternal sense of optimism and served as a brutal reminder of all that the city wasn't, but perhaps also because they echoed the death of his own father when he was fourteen years old.

The mood of the room lifted with the news of Enoch's recovery. Those gathered finally reached for the cookies and soft drinks without feeling guilty. And then came the crackle and pop over a small radio receiver that one of the officers carried, followed by the flat voice of a dispatcher:

"Officer down. . . ."

Buchanico, who had spent twenty-nine years as a police officer in the city, twenty-one of them in uniform, strained to hear the words as if they were some kind of macabre joke. How could another police officer be *down* in a different part of the city? Wasn't the shooting of one officer enough of a sacrifice to the city tonight? He grabbed the radio and went outside so he could better hear the toneless words of the dispatcher.

There were more crackles and pops over the radio, then the words:

"Officer assist."

And Buchanico knew what those words meant. The officer was in trouble, terrible trouble, going down, choking on blood and spit and fear on a shitty street corner somewhere, and right then and there, standing outside by himself, Buchanico knew what was going to unfold. He had been through these scenes before, too many times before, too many goddamn times, and they never, ever got easier, the panic and confusion and anger and frustration, the horror of an officer slipping away in a darkened city street, the horror of his family as they drove in a frantic rush to the hospital entrance and immediately knew from the avalanche of lights from the police cars and the television vans that they needed to start planning a funeral.

The moment Cohen had heard the initial call from the police dispatcher, he knew too that the officer was not going to make it. They had been lucky with Enoch, and Cohen knew that in the city, luck never came a second time.

"These guys are getting their brains beaten in," said Buchanico, his eyes welling with tears as he stayed outside and waited for the mayor to arrive. He knew how fellow officers felt about the mayor, how many of them felt rejected by him, how they hated him and didn't fall for his charm and disarming self-deprecation for a second and were convinced that he was far more interested in the bright lights of *The New York Times* and *Good Morning America* than he ever was in standing up for the men in blue who had to put up with these streets night after night after night. In previous contract negotiations, the police had always done a little bit better than everyone else, gotten a little bit more. After all, they were police officers. But this administration—the Rendell administration—had been different, particularly with that bloodless prick Cohen as head henchman. The restoration of fiscal balance became more than just a campaign catchphrase, and the once sacrosanct police department had gotten starting salaries cut and paid holidays cut, just like everyone else who worked for the city. Buchanico knew that this latest round of shootings would only add to the fury of the officers in the department and would only enhance the mayor's image as cold and calculating and obsessed with cementing his image as America's mayor and favorite budget cutter. Buchanico felt some of that rage himself, particularly in a surreal moment such as this, in which two officers had been seriously wounded within hours of each other in different parts of the city. But he also knew there was another side.

II

Buchanico had seen it five months earlier, when Philadelphia Police Officers Robert Hayes and John Marynowitz had been shot during a routine traffic stop. Buchanico went to the Albert Einstein Medical Center, where both officers were in surgery. Marynowitz had been shot in the head and shoulder, and Hayes had been shot through the eye. The police sergeant knew that the mayor had to come to the hospital.

Rendell was furious when Buchanico came to his house to pick him up. It was late; he wasn't even dressed, meaning he had to trudge upstairs to put that stupid blue-suit uniform back on. Buchanico remembered him as being livid the same way a big kid is livid when he is forced to do something he desperately doesn't want to do and can taste the very dread of it on his tongue. On the way to the hospital, Rendell said that he would just be in the way, that this was "no time for politicians," that the only reason politicians showed up at events such as this was to grandstand before those television cameras with solemnity and stoicism so the public would think they actually gave a shit about something. When they neared the hospital entrance, Rendell insisted that the car lights be cut and they use a side entrance to avoid the media. And Buchanico knew what drove that anger, which really wasn't anger at all but the pain of having to look into the eyes of the small children who belonged to these officers, with their nubby brush cuts and their rounded faces and their smooth cheeks, and somehow say something to them.

But the minute Rendell got to the hospital, all that anger evaporated as if it had never been there. As Buchanico watched, it was obvious the mayor intuitively understood the needs of those children better than anyone else, knew what to say to them, knew how to be playful with them, knew how to kibitz with them as if he lived down the block. During his career, Buchanico had seen a string of mayors come to hospitals to console families in times of tragedy. He had seen their awkwardness and their stiffness when they were trying to be heartfelt, but never had he seen anyone relate to those children the way Ed Rendell did.

Officer Hayes had three boys, and when one of them asked the mayor whether he really was the mayor, Rendell pulled out his city ID card as proof. When one of them went to the snack machine and got a package of Reese's peanut butter cups, Rendell gave his immediate seal of approval with the words "good choice." When another got a pack of gum, Rendell seemed incredulous. "Is that all you want?" When the children insisted on special *Jurassic Park* meals from McDonald's, he immediately dispatched an officer to find an open McDonald's at 2:00 A.M., and when the food arrived, he teased the children about their junk food snobbery because, after all, there had been an open Roy Rogers a lot closer. He told them about his own son, Jesse—the school he went to, the activities he was interested in. He never provided Officer Hayes's boys with false hope. He promised no miracles. But as each minute ticked by, as those three little boys tried to cope with the swirl of what was happening, he provided them with the one thing they perhaps needed most—a friend who, as if by accident, also happened to be the mayor. The two youngest boys, Sean and Ryan, didn't really understand what was happening, the mayor felt, and seemed to welcome the attention they were getting, and there was some mercy in that.

But the oldest boy, who was ten and named Robert Hayes Jr., after his father, was frightened, so terribly frightened.

Rendell watched as Sean and Ryan went home to bed. And he watched as Robert Jr., after being up all night, finally fell asleep on an oversize hospital chair, finding peace in the ebb and flow of that night as hope fell and rose and fell again. The mayor was there at 3:00 A.M., when the doctor told those gathered that Officer Hayes had a fighting chance of making it. He was there at 5:30 A.M., when the doctor burst in to say that Officer Hayes was about to go into cardiac arrest. He was there forty minutes later, when Officer Hayes was pronounced dead. He was there when the doctor awoke Bobby Hayes Jr. from his sleep to tell him that his father had died. And he was there when Officer Hayes's wife, Joanne, after receiving a dutiful string of condolences, quietly mused aloud that in four days, *four days,* those three little boys with their daddy-boy looks and nubby brush cuts would have gathered round to celebrate Father's Day.

About an hour later Rendell went to a hotel ballroom to receive an award from the local branch of the Red Cross. He walked onstage with his familiar waddle. He looked tired, a little bit gray, not too different from the way he usually looked. There was supposed to have been a videotaped roast of the mayor, but given the events of the previous night, Rendell had insisted on its cancellation. He started off his remarks by apologizing for forcing such a sudden change in the program. He scratched his shoulder slightly, as if his usually infectious body language was spent and out of rhythm, and then he began to speak.

"As I was standing here listening to all the things that the Red Cross does, and all the people—" Suddenly he stopped. Tears came to his eyes, and he dabbed at them with one of his fingers as if trying to stop any further flow. But he didn't seem embarrassed or ashamed, and it wouldn't have mattered anyway, because those tears still would have come. For the next ten seconds, he didn't say a word, and then he continued.

There are times people say, "You have to have the toughest job in the city." You know, last night I just thought about how tough it is to be a policeman or a fireman, because no matter how tough it is for us in our jobs and whatever—the pressures we operate under—none of us leave the house in the morning and don't know whether we're coming back at night.

It's a gratuitous death; it has nothing to do with anything. It was needless, it was senseless. It was part and parcel of the fact that we have become such a violent society, part and parcel of the fact that there is less respect for law and order and for decency than there was, and they're all tremendous challenges, and obviously as a mayor those are challenges which on a local level I have to address, but if you want to know a tough job, it's that policeman or fireman.

There are tough jobs all over the city, and we're all trying. The thing that's frustrating about my tough job are the things we can't do. It's not the things we can tackle and have the ability to try to change. Those aren't the frustrating things because we can change them or try to change them. Last night as I was there for six, seven hours, it was enormously frustrating to me because there was nothing I could do. . . .

When I look at some of the problems, like the violence, the violence-prone society—when I look at the problems of increasing lawlessness, the breakdown of family life, some of the things that have happened to American cities that really municipal government and the mayor and the city council and business leaders, no matter how properly motivated, can attack, those are where the real frustrations are.

All of it doesn't mean we stop trying. To the contrary, we redouble our efforts, and we're all in it together.

Not everyone realizes it, but it is the case.

"There's nothing more sickening, nothing," said Rendell later that afternoon, staring out the window of his office into the courtyard of City Hall, somber and subdued, as if he were searching for something so far away that not even he had any idea of where it was—beyond the courtyard, where every afternoon the flutist looking for handouts played his haunting rendition of "The Battle Hymn of the Republic," beyond the spires of the skyscrapers built during the downtown boom of the 1980s and the three-story row houses built during the industrial boom of the early 1900s, beyond the leather and lace glory of South Street and the carcasses of the abandoned factories that once defined the very soul of the city, beyond the splendidly restored brick of Society Hill and the blocks that looked liked Dresden after the bombing. Was it the memory of the doctor gently jarring that little boy awake from his sleep to tell him his father had died? Was it the memory of the death of his own father when he was a young teenager—the call at school from his uncle telling him he had to come home, the ride on the subway with his chest pounding and his mouth dry, and then the news that his father, who had been perfectly fine that morning, who had played football in the park with him the previous Sunday, had died outside their apartment building in New York while hailing a cab.

"Gratuitous, senseless, fucking violence," he had said that afternoon in June as he stared out the window, still searching for that far-off point. Now, on a brisk November night, the scene was repeating itself.

When the mayor himself arrived at the back entrance of Lankenau Hospital at about 8:55 P.M., both Buchanico and Cohen were there to meet him.

"Another officer has been shot," Cohen told Rendell as he got out of the car.

"Oh God," said Rendell.

He went into the room where Officer Enoch's family was waiting—his mother gently fingering the well-worn black cover of the Book of Psalms, his eight-month-old nephew clutching a cookie with thick and stubby fingers, his brothers, his sisters. Rendell, with one leg propped up on a chair like a football coach, made small talk with family members and tried to keep them going until the surgeon came out with the newest update. In the meantime, he received intermittent reports on the condition of the other officer who had been shot. Information was sketchy, but the shooting had taken place in front of an automatic teller machine on Spring Garden Street in the Fairmount section of the city, and the officer's name was Stephen Dmytryk. He had been on the police force for fifteen years, was married, and had two children.

"Head and shoulder," said the mayor quietly, his voice trailing off so that it was difficult to hear.

"The other officer OK?" asked one of Officer Enoch's family members.

"The officer was shot in the head and shoulder," said Rendell.

From around the table came a collective gasp. "Oh my God," said one.

Almost simultaneously the doctor who had performed the surgery on Officer Enoch came in to brief the family. He was dressed in a surgeon's green gown, and the protective slippers he wore over his shoes were flecked with blood. "We're all finished up," he said. "He's got a lot of injuries. He's gonna be sick for quite a while."

Then he turned away to speak privately with the mayor and various police officials, this time in much more detail, outlining the path that the bullet had taken through Officer Enoch's body—through his chest about an inch below the left nipple, taking away part of the liver, the pancreas, and the stomach and then lodging in the spinal column. Rendell asked about paralysis, and the doctor said that based on a neurological evaluation of the officer done right before the surgery, there were no indications of any.

Just a day earlier the U.S. Conference of Mayors had held an emergency meeting on violent crime. Representatives of nearly thirty cities, including Philadelphia, had been at the Chicago meeting, the ostensible purpose of which was to develop a cogent and united strategy for pushing an effective anticrime bill through Congress. Its timing could not have been any more propitious, or more cruel, given that there had been thirty-four killings in Chicago the previous week alone, including the death of a four-month-old baby. But as at all gatherings of politicians, pungent self-congratulation quickly began to suffuse the room, and there seemed to be a built-in presumption that the mayors and police chiefs and staffers, just by the very act of their coming together in their dark suits and crisp uniforms, had somehow solved the problem, or at the very least should be given an enormous amount of credit for gathering together to try to solve it. Rendell himself, all too aware of what happens at virtually any meeting in which more than one politician is present ("a complete and total waste of time" was the operative phrase he used) had elected not to go, dispatching instead the city's police chief, Richard Neal, and the mayor's deputy chief of staff, Ted Beitchman.

According to Beitchman's summary memo, the mayor's instinct had been right: the meeting had been a three-hour waste of time, the realities of urban crime and urban life taking a backseat to ego, starry-eyed ideas that would never pass muster in Washington, not to mention the endless jockeying for a sliver of the media spotlight. Roughly thirty suggestions on how to solve urban crime were made, ranging from the destruction of guns after court proceedings to the coordination of a nationwide campaign against the National Rifle Association, and that was before lunch. After lunch, Jerry Abramson, the mayor of Louisville, Kentucky, and the president of the U.S. Conference of Mayors, presided over a press conference at which he introduced every single one of the fifty-odd mayors and police chiefs attending the meeting. After that, he enumerated all the suggestions that had been made, regardless of their merit. After that, he gave the floor over to San Francisco mayor Frank Jordan. Jordan in turn had a whole agenda of his own: when he got to the issue of curfews for underage children, according to Beitchman's memo, Mayor Richard Daley of Chicago "was heard to mutter not quite far enough under his breath, 'This is bullshit.' " Fortunately the whole thing sank rather rapidly, and the good news about the conference, Beitchman wrote in his memo, was that "there wasn't a line about [it] in the *Inquirer, New York Times, Washington Post,* or *Wall Street Journal.*" But now, as Rendell stood outside a hospital fielding questions about the medical condition of two fallen police officers, the price of that rhetoric and posturing seemed greater than ever.

In a macabre trading of information, he reported on the condition of Officer Enoch while reporters in turn gave him the latest updates on Officer Dmytryk. "This is a Wild West night," said the mayor in response to a question. "There are far too many guns out there and far too many people who shoot their guns without fear." As the impromptu press conference ended and Rendell turned around to go back into the hospital, police official James Golden quietly informed him of the condition of Officer Dmytryk. "A priest has been called for the officer," he said.

Rendell shook his head slightly and walked slowly into the brightly lit hallway of the hospital without saying a word, as ashen as the rumpled gray suit he wore. His brown eyes, usually sprinkled with the mirth of amusement or the explosive rage of too much to do and never enough time in which to do it, just looked tired and puffy. He shuffled back into the waiting room so he could stay with the members of Officer Enoch's family until they could go up to the intensive care unit. Over the cooing and fidgeting of that little eight-month-old nephew, Rendell told the family about Officer Dmytryk. "[He] must be in bad shape because they have just called for a priest."

A brother of Officer Enoch's came into the room, seething with anger. In the presence of the mayor, he tried to be polite, but the words spit out of him anyway. "A lot more can be done," he said. "Drugs gettin' out of control in this city, and nothin's being done about it."

Rendell said nothing, and moments later he was given another update on Officer Dmytryk.

He was dead.

A few minutes later a nurse came into the room to take the Enoch family to intensive care. Enoch's mother, her face soft and gentle, gazed at the mayor as he clasped her hand. "Thank you so much for coming."

"He's gonna be fine," said the mayor, bending over slightly, putting his arm around her shoulder almost as if she were a child. "It's not going to be easy, and it's not going to be a short-term thing, but he's gonna be fine."

And then off he went in the autumn night, racing away from one hospital emergency room to another. From his familiar place in the front passenger seat of the car, he called his wife, Midge, en route, letting her know, in a weary, barely audible voice, what had happened. Then he fell silent as the car sped through the spine of the city, down City Line Avenue, then onto the curving slope of the expressway that runs alongside the river, the flashing lights of the police escort spreading long and skeletal fingers of red and green over the gingerbread houses of Boathouse Row and the fallen majesty of the Waterworks and the pale-yellow marble of the art museum. The caravan pulled off the expressway and continued on its speeding path toward the hospital, down the flag-lined boulevard of Benjamin Franklin Parkway, built in the throes of the city-beautiful movement of the early 1900s to resemble the Champs-Élysées; past the grand gray façade of the free library, modeled after the palaces on the place de la Concorde; past the rounded brownstone eminence of the cathedral constructed in the mid-1800s to satisfy the religious needs of the burgeoning throng of Irish immigrants—the city so quiet, so still and immutable except for the sound of the sirens tunneling down the narrow streets like the gossip of the dead.

Rendell peered out the car window, his shoulders slumped, the reflections of the boathouses and the art museum and City Hall spinning off the shadow of his face in a wash of red and green from the flashing police lights.

He arrived at the emergency entrance of Hahnemann University Hospital around 10:15 P.M., getting out of the car wearily and then going past the reporters without a word. Once inside, he was given a briefing by police officials on what had happened—how there had been a stakeout of the cash machine because of a recent rash of robberies, how the two officers had witnessed a robbery and approached the suspect, how the suspect started firing, how Officer Dmytryk went down without ever getting a shot off, how he was hit twice in the chest and once in the head. "He was not responsive when he came in," Deputy Police Commissioner Thomas Seamon told the mayor.

The mayor in turn reduced the language to its most basic elements: "He was DOA."

After the briefing, Rendell went to a small, windowless room in the emergency wing of Hahnemann to meet with the officer's wife and two children. Their eyes were red from crying, but in their faces was anger, the anger of how this could have happened and why it had happened and who in the name of God was finally going to do something about it. When the mayor came in, they barely looked up.

"Did they get the trigger man?" asked Dmytryk's son Stephen, his voice urgent and rapid, his hands turning open and shut, open and shut. "Did they get the trigger man?" he asked again, this time with an almost frantic edge.

Rendell patiently, almost clinically, explained the circumstances of what had happened. He said that one of the suspects had been shot and killed by the police, and the other one had gotten away. "They're gonna catch him," he promised the family. "They're gonna catch him." And then he mused aloud over the issue of gun control and how it amazed him that there could even be debate in Washington over instituting a five-day waiting period before the purchase of a handgun. The family had no reaction, as if the mayor's presence had become immaterial.

"I want to see him one more time," said Mary Ann Dmytryk of her husband. A social worker escorted her out of the room, leaving the mayor with the officer's daughter, Stacy Ann. There was a slight pause, and then Rendell turned to her, struggling to retain some measure of composure. He spoke softly, with the same familial presence he had displayed when he had spoken to the mother of Officer Enoch just an hour earlier, but there was an urgency now. "As bad as it is for you, it's gonna be worse for your mom, so you've got to help her."

He walked from the room into a hallway crowded with hospital workers and police officers leaning against the white walls. They looked at him, beseeching him with their eyes as if they expected him to do something. But he looked away, and for a split second it seemed as if Ed Rendell didn't want to be the mayor anymore, didn't want to be the one to supply answers when there were no answers, didn't want to be the one overflowing with optimism when there was nothing to be optimistic about, didn't want to play the cheerful fool when there was nothing to be foolish about, didn't want to be the one to tell a daughter that he was sorry her dad had died in the line of duty when the words seemed so empty and worthless. "Goddamn" was all he said as he walked down that hallway, his eyes filled with tears and his head still tilted toward those white walls so he didn't have to look at anyone. "Goddamn."

At 11:00 P.M., Rendell left the hospital to go back home. The car went back past the cathedral, past the fountain at Logan Circle where a homeless person lay shrouded in a steam of vapor, back onto the Ben Franklin Parkway toward the shimmering majesty of the art museum with that marble as pale as champagne, then onto Kelly Drive where it hugs the east bank of the river. To the left, like a scene out of Norman Rockwell, were those gingerbread boathouses as jaunty as Christmas trees. To the right, like a scene out of the American city, were the crisscrossing lights of a dozen police cars searching the alleys and crevices of the night for someone who had just become a cop killer.

Rendell was in the middle of his four-year term as mayor. If he ran for reelection and won, the job would be his until the third of January in the year 2000. There was a kind of inspirational and historic symmetry in that, in being the man who for better or worse would guide the city out of the twentieth century and into the twenty-first. But as his driver dropped him off at home, it was obvious that the events of the night had cut deeply into his core. "If I have to go through any more of these," he said to her, "I don't think I want this job for another six years." But the next day the mayor was back at work.

And so was the city.

No More Money

ONE

Ego and Id

I

Less than twenty-four hours before the new job became his and the grace of speculation gave way to crisis, David L. Cohen was ensconced in a suite of offices on the second floor of City Hall doing what he always seemed to be doing: sorting out the mess that had been unceremoniously handed to him by someone else. He was quite brilliant at it.

Municipal government in Philadelphia had never been known for the hum of its efficiency. It was Lincoln Steffens, in his oft-cited quote, who had once described the city as "corrupt and contented." But even this sight seemed more peculiar than normal, as if occupying forces, finally realizing the futility of the war, had staged a midnight evacuation. Rooms that should have had furniture in them were barren. What few desks did remain had been emptied so that nothing was left, not even a paper clip. In the aftermath of the upheaval, a few items had been left behind. A half-filled

bottle of wine lay inside the drawer of one file cabinet, and given the for-
tune at the end of the administration of the city's outgoing mayor, W. Wilson Goode, it seemed remarkable that the contents hadn't been downed in
one merciful gulp. A pile of binders in pale blue covers had been unceremoniously dumped on top of another file cabinet, as if whoever had put
them there just hadn't gotten around to throwing them into the trash. They
seemed innocuous enough, binders that might contain press releases announcing ribbon cuttings and holiday street festivals and other events that
so often had passed for earth-shattering milestones in the sputter of a city
on the brink of bankruptcy. But as David Cohen thumbed through the
binders, he discovered they contained something else altogether: the executive orders that Mayor Goode had enacted during his tenure. Many of
them were still in effect. They still had a significant impact on the 1.6 million people who lived in the city. Cohen gave a short burst of laughter that
sounded a little bit like a car alarm, rising out of nowhere in the silence of
the office he was about to inherit. Then he just shook his head, his way of
acknowledging that he was entering a world where rules of logic and reason did not have the remotest application, light years beyond the Peter
principle or Murphy's law or anything else commonly used to explain failure. Why had someone left the executive orders of the mayor of America's
fifth largest city in a heap on top of a file cabinet?

Why not?

Dressed in gray jeans, a plaid work shirt, and sneakers on a Sunday
morning, Cohen labored methodically to restore some semblance of balance and order. With all the details to attend to before tomorrow's mayoral
inauguration at 10:00 A.M. at the Academy of Music, he hadn't slept in
nearly seventy-two hours, and that was a literal calculation. But with the
exception of a skin color that looked like instant oatmeal, he didn't seem
affected in the slightest. He went about his unpacking, unwrapping the little trinkets and memorabilia that he had brought with him from his former
employer, the prestigious law firm of Ballard Spahr Andrews & Ingersoll,
where he had been a legend by the time he was thirty. But the phone kept
ringing. And when the phone didn't ring, the beeper he wore on his belt
like a six-shooter went off. The mayor-elect, Edward G. Rendell, was calling with the breathless agitation of a child. He was supposed to give an
inauguration-eve phone interview to one of the local radio stations, and he
didn't have the right number. Cohen had it at his fingertips, as if he had
been expecting the call. He continued to unpack, delicately lifting each

item from the paper towel in which he had wrapped it—a tray for memos and correspondence, a little wooden box with a calculator inside—and arranging them in the room so they stood at perfect right angles. He seemed unfazed by the thick coat of grime on the windows, which looked as if it had been there since the signing of the Declaration of Independence, or by the cockeyed view showing little more than the dark rumps of other buildings, or the way the air conditioner was held in place with a concoction of plywood, gray duct tape, and old rolled-up newspapers that had turned yellow. The scalded-brown color of the shades, as if someone had once tried to iron them flat, didn't seem to bother him. Nor did the yap of the beeper at his belt. He just went on.

Little by little his office began to take shape. On the left was the framed picture of the man who had been perhaps the greatest inspiration in his life, former federal judge Joseph S. Lord III. Cohen had clerked for him after law school, in the early 1980s, and at the bottom of the picture was an inscription that said, "If every judge had colleagues like you, the law would approach perfection, and so would friendship." On the ledge behind the desk were pictures of his two children, Benjamin and Josh. On the right were framed diplomas from Swarthmore College, from which Cohen graduated in 1977, and the University of Pennsylvania Law School, where he had been among the top three in his class. Since law school, his only professional job had been at Ballard Spahr. He had loved it there, and up until the aberration that had landed him in the Dr. Seussian world of City Hall, where hallways stopped and stairways went nowhere, he had never shown the slightest inclination to leave. "I'd be crazy if I didn't have a little bit of the feeling, Have I done the right thing here?" he said on this Sunday at the beginning of January in 1992. "There's no doubt about that."

Cohen then fell back to work, so deeply shrouded within the cocoon of the task at hand that he didn't even seem to hear the questions of others, much less respond to them. He was like that for hours, but then, just as nighttime fell, he grabbed his coat and left the building. He headed west on Market Street until he came to a stunning skyscraper that took up much of the block of Seventeenth Street. He searched his wallet for his security card and inserted it into the neat little slot, whereupon a responsive and gleaming elevator whisked him to the forty-sixth floor. He got off the elevator and opened the doors to the Ballard Spahr law firm. He went to the corner office that was still his, but, with overtones of "Cinderella," only until the stroke of midnight. After that, he would have no association with

Ballard Spahr, beyond memories and friendships. After that, he would draw a paycheck from the city of Philadelphia at a pay cut of well over $200,000 a year.

He began to pack up a few remaining things, but as he did, he was momentarily drawn to the window. It was a brisk and serene night with an unfettered view stretching west to the Schuylkill River and east down Market Street to City Hall. In the quiet splendor of that office, suffused with shades of cream and gray and beige, any decision to leave, even for lunch, seemed unfathomable. For someone like David Cohen, it was hard not to think something quite terrible had happened. Behind the veil of work and compulsion and perfection, he had gone mad.

By any stretch of logic, this office, so removed from all the trouble that routinely took place so far below, should have been his forever. "I am basically an extremely conservative, steady person," he had said earlier in the day. "It would not have been shocking to me that I would have spent the rest of my life [at Ballard Spahr] and literally not left. That would not have been an unexpected result for me." It was true that he had gone on a reduced schedule at Ballard to serve as campaign manager when Rendell had run for mayor the previous year, but even then he had managed to bill close to two thousand hours, and it had been assumed he would return to the firm full-time once the election was over.

Certainly the senior partners at Ballard Spahr were hoping that, for it wasn't simply by a stroke of hyperbole that Cohen was known at the firm by the acronym COE—chief of everything. Nor was there anything accidental about the nature of his success. Even in law school at Penn, his aura had been considerable. Fellow students recognized it—his nickname then was Chief Justice Cohen. Some students couldn't stand him, were repelled by his alacrity, but others marveled at the way he read not only all the cases that were assigned but all the footnotes, carefully underlining everything in a rainbow array of color-coded markers. They even liked him outside class, amazed, even puzzled, by the lack of pretense in this kid from Highland Park in northern New Jersey whose father had spent much of his life as a salesman for Bulova.

If fellow students found him special, so did his teachers. One in particular was Arthur Makadon, who was also the hiring partner for Ballard Spahr. Makadon taught Cohen appellate advocacy, and almost instantly he recognized something uncanny about this second-year law student, something that went far beyond his work in class. It wasn't simply his base of knowledge—plenty of students at Penn had that from their endless hours of studying and their impressive genetic strands of neurosis and paranoia. Plenty of students functioned with no sleep. What Makadon saw in Cohen wasn't the earnestness of an extremely hardworking law student but an ability to size up events in a way that was remarkably suited to the realities of the world. Although he was still in his early twenties, Cohen somehow understood, even in the artificial atmosphere of law school, precisely what it took to get things done, how to get from point A to point B without getting diverted by anything in between. To Makadon, it was remarkable to see someone who had mastered that elusive side of life at such a young age, who already seemed so unfettered by idealism, impulse, or dreams but instead was completely practical, not a brilliant legal scholar but, in a world measured by production and results, something far better—a brilliant pragmatist. "Who was I to ask law students for practical advice?" remembered Makadon. "He was the one exception."

A city power broker in his own right, Makadon would ultimately bring Cohen and Rendell together. In the beginning at least, particularly given that Cohen had no experience in politics save a stint in the office of a New York congressman between college and law school, it seemed like a mismatch. But Makadon knew both men intimately. If it was he who had discovered the gift of David Cohen as corporate litigator, it was also he who had discovered the gift of Ed Rendell roughly a decade earlier, when they had worked together in the Philadelphia district attorney's office. Perhaps on the theory that opposites really do attract, instinct told him that this was a political marriage that would endure and maybe even thrive.

Cohen's wife, Rhonda, who was a year ahead of her husband at Penn Law, remembered the same quality that Makadon witnessed, an almost mystical ability to know precisely what is important. Already married, they had breakfast together on the day of a major examination in a course they both were taking. David started firing potential questions at her. He cited material from the footnotes, and Rhonda told him he had gotten it all wrong, his studying had been completely off the mark. *Footnotes—who on earth would base his studying on the footnotes?* Later that day she got the exam and saw the questions. *The footnotes—the damn footnotes.* It was as if he had written it.

As a summa cum laude graduate of the University of Pennsylvania Law School in 1981 and executive editor of the *Law Review,* he could have gone anywhere in the country. Law firms beckoned and hoped to impress him. At least one had him picked up in a limousine outside the federal courthouse in Philadelphia—a senior partner at the firm had thought Cohen would be flattered by the attention. Instead he was mortified and after the lunch insisted that he be dropped off a block from the courthouse so no one would see him. Makadon desired Cohen as well, for Ballard Spahr. But since he knew David Cohen and understood better than most the basic paradox of his personality, he also knew how laughable it was for anyone to think that Cohen might be dazzled by a limousine. In law school, Cohen was the master of his domain. Outside that sphere, he was so rounded and average that it was hard not to wonder whether some piece of him—the piece that seeks flamboyance and extravagance for the sheer frivolity and fun of it—had somehow been removed at birth. In a certain way, it made David Cohen seem very, very bizarre.

Makadon, knowing that one of Cohen's outside interests was sports, sought his attention by sending him *The Breaks of the Game* by David Halberstam. It worked, and Cohen agreed to the job at Ballard by hiring a woman to go to the offices with a bouquet of balloons and sing his words of acceptance.

Among the various gifts that Cohen received during his tenure at Ballard Spahr was that little wooden box with the calculator inside. On the front an inscription read, BILLING KING. The general rule of thumb at Ballard was a secretary for every two lawyers to handle the paperwork and filing and all the rest. But David Cohen didn't have just one secretary to handle the volume of work he produced. He had two. He billed close to four thousand hours, the legal equivalent of winning a batting title by a hundred points while hitting .450. But it wasn't just his prodigious capacity for work that made him so good at what he did. It was his patience as a negotiator, the way in which he determined the result that he wanted and then, as Makadon put it, exhibited a "willingness to stay with something forever"—until he got there. In the meantime, he never got frustrated. He never personalized or railed or sought vendettas. Once again the normal human impulse, to get angry and become agitated, never even surfaced. He went in for the kill by listening, by making eminently clear that he really didn't mind, he could sit in some shitty conference room like a prisoner of war for a year, maybe two, without a single speck of emotion other than affability until he got the result he wanted. Other lawyers would have gone mad. They would have relished the delicious moment when they reached across the table and strangled the pinstriped bastard on the other side who had made their lives so miserable for so many months. But not David Cohen. "I saw him sit with lawyers I couldn't even bear to be in the same room with for days and work out a resolution," said Makadon. "It was amazing to me."

Rhonda Cohen also worked at Ballard Spahr. In 1985, both she and her husband suffered personal trauma when their first son, Benjamin, was born, in a true medical rarity, after an ectopic pregnancy. Benjamin would go on to become a happy and enchanting child, but the initial period of his life was a nightmare. He spent more than a year at Children's Hospital of Philadelphia, where he was on a respirator for much of that time and enduring operation after operation. Cohen's routine, according to Makadon, almost never varied: he arrived at the hospital at 5:30 A.M. to be with Benjamin, got to work around 8:00 A.M., and worked nonstop for the next twelve hours, then returned to the hospital for several more hours. Makadon was Cohen's closest friend in the firm, but never once did Cohen discuss his feelings. The quality of his work never faltered. He never sought a sympathetic ear. His outward demeanor never changed.

Makadon couldn't think of a worse ordeal than those daily hospital visits. He also knew he could never have handled it the way Cohen did, by somehow managing to compartmentalize every single speck of it, as if, in the sphere of work and cases and thousands of billable hours, the emotion of what he was feeling had no place and was somehow separate and distinct.

By the time David Cohen was in his mid-thirties, he was one of the top business getters in a firm filled with notable rainmakers. He was making hundreds of thousands of dollars a year, and yet he showed little inclination to parlay it into something, to do something with it. He drove an old-model Saab. He lived with his wife and two children in a house on Lombard Street in the downtown section of the city that was shockingly modest for a family that was producing close to half a million dollars of income a year. He had a style of dress distinguished by the holes in the soles of his black shoes and the fraying collars of his button-down shirts. As the man he was about to go work for, Ed Rendell, would later say of him with true awe, "If you took David to a motel room, and there was a beautiful naked woman on one bed and a legal brief on the other, there would be no question. He'd head straight for the legal brief."

In the sublime silence of this Sunday night that would be the last silent night for the next four years, the moment of reckoning had come for David Cohen. As he quietly continued to pack what little was left, the grand tower of City Hall, some 548 feet high and until the mid-1980s the single high-est point in the entire city, loomed from the window. It was a strange and remarkable building—Walt Whitman once described it as both "weird" and "beautiful"—positioned in such a way, smack in the middle of Phila-delphia, that much of the downtown vehicular traffic had to circle around it in forced homage.

Started in 1871, at a very different period in the city's life, it took thirty years to build and at completion was the largest office space in the United States. Presumably it was built to symbolize the magnificence of govern-ment. The council chambers on the fourth floor were larger than the House of Lords in London. The walls on the first floor were twenty-two feet thick, and the twenty-seven-ton cast-iron statue of city founder William Penn, designed by Alexander Milne Calder, was, and still is, the largest single piece of sculpture atop any building in the world. But over time, as both the city and its government began to unravel, City Hall began to symbol-ize something else entirely, not a citadel for the majesty and machinery of government, but a symbol of the very mockery of it—a favored place for suicides (either from the 360-foot-high observation deck or from the six-story stairwell on the inside), knee-deep bird droppings, basement rats so big that only psychotic cats dared to stalk them, and false fire alarms so routine that no one bothered to budge.

In its mass of contradictions, City Hall was ornate enough to rival Ver-sailles, with its red Egyptian-marble columns and alabaster walls; de-pressing enough to rival a local jail with the soupy gloom of its dimly lit hallways and cigarette-stained floors; bizarre enough to rival a psychiatric ward with the disparate elements housed within it. The mayor and his im-mediate staff had offices there, of course, as did the seventeen members of the city council and their staffs. The majority of the city's criminal court-rooms were in City Hall as well. As a result, it wasn't unusual for the solemn flow of a meeting in the mayor's Cabinet Room on the second floor to be interrupted by the wail of a convicted felon. Among the hundreds of sculptures decorating the exterior of the building were four figures, Folly, Repentance, Pain, and Prayer. They were placed over the western archway in the hopes that prisoners being led into the building would see them and perhaps feel some inspiration to lead a proper life. In this regard, they also seemed apt figures for David Cohen.

In the comforting cubbyholes of Ballard Spahr, where everything spoke of order and rational flow, cases in, cases out, cases won and cases lost, hours and minutes billed, it was easy to feel control over the world. From the forty-sixth floor, even the city below seemed somehow innocent and workable—the slow trickle of cars, the tiny buildings, the lines of trees running up the straight and narrow streets, the imprint of a city still very much the same as the one William Penn laid out in the late 1600s, with its visionary grid of streets and squares and the natural boundaries of its two rivers, the Delaware to the east and the Schuylkill to the west.

For all of Cohen's success as a lawyer, there was something totally untested about him, particularly when it came to the glare of public service and his ability to deal head to head with elected officials who had spent a lifetime perfecting the art of bullying and manipulation and castration so quick and bloodless you didn't even know you had lost your essentials until you walked out of the room and noticed you were a little bit lighter.

Cohen was the chief of everything at Ballard Spahr, but the source of his fame at the firm had little to do with boldness and leadership and the indefinable art of personal interaction. He was known for how, in a case involving twenty different partnerships, he had kept track of every single one of them. He was known for being the first one to work in the morning and the last one to leave at night. He was known for the way he learned the nuances of group insurance by reading some five thousand pages on it. He was known for the way he sat in the firm library and researched a statute not for one state or five states or ten states, but for all fifty. He was known for the way he personally inspected every piece of mail his secretaries typed up for him, even the envelopes. All those qualities had made him a legend, the man who got things done. But in the house of horrors of City Hall, where nothing ever got done, what good could David Cohen possibly do?

As he stood at the window, he rationalized his decision for leaving by noting that the corner office had never really been his anyway, since Ballard Spahr had moved into the building only earlier the previous year. It was the careful, clinical thing to say. But for a moment the most uncommon of expressions, a flickering of self-doubt, flashed across his face. He uncharacteristically lingered at that window for a few seconds more, as if trying to find some solace and meaning in the tiny twinkling lights of the city. "There I'll be, right down there," he said quietly, but there was something tentative in the way he said it, as if he were packing and moving not to the job and the challenge of a lifetime but to a cabin in a forbidden wilderness, without food, electricity, or running water.

It wasn't a keen sense of public service that was driving Cohen to do what he was doing. Although he was intrigued by the challenge of somehow trying to right the capsizing ship of a major American city, that really wasn't his primary goal. Instead, he was motivated almost solely by loyalty to the man who was about to become the 127th mayor of the city of Philadelphia. When Rendell asked him to take on a specially created job within the administration, everybody who knew David Cohen also knew that he would say yes. Cohen adored Rendell and seemed willing to do anything for him. But given their respective styles and their respective temperaments, the way they did things and didn't do things, Cohen's leap into public service seemed all the more like a free fall into a swimming pool that a city maintenance worker had forgotten to fill with water.

II

It isn't unusual for grown adults to be awakened in the middle of the night by nightmares of being back in college. Usually the nightmares have to do with failing to study enough for an exam, maybe even missing it altogether because the alarm clock didn't go off. Ed Rendell had a recurring dream about his days as an undergraduate at the University of Pennsylvania in the 1960s, and like all dreams, it was tailored to the needs of his personality. In his version, the course at hand was astronomy. There were three days to go before the exam, and as Rendell himself explained it, the source of his anxiety was really twofold: "Not only haven't I studied; I can't even find the book."

As an undergraduate at Swarthmore, David Cohen took time off to work in the office of Congressman James Scheuer and graduated in the top 10 percent of his class. As an undergraduate at Penn, Ed Rendell got enormously involved in school government, had poor grades the first semester of his sophomore year, while he was being rushed for a fraternity, and was remembered by at least one professor not for the zeal with which he approached Penn academics but for the zeal with which he approached Penn co-eds. The fraternity he belonged to at Penn, Pi Lambda Phi, was known on campus as the Jewish animal house, and when Rendell joined it, it was under suspension for branding the Pi sign on the virginal buttocks of its pledges.

After college, David Cohen went to one of the nation's finest law schools—the University of Pennsylvania. After college, Rendell applied to Penn Law School, but despite being a Penn alumnus, he did not gain acceptance—the classic case of a very smart person with unique powers of memory and reasoning who saw college as a gilded fraternity house: he said he scored a 710 on his law boards, placing him the second highest of the Penn graduates applying for admission. But his grade point average, a 2.5, placed him 201st. Rendell went to Villanova Law School instead.

At Penn Law School, David Cohen became a legend because of his hard work and mature judgment. At Villanova University School of Law, Ed Rendell became a legend because of the apartment he lived in on Lombard Street. A frequent guest dubbed it the Ape House, an appellation Rendell did not even begin to dispute. "Oooh, what a pigpen," he recalled fondly. As for his future after law school, many agreed that it would be great, or at least interesting, as long as it had as little to do with the actual practice of law as possible.

David Cohen started going out with his future wife, Rhonda, at Swarthmore after they began to work on the school newspaper together. So worried was Rhonda about dating a coworker that she made him promise he would not quit the paper if they broke up. Ed Rendell's dating patterns in college were guided in part by the urgings of his mother, who seemed largely interested in his marrying someone rich. As a result, he went out with a stream of women who were pampered and obnoxious, albeit very rich—until he met Midge Osterlund. At the time, one of his closest friends, Dave Montgomery, who went on to become president of the Philadelphia Phillies, was on a date with Midge, and Rendell was with someone else. Rendell asked Montgomery how things were going with Midge, and when the response was lukewarm, Rendell proposed a trade: he would give Montgomery the dating rights to the woman he was seeing in return for rights to Midge. As an added incentive, Rendell agreed to throw in a couple of Peter Paul Mounds bars.

Midge had first met Rendell at the Ape House on Lombard Street, where, she remembered, his idea of doing dishes was to fill the bathtub with them and proceed from there. She was a junior at Penn from a Catholic family in Wilmington, Delaware, where her father, like just about everyone else in that city, worked for Du Pont. Rendell, in law school at that point, was a Jew from Riverside Drive on the Upper West Side of New York. She was blond and athletic with just the right touch of sass; he was dark and handsome and jutting-jawed with enough gestures and spontaneous outbursts to make a drum major jealous.

There was nothing casual about their on-again, off-again romance, nor was there anything remotely casual about him. She remembered sitting in awe and disbelief on one of their first dates, at a Penn basketball game, as he screamed and yelled. She remembered the way he ate, voraciously, with his fingers. She was intoxicated by his intensity and yet in another way was so overwhelmed by it that she broke up with him in the fall of her senior year at Penn. "Certain things about him were too intense," she remembered. But he continued to pursue her. And bit by bit she relented. In 1970, he proposed to her, and she said yes—because he was Ed Rendell, because it was hard to think of anyone else in the world quite like him. She later quipped that of all the Jewish men in the world, she "married the one who didn't care about money." It was true. Ed Rendell didn't care about money. But he did care about other things, with as much zeal as anyone who has made millions on Wall Street cares about money, and the intensity that Midge Rendell saw others had seen as well—galvanizing when it was focused, scary when it dissolved into temper tantrums and fits appropriate to children. "He was different," said Midge Rendell in recalling her first impression of him during those courtship days at Penn. "Everything about him was different."

There had always been something devilish and dramatic about him, the way he memorized the names of all the U.S. senators when he was a little boy, the way he loved to play football in the rain in high school because it felt so heroic, the way he once tried to get the guests to leave his Christmas party in the wee hours of the morning by serving them a special hors d'oeuvre of dog food mixed with mayonnaise, the way his eyes moistened when he talked about the death of his father. He couldn't sit still for more than a minute or two, and there was a perpetual frenzy to him. But he also possessed his own vision—not making money or excelling within the closed world of a corporate law firm as David Cohen had done, but something far riskier. He was one of those people who seemed destined for one of two things in life—early success or an early heart attack.

Much of Rendell's persona came from his father. An ardent New Dealer, Jesse Rendell took his son to Zabar's, the delicatessan over on Broadway, where they cupped their ears to a radio and listened to the 1952 Democratic National Convention. Emotional and full of life, Jesse Rendell wept when Adlai Stevenson was beaten by Dwight Eisenhower in the general election later that year. He lived and died each fall with the New York Giants in football and each spring with the New York Giants in baseball, and during the short period of time father and son were together, Jesse taught Ed to seize the intensity of the moment as if there might never be another one. When he died of a heart attack while hailing a cab, there was a sense of absolute shock in the family. Just two days earlier Jesse Rendell had played football in the park with his two boys. Nothing seemed wrong with him. But looking back on it later, Ed Rendell realized that his father, in his voraciousness for life, had also done everything wrong from a physical standpoint, smoking four packs of cigarettes and drinking a fifth of liquor virtually every day. By most accounts, Rendell's mother, Emma, had the opposite temperament of her husband's. When Ed and Midge started dating, they would go to New York to visit her. The apartment was dark, Midge recalled, and Emma was invariably in bed watching television. When she did rise, it was to walk over to the closet and see where Midge bought her clothing, since Emma's family had been in the fashion business. Other than that, Midge could not recall seeing Emma actually out of bed until she and Ed decided to get married. "I'd kind of have to peek into the bedroom to say hello to this woman," said Midge. "It was the weirdest thing."

What money the Rendell family had growing up in New York did apparently come from Ed's mother's side of the family. She was a Sloat, of the fashion-designer Sloats, makers of a popular line of women's skirts. Ed's father worked as a middleman in the garment district, buying raw material from textile mills and selling it to manufacturers. He never made much money, but as Rendell later recalled in a lengthy profile in *The Philadelphia Inquirer,* he "strove mightily to keep our standard of living up to that of my mother's family." The family's apartment at Eighty-first Street and Riverside Drive had thick walls and a wonderful view of the Hudson River and was eventually sold to actors Eli Wallach and Anne Jackson. From the fourth grade on, Rendell and his brother, Robert, went to private schools. For high school, Rendell attended the prestigious Riverdale Country School. He was asked not to return at the end of his sophomore year for what he described in the *Inquirer* profile as "just little stuff. You know, disrupting classes, things like that. The worst thing I did, I dumped tuna fish on a teacher at lunch, somewhat accidentally, somewhat deliberately." He was readmitted to Riverdale for his senior year, in time for the editors of the 1961 yearbook to prophesy, "Eddie has a good chance for success in politics, his chosen profession." Then he went on to Penn and law school at Villanova.

After graduation from law school, in 1968, Rendell went to work for the district attorney's office in Philadelphia. If the legend grew around David Cohen for his ability to negotiate hour after hour, day after day, without ever personalizing and letting his emotions go, the legend grew around Ed

Rendell for exactly the opposite reasons. He once impulsively picked up the phone and screamed at the governor himself for releasing a convict in a prison-furlough program, according to the *Inquirer* profile. To make a point during a trial, he once dug his heel into a defense attorney's instep. When he got angry, he put his foot through the door of his office and tossed furniture and punched holes in walls.

He quickly worked his way up the hierarchy, becoming chief of the homicide unit. But then he left the office, and in December 1976 he decided to oppose the Democratic incumbent, District Attorney F. Emmett Fitzpatrick, in a primary race. It seemed a laughable campaign, filled with chutzpah and hubris, and no one gave Rendell much of a chance. "Ed who?" chortled Fitzpatrick when asked about his opponent. But Rendell refused to give in, sweeping the city away with his ability to talk to anyone for five minutes and make the person think a friendship had existed for years. Momentum built, and he coasted to easy victory in both the Democratic primary and the general election.

He became enormously popular. He wasn't afraid to take on judges for perceived ineptitude and handing out light sentences. Reporters adored him, not simply because of his warmth but because he was immensely helpful when they sought his assistance on stories exposing the ineptitude and the corruptness of the city's judicial system.

He had the swagger and the hard-jawed look of a hard-assed prosecutor, but behind the bluster was also a certain hesitation and weakness, particularly when it came to his own political career. He ran for reelection in 1981 and won in a landslide. The following year he had a clear opportunity to win the Democratic nomination for governor. But he backed off, only to watch a little-known Democratic challenger nearly topple the Republican incumbent. The decision gnawed at him. He was still the district attorney, but those who worked for him said it became increasingly clear that he had little interest in the job anymore. The esprit de corps with which he ran the office, his ability to hire the best talent away from the public defender's office, the personality that engendered such loyalty that you didn't really mind when he made you a promise you knew he couldn't possibly keep— all of it began to ebb. Those who worked for him could tell he was preoccupied with what he was going to do next to further his career. He finished his term as district attorney and ran for governor in 1986 in the Democratic primary, and he got trounced. The qualities that had made him so appealing in Philadelphia—the frat-house twinkle in the eye, the five o'clock shadow that appeared like a thundercloud, the viper's tongue that could make mincemeat out of judges—became an impediment in Altoona and Aliquippa and Allentown.

A year later, in 1987, he announced that he would run for mayor against the incumbent, W. Wilson Goode, in the Democratic primary. It was a terrible decision, and the campaign was even more of a disaster than the governor's race. He appeared flat, almost dazed, going through the motions without the passion that had once been his trademark, reading from press releases and position papers with all the spirit of a telemarketing salesman. Roughly a month before the election all his closest advisers knew he was going to lose, in part because of the monolithic nature of Goode's black voting base but also because it had become clear that Rendell had no real interest in the job of mayor beyond that it meant he would be getting back into politics.

But in the debacle and ashes of the 1987 mayoral race, something momentous occurred. It happened early in the campaign, before there even was a campaign, during a strategy meeting at Rendell's house. The subject of staff came up, and when it came time to recommend a press secretary, Makadon, in his ever expanding role as power broker, fund-raiser, and political adviser, piped in and said he had someone in mind whom he knew quite well, a guy named David Cohen.

At first, there was some confusion among the group that had gathered. There was a David Cohen who was highly active in city politics. He was a city councilman who was considered vituperative and unpredictable, so why on earth was Makadon suggesting him? No, not that David Cohen, said Makadon. Another David Cohen, a guy who was a thirty-one-year-old law partner in his office. But at least the other David Cohen knew *something* about politics, was actually *in* politics. What the hell did this David Cohen know about anything except being a corporate lawyer, which meant not knowing anything at all?

"Who the fuck is he?" said political strategist Neil Oxman to Makadon. "Do you know what the campaign is about? Do you think this is for amateurs?"

A week later someone with lengthy experience in politics wrote a draft of Rendell's announcement of his candidacy. It needed considerable rewriting, so Rendell decided to talk to David Cohen, and he hired him as his press secretary. Makadon knew that Oxman was basically right. It was a risky move. Rendell really should have taken someone with prior campaign experience. From a political vantage point, who the fuck was David Cohen?

To the reporters covering the campaign, Cohen was initially something of an oddity, too young, too boyish looking, too insulated and buttoned-down ever to enter the dark and treacherous tunnels of city politics. He adapted quickly, though, earning high marks for credibility and prompt responses to questions, but given the whole tenor of the campaign something about what he was doing still seemed out of sync, just as something about what the candidate himself was doing *was* out of sync. "I became convinced that Ed didn't want to be mayor any more than I wanted to be mayor," Cohen admitted after the election was over. "He had simply wandered from one losing campaign to another because he didn't know what else to do."

III

By the summer of 1987, Ed Rendell had been given up for dead, a fallen politician wandering about in a fallen city, the lumbering walk that had once been so endearing, so strangely lovable in a way, now seeming more like a limp. Embarrassed by Goode in the Democratic primary, he went back to private life and practiced law. Sitting behind a shiny and empty desk, playing with a little pile of paper clips that his secretary had set out for him, bending the metal ends back and forth, he seemed lost. There was something sheepish about him, something insecure, and he talked of how strange it was to go home at night and watch television with Midge and their son, Jesse. Those who knew him and saw the law firm he worked at, Mesirov Gelman Jaffe Cramer and Jamieson, or saw him socially after work, could feel the anxiousness that still welled inside him, the bolts of energy still running through him, but with no place to go. He held court. He gave opinions, but fewer and fewer were inclined to listen. It was hard not to feel sorry for him, hard not to think of him as one of those baseball players who after that great rookie season just fade away because the timing of the swing has gone sour.

"Ed was a lost soul,"Arthur Makadon remembered. "He was back in the Mesirov firm trying asbestos cases. It was just awkward."

Rendell himself, despite his outward buoyancy, knew what it was like to hit rock bottom. In 1988, he was the head of the Michael Dukakis campaign in the Pennsylvania presidential primary, and because of that he thought he would be named a "super" delegate to the Democratic National

Convention in Atlanta. Rendell had been a fixture at the Democratic conventions since 1980 and had even addressed the delegates when he had
been district attorney. (He was the first to admit that no one paid attention.
"Thirty seconds into my speech, it dawned on me that I could have been
reading the best parts of *Lady Chatterley's Lover* and it wouldn't have
mattered. Not a *fuck* or *put it in her* or anything. No one was listening.")

In 1988, Robert Casey, then the governor of Pennsylvania, and Mayor
Goode didn't want Rendell as a super delegate. If he wanted to come to the
convention, he could come as an alternate. Rendell had thought he was still
big enough politically that various Democratic forces around the state—
the governor, the mayor—would have to show him respect. He thought he
still counted for something, had some clout. Instead, as Rendell later put it,
he was "squished like a bug."

There were other moments as well, like the time he found himself trying to photocopy something at his law firm as if he were little more than
an office clerk. Rendell was not very good with machines. In fact, he hated
them, and they hated him, and when the copy machine at Mesirov Gelman
failed to respond to his increasingly desperate commands, he couldn't take
it anymore. *"This is how my luck has been for two years!"* he wailed as he
banged his head against a wall.

While others deserted Rendell after 1987, David Cohen did not join the
ranks. They remained close friends, and when Rendell decided in 1990 to
run for mayor again, Cohen was there, this time in a much greater role, as
campaign manager.

Like many others in the city, Makadon had a crisp and distinct reaction
when Cohen told him that Rendell was thinking of running for mayor
again and that he was thinking of helping him: "You must be out of your
mind."

Rendell's initial efforts seemed futile, almost painful. He held a dinner
at the Union League on South Broad Street, hoping to raise money so that
he could be ready to announce his candidacy officially if the outcome of a
poll that was being taken and paid for by an old classmate from high school
proved favorable. But for the thirty-five people who gathered at the dinner
in the cold shadows of one of the club dining rooms, there was hardly a
sense of buoyancy. They liked him. Anyone who met Ed Rendell for more
than a minute liked him. But when it came to raising money, how could
they convince anyone that he wasn't a perpetual loser? They also knew
how high the stakes were this time around. "This guy was looking at death

at the time," said Alan Kessler, who had an office near Rendell's at Mesirov Gelman and was a key political fund-raiser. "He knew that this was pretty much it for elective office."

When the poll was done, it showed something that perhaps only Rendell himself had believed—he could win the Democratic mayoral primary. Like a Fuller Brush salesman selling his wares out of a suitcase, he carried that poll from office to office, showing the white men in the dark suits who contributed the money and also raised it that he was back and his time had finally come. On the basis of that poll, money was raised. On the basis of that money, bits and pieces of momentum were gained, but it still wasn't easy. He announced his candidacy against a backdrop of humble and quaint row-house homes on Myrtlewood Street, but there was hardly a sense of anticipation in the air. Cohen watched the proceedings nervously, convinced that the media, the first time they mentioned Rendell in their stories, would immediately refer to him as a two-time political loser vainly trying to make a comeback. His fears were not unfounded. "Edward G. Rendell, the former district attorney who has not won an election in nine years, yesterday became the first official candidate in the 1991 mayoral campaign," wrote the *Inquirer.* But bit by bit, the tag of "loser" began to fade. People who had stopped listening began to listen again, and when they did, they heard a different man, someone who finally had a sense of who he was and what he was and what he should be, someone who spoke about the city deep from his heart and not as if Cohen had just handed him a position paper about it. Humiliation, as it turned out, had been very good for him, for it had forced him to seize the one quality that had proved most elusive in his life—a sense of purpose beyond the immediacy of the moment.

"Somehow," recalled Neil Oxman, "he woke up in 1990 and said, 'I'm going to do this the right way.' "

As he campaigned, he did something he had never really done before in his entire life in any genuine way. He listened much more than he talked, and in a city so far down at its heels, there was no shortage of what needed to be done. Ten-year-old members of the Fishtown Soccer Club asked him to fix up the field they played on, which had been reduced to hard-packed dirt. Thick-fingered butchers in white shirts and bloodied aprons at the Thriftway supermarket over in Port Richmond asked him to please re-member that not all union men were scofflaws. A black woman outside Helen's Wig Fashion in Point Breeze asked him whether there was any way of finding jobs for young kids so they wouldn't roam the streets. A man in his thirties at a shopping center in North Philadelphia told him that he and his family were economically drowning. "We're sinking every day," he said. "The slightest thing that comes up, we're in the hole. We're under the gun. We worry to the point where we're thinking of moving out of the city." But he didn't want to leave. "I have lived here all my life. I know no other place."

When Rendell spoke about the city, there was a passion in his voice, and not some thin veneer of playacting. He didn't minimize the city's problems, particularly its financial ones, but instead of deflecting and blaming and saying the answer lay in increased help from the federal and state governments, he said that the city had no right to ask anyone for anything until it got its own house in order. Radical change must come from within, he said, and voters admired him for that.

The unpredictable factors of political luck, which had not kicked into place in the nearly fifteen years since that first district attorney's race, suddenly went to his advantage. Those who should have dropped out of the race in the Democratic primary stayed in. Those who should have stayed in dropped out. Instead of facing a single black candidate head-on, he faced two black opponents. They splintered the city's formidable Democratic black vote, and Rendell coasted to easy victory in the primary. In the general election, his opponent was the legendary former mayor of the city, Frank L. Rizzo. But Rizzo died suddenly over the summer, and Rendell's path to victory became effortless. He won the general election in a landslide with nearly 65 percent of the vote, and there he was on January 6, 1992, at the head of the line at the Academy of Music on Broad Street, about to give his inaugural speech as the newest mayor of the city. Pacing back and forth in the Academy's reception room backstage, he shaved and then gargled with mouthwash. He went over a few last-minute details with Cohen, then left the reception room a few minutes before 10:00 A.M.

"Here we go," he said in a voice that was nervous and almost bemused, like a parent suddenly finding himself in the lead car of the newest roller-coaster ride at Six Flags with no time to take it all back. It was a crowning moment, taking place in this splendid hall where for ninety-two years the Philadelphia Orchestra had spun symphonies and concerti as magical as any on earth. In a box to the left sat Rendell's family, Midge beaming and vindicated after those dark election losses of 1986 and 1987, when her husband had lost those two elections back-to-back. Next to her was their eleven-year-old son, Jesse, at that age of perpetual gawkishness, when the blue blazer and the button-down shirt and the penny loafers all seem slightly out of kilter.

In the fourth row sat some of Rendell's closest friends and advisers: Cohen, Oxman, Makadon. The three had spent endless hours together during the campaign, acting more like fraternity brothers than grown professionals, needling, cajoling, screaming, cynical and suspicious of any need or suggestion that didn't come from the sanctity of their own lips, but as Rendell moved to the podium, they were clearly overcome with emotion, and their eyes seemed moist.

Behind Rendell on the Academy stage was a short row of state power brokers—Governor Casey and U.S. Senators Harris Wofford and Arlen Specter. Certainly they could do a great deal to make or break Rendell's term in office with their power of the purse strings. But they didn't wield nearly as much clout as the group that sat behind them on the stage, a mélange of city council members and city commissioners and city judges with necks too big for their shirt collars and dresses more suitable for a high school prom than an inauguration. Over the past decade, more than a dozen of their former brethren had been sent to jail for selling their offices to a variety of bidders. But this group still had power, the kind of power that if dispensed vindictively and capriciously, as it usually was, could make Rendell's life as mayor miserable.

Mixed in with this group was someone who wasn't a council member or a commissioner or a judge. Relegated to the back of the stage, he seemed virtually anonymous, an afterthought. But eight years earlier in this same hall, with many of the same people watching and wondering, he had ignited the city with his own best intentions.

We are a diverse people and we share a deep optimism about our future. Today, we begin to shape that future. Let the word go out loud and clear: Philadelphia is on the move again.

The man who said those words was the son of a North Carolina sharecropper. He was also the city's first black mayor, W. Wilson Goode. During his first hundred days in office, he promised to attack the problems of the city with a swiftness and a savagery never witnessed before. He did not produce as much as promised, but his best intentions continued to generate enormous goodwill, until one of the strangest and most horrifying days in American urban history, May 13, 1985, when police dropped a bomb on a West Philadelphia row house containing members of the radical group MOVE. Paralyzed by fear, torn by a set of choices that offered no easy answer, Wilson Goode sat in front of a television set in silence hour after hour after hour, watching a fire burn out of control until sixty-one homes had been reduced to rubble and eleven people had died.

From that moment on, the best of intentions were not enough to save the mayor. The city, like a living creature, began to devour him. The problems of the homeless, crack, a sinking economy, race, and his own tragic indecisiveness did him in without remorse. "He still stands around believing in the power of good intentions, which are fine if you're running a soup kitchen, but not if you're running a hard-luck city teeming with a mutant strain of political hacks," wrote Steve Lopez, a columnist for the *Inquirer* and the city's leading voice. By the time of Rendell's inauguration ceremony, Goode was like a ghost, the wisp of a man who had once stood in this very same building and had said in that confident and clear voice: *"Philadelphia is on the move again."*

For much of the inauguration ceremony, his eyes were dull and his lips tightly pursed, whatever emotion he had started with as mayor seemingly drained by the end of his administration, when everyone, even those who had worked side by side with him, seemed determined to betray and humiliate him with endless anecdotes about his isolation and incompetence. Shortly before the ceremony, Goode had seen Cohen backstage. It seemed like the perfect time for something private and maybe even inspirational, the passing of the torch from the outgoing administration to the incoming one.

"Hi, David."

"Hi, Mayor."

"Good luck."

That was it.

The only change in Goode's expression during the ceremony came during a prayer, when he closed his eyes so hard it almost seemed to hurt. That was Goode's final act as mayor. The job, mercifully perhaps, wasn't his anymore. Someone else could stand before the gathered crowd, promising miracles and betterment and the best of intentions. Someone else could imbue himself with the notion that the impossible, the salvation of a dying and obsolete city, was still possible.

IV

When the moment was finally his, Edward G. Rendell, then forty-eight, shuffled to the edge of the stage of the Academy of Music. With both hands firmly on the podium, he made the speech that he had waited a lifetime to make.

Make no mistake, our situation is worse than we thought it could ever be. Projected deficits in the years ahead number in the hundreds of millions of dollars. And the shame of it is that those deficits do not even begin to tell us the costs of their consequences. These costs—the costs of unsafe streets, of dirty neighborhoods, of struggling schools, of shut-down health clinics and recreation centers—these costs are simply incalculable.

We have put off difficult choices for far too long. We have been too willing to accept the old way of doing things. In the face of long-term challenges, we have opted for short-term fixes. And we have shown virtually no courage or backbone in standing up to pressure against outside interests.

Change must surely come, but the good news is that if it does come, this city cannot only survive; it can come alive again with a thriving economy, strong neighborhoods, and a dynamic downtown that can serve as a magnet to conventioneers, tourists, and suburbanites alike.

To make this change a reality, I want to issue a few challenges:

To everyone involved in government, to no longer accept the old way of doing things, but to challenge them, change them, and get results.

To the seventeen city council members on this stage with me today, to put aside politics, partisanship, and personal gain to forge a working relationship with me second to none in this city's long history.

To our municipal unions and their four fine leaders, to join with us and help this city survive and flourish as other unions have joined together with their employers to keep those businesses afloat.

To the people of Philadelphia, to be willing to accept short-run sacrifices and pain that will allow us to get through the near future and lead to tremendous long-run gain for all of us.

And lastly, a challenge to myself, to stand tall, to stay the course, and make the difficult choices unflinchingly, regardless of what the pressure to do otherwise might be and regardless of the political risks involved.

I cannot and will not falter.

We cannot and will not fail.

The stakes are too high.
The cost of our failing is unthinkable.

Roughly twelve hours later, the pomp of the day finally tucked away, Ed Rendell appeared at an inauguration party at the city's Reading Terminal Market. Amid the pungent smell of spices and fish from the rows of eclectic food stalls, he was greeted by a Chinese dragon spinning its papier-mâché tail, then by the furry green fuzz of the Phillie Phanatic mascot. A crush of people surrounded him as if he were a boxer making his grand return to the ring, and his brown eyes were electric and lit with a little boy's anticipation. Through perseverance and luck and the strength of his own confidence, he had made a startling comeback in a city that had given him up for dead. As he walked across the concrete floor, people reached out to grab his hand and touch him. For some, it was a matter of connecting with someone who was now important. For others, it was the simple act of reaching out to someone who, after all he had been through, was still the same old Ed.

Rendell reacted to it all without a trace of self-importance. He blew kisses. He posed for pictures. He squeezed arms. He didn't turn down a single request for attention, regardless of where it came from, but he also paid attention to his own needs. When a resplendent plate of pastries was brought his way by a waiter, his eyes turned almost moist."I'll take two!" he said, grabbing at them as if he had just heard a rumor that the caterer was about to leave the country. Music pulsated from a stage that had been set up in the center of the terminal, and Rendell joined in with relish. He clapped as the band played "In the Midnight Hour." He got up onstage and sang the old Beatles song "Twist and Shout" without a twitch of self-consciousness, even though his singing style resembled a doglike croon. He did a little chain dance to another song. When the leader of the band yelled to the feverish crowd, "How many people are happy that Ed Rendell is the mayor of Philadelphia?" the applause in the room was loud and strong, except for one tiny voice of dissent.

"Not me," said Rendell with a devilish smile on his face.

At the stroke of midnight, a cake in the shape of the city was brought out, and it didn't take long before little chunks were being stuffed into Rendell's mouth as if he were the groom at a wedding. From several feet away, Bob Brady, the chairman of the city's Democratic party, watched the proceedings with a grandfatherly benevolence. Political decorum would dictate that chunks of cake should probably not be forced into the mouth of the mayor of the fifth-largest city in the country even under the most joyous of circumstances. But Brady had been down this road many times, and he seemed to know instinctively that the best night of a mayor's life was usually this very first one. "Let 'im have fun," said Brady. "Tomorrow he'll wake up and say, 'I'm the fucking what? What the fuck happened?' "

Behind the swell of hope and optimism lay the unraveling of a once glorious American city. And there were also issues of Rendell's character. Several weeks before the election in November, Cohen had gotten word from a variety of sources that the *Inquirer* was delving with a vengeance into allegations that Rendell had engaged in acts of sexual harassment while district attorney. Cohen received nearly thirty phone calls from individuals who had either been contacted by the newspaper or were aware of the investigation, and so he knew intricate details of it: the names of the reporters assigned, the supervising editor, and the kinds of allegations being pursued. He knew that the investigation had generated considerable controversy within the paper's newsroom—some thought it was a legitimate story; some thought it had nothing to do with anything. Cohen questioned the timing. Such rumors were not new. Virtually every time Rendell had run for office, they had cropped up. So why all of a sudden were they being vigorously pursued? The more Cohen learned, the more he became convinced that the paper was conducting a kind of witch-hunt, contacting a secretary in one instance to ask her whether Rendell had once chased her around the office in the nude. The paper never published a word of what it learned or didn't learn. But from this episode alone, it seemed likely that questions of Rendell's character and behavior were not simply going to disappear.

As Ed Rendell danced and sang and rocked back and forth in a red cap that said RIZZO'S PIZZA on the front, David Cohen stood on the fringes, away from the music and the stage. He wore a tuxedo, but given the way his eyes scanned every detail, he might as well have been at the top of a ridge dressed in dark glasses and camouflage, armed with binoculars and a map pointer. He too received his share of congratulations, but whereas there was a grace period for the mayor, there was no grace period for him. Much of his evening, in fact, had been taken up with people who wanted jobs with the city now that a new mayor was coming into office. Amid the pulsating swell of the music, one such job seeker came forward to ask Cohen whether he had received his covering letter and résumé. Cohen listened to the name thoughtfully and then politely offered acknowledgment: "Buff-colored paper with a signature on the left-hand side."

It *had* been buff-colored paper. The signature *had* been on the left side. How could anyone have remembered that? *Why* would anyone have remembered that? "That's right," said the man with a strange look on his face. Cohen gave a modest shrug. After all, why wouldn't he have remembered the résumé?

There had been only four thousand of them.

It was a grand party and a grand day, and no one begrudged the mayor a single second of it. When he woke up the next morning and went to work, the first item on the agenda, among roughly a thousand, would be how to somehow right the city's financial condition and stave off bankruptcy. Beyond that, one could already feel the first rumblings of the war with the unions that would take place in the coming summer, not a war simply about the usual territories of wages and benefits but a war over the ability of government to reclaim itself and act as an instigator of bold change, not an impediment to it. These were immediate crises that might somehow lend themselves to reversal with ample amounts of luck and miracle. Beyond them lay problems that seemed impervious to hope or even the barest outlines of solution.

There was the disgrace of public housing, where the vacancy rate hovered at 20 percent and children got third-degree burns from exposed pipes that melted the skin in a sizzle. There was the shame of the schools, whose teachers taught with contempt in a system where 60 percent of the elementary school students lived at the poverty level. There was the flow of manufacturing jobs, 80 percent of which had been lost, and there was the vast industrial heritage of the city, whose once proud moniker, Workshop of the World, was now just a cruel taunt. There was the despair of the neighborhoods, where in many cases the only answer to these once sturdy blocks, as bleached of life as a skull in the desert, was to borrow a chapter from Vietnam and save them by demolishing them. There were the pockets of despair in the city's black neighborhoods, where heroic grandmothers who had already raised their grandchildren were now raising their great-grandchildren and were hoping to veer them somehow from the path of dice games and drugs and drive-by shootings that had become rhythm and regimen. There were pockets of anger in "changing" neighborhoods, where those who worked and suffered through the wage tax and believed and luxuriated in the heartbeat of the city felt they were being driven out by those who didn't work and didn't care and had no respect for themselves, much less for anyone around them. There was the fear of the men and women who worked at After Six stitching tuxedos or at Whitman's making chocolates or over at the navy yard at the foot of Broad repairing ships suddenly being told to find new lives and new means of employment because these places were closing up for good.

"There's so much work to be done," said Nellie Reynolds, who had lived her whole life in the city and had been a longtime activist on behalf of housing for the poor. "The city looks like it has gone to the dogs. Everybody looks to the mayor like he is the gospel, but everyone knows that it's going to take more than one person to clean up this mess." But in the giddiness of that inaugural night nobody seemed to believe that at all.

Shortly after Rendell's victory in November, political strategist Oxman had written a confidential memo with fourteen points that the new mayor needed to tackle to succeed. The memo had a political framework, but it went beyond politics and urged Rendell to do what was right, regardless of how hard that might be, regardless of the virulence with which others might fight him. The very life and future of a city was at stake now, and the hard choices, the choices that no politician made anymore, must become the only choices.

"Remember, Ed Rendell has won a huge mandate for change," wrote Oxman. "You can take over everything. Fuck them all."

TWO

The Number

I

It was somewhere around 2:30 A.M. when David L. Cohen and F. John White ran the model through the computer to discover whether there was even the slightest prayer. White was the managing director of a company called Public Financial Management, which specialized in helping municipalities discover creative financial paths out of seemingly intractable financial disasters. He knew the hidden arteries and veins of big-city finance as well as anyone else, and so did Cohen, who, by the arduous and tireless embrace of foot-thick documents, had become the city's leading budget expert. They were in White's corner office on the sixteenth floor of a downtown office building, huddled over the computer next to White's desk, and the sense of anticipation was palpable. After hundreds of hours of interviews with city department heads, a few of them fruitful but most of them ending in *Waiting for Godot*–like curlicues—*Is this your budget? Is this not your budget?*—they were finally going to get a number, *the* Number, that would quantify the extent of the city's budget mess and show the cumulative deficit over the next five years if no corrective action was taken.

It was January of 1992, shortly after the inauguration, and of all the activities that Cohen might seize during the four years of the mayor's term in office, none was as important as this. Without the Number, they could not even try to begin to move the city forward. Of course, once they had the Number, it might also become apparent, less than one month into a term in which there were still forty-seven left, that they would *never* be able to move the city forward. Perhaps it would be better, as the previous administrations had done, to get out the pad and abacus and fairy dust and number blocks, make a calculated guess, and spin tales better than those of Charles Dickens.

Sitting at the keyboard, White punched the requisite data into the model—projected revenues based on the various taxes that the city levied, various fees the city charged, state and federal aid; projected obligations based on salaries and benefits for city workers and the cost of services that the city purchased from outside vendors. The computer paused momentarily and then returned the Number.

Emotional reactions to budget-forecast models were not part of the financial vernacular, particularly for someone like White, who saw weird numbers all the time. Numbers, after all, were numbers. But *what was this*? Then it became obvious what had happened. In the lateness of the hour, he had simply made a clerical mistake, punched in some incorrect data. With Cohen still next to him, he went through the same procedure.

The computer again paused momentarily, then returned the Number once again.

John White looked at it, and so of course did Cohen, and they quickly noticed the same thing. It was exactly the same as when White had punched in the data the first time. There had been no clerical error. There had been no mistake.

$1.246 BILLION

That was the Number glaring at them from the computer screen. That would be the budget gap over the next five years if nothing was done: *one billion two hundred forty-six million dollars*—a budget deficit bigger than the entire budget of Boston or Houston or Baltimore.

John White looked at David Cohen. David Cohen looked at John White. "Holy shit," said White. "This is bad."

II

It was still occasionally called the City of Firsts, and it was more than mere promotional gimmick, even though so many of the firsts had occurred so long ago that few who lived in the city were aware of them—the first public school in the colonies, the first American paper mill, the first stone bridge, the first botanical garden, the first volunteer fire company, the first American magazine, the first American hospital, the first American insurance company, the first American stock exchange, the first American theater, the first production of an American play, the first carpet woven in America, the first piano made in America, the first American corporate bank, the first daily American newspaper, the first circus, the first balloon flight, the first public building lit by gas, the first American-made lager beer, the first screw-propeller steamship, the first American minstrel show, the first Republican National Convention, the first American zoological society, the first American merry-go-round, the first women's suffrage demonstrations, the first telephone book, the first Salvation Army in America, the first black newspaper, the first revolving door, the first Automat, the first Girl Scout cookie sale, the first city wage tax.

It was perhaps a symptom of things to come that the last of these firsts occurred in 1938. Even then there were serious signs of implosion and decay, the beginnings of a two-tiered society in the city, the haves and the have-nots, the rich and the poor, nuggets of wealth surrounded by rings of decline. But in the headiness of the American era, particularly after World War II, the signs were largely ignored. Outwardly, at least during the 1950s, the city still managed to sustain itself rather well, and nothing but growth seemed to be on the horizon.

In 1960, an enthusiastic plan by the City Planning Commission predicted that the population of Philadelphia would be a minimum of 2.25 million by 1980 and perhaps as high as 2.7 million. The plan predicted a robust increase in manufacturing employment, with the exception of jobs in the textile industry, and an increase in citywide employment above the magic one million mark. Printed lovingly on the finest paper, the plan was bold and energizing to read, a testament to the optimism of the American spirit that existed then not just in regard to the city of Philadelphia but in regard to all American cities, the idea that nothing could diminish regardless of what evidence there might be to the contrary. It was also one of the most wrongheaded documents ever created, a symbol of the dangers of urban myopia. By 1960, conditions in many American cities were already alarming. A social upheaval was taking place, but still no one wanted to listen to those who recognized it and issued warnings. White middle-class flight to the suburbs fueled by the crafty and relentless engine of federal policy; black migration by the millions from the South spurred by the dream of industrial jobs that were already dwindling and beyond reach; the rapid loss of manufacturing to nearby locales, where the land was cheaper and more plentiful for efficient, one-story assembly lines; the shift from downtown shopping to suburban strip malls and to the latest retail invention, the indoor shopping mall; the ravages of the slums and the ignoble record of urban renewal—these were just some of the evident problems that would multiply exponentially over the next thirty years.

"The modern city can be the most ruthless enemy of the good life, or it can be its servant," President Lyndon Johnson said in 1965. "The choice is up to this generation of Americans. For this is truly the time of decision for the American city." The generation Johnson beckoned to clearly responded. By leaving.

In 1950, ten of the country's twelve largest cities reached their highest populations ever. After that moment, the American city was never the same. By 1966, the proportion of nonwhites living in cities of more than 250,000 had nearly doubled, to 23 percent. For the vast majority of these residents, it was a wrenching and almost horrifying transition to urban life, and this was a demographic shift that only intensified in later decades. Between 1950 and 1990, the population of Detroit dropped 44 percent while the proportion of minorities increased to 79 percent. The population of Cleveland dropped 45 percent while the proportion of minorities increased to 53 percent. The population of Milwaukee dropped 15 percent while the proportion of minorities increased to 39 percent. The population of Chicago dropped 23 percent while the proportion of minorities increased to 60 percent. The population of Newark dropped 38 percent while the proportion of minorities increased to 82 percent. In Philadelphia, the population of the city dropped 23 percent from its peak, and the proportion of minorities increased to 45 percent.

For many of these minorities, the move to the city was beset with hostility and alienation. Instead of finding the promised land, they found only the sealed-off physique of the ghetto, and what made these statistics even more distressing were studies showing that the incidence of poverty in cities was growing. Between 1980 and 1990, according to one such study, the number of blacks living in urban ghettos had increased nearly 40 percent, from 4.3 million to 5.9 million.

Philadelphia itself continued to compile firsts during the 1970s and 1980s, but they were different firsts: the first city in the country to have as its mayor a former police chief who didn't have a high school education and once wore a nightstick in his tuxedo cummerbund; the first city in the country to be sued by the Justice Department for systematic police brutality; the first city in the country to have a mass murderer who was fond of torturing his victims and also invested rather well in the stock market; the first city in the country in which a remarkable number of people thought the statue of a movie prizefighter belonged at the top of the steps leading to the art museum.

After 1960, the city of Philadelphia did not gain a minimum of 225,000 residents, as the Planning Commission had so rosily predicted. Instead, between 1960 and 1990, the city *lost* 400,000 residents. Once the country's third-largest city, by 1990 it was only the fifth largest, with 1.58 million residents, and the number of inhabitants in the city was the smallest since 1910. Beyond sheer population loss, an analysis of the numbers showed a nearly 30 percent drop in the number of middle-income families. The phenomenon only reinforced a place that had the demographic look of a lopsided sandwich, a thin piece of bread on top and a thick piece of bread at the bottom, but less and less meat in between to provide consistent nourishment and sustenance. Unless the trend somehow reversed, the middle-income would continue to leave a city that held no hope for them, beckoned by the suburbs and the most enduring American dream of all— private lot, private lawn, and private home. The small percentage of wealthy who could afford burdensome taxes and private schools would feast off a city that had wonderful shops and restaurants and privileged oases in which to live. The low income would always live in a city that by any standard of decency and morality had become unimaginable.

By 1990 in Philadelphia, 20 percent of the entire city was at the poverty level. Sixty percent of its children had been born to single mothers. Fifteen percent of them had had little or no prenatal care. Thirty-five percent of them were not adequately immunized. One in eleven had a case open with the city's Department of Human Services, the agency charged with protecting abused, neglected, and dependent children. In the city's public school system, 40 percent of those enrolled dropped out in high school.

There were also the compounding effects of the problems that arose during the 1980s that no one could have imagined: the number of AIDS cases in the city had gone from zero to more than 2,200; the number of people in treatment for cocaine abuse had gone from 117 to 10,480; the number of inmates in the city prison system had gone from 2,722 to 5,178. In 1981, there had been no city agency to serve the needs of the homeless. In 1990, with an estimated 5,000 people on the street at any given time, the city was budgeting close to $37 million to care for them. In 1981, the city had budgeted $510,000 for demolishing dilapidated buildings and industrial sites. By 1990, due to abandonment and population loss, that figure had increased more than tenfold, to $5.3 million, but it was still a losing battle. By 1992, there were 27,000 vacant residential buildings in Philadelphia, roughly 6 percent of the city's residential stock, and 15,800 parcels of vacant land. Another problem in the city that flourished was murder, which reached an all-time high of 500 homicides in 1990.

The number of jobs, instead of reaching the one million mark that the planners had predicted, had plummeted to about 750,000. Nearly 19 percent of those jobs came at taxpayers' expense, through the federal government, the state government, the local government, and the school district. In 1960, there had been roughly 300,000 manufacturing jobs in the city. By 1990, that figure had dropped to 85,000, and all these employment figures reflected the enormous shift in jobs from city to suburbs that had taken place over the past thirty years.

In 1959, 59 percent of the region's jobs had been within the city limits. By 1990, only 32 percent of the region's jobs were in the city. And this wasn't a trend unique to Philadelphia but was similar in virtually every major city in the country. In 1960, per capita income had been 5 percent greater in metropolitan-area cities than in their suburbs. In 1987, per capita income in central cities was 41 percent less than that of their surrounding suburbs. The revolution had come, the determined American march from city street to cul-de-sac was virtually complete, and by the 1990s people such as Ray Flynn of Boston and David Dinkins of New York and Tom Bradley of Los Angeles and Michael White of Cleveland and Ed Rendell of Philadelphia and Richard Daley of Chicago were left holding the broken pieces of what was left.

Out beyond the central business district, in the endless miles of built-up neighborhoods that some of us call the "grey areas," the rot goes on unchecked.

These words, uttered in 1959 by a Harvard professor named Raymond Vernon and reprinted in a Senate subcommittee publication, had been left to languish on the shelf of the urban studies section at the college library. Thirty years later they formed the urban motto.

III

In 1992, the City of Firsts needed an emergency jump start, something to restore credibility, any credibility, in government. Rendell had a narrow window of opportunity, and he needed to seize on something that offered the possibility of real change. However horrifying the Number was, the budget offered that opportunity. He could gain mightily from fixing it, but he had to do it in a way that was real. Creative budgeting, perhaps the most powerful and useful invention of modern politics, would not do philosophically or practically.

In May 1990, his predecessor, Mayor Goode, had introduced a budget so far-fetched and full of holes that the city controller responded to it by stating, "It may only be balanced for about seven hours." A month later, when Moody's Investors Service dropped the city below the level recommended for investors because of numerous uncertainties over the budget, Philadelphia became the only major city in the country to achieve junk-bond status. "Wilson will occasionally tell me I don't know how bad it is," Rendell had said privately of Mayor Goode several weeks before his own elevation to mayor. "What I think Wilson really means is 'Eddie doesn't know how badly I fucked it up.' It's like bailing out a boat. When you're three quarters done, are you going to find out there are two other leaks?"

Shortly after winning, that's exactly what Rendell did find—leaks, so many of them that it was hard to believe the boat had ever floated. Within weeks of his victory, *City and State* magazine came out with its annual survey on the fiscal soundness of the nation's fifty largest cities. Smack at the bottom was Philadelphia, and those who made a living studying municipal finance only rattled the death knell even more. The situation facing Rendell, said Rutgers University political scientist Ross Baker, is "one of the most hair-raising municipal horror stories in the country."

It didn't help that three of the city's budget analysts did not have computers powerful enough to analyze financial records. Or that city sanitation crews, because they lacked two-way radios in their trucks, could not get in touch with their supervisors when they had a breakdown and so used an emergency notification system that consisted of quarters fed into a pay phone. Or that payroll clerks filled out employees' daily time reports by hand. Or that marriage licenses languished in boxes and took months to file properly. Or that half a million dollars' worth of prison uniforms sat in a basement because someone supposedly did not like them. Or that the police department couldn't hire sketch artists but instead under union rules had to give police officers art lessons. Or that the Department of Human Services paid a provider nearly $115 a day for a camp program that, as Rendell put it, was roughly the same as a discounted rate per night at the Four Seasons Hotel.

Beyond the man-made problems, the city's financial crisis was further heightened by the areas in which the bulk of the money was being spent. In justifying their handling of the budget, Goode and others had argued that the city's financial position was not a reflection of bad management but a reflection of an unprecedented and frightening social upheaval that was taking place in America's cities. Costs of traditional municipal services had been held in check, but costs in four specific areas—health, prisons, courts, and child welfare—had gone up exponentially. The state of Pennsylvania did not assume the major burden of costs in these areas, and there would not be much help from the federal government. The amount of federal funding to the city was half what it had been ten years before when adjusted for inflation, and the number of federally funded city workers, nearly forty-five hundred at its peak, had dwindled to zero. If the federal government would not help to the degree that was necessary and the state would not help, should the city simply follow suit and turn off the spigot?

Rendell discovered that the immediate budget deficit wasn't $150 million but was closer to $250 million. He found out about the weekly cash meeting, at which the city, like a mom-and-pop grocery store staving off bankruptcy, went through a list of bills and figured out who had to be paid (the electrical contractor rewiring city office space was going to walk if he didn't get something) and who could be stiffed for another month or two (already $7 million in the hole to Catholic Charities, what was another $500,000?). In a macabre briefing with reporters, the outgoing city finance director predicted that when Rendell took office in January, the city would have only $36 million of its $2 billion budget left in the treasury, good for roughly a week and a half of routine spending. After that, there wouldn't be money for anything, not the salary of a city sanitation worker or the cost of cleaning up after a sudden snowstorm. On the eve of the inauguration, right around Christmastime, the city had $104 million in unpaid bills.

Merry Christmas, Ed Rendell.

Presumably, on paper at least, there was a way for the city to raise revenues sufficient to meet the needs of the budget: it could increase city taxes. Like a bolt of drugs to an addict, it would ease the pain and cause a momentary sense of relief. But once the rush was over, the need would be even worse than it had been before. In a decade of imposing such tax increases, the city's tax base had dropped $2 billion. Another tax increase, large or small, would hasten the exodus beyond all hope.

But as Rendell and Cohen and White and city budget analyst Mike Masch got over the initial terror of the Number, something strange happened. They were seized by a sense of opportunity that was both breathtaking and unprecedented, perhaps a little bit crazy. It fell largely in the area of personnel and in the amount of money the city paid its unionized workforce each year, not simply in salaries but in health benefits and paid holidays and disability and legal-fund contributions and funeral leave and a host of other items that the unions had negotiated over the years as a legal kickback for labor peace. What that meant was challenging the city's unions in a way in which they had never been challenged before. It also became clear that savings could be achieved by reining in city departments that seemed to find contrary to their purpose such budgetary practices as monitoring where the money went each month and actually meeting financial projections.

But the option of a bitter confrontation with the city unions wasn't an easy one, particularly in a town such as Philadelphia, where the cause of workers' rights had been fought with tears and even blood for nearly 150 years, stemming from a time when immigrants were paid sixty-three cents an hour for a fourteen-hour, six-day work week, with July Fourth as their only holiday. White knew intimately about the role of the unions in the city. Every day he was reminded of it by the picture in his office of a handsome and strong-jawed man who had helped lead a legendary strike against General Electric and Westinghouse in 1946 on behalf of the United Electrical Radio and Machine Workers of America. The strike went on for nearly a month and a half, and when union workers defied a court injunction limiting pickets, the police rode on horseback into the crowd of strikers to break up the blockade. The next day the pickets came back with bags of marbles to trip the horses with, and as the police flailed away with billy clubs and chased strikers across lawns, horrified residents opened their homes as sanctuaries. Some ten thousand people crowded around City Hall in a show of sympathy with the strikers, and finally, after fifty-seven days, the strike was settled when workers accepted a raise of $1.48 a day. The man in the picture was John White's father, Francis, and John was proud of his part in providing the worker with a better life in the city. But he also knew that times had changed. According to historians, the Philadelphia strike of 1946 represented the apotheosis of plant unionism in the United States. Companies responded by using their political clout to dismantle the power of the unions, and on a far more visceral and damaging level they began to take thousands upon thousands of jobs in the cities and move them to places where they didn't have to grapple with the unions because, praise the Lord, there were none.

                                    IV

The pivotal mechanism that had been created to deal with the city's enormous financial problems was a somewhat sad and sexless-sounding document called "City of Philadelphia: Five-Year Financial Plan." (In private, Rendell at least tried to brighten it up a little bit by calling it "City of Philadelphia: Five-Year Financial Plan—No Way Out.") Its creation was a requirement of an equally sad and sexless-sounding agency called the Pennsylvania Intergovernmental Cooperation Authority, which had been set up by the state legislature in June 1991, when the city was running a deficit of more than $100 million. Empowered to borrow hundreds of millions of dollars on the city's behalf, the state agency offered the city a way out of its crippling debt. But given the city's history of empty promises and phantom revenue streams that never flowed, it was not going to simply hand the money over with instructions to have a good time and try not to spend it all in one place. *Accountability* wasn't some catchphrase but was a requirement, and if the state agency didn't like the five-year plan and thought it was financial junk, it would reject it and the city would go into bankruptcy. It was as simple and as stark as that.

On a Wednesday night in the middle of February, after a series of grueling and painful twenty-hour days, the five-year plan was finished. All the pages, several hundred of them, were neatly laid out in twenty-eight little stacks at a ten-foot table in the conference room of Public Financial Management, each stack representing a different city department or public agency that did business with the city. The plan was so laden with charts and dotted lines that it would reduce the most earnest mind to a state of confusion. Even Cohen's wife, Rhonda, or Saint Rhonda as she had been dubbed during the campaign because of her blissfully even temperament, could barely muster excitement when her husband brought it home enthusiastically, as if it were the newest Grisham novel. But despite its turgid weight and volume, the five-year plan did carry a manifesto for dramatic and radical and unprecedented change in an American city. "What occurs in the next five years will determine our City's fate for the next quarter of a century," said the introduction.

From the conference room of PFM on this otherwise dreary night came the simmering sense of something powerful. Perhaps the very setting—a conference room with blue velvet chairs the size of bumper cars, in which lawyers and financial wizards moved about with the quiet confidence of their professional pedigrees—only skewed the real sight lines. For these men, the city would always work. They would always be in a place where the air was climate controlled. If they didn't find success here, they would surely find it someplace else. They lived in the city, and they loved the city, but they never had the sickening sensation of feeling trapped within it. And from this room, with a kind of schoolboy breathlessness, flowed a current that hadn't been felt in the city in years, a feeling that somehow, in some way, something within it could actually be changed.

Near the stroke of midnight, Cohen and White and the others who were there decided to call it quits. Cohen's red tie was pulled down, and the bleak stubs of a five o'clock shadow spread across his boyish face. His hair was greasy and his face puffy, reflecting the look of a man who hadn't slept in the past twenty-four hours, which in Cohen's case wasn't exactly true. He had actually slept about ten hours—in the past eight days. As he left the building, he had that furrowed look on his face, the look of a man with numbers whirring through his mind, a man searching for anything that might have gone undetected—a number off, a word out of sync, a fact over here that did not line up with a fact over there.

Down the street in the quiet night, a city trash truck went about its business picking up garbage. The grind of machinery supplied comfort, a presence on the otherwise deserted block. It was also hard not to notice the diligence with which they cleared away the debris, even at this late hour.

Suddenly, as if jolted by something, David Cohen started talking. "It's crazy!" he shrieked. "What are they doing out here at eleven-thirty at night!!" It wasn't their safety he was worried about, or the fact that they might be making too much noise. He knew, as surely as he knew anything, that they were working overtime, and the city was paying them time and a half.

He got into his car and headed south to Lombard Street. Neither his wife nor his children were up when he got home. Given that he had averaged about seventy-five minutes of sleep per night during the past eight days, he had a right to be tired. So he showered and got into bed, but still he wrestled with rest. The unions, the media—all would get copies of the five-year plan later that day, and Rendell himself would go on television to give a live address and present details of the plan to the public. Details, details, so many details, so many chances for screwups—unless he could master all of them. . . .

Several hours later, in the darkened gauze of the night, a nondescript black sedan with an ugly red interior parked across the street from City Hall. With the light from the streetlamps weakly splashing on the pavement, the man getting out of the car walked briskly and firmly. He opened the door at the northeast corner and then ascended the steps to the second floor. The sound of worn sole against hard floor majestically echoed, but only he was there to hear it. The time was 3:30 A.M.

David Cohen was back at work.

Sitting at the head of a large oval table in the Cabinet Room at 8:15 the next morning, Ed Rendell already looked exhausted. Lack of sleep had reduced his eyes to narrow slits, and his body looked pale and almost bloated, like a raft lost on the ocean. He would spend this day much as he had spent the previous one, pushing and pumping and pimping the five-year plan, trying to convince just about anyone willing to listen that this was an authentic blueprint for attacking the city's fiscal problems, not some glossy document that beyond the charts and the numbers read like pulp fiction. But he also knew that the measures he was seeking, particularly in a city in which the working person was a conquering hero, were draconian. Among other proposals, the plan called for a union wage freeze and drastic cutbacks in virtually every benefit that had been successfully bargained for over the years.

"Nobody wants to be viewed as a prick or a bad guy," he told a group of local labor leaders from the city's Building and Construction Trade Council in the privacy of the Cabinet Room. "Neither do I. I didn't cause this mess. I'm faced with the responsibility of trying to do something about it.

"There's a lot of pain," Rendell conceded. "A lot of people will be yelling at me. I understand that."

But Pat Gillespie, business manager of the council, wasn't sure whether Rendell really understood at all. "They don't trust you," said Gillespie, a handsome, husky man with a smile like an angel and a mouth like Madonna's. "It's not you personally. The city government has lied to them consistently. They've had it stuck up their ass."

But Rendell clung hard to the numbers in the five-year plan, and the more he talked, the more convincing he became, the timbre in his voice not one of theatrical fist pounding but more a kind of common man's incredulousness at just how rotten the system had become. Although he had been trained as a lawyer, Rendell spoke like a talk-show host—instantaneous warmth, humor, accessibility, and unpredictable volcanic explosions every so often, just to keep viewers glued to the screen.

"There hasn't been a bad day for these guys in thirty years," he said of the municipal unions, and he excitedly rattled off the wage increases they had gotten during the past three years despite a crippling recession. "Who do you know who got five, six, and eight in the last three years?! Who do you know?!"

There was no answer. If the city workforce didn't buy into what he was proposing, the alternative was really quite easy: as much as a sixth of the workforce—four thousand of twenty-four thousand employees—would have to be laid off once the contracts expired four and a half months from now, at the end of June.

"I've never been in a union, but when confronted between a wage freeze or no job, it's a pretty easy choice. Look at fiscal year ninety-two. There will be a two-hundred-sixteen-million-dollar cumulative deficit. If we do nothing [for the next five years], change nothing, freeze wages, put in inflation, we will have a one-point-two-billion-dollar deficit. A one-point-two-billion-dollar deficit, and this city will be destroyed."

Afterward, in the privacy of the mayor's office, Rendell and Cohen went over the speech to be televised that night. Most of the points they discussed were minor, centering largely on who in the political world had to be given credit regardless of whether or not they actually deserved credit. Rendell wanted to be slightly discerning, but Cohen's instinct was to err on the side of total inclusion. Rendell, after pondering for a moment, agreed. The names—"suck points" as Rendell called them—went in.

While Cohen sat still, making the changes at the round table, Rendell walked around the office, throwing a football into the air and then catching it. He sat at the table briefly, the football clutched in his hands, but before long the football popped out, skittered across the table, and headed straight for Cohen's head. It missed him by inches, a drive-by football.

"Sorry, David," said the mayor somewhat sheepishly.

Cohen didn't seem to notice.

When it came to the last line of the draft, Rendell felt there should be something new. Up to this moment, all the private briefings on the five-year plan had gone well, remarkably well, but the most important briefing of all, with the leaders of the four municipal unions, was not until that afternoon. And he knew better than anyone else that the five-year plan, as pretty as it looked on paper, could quickly dissolve into a public blood-letting. Given his view of the media, he could hear them filing down their incisors, making them razor sharp as they looked for the sweet and the meaty parts of the plan, the parts that could be torn to bits, this number off, this projected savings pie-in-the-sky voodoo, eager to portray the new mayor in the very stance he hoped to avoid—locked in some epic do-or-die struggle against the city workforce. So for the moment at least, Rendell thought it might be better to end the speech this way:

Thank you. Good night. I'm going away for a month. You can reach me in Aruba. I made a plan, and now I'm out of here. I'll be back to watch the NCAAs in basketball.

Several hours later Rendell braced himself for the briefing with the city unions. Hoping to establish a spirit of cooperation, he carried with him individual letters to each, asking for productivity suggestions. If any of them could come up with ways to save money that would lessen the impact on salaries and benefits, he was all for it. The meeting was set for 5:30 P.M., but as minute after minute ticked by after the appointed time, it became apparent there was a problem. As the mayor stood in a holding area between his private office and the Cabinet Room, his good mood, which had lasted the entire day, began to crumble. He didn't get angry but seemed chagrined, like a little boy whose plans for a memorable birthday party, with hats and noisemakers and jam-packed treat bags, had dissolved when no one even bothered to return his invitation. "I guess nobody's showing up," said the mayor quietly, and he was precisely right. Nobody from the city's unions was showing up, and Rendell knew immediately the symbolism of that.

"This is the story," said Rendell, whose instinct for news was as keen as any reporter's. "The rest is all bullshit." He looked sadly at the letters he had so carefully planned to hand-deliver, the perfect olive branch that had been met with a cigar-size middle finger, a very bad omen of things to come. He patted them gently and then put them away. "I guess we'll have to send these."

An hour later Rendell was in the studio of a local television station. He was moments away from giving the most important speech of his life, one that would be watched by hundreds of thousands, but the impact of the snub by the unions still gnawed. "I'll tell you one term may be enough, more than enough," he said, his month and a half as mayor more like a millennium. And then, at exactly 7:00 P.M., as the on-the-air light went on, a new spirit seemed to float into his body. Weariness was replaced by comforting strength, and of all the political skills that Ed Rendell possessed, his most valuable may have been the way in which he conveyed horrific news. The city was on the brink of bankruptcy. An ugly confrontation with the municipal unions seemed inevitable, no matter how much he tried to delay it. The Number hovered like a guillotine. People were fleeing the city by the thousands, and so were jobs. But he made all of it somehow sound like a wonderful opportunity for change and renewal if everyone in the once-shining city would put aside petty differences and come together. The unions would have to sacrifice, but, he also announced, cabinet members and appointed officials, including himself, would take an immediate 5 percent pay cut. "Everybody is going to have to be part of the solution," he said, and he firmly established that the city's efforts to right itself financially must finally come from the city and not in bailouts from the state and federal government. "The only resources that we can rely on to solve our problems is ourselves."

The unions hated what he had to say, but in the corridors of the state capitol and the equally important offices of Wall Street, the response was unprecedented, what one called "a new day." Rendell himself was aglow afterward, but he knew the moment would not last, because moments such as these in the life of the city were always just that. Moments.

V

"Go! Go! Go!"

The mayor ground his teeth as he said it, spitting the words with such venom that they came out like little projectiles, capable of rocketing across the wide berth of his office and causing punctures in the wall. It was now April Fool's Day 1992, but the time-bomb look on his face, menacing and slightly contorted, indicated that any kind of prank would be highly risky. His meeting with Deputy City Representative Kathleen Sullivan was supposed to have begun at 9:15 A.M., and he was forty-five minutes late, meaning that well before noon his jam-packed schedule had already begun to unravel hopelessly. His mood only meant trouble.

The five-year plan had not yet been approved, which meant that the city was still teetering on the brink of insolvency. The union negotiations were totally up in the air, and so was the budget. But none of that had any standing at this particular moment. Sullivan was responsible for organizing various events that promoted the image of the city, and she cut to the chase. What about Mickey Mouse? Would the mayor stand with him or not?

Oh Christ, not that frigging mouse again.

As soon as Sullivan mentioned the name, a kind of sickened look crossed his face, as if he had just been stung by something. He had been mayor for three months, and in that short time he had accepted the degree to which the job involved groveling, begging, proselytizing, and grace in the face of foolishness. But even so, couldn't he still retain some shred of self-respect? Spending time with dignitaries from Chile and Hungary and Cameroon was one thing. They usually left behind nice gifts—bowls, vases, pictures, fancy coffee-table books that fit in perfectly with the teak walls of the mayor's office. But what the hell did Mickey leave behind besides pictures of Minnie and those damn mouse-ear hats? When an important official came to town, the city liked to give them something, usually a miniature Liberty Bell. The bells cost money, and the mouse wanted one? You had to hand it to him. Beneath that squeaky voice, the mouse had *cojones.*

"We have to try to keep a little bit of value in my appearance," he said to Sullivan with plaintive weariness. "Standing next to Mickey Mouse is not a great deal."

Sullivan pressed on, trying to convince him that it would be worthwhile for him to do exactly that as part of a Disney promotion. The event was to take place on Market Street near the Liberty Bell, and thousands of kids would be there. For a city that was trying to establish itself as a tourist destination, the slightest snub of Walt Disney might be fatal. But Rendell was firm. If Disney chief Michael Eisner was playing the mouse, he told Sullivan, then he might do it. In the absence of that, he had made a decision, and that was that. Mickey would get over it, and for God's sake he shouldn't take it personally. "I'd do the same for Bugs Bunny," the mayor told Sullivan.

In the midst of the Mickey Mouse meeting, Police Sergeant Buchanico, the head of the mayor's security detail, walked in to give a status report on the various demonstrations taking place at City Hall. Demonstrations at City Hall were obviously not new, but today it was important for the mayor to have a road map since there were four going on simultaneously. When he stepped outside the office, Rendell would at least know who was screaming and why and not risk giving the right assuagement to the wrong demonstrators.

Around the corner, in the Reception Room, hundreds had gathered to disrupt the board meeting of the Philadelphia Housing Authority. This demonstration was not wholly unexpected, since the PHA, ostensibly responsible for administering public housing in the city for some eighty-thousand residents, had been under siege for close to twenty years.

The Reception Room was one of the most elegant in all of City Hall, with almost every inch of the towering walls covered by portraits of the city's mayors, stretching back to the 1700s. Now, however, the atmosphere was charged, pent-up emotion ready to burst, angry single-mother tenants lashing out at stone-faced board members trying to maintain order. The board was set to vote on whether to study the possibility of abandoning high-rise public housing in the city. Given the inherent social ills of high-rise public housing and the cynicism with which it had been constructed in city after city across the country, designed to pack the highest number of poor people into the smallest landmass possible, it was an idea that made infinite sense. But given the housing authority's legacy of neglect, corruption, and contempt for those it was supposed to serve, tenants had ample cause to be both scared and livid. Board members sitting at a long table at the front of the room like rejected apostles asked for quiet, but it was pointless. "We do not want to be nice!" yelled a member of the audience to loud applause.

Two floors up, two demonstrations were taking place inside the chambers of the city council. One was by children and youth advocates, replete with signs that said STOP KILLING BABIES. The other was to protest possible budget cuts in the city's Department of Health. Back downstairs, a small group of people had gathered in the hallway outside the mayor's office. Since they were not very well organized, with no signs or bullhorns or designated screamers, no one gave them much credence at first. But the more they talked, the more others began to listen, including an increasing flock of reporters scurrying from the press room across the hall. (As Rendell would point out on several occasions, the guy who decided to put the City Hall press corps right across the hall from the mayor's office was a real "smack ass.")

The story these demonstrators told was as harrowing as it was astounding: the city, in its eagerness to eliminate crack houses in a blighted area of the city known as the Badlands, had mistakenly demolished the home of a fifty-nine-year-old maid named Helen Anthony. The day before, Anthony had left for work at 7:45 A.M. When she returned home, at around 4:35 P.M., police were on the scene and refused to let her inside. She left and came back in a panic with relatives, only to find that her home had been demolished, except for a blue foundation wall on which several dresses, a white skirt, and a gray jacket hung neatly on a hook above a rubble of bricks and jagged wood. "I can't tell you," said Anthony before breaking into tears. "When you don't have nothing, when everything is gone . . ." Her frame was frail and gaunt, the look on her face bleached and painfully tired, and she clutched a purse hard against her chest.

City officials maintained that they had a legal right to tear down the house because it was structurally unsafe and imminently dangerous. They also said that they had found bloody heroin needles and dog feces on the first floor and they could not imagine that anyone could live there. Somehow Anthony had survived on this drug-infested corner of Germantown and Stella for twenty-three years, close to ten of them as a widow. She put up boards of thin plywood as protection against the crack addicts, but the effort was in vain. The addicts did what they wanted when they wanted. So Anthony lived mostly on the upper floors with her wedding pictures and her children's trophies. City officials later conceded that they had made a mistake. It was also a public relations disaster, exponentially intensified by the fact that a *48 Hours* film crew, there to witness the city's ostensibly noble efforts to take swift action against drugs, now had the entire Helen Anthony fiasco on tape.

Rendell seemed to take the demonstrations in stride, much as he took in stride the fact that the round table in his office, at which he did most of his paperwork and held most of his meetings, had disappeared. The table had been made by a prisoners' work cooperative in Philadelphia. Rendell had showed it off with considerable pride on the day of his inauguration, but while undergoing a little refinishing, it had fallen apart. "It was supposed to be a twenty-four-hour job to fix it," said the mayor. "It's now approaching twenty-four days."

Rendell presided over his last meeting of the day at 10:00 P.M. It took place in the den of his home, under the watchful eye of a bronze Buddha that looked strikingly like the mayor. The Buddha dressed humbly, but Rendell himself wore a purple sweatshirt and blue sweatpants.

"Let's see," said David Cohen, mulling over the day's events. "Two billion for children and youth and health, eighty thousand to buy a woman a new house. A couple of hundred thousand for PHA. For two and a half billion, we could have solved four demonstrations today."

The ostensible purpose of the meeting was to discuss the most effective use of lobbyists on behalf of the city and the most effective way in which the administration could push through its agenda at the state level. It was suggested that Rendell meet privately with Governor Casey when he came to town at the end of the month. Of course seeing the governor was a good idea. More than ever, good relationships between the city and the state were crucial to any chance of future success. But there were complications.

"One of the reasons I can't see the governor is because I'm seeing a mayor from Chile and the president of Botswana," said Rendell. Sitting so comfortably in a chair in his den at five minutes to midnight, feeling a sense of peace and the security of knowing that he had at least another five hours, maybe six, before it all started over again the next day, he rolled his eyes and shook his head.

"I do some unbelievable shit."

The next day, the inexhaustible Kathleen Sullivan was back with Mickey Mouse. The day before, the mayor had been strident. Now he just seemed defeated and tried one final time to make her understand it all from his perspective.

"It's appearing next to a mouse," he said sadly.

"Why, you've been in worse company," she shot back.

"But not with my picture in the paper."

When that didn't work, Rendell made an appeal to practicality: why appear with a fake mouse when there were several real ones rummaging around his office on a daily basis? That didn't work either. Sullivan shook her head in disappointment. She also saw a clear case of scandal: Why, she

wanted to know, was the mayor seemingly willing to appear with the Diet
Pepsi Uh-huh girls and not Mickey Mouse? He looked at her for several
seconds with an expression that was somewhere between a grimace and a
cry for help. He was thinking, as if pondering the possibility of a Justice
Department bias suit on behalf of the world's most beloved mascot. In a
deposition, how *would* he explain that appearance with the Pepsi Uh-huh
girls? It was never easy.

"All right. I'll do the fucking mouse."

Not all his meetings were like this. Some were even more bizarre, and
many were wrenching and sober. The five-year plan and the union negotiations and the city's attempts to balance the budget were important enough
to occupy his attention for all of 1992. But hovering over Rendell, always
in the back of his mind, was something else even more crucial and vital to
the lifeblood of the city than any of these issues, the very essence of its
soul. Looming was the future of the city's largest smokestack employer,
still holding on to the kind of industrial jobs that had built this city and
dozens of other cities like it. Looming was the fate of the yard.

THREE

The Yard

I

Beyond a wife and six children, ranging in ages from three to sixteen, Jim Mangan had no constituency. When he pondered the future of the navy yard, he didn't worry about how to convert the fears of a workforce into votes by making assurances that could not be kept; he had more personal concerns: the cost of clothing, the price of food, the payment of the mortgage on the modest home on Haworth, the feelings that would overwhelm him if that moment came when he no longer had a job and, in the absence of finding a comparable one in a marketplace uninterested in his skills, would no longer be able to provide for his family.

He was a quiet man, thirty-seven years old, with a wryness that served him well in terms of the fate of the yard or at least took off some of the edge of hurt and fear. His voice had the raspy roughness of the Philly twang, various words filed off to a blunt point. He smoked his cigarettes to the stub, and he yearned to move from the cramped house that he had bought over in the Frankford section of the city because that was all he could afford. He was in many respects a working man in what had been a working city, but he also had a philosophical and intellectual side that seemed incongruous among the uniform porches and men in undershirts that dominated his neighborhood. He was perfectly at peace talking about Plato's philosophy of government or watching, with a bemused smile on his face, the bizarre wonders of the legislative process as it unfolded on C-SPAN.

He heard the politicians give their fighting chants that the navy yard would stay open even though a federal commission had voted for its closure. He knew how many of the workers, particularly the old-timers, still believed that, still believed that if they did a good job, the Navy or the Pentagon or the Defense Department or someone in power would see the error of their ways. Given the strain of forced career change, particularly for men and women who had survived by the strength of their hands and did not have the college degrees and the computer skills that every employer seemed to want, it was easier, perhaps even safer, to run from the truth. Just about everywhere you looked now, the news was bad for the working man, particularly for the working man who had made his wages off heavy industry. The U.S. Bureau of Labor Statistics, in its exhaustive occupational forecast, predicted a 3 percent drop in the number of manufacturing jobs nationally while the number of jobs in the service sector was expected to rise 35 percent. Occupations requiring little formal education, the report said, were expected to "stagnate or decline."

Counselors who were acting as liaisons with the workers at the yard, trying to advise them of possible career alternatives, reported increased alcoholism, drug abuse, and heart attacks. In the immediate aftermath of the decision to close down the yard, one counselor remembered a worker who had to be rushed to the hospital after he was found outside the union hall in tears, picking at his hands and talking of suicide.

Mangan understood those feelings. As much as he concealed it, he knew what it was like to feel helpless, but he firmly believed that the yard was going to close regardless of how much rhetoric was spilled by politicians. He believed it because of what he knew about the yard's history, how the place had been invented and sustained for a different place and a different time and never updated to handle the needs of the modern nuclear navy. Like so much else about the city, the original advantages of the yard—

proximity to the great coal mines and steel mills of Pennsylvania, the skills of a built-in workforce that knew shipbuilding inside and out—made no difference now. Steel and coal were struggling industries in the state, and shipbuilding had been worn to a whisper. In the late 1800s and early 1900s, at least eight different shipbuilders had filled the arc from Philadelphia to Wilmington on the Delaware River. But one by one they had dropped away, the business of commercial shipbuilding in America swallowed up by the Japanese and the Koreans, who could build a private commercial vessel for one-third the cost with cheaper labor and cheaper materials.

In the spring of 1992, as Ed Rendell presided over the city, the navy yard was still holding on, visible from a grimy green bridge on Interstate 95—spindly-legged cranes and massive dry docks and lines of gray ships settled along the piers like a faded showgirl chorus. In 191 years, the navy yard, the nation's first, had outlived thirty-nine presidents and nine wars. Of all the institutions of the city, it may well have been the most important and certainly the most overlooked. Over a million visitors flocked to the city each year to see the crack in the Liberty Bell and wander Independence Hall. Few, if any, even knew that there was a naval shipyard in Philadelphia. But in those dry docks wide enough to fit the keel of an aircraft carrier, in those cranes taller than a seventeen-story building, lay the greatest American spirit of all, the magnificent spirit of work, of fathers and mothers and sons and daughters and brothers and uncles and cousins coming together from row house and neighborhood to make something spectacular with the labor and skill of their own hands and hearts. Not just a part of the city for nearly two centuries, but the very definition of it.

II

The 74-gun USS *Franklin* was the first of the 119 ships that the yard built and gave birth to, 188 feet long at delivery, weighing 2,257 tons of wood and beam, gliding into the clear of the Delaware at precisely 3:15 P.M. on August 25, 1815. At the sight of the launching, the men who had built it, as one chronicle of the time reported, "threw their caps as they would hang them on the horns o' the moon, shouting their emulation."

"I believe it is time this country was possessed of a Navy," Joshua Humphreys, the son of a Quaker farmer and America's first great naval architect, had written twenty-two years earlier, in 1793, to Robert Morris, a Philadelphian and financier of the Revolution. Humphreys started with a little shop on Swanson Street in the southern part of the city below Catharine. He was an apprentice to a master shipbuilder who died before the apprenticeship was complete, but Humphreys's gift was such that in the late 1700s he designed six frigates notable for their speed and power: the *United States,* built at his own private shipyard in Philadelphia; the *Chesapeake,* at Norfolk, Virginia; the *Constellation,* at Baltimore; the *President,* at New York; the *Constitution,* at Boston; and the *Congress,* at Portsmouth, New Hampshire. Of all these seaboard cities, none became a greater builder of naval ships than Philadelphia.

In 1801, the Philadelphia Naval Shipyard officially opened at the foot of Front Street, and that is where the *Franklin* was built and launched. Seventy-five years later the yard moved to its current location in the southern part of the city, an inhospitable swath of land known as League Island. There wasn't much to recommend League Island from a human standpoint or even from an animal one. Only the muskrats sought pleasure in its marsh, and a syndicate of boosters from New London, Connecticut, hoping to lure the navy to build a new yard in their home port, floated claims in Washington that League Island was awash with fever that would surely strike all those who worked there. But the fresh water of the Schuylkill and Delaware Rivers protected the ironclads from rust, and its inland position, some ninety-five miles from the place where Delaware Bay meets the Atlantic, offered sound protection from attack. Most important of all perhaps, Philadelphia could legitimately boast of itself as the greatest and most diversified manufacturing city in the United States.

The steel and iron needed to build the new ships of the modern navy were close at hand, and so was an inexhaustible supply of skilled labor. So the yard was built there, thriving in times of war, when nearly fifty thousand men and women crammed its gates in traffic jams that ran the length of Broad Street from City Hall to the nexus of the yard entrance, barely hanging on in times of peace and power politics, when slow-drawling politicians from Virginia and Mississippi tried to sweet-talk and strong-arm military brass into closing it down so ship work could go to yards in their own states. In 1970, the yard built its last ship from the keel up, the 18,646-ton USS *Blue Ridge,* a specially designed amphibious command ship. But the yard continued to endure, shifting from the building of ships to the huge task of overhauling and modernizing the navy's fleet of nonnuclear aircraft carriers.

Even on the grayest of days, when the city seemed too tired and too beaten down to ever pick itself up, a certain sensation still stirred in the motorist who saw the yard from that grimy green bridge. The yard was quiet then, in the spring of 1992, almost ghostly, but memory and myth and the considerable powers of nostalgia took hold, and if you knew any of the stories, it was impossible not to think about them. You imagined that insufferably hot July day in 1837 when the banks of the Delaware filled with some two hundred thousand people, butchers and bankers and drunkards in the momentary suspension of inebriation, watching in awe as the largest ship ever constructed in America, the 120-gun *Pennsylvania,* 3,234 tons and 283 feet from keel to masthead, was launched from the yard. You imagined the thousands who had overflowed the decks of the *Kansas* and the *Maine* and the *Georgia* for a Sunday-afternoon sailor dance in 1919, at which the piano player drummed "Stars and Stripes Forever" and "Ain't You Coming Home to Old New Hampshire, Mollie" in earnest but soft spirit to not offend those who disapproved of dancing on the Sabbath. You saw Hedy Lamarr taking a bite out of the sandwich of a surprised shipbuilder and Judy Garland singing two whole choruses of "For Me and My Gal" right after the lunchtime whistle. You could still hear the sounds of ships rising out of the dry docks like the Egyptian pyramids, steel and iron shaped and hammered by a cast of thousands—

The *Franklin.* The *North Carolina.* The *Dolphin.* The *Raritan.* The *Pennsylvania.* The *Vandalia.* The *Relief.* The *Dale.* The *Mississippi.* The *Princeton.* The *Germantown.* The *Susquehanna.* The *Wabash.* The *Arctic.* The *Shubrick.* The *Lancaster.* The *Wyoming.* The *Pawnee.* The *Tuscarora.* The *Juniata.* The *Miami.* The *Monongahela.* The *Shenandoah.* The *Tacony.* The *Tonawanda.* The *Yantic.* The *Kansas.* The *Neshaminy.* The *Shackamaxon.* The *Pushmataha.* The *Swatara.* The *Antietam.* The *Omaha.* The *Quinnebaug.* The *Henderson.* The *Relief.* The *Dobbin.* The *Sand-piper.* The *Vireo.* The *Warbler.* The *Willet.* The *Kearsarge.* The *Constitu-tion.* The *United States.* The *Minneapolis.* The *Aylwin.* The *Cassin.* The *Shaw.* The *Campbell.* The *Ingham.* The *Duane.* The *Taney.* The *Philadel-phia.* The *Wichita.* The *Rhind.* The *Buck.* The *Washington.* The PT 7. The PT 8. The *Terror.* The *Butler.* The *Gherardi.* The *Andres.* The *Drury.* The *New Jersey.* The *Scott.* The *Burke.* The *Enright.* The *Coolbaugh.* The *Darby.* The *Blackwood.* The *Robinson.* The *Solar.* The *Fowler.* The *Span-genberg.* The *Currituck.* The *Rudderow.* The *Day.* The *Wisconsin.* The *Crosley.* The *Cread.* The *Ruchamkin.* The *Kirwin.* The *Antietam.* The *Los Angeles.* The *Chicago.* The *San Marcos.* The *Princeton.* The *Valley Forge.*

The *Whetstone*. The *Dhalgren*. The *Pratt*. The *Okinawa*. The *Guadal-canal*. The *Guam*. The *New Orleans*. The *Newport*. The *Manitowoc*. The *Sumter*. The *Blue Ridge*.

As you continued over the bridge on Interstate 95, past the jumbled stench and sprawl and spew of oil refineries and the endless fields of row houses where many shipyard workers once lived, as you entered a city that seemed so shiny and steely on one side and so dilapidated and deflated on the other, simultaneously resurrected and obliterated, you thought about the yard as it was now, in 1992. Regardless of nostalgia, its fifty-two miles of streets were nearly deserted, its dry docks virtually empty, its cranes at a standstill.

In a commemorative book that had been prepared for the 150th anniversary of the shipyard in 1951, Secretary of the Navy Francis P. Matthews wrote, "I have every confidence that one hundred and fifty years from today Americans will repeat this salute to the Philadelphia Naval Shipyard when it celebrates three hundred years of distinguished service to the fleet and to the nation." But Matthews was wrong. Forty-one years after he wrote those words, the yard was on its knees, laboring mightily and, some thought, fatally this time to save itself from becoming another relic of the city, a symbol not of the magnificence of work but of the very absence of it.

Rumors had coursed through the workforce over the years that the yard was on its last legs, ready to be shut down by a navy brass in Washington that found it outdated and ill-equipped to handle the needs of the modern nuclear fleet, but after a while those rumors seemed as much a part of the territory as were the whine and heat and claustrophobia of the ships' crawl spaces. Somehow, in some way, another ship always came trudging down the Delaware needing an overhaul and the Philly finish. The old-timers had been there long enough to know that nothing was more subject to old-fashioned horse-trading in the corridors of Washington than military contracts—who got them and who didn't get them and who had them taken away after they did get them. But scream and cry and threaten as politicians always did when it came to the need to cut spending and reduce the fatty tissue of pork, the old-timers knew that no politician was dumb enough to touch the yard, not with its legacy and its history. "In 1985, when I was working as a pipefitter, I went to one of the older fellows in the shop about a rumor that the yard was closing," a shipyard worker told the *Philadelphia Daily News*. "He was puffing on a cigar and he said: 'Listen, kid, this place has been shutting down for 240 years. It ain't never going to close. So shut up and get out of here.' "

But it was different now, and the latest volley of rumors about the impending closure of the yard—that it was real this time and not some private game of battleship between Republicans and Democrats in Washington—had never been this intense. In April 1991, Defense Secretary Dick Cheney proposed closing thirty-one major military bases around the country, including the Philadelphia Naval Shipyard. The navy yard had been on closure lists before, and this one still needed approval from Congress and the president, but there was something different about this announcement, particularly since it was made by a Republican administration and the leading senator of the state, Arlen Specter, was himself a Republican. "There's a bad feeling this time," said a shipyard worker named Gene Smith, echoing the feelings of thousands of military and civilian workers, and newspapers covering the story came up with a chilling statistic: if in fact the yard and base did close, the net effect in the region would be a loss of forty-seven thousand jobs and a hike in the unemployment rate from 6.5 to 8.5 percent.

As soon as Cheney produced his list, politicians from all over the state went on the offensive. One promised a "war bigger than the Persian Gulf" to save the yard, and others quickly added their own versions of outrage and vitriol. The most sincere expression of what the yard meant came at the beginning of June 1991, when six women dressed in red, white, and blue attended a federal hearing on the proposed closure and somewhat mysteriously hauled a large plastic bag to the front of the room. Inside were 100,000 signatures on petitions begging that the yard be saved. Quietly and methodically the women had gone to bowling alleys and supermarkets and Phillies games to collect them.

On the last Sunday in June, when the decision on the fate of the yard was to be announced, Pat D'Amico, one of the women who had fanned out all over the city collecting signatures, cooked a big family dinner. She had grown up in the southwest section of the city in an Irish Catholic neighborhood, and beyond belief in God and pub the only other automatic assumption in life was that when you got old enough, you could always go to work at the yard. She had fulfilled that prophecy. So had her father, her husband, her brother, her sister, her father-in-law, and her brother-in-law. That previous Friday rumors had floated that the federal Base Closure and Realignment Commission, in charge of deciding on Cheney's recommendations and overwhelmed by the outpouring of support for the yard, not to mention crucial data showing its efficiency, might keep it open. The vote was televised live, and Pat D'Amico and her family watched. The decision was stunning: a unanimous seven votes. In favor of closure.

As the impact of the vote set in, Pat D'Amico thought that what had just happened could not have happened—that somebody would listen and grasp the importance of the yard, not just as a place that efficiently and expertly overhauled ships but as a place that was too much a part of the city's lore, America's lore, to be rendered silent. "You kind of thought in your heart of hearts that this is America, that this is the United States, and somehow somebody would have to say that this couldn't happen," she later told an interviewer. "You really didn't think that this was really possible, and I had a really naïve belief, I'm sure, that somehow my government wouldn't do this to me."

But her government had done it, to her and to her city.

Sponsored by Senator Specter, a suit was filed claiming that the criteria used by the navy to close the yard had been faulty and filled with purposeful omissions. In effect, the suit argued that the fix had been in, that the navy had vowed to shut the yard down regardless of how efficient it was compared with other yards around the country. Other politicians and union leaders fell in line behind Specter, their battle cry once again brimming with confidence. They claimed the suit was on sound enough legal ground to keep the yard open, and many of those who worked there were flooded with a sense of hope or, at the very least, ammunition for their own self-denial.

But one politician who did not join the bandwagon was Ed Rendell. When he took office, he spoke little of the navy yard publicly, and much of the reason for that was purely practical. With the city sinking financially and the union negotiations heating up, to give time to anything else was difficult. But he was aware of what was happening at the yard, and as he heard Arlen Specter and other politicians fire away about the merits of the suit and how it would be the yard's savior, he saw their pronouncements as political and more than just political, as a form of cruel and unusual punishment of the workers, supplying them with the one emotion they could not afford to have—a misguided sense that their careers and futures were eternally safe.

The navy had previously agreed to send one final aircraft carrier to the navy yard, the *John F. Kennedy,* for overhaul. Because of the amount of work an aircraft carrier overhaul required, such a job would keep the yard open until the fall of 1995. But no more work was scheduled after that, and Rendell privately believed that it was ludicrous to think the navy was going to supply any. Instead, the yard would close in September 1995 once the work on the *Kennedy* was completed, at just about the same time his term as mayor would end. As a result, the issue for him wasn't how to keep the yard open but what on earth to do with the massive facility when it closed and, equally problematic, what to do with the nearly ten thousand workers who, outside of some miracle, were destined to lose their jobs, their livelihoods, and their way of life.

III

Had Mangan's mind-set been different, he might have been able to convince himself of a different fate. During the spring of 1992, there were even some glimmers of hope, if it was your inclination to be hopeful. Vice President Quayle, at a political stop in Wilmington, said the administration was looking into the possibility of using the yard to service and maintain the navy's fleet of cargo and support ships. In addition, the lawsuit filed by Senator Specter had made a miraculous recovery from the dead. The previous November, it had been dismissed by a federal judge on the grounds that Congress had clearly worded the base-closure law to preclude any court appeal. But in April 1992, a federal appeals court revived the suit on the grounds that various aspects of the decision to close the yard were appropriate for judicial review. "Their jobs are a lot safer today than they were yesterday," said Bruce W. Kauffman, a former justice of the Pennsylvania Supreme Court, arguing the case for the plaintiffs.

But Mangan was still reluctant to put much stock in such comments. He knew what these bromides of optimism were largely about, telling workers what they so desperately wanted to hear, giving them a scrap of good news that they might well remember in the voting booth later in the year, when Specter was up for reelection in a nasty dogfight against Democratic challenger Lynn Yeakel. His memory for political semantics was a good one, and he could still recall being at the once thriving Frankford Arsenal in 1975 when Walter Mondale, running on the ticket with Jimmy Carter, vowed that that facility would never close. In its heyday during World War II, the Frankford Arsenal had employed more than twenty-two thousand people and had produced eight million bullets a day. Much like the navy yard, it had not equaled such dizzying heights of production and employment since then, but still, there was Mangan at the arsenal listening to a political speech in good faith, and there was Mondale, as honest a man as you could ever find in all of government, promising that the arsenal would stay open, which of course is exactly the opposite of what happened after Carter became president. Carter did decide to close the arsenal in 1977, and it was after that that Jim Mangan generally stopped voting for mainstream candidates and listened to what politicians said as if it were some form of exotic theater. "It starts to sound like a rerun after a while," he said of the battery of politicians and lawyers coming to the defense of the yard. "There's nothing they can do."

There was always a certain fatalism to Mangan, measured by the way he sometimes sat on the couch in his living room with a quiet expression on his face, as if fighting off some personal demon inside him, or by the way he consistently acted as though what could go wrong not only would go wrong but already had gone wrong. But the stirrings inside him, of what it meant for a man to be a provider for his family and what it meant to no longer be able to do that, were not imagined.

Unlike some of the old-timers, who had worked there for twenty or twenty-five years and had developed a deep and abiding love for the yard, Mangan could not confess to such feelings. Many of the workers came from neighborhoods so close that they could almost reach out across the bed and touch the steel of the dry docks. Son followed father who had followed grandfather, but Mangan was different. He grew up in the neighborhood of Mayfair in the city's northeast, some ten miles north of the navy yard, and his father was a computer programmer who liked nothing better than to read quietly and surround himself with books. Mangan himself went to Catholic grade school and then to Central, the area's most prestigious high school. He considered college but decided against it and instead went to a trade school to learn air-conditioning and refrigeration. He spent six and a half years at a company that made specialized air-conditioning equipment to keep computer rooms dry. When the company moved to the suburbs, Mangan elected not to move with it. Instead, in 1981, when he was twenty-six, he joined the yard, going to work in an apprenticeship program as a welder.

Mangan never thought the yard would be the place where he finished his career, and in the back of his mind he always dreamed of following in the footsteps of a grandfather who had run his own business, a bar called Jim's over at Tulip and Venango. His grandfather, who died before he was born, was a go-getter and an entrepreneur, a man who wasn't afraid to take a chance if he thought the chance was right, and Jim always thought his life might have turned out differently if his grandfather had lived and had imparted to him some of the secrets and the confidence of that spirit, helped him to reverse the fears and dourness that sometimes seemed to cloud over him.

But still, the yard wasn't at all a bad place to be in those early days. The dry docks were filled with ships needing repair, and the first of the gigantic aircraft carriers, the *Saratoga,* was in for overhaul as well. Mangan cut his teeth on the *Saratoga,* a half-billion-dollar job so massive that, as a reporter for the *Inquirer* wrote, it was "hard to tell whether the insides are outside or the outsides inside." As an apprentice, he learned the rigors of what welders did, using their torches to cut holes called rip-outs so huge turbines could be taken out and sent back to the manufacturers for rebuilding; patching up the hull; crawling into darkened shafts deep in the innards of the ship to work on the deep tanks. He quickly formed respect for the men who had spent their professional lives routinely doing what he was just learning to do. In the romance of the trade, laboring on a ship was called working on the iron, but to Mangan it was little more than what he termed a euphemism for work that was too hot in the summer and too cold in the winter and perpetually smoky and dirty. If you weren't at dizzying heights, you were in tiny and confined spaces.

The worst job of all was working with preheated metal in the summertime. The metal would be warmed with strip heaters that look like the coils of a toaster. A temp stick would be placed on the metal like a stick of butter, and once the temp stick melted, you knew that the metal had reached a temperature of 150 degrees and was ready for the weld. Mangan had to do this work on every possible part of the ship, from the lowest tank to the uppermost reaches of the flight deck. There was a pay differential for such misery, so-called hot money, just as there was "high money" for working so far up the mast that you had to be tied to it. The extra cash was nice, but it never made the work any more palatable. "I'm convinced it takes years off your life," he said, referring in particular to the times when he had worked on an area of the ship that a week later had been sealed off because of possible asbestos contamination. Scariest of all was working on the deep tanks: they fanned out from the center of the ship far below the main deck, and just finding them was tortuous and difficult. To get to the tanks, he had to go through a series of manways, then pull down the welding shield, then straddle a board that meant a fall of thirty feet if you happened to slip off of it. On one occasion, he got stuck in an area of the tank called the inner bottom but was somehow able to extricate himself.

Industrial accidents were not uncommon. While the *Saratoga* was in the yard, ten people were injured, three of them critically, when a valve on a steam line carrying twelve hundred pounds of pressure blew open in one of the boiler rooms. Metal fragments from the line hit some workers, and a spray of hot steam hit others, causing critical burns. An accident such as this was hardly comforting, but Mangan persevered, and so did the yard. The aircraft carrier *Forrestal* followed the *Saratoga,* and the *Independence* came after the *Forrestal.* He had a little trouble catching on at the beginning, but he learned quickly as he proceeded up the steps of his apprenticeship. "I was no surgeon," he admitted, but he generally hit the weld right the first time and had little rejected when his work was inspected. If the labor was dirty and scary, it was also challenging, and at the beginning at least there was a considerable amount of pride associated with it. It also offered good pay and good benefits and ample opportunities for overtime.

But then Mangan took the chance that he had been thinking about for so long. He left the yard in 1986 to open up his own business in air-conditioning repair and service. He lasted for a year before it all went sour. He went back to the yard and to welding, but with no regrets. "I learned a lot the year I was out" was the way he justified it. "I learned a lot about my failings." He settled back into the routine of the yard, back into the work of preheated metal and deep tanks and hot money and high money. In a bountiful year, with the overtime still flowing from carrier work, he made almost $45,000, but at that point there already was the churn of uncertainty.

By 1990, the rumors plaguing the yard were all over the place. Mangan neither dismissed them nor listened too closely until 1991, when in his capacity as a shop steward for the boilermakers' union, he traveled to Washington with a contingent of local labor officials. All that day they talked to members of Congress, and it became abundantly clear to Mangan that not only did the navy want the yard closed but it had really wanted the yard closed twenty years earlier. He returned from Washington with a feeling in his heart that few others shared or at least shared publicly. He went about his work, but the pride he had once felt came to be replaced by the sensation of knowing that as far as his livelihood was concerned, he was living on borrowed time.

In his stronger moments, as if trying to talk himself into what he was saying, he claimed he had worked out a scenario for himself whereby, if he didn't find another job before the yard closed, he would take the severance pay that was offered, run through the unemployment that he was entitled to, and go on welfare. Given the state of the economy, he said he wasn't bothered by that. There had been a certain point in his life when he had perhaps drunk a little bit more than he should have, and he had realized the degree to which his life had been guided by fear—fear of failure, fear of ridicule. After he stopped drinking, he also changed the pattern of his life. "I don't worry," he said. "I live one day at a time. I've lived from one paycheck to the next for so long I don't know anything else." But at other times—particularly down at the yard when everybody was waiting for the next overhaul to come in and the trickle of work was so damn slow that all you had was time on your hands to think, to think about all the things you never wanted to think about—he confessed to other thoughts. "In my quieter moments, it's scary as hell."

He sat in the living room of his home on Haworth when he said that, and later he moved outside to sit on the front steps. He paid $21,900 for the house in 1981, and while it wasn't exactly what he wanted, it was still a home. He could still make the mortgage on it, and it still offered security. Rain fell in little drops from a gray sky, and a swirl of cool air broke the heat. The block, lined with identical-looking single-family homes like the ones in a game of Monopoly, hummed and flowed with mothers and fathers and girls and boys on bikes. Jim Mangan had never sorted out how much he really liked the navy yard, but it meant a paycheck, a steady one, and it meant benefits, and it made him a good provider. It was one thing to do something else with your life because that was your choice. It was another thing to do something different with your life because you had no choice.

Linda Mangan sat on the steps with her husband, and they were joined by their two youngest daughters. Framed in that moment, they presented a Norman Rockwell portrait of an American working-class family in the city, children interlocked in the loving arms of mother and father so as to become one, watching and laughing at the simple comings and goings on a block paved with red brick.

It was Jim Mangan, with his own quiet and laconic wisdom, who saw the ingredient missing from it all. "What happens when all the jobs have left?"

IV

For the Rendell administration, in the spring of 1992 the answer to that question manifested itself not only in the fate of the navy yard but in the more immediate fate of a place called Sovereign Oil.

In 1909, of the 264 different classifications of industry as determined by the Bureau of the Census, Philadelphia was represented by 211 of them. It led the nation in the production of hosiery and knit goods; carpets and rugs other than those made from rags; fur-felt hats; locomotives; dyed and finished textiles; shoddy; upholstery materials; streetcars; oilcloth and linoleum; sporting goods; saws; and surgical appliances and artificial limbs. The Englishman Arthur Shadwell, after completing a study of industrial life in England, Germany, and the United States, called Philadelphia "the greatest manufacturing city in the world," and in the late 1800s a delegation of Japanese businessmen visited the city for a three-week tour of its great manufacturing plants.

They traveled to Baldwin Locomotive on Broad, where twenty-five hundred employees churned out an engine in twenty days. They went to Cramp and Sons Steam Ship Yards, where four different vessels were being built simultaneously, and they studied tools they had never seen before: noiseless punches, extra-strength sheers, angle iron cutters. They went to Henry Disston and Sons' Saw Manufactory at Front and Laurel Streets and marveled over the use of emery stone for polishing. They went to Excelsior Brick Works at Broad and Germantown, where nine large kilns produced seventy thousand bricks a day. They went to J. B. Lippincott and Company, publishers and booksellers, on Market above Seventh Street, where sixteen presses were in simultaneous motion, and they especially admired the machines that were being used for folding, automatic cutting, embossing, and stamping. Everywhere they went in the city, they saw something unparalleled in the fields of manufacturing and production, something you could find only in a city that was teeming with the marvelous twins of innovation and entrepreneurial spirit. When a salesman at Lippincott asked the Japanese whether they might like a copy of the British translation of Simonin's *Science of Mines, Metallurgy, and Engineering,* they declined.

"No, no," replied one of the guests. "We want only American books on American engineering. We want everything American."

Baldwin Locomotive wasn't in the city anymore. Neither was Cramp and Sons. Neither was Disston. In 1909, Philadelphia was the largest

manufacturer of textiles in the entire world, and one third of all wage earn-
ers in the city worked in some area of the field. By 1992, employment in
the textile and apparel industry had shrunk to a minuscule thirteen thousand, or 2 percent of the city's total employment. Given the trend of the
last decade, when eighty-eight thousand manufacturing jobs, or two out of
every five, were lost, it was apparent that the decline would only continue.
The Workshop of the World had become the Manufacturing Mausoleum
of the World.

Sovereign Oil, an abandoned industrial site about two miles north of
City Hall in what was known as the American Street Business Corridor,
embodied the futility and the tragedy of the city's manufacturing death. On
a Thursday morning in the middle of May 1992, in a rare break from the
business of the budget and union negotiations, nine people were deep in a
summit at the mayor's conference table. They spoke in the blunt and agitated tones of an emergency about which something has to be done and
done right away. Sovereign Oil had been in the business of buying
shipments of oil in bulk, blending the oil, and then selling it as various
byproducts. But then, in May 1990, the company closed and filed for bankruptcy, and the place became a horrifying mess with an eight-foot bouilla-
baisse of oil and water flooding the basement.

The city tried vainly to get Sovereign's owners to clean up the site. But
the efforts only underscored the utter impotence of a system of laws and
rules and procedures that seemed designed to provide city bureaucrats
with jobs and private lawyers with fees. The city's Fire Department, Law
Department, Department of Licenses and Inspections, Commerce Department, Water Department, and Managing Director's Office were all involved at various stages, and the collective result of their warnings and
citations for code violations and threats against an owner who was apparently too broke to pay a fine but too rich to drive anything less than a Mercedes, had been little. The judge hearing a civil suit filed by the city against
Sovereign had ordered fines and the removal of materials that might cause
an explosion or a fatal injury, but according to records, little had been
done.

When in May of 1992 the situation had finally become enough of a crisis for the mayor's office to get involved, at least four fires the previous
month had been set to rubbish that had been dumped around the exterior
of the building. The interior had become a clubhouse for crack users and
prostitutes. There were so many leaks in general that oil routinely seeped
through the walls of the building. Every time it rained, oil bubbled from

the ground as in the opening scene of *The Beverly Hillbillies* and trickled into the nearby Delaware. Oil byproducts also spilled into the street, causing at least one car crash.

Two days after that summit meeting, on a gray, rain-soaked morning, Cohen, City Council President John Street, and other public officials visited Sovereign to assure neighbors and local businesspeople that the site would finally be cleaned up regardless of who had to pay for it. In 1910, when Philadelphia had been at the height of its manufacturing glory, the building and site had been used as an engine house by the Reading Railroad. Eighty-two years later the yard outside was filled with discarded tires. At one point, a fence had been put around the property to prevent such dumping, but in a city where people scavenged for parts and supplies they could not afford, the fence had quickly been stolen, and the pile of tires had just multiplied. Thick lumps of asbestos insulation, syruped with oil, lay in a corner of the loading dock. Tiny shreds of green and clear beer-bottle glass covered much of the surface, along with a sock, a Marlboro box, a single work glove, a can of Blackjack roach and ant spray, and a margarine box. The interior of the building was huge and pitch-black once the natural light from the loading dock fell away. Like an underground cave, its shape and circumference were impossible to fathom, as if it might have gone on for miles. The only sound came from the rainwater seeping in through holes and cracks in the roof and drawing puddles around hundreds of little caps that had once been used to seal bottles of motor oil. There was little to see in the absence of light, and yet there was something mesmerizing about that darkened cavity, a hope that if you stood before it long enough and stared into its emptiness, you might gain some explanation of how something like this had been created and perpetuated in what was supposedly the world's most advanced society.

No, no. We want only American books on American engineering. We want everything American.

Had those foreign visitors been standing on the loading dock of Sovereign Oil, watching those little caps float in the rainwater like drowning bugs, what would they have thought of America and the once great city that had embodied it now?

There was a bitter irony about a city's being forced to pay even a cent for the cleanup of an industrial site that far from providing a decent wage for a single resident had only created havoc. Rendell knew that the fundamental issue underlying the future of the city, his city now, was jobs—how to hold on to the ones that were still there, how to create new ones. Even in his short span in office, a mere four months, he had become remarkably effective at pumping hope into the veins of the citizenry. And more than just hope, there had been progress, the likes of which had not been seen in nearly forty years.

As it turned out, the five-year plan for the restoration of the city's financial health that Cohen and White and others had worked so hard over had not been for naught. After an exhaustive review, in which every assertion had been challenged and reviewed and then challenged again, it was approved by the persnickety faces of the Pennsylvania Intergovernmental Cooperation Authority. Toward the end of May, $475 million in bonds was issued on behalf of the city, and a major rating agency actually increased the city's credit rating, placing it at a level reserved for speculative investments instead of at one reserved for investments that are in imminent risk of default. PHILADELPHIA IS NEARING SOLVENCY said the headline in *The New York Times,* and Randall M. Miller, a professor of history at St. Joseph's University, called the city's turnaround "downright startling." But the need was still voracious.

Sovereign might have been the worst of the city's abandoned sites, but it wasn't the only one. There were thousands of vacant sites, and outside the womb of Center City they were as easy to find as crack vials or cigarette butts. Rendell also knew that the effects of vacant lots and vacant factories could be more than simply dispiriting. In certain working-class neighborhoods—the ones that had gained the most from the city's manufacturing legacy and had lost the most in its decline—a single isolated act in the heat of Rendell's first summer as mayor could turn into something combustible. And deadly. And irreversible.

FOUR

The Racial Trifecta

I

It was a summer night in July 1992, one of those nights so thick with heat
it was hard to breathe, as the mayor made his way to a grimy gymnasium
in a neighborhood as far away from the nerve of City Hall as a crumbling
fort in the ruins. The route he took, beginning at a boxy hotel on the
straight edges of suburbia, was transformed into a painful communion of
what was no longer there and what had somehow managed to survive—red
zigzags of graffiti on a boarded-up doorway underneath a stone inscription
commemorating the St. Joseph's Home for Orphaned Boys; the bruised
red brick of the stillborn Penn Ventilator Company rising to nowhere in the
stench of the heat; tidy lines of trash underneath a bridge at Allegheny, as
if someone had taken the time to arrange them. And then into the shut-off,
shut-out neighborhood known as Kensington, at Allegheny and F, where

women in tank tops stared from the narrow doorways of the brick row houses and kids with hair as slick as seal coats sucked down cigarettes. They briefly looked up when the mayor's car came down the street. They saw Rendell through the dull sheen of the window, and they gestured to one another almost in a special sign language indigenous to the neighborhood, and they pointed in the direction of his car. They didn't wave and they didn't smile, but they looked almost bemused, as if a fat possum had just been sighted sniffing for food.

The mayor's coming to Kensington because someone got killed. He's going to preach peace and harmony, tell us how we have to get along with the spics who are taking over goddamn everything, just like they told us we had to get along with the niggers.

Big fucking deal, Mr. Mayor. Big fucking deal.

II

Robbie Burns worked part-time at a pharmacy in Kensington. He had recently gotten his degree in radiation technology and was now planning to take graduate courses. At six feet five inches, he was taller than the others who hung out at the corner of Rorer and Westmoreland on Saturday nights, and that may have given him an aura of toughness. But to those who knew him, that wasn't at all a distinguishing characteristic of Robbie Burns. He stood out not because of his size but because, unlike so many others, he was planning a career and saw hanging out on the corner as a way of passing time, not a way of life. As a friend of his put it, "He was the only one who made it out of here."

Sometimes the whites who hung out at Rorer and Westmoreland just hung out. Other times they drank more than they should have from their open containers. Occasionally they engaged with the Latinos who came upon the corner and were equally ready to rumble. The conflicts between the two groups had to do with the unwritten laws of the playground and the territory of the street corner, who had the right to be there and who did not. But the root of it lay in the joblessness and hopelessness of a city neighborhood that now engaged in the endless no-win contest of who the hell to blame it all on, working-class whites pitted against Hispanics, Hispanics pitted against working-class whites in a game of who had more of a right to nothing.

It was somewhere around 4:00 A.M. when a brown car, maybe a Chevy,

maybe a Buick, appeared near the corner of Rorer and Westmoreland. Two
Hispanics exited from the car and engaged in a fight with various whites
who were hanging on the corner. There were also indications that one or
both of the Latinos may have been struck in the head with bottles. They got
back into their car, but they weren't finished, and once Robbie Burns realized what was happening, once he saw the outline of the gun in the lowered window, he pushed a younger friend out of the way to avoid the line
of fire.

The police radio call about the shooting went out at 4:00 A.M., the scratchy
syncopation of the words sounding like a thin cover of tin on a boiling
cauldron, revealing everything and nothing at the same time.

"Man with a gun, shooting, hospital case."

The first patrol car arrived at the corner of Rorer and Westmoreland at
4:04 A.M., four minutes from radio call to arrival, and it is there the officers
found Robbie Burns, his frame sprawled on the sidewalk, a single bullet
buried in the right side of his head. Burns was rushed by a rescue squad to
Temple Hospital, and doctors well versed in the mortality of blood and
bullets worked feverishly on him, but their efforts didn't matter because
Robbie Burns was dying.

Within the neighborhood of Rorer and Westmoreland, pandemonium
and hysteria erupted. Shortly after the shooting, officers at a nearby hospital observed two Hispanic males entering the emergency room for treatment of head wounds. Witnesses in the Burns shooting were immediately
transported to the hospital, where they identified the men as the ones involved. They also identified a vehicle in the hospital parking lot as the get-
away car. But it actually belonged to a nurse on duty at the hospital that
night. And the suspects they fingered with such quickness were quickly
able to prove to detectives that they had nothing to do with the shooting. It
seemed clear they had been fingered merely because they were Latinos,
and the police had no choice but to release them.

At 8:25 A.M. that Sunday, Robbie Burns was pronounced dead.

News of his cold-blooded killing moved quickly across the tight webs
of Kensington. So did news of the release of the two Latinos, but without
the police justification for their release. A crowd of about fifty people gathered at the corner of Rorer and Westmoreland on Sunday morning in
protest. They were peaceful and dispersed after about an hour. At about
2:30 P.M., another crowd gathered, this one loud and unruly. The demonstrators started marching, and before police had time to seal off the area ef-

fectively, a blue Mazda moved westbound on Allegheny in their direction. The driver was a twenty-four-year-old Hispanic named Michael Rosato, and with him were his wife and six-year-old son. He could have turned around when he saw the crowd, but he did not, and so set himself on a direct collision course with the demonstrators. His car was engulfed. His windshield was smashed. Shots erupted from inside the car. One man was hit in the left thigh, another in the stomach, another in the buttocks. Rosato sped off with police in pursuit. When he was stopped, the officers found a .38-caliber silver revolver underneath the seat.

In less then twenty-four hours, four whites had now been shot in Kensington, one of them fatally. Wild rumors sped everywhere; building in intensity were the accusations that the police had actually had in custody but let go the two suspects in the Robbie Burns shooting. The demonstrators, unsteady and unpredictable on account of youth and drink, refused to disperse. "If they love Puerto Rico, send them back to Puerto Rico. I'm tired of our boys lying on the street," someone said. Desperate to get the crowd to go home, a contingent of five police officers went to Robbie Burns's home and asked relatives to come and speak to the crowd.

"Robbie don't want this," said Burns's stepfather. "Please go home. I beg you, go home."

His words calmed the crowd to some degree, but they also wanted the mayor. Through an intermediary, Rendell agreed to meet with the community the following night, giving him twenty-four hours to defuse the feelings of anger and alienation and disfranchisement that had been building in Kensington over weeks and months and years, allowing him time to negotiate the narrow racial tightrope strung between working-class white and Hispanic and to appeal to all, to try to convince them that they all live under the roof of one city, despite the almost inevitable result that at least one side would feel betrayal and outrage.

Even without the shootings, this was an area of the city that had been tired and turned off by the endless parade of politicians whose promises were never kept. With the shootings, the odds of reaching any kind of common ground with the white working-class residents seemed impossible. At best, they would not listen. At worst, they would mercilessly heckle him and boo him off the stage while the entire city press corps licked its fingers. And in the meantime, during the twenty-four hour reprieve that he had been given, there might be more killings, more vigilante justice at the point of a gun. He needed a miracle, something that would reduce the heat and divert attention.

Ed Rendell was not a particularly religious man. He was Jewish only in the most nominal sense, and he looked forward to various Jewish holidays not because of their religious significance but because they meant he had a valid excuse to stay home. In his office one spring, he voiced his own version of the Four Questions of the Passover seder by asking, "Why is this night different from all other nights?" and then answering with a refrain of "the NCAA finals."

But he still knew better than anyone else the powers of divine intervention.

III

In the city that Lincoln Steffens had also called "the most American of our greater cities," no area embodied the tradition of industry and the white working class better than Kensington, with row house and church steeple and narrow street and the El and the spew of factory smokestacks all within its boundaries. The first American textile mill opened in Kensington. So did the country's first building and loan association. Around 1900, close to 100,000 people filled its row-house corridors, an assemblage of Irish, English, Scottish, and German immigrants pocketed in a neighborhood two miles northeast of the grand spire of City Hall, and the estimated worth of its manufactured products was said to be $100 million annually. "A City Within a City," touted one local booster, "filled to the brim with enterprise, dotted with factories so numerous that the rising smoke obscures the sky. . . . A happy and contented people, enjoying a land of plenty."

It wasn't nearly as rosy as that. Conditions were often brutal, but one thing Kensington always promised was work, its factories alive with what America wanted and could get only from the American city: novelty toys and miniature pianos and beer and textiles and carpet and dyed goods and gingham and diapers and hosiery and yarn and silk upholstery. By 1920, the population had ballooned to 155,000, and Kensington led all American cities in the value of its carpets, rugs, hosiery, and knit goods.

With the Depression and the postwar shift in factory production from the gritty neighborhoods of the cities to the placid suburbs and the South and the third world, the steady might of Kensington began to crack. The multistory factories built there weren't desired anymore. In the age of automated mass production and robotic assembly lines, they were unwieldy and technologically obsolete. Businesses wanted plentiful space for factories that the suburbs could easily supply. They also wanted to avoid the contentiousness of unions. The population of the area, which in 1950 was 149,000, dropped to 95,000 in 1990, a loss of 36 percent. The factories that reflected the very heart of the area, its very essence, were abandoned.

For much of its history, race had not been much of an issue in Kensington, largely because of its refusal to accept blacks. There were blacks who worked there in the mills and the factories, but as author Peter Binzen noted in *Whitetown, U.S.A.,* they weren't likely to be assaulted as long as they observed the unofficial curfew and were out before sundown. But in the 1960s, as the dynamics of race in the city changed and the percentage of blacks in the population multiplied, Kensington reacted violently. In October 1966, after a black family rented a home near a local high school, there were five nights of riots. The family ultimately moved away, but the issue of race in Kensington did not. Between 1980 and 1990, the Latino population of Kensington and the adjoining neighborhood of Fishtown increased by more than 40 percent while the number of whites decreased by nearly 14 percent.

In looking for ways to displace their anger and frustration, young whites in Kensington seized upon Hispanics as the culprits, and Hispanics all too willingly returned the fire. It was one thing to have to share the neighborhood with them, and as long as they never crossed the invisible border of Front Street, things would be OK. But it was another to watch them encroach upon their playgrounds and favored street corners as if they somehow had a right to be there, particularly when these were the only reliable institutions they had left. "Scum." "Animals." "Not human." That was the way some of the young whites referred to Hispanics. In response to Hispanic encroachment, a group called the Swoop Troop was formed, a kind of makeshift SWAT team. SPICS GO HOME said giant-size graffiti on a wall.

In the early 1950s, a sociologist named Peter Rossi had visited Kensington to do research for a book he was writing on why people move, and he found, much to his amazement, that residents of Kensington did not want to move despite its dearth of amenities. He found the loyalty to it astounding and the rituals of the place—buying soft pretzels under the El, going to soccer games over at the Lighthouse Field—had a hold that was almost spiritual. But over time, that sense changed—a neighborhood in the city that was no longer a place to live in but a place to escape from if you were somehow lucky enough to have the means of escape. "Kensington today is a passed-over, deteriorated, forgotten section of industrial Philadelphia," wrote Jean Seder in a book called *Voices of Kensington.* "Almost all the mills have gone. They've moved South, or gone out of business. Pe-riodically the children set fire to the empty shells of factories, and the city levels the ruins into another empty lot."

IV

Rendell did not equivocate, nor, unlike some politicians, did he seem the slightest bit insulted by it. Placing himself in their own shoes for a mo-ment, he wondered why anyone in Kensington would be remotely happy to see him. He could make a few promises, increase the presence of the po-lice, repair a basketball net, and patch up a rec center roof. But how could he do what was needed most—make the echoes of those factories and mills into real sounds again? If it were just he and a group of public officials up on the stage of the McVeigh Recreation Center gym tonight, the crowd would be inclined to scream and yell, heap the legacies and histories of their anger on him.

That's why he called the cardinal.

"I don't know these people as well as you do, but I know them from my days as district attorney," said Rendell in a meeting with advisers in City Hall that Monday morning. "They probably don't believe in God, but they are not one hundred percent sure."

Several hours later Rendell spoke with Cardinal Anthony Bevilacqua over the phone and made his pitch for accompaniment. "We have an enor-mously difficult problem in the Kensington area. Essentially what it is is a recurring problem; it's Hispanic and white. It's a very, very explosive situation. These are the hardest hit whites in the city of Philadelphia, and they blame their problems on minorities, which is not correct. They share everything in common with minorities in confronting problems."

Bevilacqua, the head of the archdiocese of Philadelphia, said he would be happy to attend the meeting and asked for some background material.

"Sure," said Rendell, thoroughly up-to-date on the changes in modern religion. "What's your fax number?"

The mayor and the cardinal met secretly in front of the Ascension of Our Lord Church on Westmoreland Street at about 8:00 P.M. Rendell quietly exited his car and then, as in one of those films about Mafia informants, slid into the backseat of the cardinal's before anyone knew what was really going on. During the short trip to the gym, the cardinal was relaxed and pleasant, his one major concern his breath, since he had just eaten a large Italian dinner with lots of garlic.

The gym was packed when they got there, a sea of white—about five hundred people pushed against the grimy green walls, women with puckered faces and sweaty brows and blond hairdos as hilly as the moguls of a mountain, men in baseball caps and droopy mustaches and fleshy arms with a dollop of a tattoo near the blade of the shoulder. Initially the gambit of the cardinal paid off. As soon as he walked in, there were oohs and ahs and breathless greetings of "Your Eminence!" He received a standing ovation, and his initial words helped to soothe the crowd. "To correct an evil or injustice, you don't perform another evil. Wrong does not correct wrong. We are all Christians, and we know the message of Jesus Christ. . . . We are called on to be people of peace. Each of us must be peacemakers."

Rendell spoke as well, and his words too seemed to have a positive effect, in large part because of their lack of pretense and bombast. "We're not going to come here tonight and promise the things that we cannot do. If you hear us say we will do something tonight, we will do it. If we keep fighting each other, keep killing each other, wasting our time on things like that, this city doesn't have a snowball's chance of turning things around."

The crowd seemed both dazzled and wooed by the duo of the cardinal in his impeccable vestments of red and white and the Jewish mayor in the creases of a blue suit, and their odd-couple fox-trot seemed to be working in an area of the city where outsiders, any outsiders, were almost never embraced. But then other public officials spoke, and the mood dissolved, the illusory moment of a united city unfettered by race and class giving way to the very rawness of race and class that now seemed destined to divide it eternally.

Sneers of distrust crept onto the faces of the women. The men placed their hands on their hips in a gesture of challenge. In the heat and humidity, a layer of mist rose toward the ceiling. Bodies in the crowd became soaked and glistened; the gym seemed more and more like an overcrowded boxing arena, gauzy and smoke-filled and ominously overcrowded, heat and suspicion and sadness and anger all vying for too little space.

Acting Police Commissioner Thomas Seamon tried to explain that the two Hispanics questioned the night of Robbie Burns's shooting had been falsely accused. "We were convinced they were not the right people," said

Seamon, the large pair of glasses affixed to his face seeming to get larger
and larger every time he spoke. People jeered and booed, belittling this
pasty-faced man with his Sad Sack jowls. He vowed that the department
would make arrests in the case as quickly as possible, and he was greeted
by more boos, more catcalls. Almost at once a dozen voices filled the
gym—

"Bullshit!!"

"We're just sick and tired."

"What's that got to do with anything?"

"Shut your mouth!"

It became clear what the people of Kensington thought of the Philadelphia Police Department. The police were spic sympathizers, shameless
panderers in the name of political correctness and ethnic diversity and all
too willing to turn their backs on the blue-collar whites who had filled the
factories and labored in the sweatshops and made this city what it was. The
cardinal sat speechless at a long table on an elevated stage at the front of
the gym, those impeccable vestments looking like a Halloween costume.
Rendell sat there too, sweat dripping down his face like thick drops of
summer rain, acutely aware that the floodgates of race and racism had
opened and would not be closed. His finger tapped over and over at the top
of a microphone, but for one of the few times in his political life his kinetic
energy had no place to go.

The meeting had disintegrated.

There were claims that the police responded to calls from Hispanics and
not to those from whites who lived in the area, claims that it was unsafe to
have a cup of coffee on the front stoop. Whenever Seamon tried to speak
and counter emotion with fact, he was shouted down. When it was announced that a Hispanic police officer would no longer serve within the
district, there were loud cheers. Within the charged crowd someone passed
around a pamphlet for the Ku Klux Klan that included a number to call in
New Jersey. "Are you Fed up with: Murders, Rapes, Muggings, Disintegrating Neighborhoods, Illegal Aliens?" it asked. "Then join the Invisible
Empire." A fight almost broke out, and plainclothes police officers had to
step in to fend it off.

The meeting ended after about an hour. Rendell walked outside, where
hundreds more angry residents had gathered. Despite the best efforts of the
police surrounding him, he became engulfed by dozens of sweat-drenched
teenagers glistening under the hard lights of the television cameras. The

blaze of the lights was blinding; every bead of sweat and every grimace was intensified and made almost surreal. The teenagers verbally confronted the mayor, but he did not shy away.

"This country is really fucked up," he said out of earshot of the media, as if there weren't anything else you really could say, and suddenly the tension of the situation melted away.

"He's human," said someone in the crowd with admiration.

Driving home that night back along Allegheny Avenue, Rendell admitted to a feeling of complete futility. There were no physical confrontations, but the sense of anger and rage had been visceral, not simply in Kensington, but in so many other swaths of the city. There had been eight murders over the weekend, and Rendell had grave concern that it was going to be a brutal summer. In his public speeches, he had talked with passion about the difficulties that cities all across the country were facing. He openly warned those who thought they were so safe and so secure in the suburbs that they had better start building towering walls to fend off those who would eventually, out of despair and desperation, besiege them.

The obliteration of Allegheny passed by, but as usual he really didn't pay attention to it, perhaps because he was tired of looking at it, tired of dwelling on something that seemed immune to the best intentions of anyone. He wasn't a miracle man, he was just a mayor, although he wasn't immune to praying for another miracle.

"What we need in this town is on every fucking weekend between now and September for it to rain," he said from the whirring quiet of the car. "I don't mean sporadic rain. It has to pour."

V

But it didn't rain the next day. Instead, there were only more issues of race and the all too predictable byproduct of racial politics, the charge of favoring one ethnic group over another pointed at the bull's-eye of the mayor.

Roughly twelve hours after meeting with angry whites at the McVeigh gym, Rendell found himself meeting with Latino leaders in the City Hall Reception Room. They claimed oppression. They claimed misunderstanding and underrepresentation in the mechanism of the city. Without even knowing it, they made the exact same claims the whites had made the night before, only with the targets of persecution reversed. "The problems are still there," one of the leaders told the mayor. "The hatreds still exist. The white sheets are coming back out."

Rendell agreed that whites in Kensington, in venting their frustrations, had chosen Latinos as a scapegoat. "The reason we don't have blacks involved is because they're not readily available to be scapegoats."

But various black leaders in the city, watching white and Hispanics dominate the headlines and personally address their frustrations to the mayor, felt like scapegoats anyway. The mayor might be trying to heal a city and hold it together in the aftermath of a terrible series of shootings, but this was no time for understanding or commiseration. To the contrary, with the mayor's belly exposed by the Kensington shootings, now was the time to launch the harpoons because in the world of city politics, no mayor was a better mayor than a mayor who was wounded and bleeding.

Rendell had been actively involved in politics in the city for nearly twenty years. He was no neophyte to the unseemly wars that had to be fought, to the compromises of racial appeasement, particularly in a city that was almost evenly split between whites and minorities. But when he became mayor, even he seemed taken aback by the power plays of racial politics between white politicians and black politicians and by how little of what they seemed interested in had to do with the common good of the city or with matters of racial injustice but, instead, had to do with amassing their own bases of power.

Rendell may have been taken aback by the power plays of racial politics, but he was also powerfully swayed by them. He had a deep commitment to the black community in the city, and while much of the criticism he sustained as mayor barely seemed to bother him, the one charge that set his temper afire was the charge of racism. But beyond commitment, Rendell also had a political need to keep black elected officials happy and contented. He did not want to raise their ire, as doing so might in turn galvanize the black community, which might in turn encourage a black candidate to run against him in 1995. He knew he was potentially vulnerable.

There was not a major decision or a major personnel move that Rendell contemplated without first screening it for racial acceptability, whether it was the selection of a new police commissioner, a new head of the housing authority, a new appointee to the school board, or a new school superintendent. He even got involved in the race of those picked up by the police in racially sensitive cases. Like ordering from a Chinese menu, if you had one from column A (the black column), you'd better be sure to have one from column B (the white column) as well.

Less than twenty-four hours after the mayor met with leaders in the Hispanic community and less than thirty-six hours after he met with angry whites, he met privately with a gathering of African American leaders in the Cabinet Room at 7:30 A.M. The ostensible purpose of the meeting was to discuss the fatal police shooting of a man named Charlie Matthews in West Philadelphia the previous month. Matthews had been hit twenty-two times by eight different officers. The police originally alleged that Matthews had shot an officer, but later investigation showed that the officer had been wounded by fire from another officer's gun. Matthews did have a gun, but investigation showed that it was not loaded.

"Does anybody care what happens to the African American community in this city?" asked Reverend Jerome Cooper, who was the first to speak. "Does anyone care when an African American is cut down? I want you, Mr. Mayor, to tell us what your moral leadership is in this case. I want you, Mr. Mayor, to tell us what we can expect."

There was the clear implication that Rendell, for what could be interpreted only as reasons of racial insensitivity, hadn't been nearly as concerned about the fatal shooting of Charlie Matthews as he had been about the fatal shooting of Robbie Burns. But the raw assertion did not take into account the radically different circumstances of the two cases. Robbie Burns was a bystander on a street corner who had been shot from a car. Matthews, apparently inebriated, had threatened a little girl in the neighborhood with a gun. When police arrived to respond to a complaint, Matthews answered the door with a gun in his hand and refused to drop it. Far from being buried, the case was in the hands of the district attorney, whose office was evaluating the charges of misconduct against the officers involved. When Rendell tried to explain the city's handling of the Matthews case to those present, discussion of it was dropped since the harpoon had already been fired anyway. Instead, the mayor was roundly criticized for his handling of another incident, one in which a black family, after moving into an all-white neighborhood, had reportedly been harassed and attacked by white residents over the July Fourth weekend. State Senator Hardy Williams accused the mayor of not reaching out to the family.

Rendell worked feverishly to remain calm, pointing out that Williams's assertions were not true. He had reached out to the family through intermediaries, and the family members themselves had decided that they did not want to become transparent symbols for the fodder of politicians. Instead, they just wanted to leave the neighborhood. In addition, when two blacks had been arrested for their involvement in the incident, the mayor, after personally reviewing the case, had ordered that a white participant be arrested as well. "We didn't try to make them into political statements," said Rendell of the family in question. "They wanted to low-key it. They wanted to leave."

But Williams didn't appear to be listening. Rather, he had a loud and distinct message: *"Many people in Philadelphia think the mayor really don't care."*

Another minister stepped in and said that the city was actually pressuring the family into leaving its home. She also claimed that the family had tried to contact the mayor's office and had been rebuffed.

Rendell leaped out of his chair at the head of the table, words tunneling out from between his teeth with venom, the pallid grayness of his face from pressure and lack of sleep bursting into a menacing red. He could no longer listen to falsehoods and badgering with a sweet smile of conciliation on his face. *"That is baloney! That is baloney! I answer every phone call and every letter twenty-four hours a day! I am not going to let untruths be spoken here!"*

Those gathered in the room seemed almost to enjoy the image of a virginal mayor responding to charges of racial insensitivity by screaming at the top of his lungs.

"He's psychotic!" said Williams in a loud whisper to another member of the group.

With the mayor more exposed and weaker than ever, the harpoons continued.

"We need something clear and stated through your office that you do have a concern for all the people in Philadelphia, not just West Kensington. Not just white Catholics," said the Reverend Paul Anderson. "A white man is shot in the head and the mayor and the archbishop are out there immediately. The perception is that these four individuals are of more value to you, possibly because the complexion of the man killed was lighter than mine."

Rendell, groping to regain control, said that maybe Anderson was right: he had not been as vocal in voicing concern about the Matthews shooting as he had been in showing concern about the Burns shooting, but it was not because of any purposeful agenda. Instead, he noted that he had been in the hospital for minor surgery on his elbow when the Matthews shooting had taken place. He then turned the discussion back to the city's handling of the family that had been harassed and asked the Reverend James Allen, the chairman of the city's Commission on Human Relations, to reiterate that the city had never pressured the family to move.

"What's the point of this?" snapped Hardy Williams.

Rendell said that it was important to make everyone understand that the city had not tried to force the family to leave.

"This is not what we're meeting about!" snapped Williams, although it was utterly unclear what the meeting was about, other than to see how the mayor would respond with three or four racial harpoons in his side.

"Come on, let's go!" Williams suddenly said to those who were gathered.

Rendell, still at the head of the table, calmly beseeched the leaders to stay, all too aware of how it would look if the press reported that a group of black leaders seeking the mayor's humane response to their concerns had marched out of a meeting with him in a huff.

But with the exception of one minister, they all left.

"Goddamn it!" yelled Williams as he left the Cabinet Room, slamming the door with such theatricality that the room reverberated.

"I was here ready to discuss," said Rendell to the lone remaining minister. "I am embarrassed for the people who got up and left. If they are men of the cloth, I am embarrassed."

He also felt that in the game of racial politics he had been set up. Although he could not prove it, the departure by Williams and the ministers seemed staged, designed to send him the unsubtle message that these kinds of contentious skirmishes would become routine unless he started paying a little bit more attention to their agenda. He knew the media would seize upon what had happened, particularly since a notice of the meeting had been placed on the public relations news wire, which went to all the major newsrooms. With the departure of Philadelphia Police Commissioner Willie Williams for Los Angeles, the mayor was also involved in the crucial process of finding a new commissioner, and he felt that the real purpose of the walkout, much like a warning shot through a picture window, was to let him know what would happen if he picked a white rather than a black replacement.

If nothing else, Rendell could take some solace in hitting the racial trifecta. On Monday, working-class whites had accused him of being callous and insensitive to their needs. On Tuesday, Hispanic leaders had accused him of being callous and insensitive to their needs. On Wednesday, black leaders had accused him of being callous and insensitive to their needs. The only elements missing were the fringe groups—Asian Americans, Italian Americans, gays and lesbians, the disabled, advocates for the homeless. But Rendell knew from past experience that their lack of participation was not a matter of restraint but was a matter of the groups' own difficulty in figuring out a way to inject themselves into this particular situation. Robbie Burns wasn't gay. He wasn't Asian. He wasn't homeless. He hadn't died in a wheelchair trying to negotiate a sidewalk that didn't have a federally mandated curb cut. But the mayor also knew that at some point during his administration all these special interest groups would be paying him visits, claiming woe and oppression and misunderstanding with such heartfelt poignancy that even the members of the press they leaked the contents of the meetings to would be reduced to tears if they weren't on deadline. Several months later Mark Segal, publisher of the *Philadelphia Gay News,* would tell the mayor with all the profound outrage he could muster, "Do you know you don't have a single lesbian in the administration?" Several months later State Senator Hardy Williams would be back in the Cabinet Room, this time claiming a conspiracy in the failure of a black police officer to get a promotion. Well trained by this point, the mayor would muster every ounce of goodwill and personally order a police review of the officer's file. The review would reveal that dismissal proceedings had been started after traces of cocaine were found on the officer's person. Several weeks later a group of Italian Americans, refusing to believe that a slip of the tongue was all that lay behind the dyslexic head of the city's art commission referring to a color as "dago red" instead of "Day-Glo red," would stomp into the Cabinet Room and tell the mayor they would march in protest unless the man was fired.

It was in the middle of the white-hot heat of that meeting at the McVeigh gym in Kensington, with those layers of mist rising toward the ceiling, that a woman in sandals and shorts had come to the front of the stage. Her name was Mary Jane Burns, the mother of Robbie Burns, and although she had lost more than anyone else in that gym, she was the least angry. "My son Robbie was a peacemaker who did not believe in vengeance or rowdiness," she said. "Everyone is doing what they can do. Take one step at a time."

The decency of those words struck a momentary chord. Rendell, on the way back home that night, seemed dazzled by such dignity in the face of such loss. "I mean if it was my son, Jesse, I'd be the loudest fucking one. I could never do what she did." But in the aftermath, the jockeying for position and the probing of the mayor's underside for weakness, the message of those words—peace, forgiveness, healing—had been forgotten in less than forty-eight hours. In the political world of the city, a city of fiefdoms and feudal lords and warring bands of self-interest, the death of Robbie Burns wasn't much of a tragedy to anyone beyond his friends and family.

It was the perfect opportunity.

FIVE

"Watch Out"

I

Between the rows of spectators and the judge's bench, in that small and claustrophobic space where lawyers perform their theatrics of shock and sympathy in the name of justice, Michael McGovern awaited the verdict.

A month had passed since the killing of Robbie Burns, and politicians in the city, realizing that they had picked the victim's bones clean and could gain no more from instant indignation, had gone on to other pursuits. The fissures of race remained, but when McGovern grappled with them in a courtroom in the continuing heat of the summer, the very trial itself revealing the soul of a city so very much torn by hate and misunderstanding, not a single politician was there to listen.

McGovern, a prosecutor of hearty vintage, was dressed in a gray striped suit that he had purchased a month ago because he thought it would bring him good luck. He had slept poorly the night before, partly because of his three-year-old's nightmare about Dracula tapping on the window and partly because the anticipation of a verdict in a murder case made him edgy. Sometimes he could gauge the outcome of a criminal trial with confidence, was so sure of the evidence and the way it played upon judge and jury that there was no need to be squeamish. But this case, *Commonwealth v. William Taylor,* carried no certainty.

McGovern approached his job the same way athletes approach major games. There was no such thing as a Pyrrhic victory. Regardless of his own performance, there was no dignity or valor in what he perceived as a loss. In the vernacular of his trade, when he took a case file and wrote the verdict across the top of it, he called it marking the file. There was a range of verdicts that a judge or a jury could hand down in any homicide case. But for McGovern, that moment of pulling out the pen and marking the file, if it was to carry any flair and flourish, meant only one verdict, murder in the first degree, which carried a minimum sentence of life in prison. Only with that verdict did all the energized performances in that small and claustrophobic space seem truly worth it, not simply for McGovern but for those he believed depended on him—the spirit of the victim, the victim's family, the city itself.

McGovern had been a prosecutor for ten years, five of them in the homicide unit. Although there were elements of the job that he found increasingly difficult, particularly the pay and the legal requirement that he live in the city because he was a city employee, he undertook his work with a zeal that at times seemed almost evangelical. He loved the challenge of a trial, particularly a jury trial, the uses of narrative and pace with a pinch of melodrama here and pathos there. McGovern believed that juries listen to evidence to a certain degree but that what they really listen to are stories, with the evidence serving as character and plot. If you didn't have a good story to tell, something with which to entice the jurors to stay with you and listen to you, you were going to lose them.

Although there were variations, the story McGovern told always had basically the same demarcations and the same outline: the story of a city he had been born in and had grown up in and loved terrorized by a strain of killers who regarded murder as a common and acceptable form of conflict resolution—an argument that had gone wrong, a twenty-two-month-old who was making too many demands, a teenager with the misguided suspicion that someone was hitting on his girlfriend.

Criminologists and other social scientists had spent tens of thousands of pages tracing explanations and answers to urban crimes such as these. Some ascribed them to the breakup of the family. Some, longing in a nostalgic way for a return to the good old days of heroin, when addicts more often than not did harm to themselves, attributed these crimes to the appearance of crack in the mid-1980s. Others traced them to the destruction of the city's manufacturing base and to the loss of jobs that not only had meant steady pay but also had provided the spiritual lift one gets from actually producing something and making something for a living. But whatever the causes, much of the life of the city seemed to be guided by twin poles of fear, fear among those who lived in it and wanted to leave, fear among those who lived outside and would never step inside because of what they believed and what they had heard. Tales of urban crime could be embellished until, with each retelling and each added detail, they took on the lore of myth.

When the crime rates of the nation's ten largest cities were compared, Philadelphia's was usually among the lowest. But the trend of the city's crimes over thirty years still revealed something shocking. In 1960, there were 6,734 violent crimes (homicide, rape, aggravated assault, robbery) in Philadelphia, a rate of 336 per 100,000 citizens. In 1990, the number of violent crimes, 21,384, had more than tripled, and because of continued population loss, the rate, 1,349 per 100,000 citizens, had more than quadrupled. In 1960, there were 150 homicides, a rate of 7 per 100,000 citizens. In 1990, there were 500 homicides, a rate of 32 per 100,000 citizens. In 1960, the rate of robberies was 101 per 100,000 citizens. By 1990, it had increased eightfold, to 808 per 100,000 citizens. In the meantime, the city's perpetual cycle of budget woes, mismanagement, population loss, and a dwindling tax base had created an equally incredible phenomenon: a drop in the number of police officers, from a high of 8,127 in 1975 to 6,140 in 1990.

Given the crime rate, McGovern had ample opportunity to refine his craft. And he did it exceedingly well, not simply because it was the posture of a prosecutor to loathe crime but also because he knew firsthand its effects on the psyche of the city. He was born and bred in Port Richmond, a neighborhood hard along the Delaware River that was next to Kensington and shared its characteristics—white, working class, held together within the rectangle of school and playground and row house and factory. His father was born in Port Richmond, and so was his mother. His father was Irish, a toll collector on the Ben Franklin Bridge who went to work every day, ate meat and potatoes when he got home, said as little as possible without being certifiably mute, and then went over to the local taproom to play pinochle and darts and drink some beer. He spent one summer week of every year in the seedy surf and sand of Wildwood on the New Jersey shore, and perhaps because he had spent nearly an entire life peering into driver's-side windows and observing outstretched palms, he never owned a car.

Mike McGovern's mother was Italian, and the alchemy of the two cultures made him a kid who had the wits and street smarts to hold his own, a good fighter and an even better talker. He fought—most kids in the neighborhood fought—but there were basic, agreed-upon rules of engagement: snitching on someone, running away when a buddy was getting the bejesus knocked out of him, cursing in front of somebody's sister. You didn't gouge or bite or use bats but fought with your fists, and the fights never lasted too long, for kids were more inclined to go down to the railroad tracks with shakers of Morton's salt, rip the covers off them, and spend all day throwing them at one another as if they were grenades.

For the first thirty-one years of his life, McGovern didn't simply live in Port Richmond. He lived in a variety of homes on the same street—Chatham Street. He lived there in 1951, when he was born, and he lived there when he went to Nativity BVM elementary at Belgrade and Madison Streets and then when he went to high school at Northeast Catholic. He lived there when he went to Villanova University and Temple Law School. He lived there when he married Mary Pat and they had the first of their four children. He lived there in 1980, when he went to work for the district attorney's office.

Between him and his parents, the McGoverns' roots in Port Richmond went back nearly seventy-five years. But there had been changes, particularly during the last ten years. Kids began to piss on his steps and then say "fuck you" when he asked whether maybe they could walk to the alley and piss there. It was a small thing, but it made him realize that the neighborhood he had grown up in bore no resemblance to the neighborhood he was living in now. He lived on the same street, but that was the only thing that remained the same. In 1985, he decided to move to the northeast corner of the city, as far away as he could possibly go without breaking the city's residency requirement.

McGovern left the district attorney's office in the mid-1980s and went into private practice for about a year and a half. But he missed the sense of doing something that he thought was noble and in the service of the city. He came back to the district attorney's office in 1988 and was assigned to the homicide unit. Many of the cases were wrenching, but none caused him greater anguish than he felt when a seventeen-year-old boy, the son of a cop from the same neighborhood that McGovern himself had grown up in, had his skull battered and his legs broken by an angry mob wielding baseball bats.

"That was like an epiphany for me," Mike McGovern said of prosecuting the killers of Sean Daily. "Everything I did as a lawyer brought me back home."

But there was no sense of homecoming, just the juxtaposition of the neighborhood that was gone and the neighborhood that now existed— Sean Daily found dead on a metal grate across the street from where McGovern had gone to elementary school, the prescribed rules of fighting that McGovern had grown up with replaced by baseball bats and guns and slow torture, the tearing off of the tops of shakers of Morton's salt and playing war hardly as satisfying anymore as the smashing of a seventeen-year-old's balls with a baseball bat.

Sean Daily was killed on May 20, 1989. A week before, a Latino had been insulted and punched by a group of whites during an altercation in the neighborhood. The incident wasn't forgotten, as all incidents of racial hatred are never forgotten, and a group of Latinos returned to the corner of Belgrade and Ann Streets seeking revenge. Most of the kids scattered, but Sean Daily wasn't lucky enough. His legs were knocked out from under him by a baseball bat, causing him to fall, and then there were swings from the bat, repeated swings, to his shoulders and his skull and his buttocks and his legs and his testicles. Like a dog that had been hit in the street by a speeding car, he somehow tried to crawl to the safety of his home. But before he got there, God took mercy on him, and he was shot in the back.

McGovern didn't tell the reporters he was from Port Richmond. He didn't want to be seen as the neighborhood's avenging angel, but that's what he was, his relationship with Sean Daily's family stretching back nearly thirty years. When McGovern was thirteen, he and a friend had set fire to some leaves. The fire spread to a tree, whose burning leaves fell onto the roof of the B and H Deli, and the fire department had to be called. Mc-Govern and his friend did what any other thirteen-year-olds would have done—they hid, assuming it was better to disappear and live on their own for the rest of their lives than ever face their parents. But their plan didn't work. The source of the prank was discovered, and it was Keith Daily, Sean's father, who knocked on the door of the McGoverns' house to tell Mike's parents that their son had narrowly missed burning down a neighborhood landmark, not to mention a damn good deli.

McGovern spent much of that trial in fever pitch. He ignored the predictable charges of racism made against him and his office by members of the Hispanic community, as well as the absurd claims that the defendants were the subject of a racially motivated prosecution. He knew that hate had no bounds in the city, and he knew that the context of the Daily case was rooted in the hate that many white kids had for Latinos and the hate that many Latino kids had for whites. But he also knew that Sean Daily was an innocent, a seventeen-year-old innocent. And he knew that Sean Daily had been tortured before he died, his body "one deep, dark contusion" from his shoulders to his buttocks, as he described it to the jury, from the repeated blows of baseball bats. One blow after another. For two or three minutes.

The case took eleven weeks in a sweltering courtroom that didn't even have air-conditioning at first, and at one point McGovern moved his family to the Jersey shore because he had received death threats. But he refused to throttle his outrage by a single decibel, and in his closing argument to the jury he took a broken baseball bat that had been introduced into evidence and struck it against a courtroom table to give the jurors an idea of the sound such an instrument makes when it is repeatedly used for torture.

"What clearer example of intent to inflict pain?" he asked. And the jury answered.

In August 1990, five of the seven defendants in the case were sentenced to life. McGovern marked their files with particular gusto, a neighborhood boy making good on his debts and obligations to the neighborhood even though he didn't live there anymore. One of the effects of having had a quiet father is the tendency to remember what little he did say, and Mike McGovern always remembered this piece of advice: "As long as you never forget where you came from, you're welcome back." For Mike McGovern, the best and truest measure of that was the number of people who tried to buy him a beer when he went back to visit. After the Sean Daily trial, when he went to Mick's Inn, he could have sat there for three days and not spent a single dollar. He was a guy from the neighborhood who still carried the neighborhood with him regardless of who he was and where he went, still Kewpie McGovern's kid regardless of how many times he got his name in the *Inquirer.* Something precious had been taken from the neighborhood, and Mike McGovern had given something back—faith in a system of laws and justice in a city that creaked and sputtered sometimes but still worked. In the absence of restoring a life, it was the best that anyone could do.

And now, two years later, in August 1992, he was telling the story again in a different courtroom with a different victim and a different defendant and a different set of family members but with the same undercurrent of frustration and racial hatred that had claimed the life of Sean Daily. There was a new mayor now, and McGovern, like many others, could feel the clouds of gloom that had hung over the city slowly lifting, as if Rendell, through the sheer force of his enthusiasm, had just blown them across the Delaware to the eternal misery of Camden. McGovern had worked for Rendell when Rendell had been the district attorney, and he knew the considerable persuasions of his charm. It was Rendell, in fact, who had hired McGovern away from the public defender's office as part of a group of young, aggressive lawyers who reveled in the daily combat of the courtroom. As mayor, Rendell was changing perceptions, and people who had thought they would never again believe in the city's future were, if not quite ready to become believers again, at least thinking about it. But from the vantage point of a prosecutor and the kinds of cases that a prosecutor tried and the kind of city that a prosecutor saw day in and day out, certain realities were very much the same.

II

He could sense the horrible feeling in Courtroom 246 in City Hall, the Berlin Wall as he described the atmosphere, blacks on one side and whites on the other. But at least the Berlin Wall was a wall, a physical impasse. This was different and somehow worse. Without a single impediment, the narrow aisle between the two sides had become impenetrable. Defense attorney Dan Rendine saw it too, particularly as the trial progressed and the tension spiked and sharpened so that it was no longer just a murder trial but a trial about polarity and division and whites seeking vindication and blacks seeking vindication. But neither attorney was there to pass moral judgment. Rendine was there to represent a defendant, and McGovern was there to convince the judge of the premeditated, first-degree guilt of that defendant, a fifteen-year-old who looked closer to ten and spent much of the trial doodling and hanging his head to the side, as if self-consciously trying to adopt a pose of carelessness and detachment not because he necessarily meant it but because that's how he thought he should act.

His name was William Taylor, and he was known as Will. He had an IQ of 72, had been in special programs in the Philadelphia public schools in fifth, sixth, seventh, and eighth grades, and was performing at a level five to seven grades below what was expected for a child of his age. His parents had never married, and he was raised primarily by his mother. When he was two, they moved to Texas, where, according to a report that was submitted to the court, he was repeatedly abused by someone his mother lived with—beaten with bare hands and struck with a belt across the back, legs, and face. He came back to the city when he was eleven, and his father noted how timid he seemed and wondered whether he might be gay, a sentiment the son seemed determined to rid him of. On a reading examination administered by the Philadelphia public schools after his return, he scored 1 percent, meaning that 99 percent of the students in his age group were more proficient. He scored 2 percent on spelling and 0.8 percent on math. It was noted that Will had a need to be "perceived as a strong and masculine figure" to overcome feelings of inferiority caused by his intellectual limitations. In November 1991, he was arrested for possession of a loaded weapon and was placed on probation. A little more than a month later, on January 10, 1992, Will set off to take his midterms at Audenried High School.

During the trial, it was never clearly established whether Will, in anticipation of his exams, took any papers, pencils, or books to school that day. He may well have thought he didn't need anything other than the pump shotgun he concealed under his Raiders Starter jacket and then placed in his locker.

School let out early because of the midterms. Somewhere around 11:30 A.M., Will and eight or nine other kids passed through the edge of Grays Ferry on their way home. Like so many neighborhoods in the city, Grays Ferry was its own social fortress, with a tradition of suspicion and hatred of blacks.

At Don's Variety at Taney and Dickinson, a little American flag had been taped to one of the windows, and inside the furnishings included a pinball machine, an ice-cream chest, and a rack for potato chips. The boys went in, supposedly to buy something to eat. They were not welcomed, either by the elderly woman at the counter or by the man with the mustache and the blue jean jacket who was sitting on a board on top of the radiator. The boys milled about, and the lady told them that if they weren't going to buy something they would have to leave. They knew they were being watched by the white man in the blue jean jacket. One of the boys, Gilbert Robinson, knocked the man's hat off as he was leaving, and Robinson was tripped in retaliation.

"What the fuck you do that for?" asked Robinson.

"What are you going to do about it, you fucking nigger?"

"Come on, what do you want to do?"

"I'll kick your fucking ass."

They went outside onto Dickinson Street. Robinson didn't know it, but the white man he was tangling with, a thirty-four-year-old named Keith Duczkowski, was a former Golden Gloves boxer.

"What are you going to do, nigger?"

They squared off in the street in an urban version of *High Noon,* a black teenager against a white man twice his age. Robinson hit him two or three times with a combination of lefts and rights. Duczkowski tried to rush Robinson and started hitting him on the back. A black man in his thirties jumped in to stop the fight. The heated ugliness of it appeared to be over.

Then Will Taylor started arguing with Duczkowski. And then, from underneath the Starter jacket, came the shotgun. It had gray tape on the handle and looked like a long pistol. Those who knew Will had seen it before. But usually he kept it at home, except of course, as his cousin later put it to police, "if we were going to a party, something like that."

"Watch out," Will said in the middle of Dickinson Street. Then he pulled down on the lever.

Duczkowski grabbed his side and fell backward, the blue jean jacket darkening with blood from a bullet wound in his abdomen. He got up and staggered backward in the middle of the street at fifteen minutes before noon, with the front window of Don's Variety still visible, with that little American flag taped to the window.

"Oh my God," he said.

Taylor stood over him. Those who had been with him had all started running, so it was just the two of them, a fifteen-year-old black boy with a 72 IQ and a history of abuse and an education that was worthless and a habit of carrying his shotgun to parties and a thirty-four-year-old white man who had a wife and three children and a job as a roofer and lived in an area of the city where blacks were still routinely called niggers.

There was a pause, and no one heard anything for a little bit. Five seconds, ten seconds, fifteen seconds . . .

The boys who had been with Will had kept on running. They didn't turn around to see what was happening, but there was no need. The sound of the blast booming down the street told them that Will had fired again.

A man living on Dickinson Street was watching a rerun of *The Fugitive* on television when he heard the shots, and he ran outside with a towel. He placed it on Keith Duczkowski's stomach in an effort to stop the bleeding.

Someone else called 911.

"They're on the way."

"Thanks, I mean I thought I heard a shot, and I, I run out the door, and all I heard was this man screamin', cryin' here."

"They'll be there. They'll be there shortly, ma'am."

"Oh, Jesus! This poor man. Oh! He's not moving! Oh come on, send it!"

"I'm gone, I'm gone," Keith Duczkowski whispered in the middle of the street with a towel and a sheet wrapped around him in a vain attempt to stop the rush of blood spreading over his clothes.

It was the last thing anyone heard him say before he died.

"I'm gone. I'm gone."

Will Taylor ran off before the police came. He found some of the kids, and they went back to a house in their neighborhood and watched some television and got a cold drink. Will thought about what had happened and told a friend that he hoped the guy didn't die. "It isn't right the guy's kids don't have a dad," he said. But otherwise he seemed calm and cool. Several hours after the shooting, a probation officer paid Will a visit. Will told him everything was fine, leaving out that he had just killed someone in the middle of the street. The probation officer was satisfied, and even after Will's arrest for murder, somehow unaware of the charges, he was still satisfied. In a note in the boy's file, he wrote, "Will appeared to be doing well." Aside from the fact that the spiral of Will Taylor's life now included the possibility of imprisonment for life at the age of fifteen, perhaps he was.

The trial ate at McGovern—the racial tension, the conflicting emotions of trying a juvenile. Both sides in the case closed ranks around their own, white witnesses determined to show that Taylor had committed premeditated murder, black witnesses trying to recant the statements they had given the police.

As much as McGovern liked aspects of the work he did—the sense of doing something worthwhile that very few other lawyers felt—there were significant constraints. As long as he worked for the district attorney's office, he was also locked into the city, which meant among other things a wage tax, a public school system that could not provide even a nominal education for his four children, a level of service that was spotty at best and nonexistent at worst, and a level of pay that left no real room for upward mobility. On the typical ledger sheet of reasons to leave the district attorney's office and reasons to stay, it wasn't even close. But then a case like Will Taylor's came along, and the qualities that made McGovern such a superb prosecutor—that religious sense of protecting the city from those who were destroying it—came rushing back.

When he gave his closing argument in the Will Taylor case, he became so heated that his voice cracked. He knew his conduct was unprofessional, but it also conveyed his emotions about the case, the image of a fifteen-year-old bringing a pump shotgun to high school midterms. His whole style was a mirror of the way he looked, compact and energized and blunt, the roots of Port Richmond as apparent and as proudly worn as an American flag in the lapel. "All we had was a fistfight in the city," McGovern told Common Pleas Judge Carolyn Temin. "No one should die over this."

"Why was Will standing over a man with his guts shot, totally helpless, with his bowels and intestines perforated?" he asked in his closing argument. Why did he fire that second shot? McGovern answered the question: because it was an act of premeditated, cold-blooded murder. "Some people can do it when they're fifteen, and some people can do it when they're ninety-five, and some people can never do it."

During the closing argument, Will Taylor looked at Mike McGovern with mild interest, the kind of interest a young teenager might exhibit while watching a television show he really doesn't care about very much, a look in that adolescent space between boredom and reluctant amusement. It was a look that crept inside McGovern, and in the privacy of his office after the closing he couldn't help but reflect on his picture of Will Taylor as a cold-blooded killer who deserved to go to prison for the rest of his life. He knew why Taylor carried that shotgun and flashed it around with as much pride as a father showing off pictures of his children. He knew how in Will Taylor's world it was a way of proving strength and gaining peer acceptance. "You look at this guy, and he's four years older than my son Michael. I love kids, and you wonder about this society disease that we have is corrupting all of us. Does it warp the young ones faster in areas where they are trapped?"

McGovern knew that a first-degree murder conviction would mean that Will Taylor would spend the rest of his life in prison. "I feel sorry for his youth because he wasted his life," he said. He also expressed sorrow for his family. But then, like a priest questioning his faith, he caught himself. "I don't play sociologist anymore," he said. "I just play with the facts on this day. I deal with the adult on trial. I deal with the act as opposed to the action."

Just as he was acutely aware of the tender age of the defendant, he was acutely aware of the racial hatred that had fueled the confrontation in the first place, cries of "nigger" on a street corner in Grays Ferry a quarter of an hour before noon, the specter of a white man and a black teenager fighting each other in the middle of the street, a black teenager standing over a white man with a pump shotgun in his hands.

"Everybody says, 'What racial hatred?' It's like saying, 'What elephant in the phone booth?' " he had noted during his closing. But none of that ultimately mattered when matched up with the image that McGovern thought about the most—the pleas of a man with his intestines hanging out met not with an ounce of sympathy or even the sound of footsteps as the shooter ran away but with another blast.

"That second shot says a lot," said McGovern, but did it say enough to convince a judge that Taylor should be found guilty of first-degree murder? Was there sufficient proof of premeditation and intent to kill, or would the judge, assuming she found Will Taylor guilty, come back with a verdict of third-degree murder instead? Although he was loathe even to consider it, that's what McGovern thought it would be, which meant that when he marked the file, the strokes of the pen across the top would lack their usual spark. It also meant that when the trial was over, when the inevitable moment came when he would have to look into the eyes of the members of the victim's family and explain to them what had happened, he would feel that he had somehow let them down, that the faith they had placed in him as a prosecutor had been misguided.

III

The morning of the verdict, a white man in white shorts and sneakers, lingering outside in the hallway, spoke to a friend and succinctly summed up what he perceived to be the thrust of the previous day's testimony. "You missed the main event. The nigger took the witness stand."

Will Taylor was brought down the hallway in handcuffs. He wore a black suit that was too big for him, looking like the concentration camp uniforms that the characters wear in Art Spiegelman's *Maus*. The suit floated on his frame. His face, still with the softness of youth, only added to the incongruity. He walked down the hallway with a look that was calm and resolute, playing out his self-perceived part to the end.

Inside the courtroom, five rows of wooden chairs were divided by an aisle down the center. The right side was completely filled with whites who were friends and family of Keith Duczkowski. The left side was occupied by blacks who were friends and family of Will Taylor. There were plenty of seats to sit in on the left side, unless you were white. Then there were apparently no seats at all. "Do I have to sit over there?" said a white woman as she walked into the courtroom and saw the seating arrangement. She shrugged and looked disgusted. Rather than go near the left side, she found a seat in the jury box.

"This is a courtroom, and I want to remind you to be calm and act with restraint," said the court crier, sensing the tension, as if the slightest gesture or movement might set off a mêlée, as if all the sad, insoluble hatred in the city between blacks and whites were focused in the silence of this room.

McGovern stood in that small and claustrophobic space between the rows of spectators and the judge's bench, his arms folded like a circumspect schoolboy, waiting for the verdict. A little bit before 10:00 A.M., Judge Temin appeared to render a verdict, the decision entirely in her hands since Taylor had requested a non-jury trial. McGovern knew virtually all the judges in the system, and after a while when you knew a judge, you could predict with regularity those willing to grant some degree of mercy and those who saw mercy as something that God could sort out once the defendant died in prison. McGovern didn't know Temin. He had never tried a major case in front of her, and he did not know what to expect.

She asked the defendant to rise. He did so, standing obediently in that ill-fitting suit. She looked at him and announced her verdict.

Guilty of murder. Guilty of murder in the first degree.

Several members from the white side of the courtroom began to applaud, as if they were at a sporting event, but they stopped when the court crier yelled, "Quiet, please!" The courtroom fell silent, the only sound the click of the handcuffs around Will Taylor's small wrists. Several sheriff's deputies surrounded him and took him away through the back of the court-room, and there was the sound of a slam of a door. Sentencing was set for November 30, but it was moot since first-degree murder in Pennsylvania carried a minimum sentence of life imprisonment without parole. The only other sentence would have been the death penalty, but since Will Taylor was still fifteen, he was too young for that. Instead of dying some day by lethal injection, he would simply die in prison instead.

Outside the courtroom, Joe Duczkowski, Keith's older brother, hugged a friend and said, "Let's go, man! Everything's made!"

Inside the courtroom, Will Taylor's mother sat in the front row, rocking back and forth, moaning softly in a kind of mantra, vomiting into a metal wastepaper basket with a black plastic liner.

Outside the courtroom, Joe Duczkowski talked about his brother's legacy as a Golden Gloves fighter and said of the verdict, "That was his last fight, and he won it."

Inside the courtroom, the sound of the vomiting coming from Will Tay-lor's mother continued. A little girl watched, then ran to the back and shielded her eyes.

Outside the courtroom, on the way back to his office, Mike McGovern said he felt the way he used to feel at law school, when actually linking the law with the ideals of justice wasn't considered some pathetic form of naïveté. "No amount of money can compensate for the feeling you get when the mother of the dead guy says, 'Thank you, God bless you, I'll do anything for you.' " He knew those feelings would not last—another case in a week or two, another pumping of emotion—but standing on Broad Street, the glowering frown of City Hall behind him, he said he felt like the best lawyer in the entire world—proud of the legal system, proud of the judge who hadn't been swayed by sympathy, proud of the family of the victim who had put their faith in him, proud of himself. He was a prosecu-tor, and he was ready to mark the file murder in the first degree.

"There will be another case tomorrow, but this guy is slam-dunked. In terms of this town, he's out of here. I don't have to worry about him anymore."

IV

Right around the corner from the courtroom, the mayor sat at the table in his office surrounded by some of the keenest and cleverest minds in the city. The verdict had been handed down only hours earlier. They were all aware of what had just happened and even more aware of how this could be a major black eye for the city unless it was immediately addressed and handled. The injustices and inequities that had been revealed must be righted. Somehow, some way, the Miss International U.S. Beauty Pageant must be saved. Somehow, Miss North Dakota and Miss Tennessee, not to mention Miss Minnesota and Miss Georgia and Miss Virginia and all the rest had to get the toothy gleams back in their smiles.

The previous day by happenstance Rendell himself had witnessed the spectacle of pageant contestants beating on the sides of a police van outside a hotel as it carted off the show's sponsor. The mayor didn't know what was going on, but the sight of those crying, screaming beauty-show contestants in such pain and agony over the loss of their dreams and their entrance fees moved him. He swung into action that very same day, at around midnight, calling a member of his staff, marshaling the forces of the city to turn the nightmare of these girls into a fairy tale. He got the hotel they were about to be evicted from to let them stay for free. He arranged for tours of the city, and he talked various restaurateurs into letting the contestants have a night on the town.

That Friday around noon, two hours after Will Taylor had been carted off to prison for the rest of his life with a single tear in each eye, the mayor held a press conference to publicize his monumental efforts on behalf of a beauty contest. "This way, ladies," said Deputy Chief of Staff Ted Beitchman, ushering the fallen contestants into the Reception Room as if they were survivors of a year-long hostage crisis. Three reporters had been in the courtroom when the verdict in the Will Taylor case was reached. Nearly twenty reporters milled about with notebooks and cameras and microphones for what one newspaper later dubbed "Beauties and the Feast," filing through the rows of the Reception Room like prep-school boys trying to coax shy girls to dance, gently bending down to get all the details from Miss Tennessee and Miss North Dakota and Miss Minnesota. The girls themselves sat in the front row, pretty and prim, the white sashes proclaiming their states running in neat diagonal lines from shoulder to sternum like cellophane wrapping on a piece of processed cheese. In between answering questions, they munched on a spread of hoagies and chicken wings, and whereas they were polite and artful, they could also feel the power.

"Are we going to a baseball game?" warbled Miss Georgia.

"Do you want to go to a baseball game?" warbled back the mayor.

At the front of the Reception Room, underneath all those portraits of mayors past, various city officials beamed like groomsmen at a wedding party. They knew they were onto something. "Talk about getting mileage!" said press secretary Feeley, watching one reporter after another sidle up to the pageant contestants. Even the wire services were there, which meant national coverage. Sure enough, that following Sunday *The New York Times* had a story with a headline that read, PHILADELPHIA RESCUES STRANDED CONTESTANTS, and the mayor was cast as a worthy hero. "I figured these young ladies from all over the country would have nothing but bad thoughts and would always remember their awful experience in Philadelphia, which was humiliating and tragic, and I didn't want that to happen," he was quoted as saying.

It was another sublime moment for the mayor, another perfect bull's-eye in the game of creating the perception of change. Eight months into the term a remarkable amount had gone well, more than anyone, friend or foe, would have predicted. But absent the one piece that could make the miracle of a reborn city truly plausible, it still was all largely illusory. Blocking the road to glory and national acclaim were the city's four major unions. Together they numbered nearly twenty-five thousand members, and the tentacles of their power reached deep into every politician in the city. They also knew what they could do with a slowdown here and a work stoppage there and the ultimate weapon of an all-out strike to create an image of the city so different from the one the mayor was groping to create—not oncescorned beauty contestants with beauteous smiles, but pictures of stinking garbage piled to the heavens on city streets and angry workers with picket signs, the portrait of a city in chaos. It was contract time, and it seemed unlikely the unions could be bought off with hoagies, chicken wings, free hotels, or even free tickets to a baseball game. They wanted more, much more.

Ed Rendell talked tough, but that was in public, when the television cameras were on and the rating agencies were in town. In private, Ed Rendell had an impossibly hard time saying no to anyone about anything. This would be the ultimate test of his term as mayor, the true defining moment. And if the best barometer of the future was the behavior of the past, then he seemed likely to flunk it.

War of the Unions

<u>S I X</u>

"Fast Eddie, We Are Ready"

I

All during the spring and summer of 1992, the legend of David L. Cohen had spread through the city like an urban version of the story of Davy Crockett, but with a pulsating beeper strapped to his belt instead of a hunting knife. Some in the administration had taken to calling him the boy wonder. "David, my lord," people said over the phone to him. There was some suggestion that perhaps the time had come to have his name in raised red letters every time it appeared in print, as Christian Scriptures do for the names of saints.

"I have to be seen with you," Bill Batoff, a prominent Democratic fundraiser, had told him when insisting that they have dinner together.

"That may be the most pathetic line of all time," said Cohen.

The *Inquirer* was the first to extol his skills, which it did in a front-page story that was so gushing and complimentary that the only thing missing was a picture of Cohen water-skiing on one foot down the Delaware with the mayor on his back while returning phone calls. Then came *Philadelphia Magazine* and ultimately the *Daily News*, all in the same reverential tone. There was some suggestion that the city get rid of its famous Thanksgiving Day Parade and the ringing of the Liberty Bell on July Fourth and just have David Cohen Day, a day on which every city employee stayed home and Cohen did all their jobs—garbage pickup, traffic enforcement during rush hour, restaurant inspections.

In a city where public officials were routinely carved and quartered, the treatment of Cohen was without precedent, as if there were truly something mythical about him, not simply in his remarkable capacity to work and get things done but also in his capacity to deny himself any of the basic pleasures of life if they ever conflicted with his work.

Quite obviously any comparison of Davy Crockett with David L. Cohen was ludicrous. Davy Crockett had survived the rigors of the Tennessee wilderness, killed a few bears and maybe a few men, but how could any of that compete with the deprivation David Cohen suffered as chief of staff when he attended a Genesis rock concert and discovered, to his absolute mortification, that the music was so loud he couldn't hear himself over his cellular phone? Davy Crockett had died an epic death at the Alamo, but during the summer of 1992 David Cohen actually went on vacation with his family to Martha's Vineyard, thereby absenting himself from the office for two whole weeks as opposed to the usual two hours, during which he went home and, instead of sleeping on a bed, presumably just went into a darkened closet and hung by his knees from the tie rack. He had claimed he was looking forward to the vacation, that he had no apprehensions about being away. But the memo he wrote just before he left, two and half single-spaced pages entitled "Vacation Memorandum of David L. Cohen," revealed the true inner soul.

   a. All of my mail (including "see mes" from Ed), with the exception of
      mail that I return to the office in accordance with this section, should
      be sent to me via Federal Express once a day. I also want to receive

copies of all relevant newspapers (Inquirer, Daily News, and Tribune), including weekend editions.

b. I will return mail, also via Federal Express, for routing. When I write
a routing message directly on the mail, it need not be copied; the
original can simply be sent to the person to whom I have routed it.
When I attach one of my cover sheets, or put "cc DLC" on the top
of a document, however, the document (including the cover sheet)
should be copied for me. The original should be sent to the addressee,
with other addressees receiving copies if necessary.

c. On some mail that I return I will simply put "to DLC." This mail,
along with my copies of the documents that I route to other people
with cover sheets, should be placed in my "in" box for me to deal with
upon my return. I would like my copies of the documents that I route
to be sorted by cabinet official.

If people insist they need to speak with me, please take a telephone
number where I can reach them during the day and in the evening, and
I will get back to them directly. For your information, the best time to
reach me is in the morning (before 10:00 A.M.), around lunch time, in
the late afternoon (around 5:00 P.M.), and late in the evening.

But regardless of the legend that was so rapidly building, even Cohen
himself privately yielded every now and then to the feeling that what he
now did for a living and the conditions under which he did it were both
bizarre and brutal. He luxuriated in work, but from that very first Sunday
in January, when he had moved in, it was apparent that the job would require a capacity for workaholic self-abuse and self-imposed torture far ex-
ceeding that which had defined his life as a lawyer. Among his office
decorations, he put up huge pictures of his two children on one of the walls,
and while it was clear to everyone that he loved his children, some privately snickered that the real reason for the size of the pictures was to help
him remember what the kids looked like since he almost never saw them.
"I've worked hard in every job I've ever had," he said one day. "But nothing in life has prepared me for the swirling chaos that goes on all the time."
And for someone as inherently obsessive about detail as Cohen, the possibilities were endless.

There was the Friday night in March when long after everyone else had
gone home to wives and kids and weekends, he sat at his desk deep in
thought with legal pad in front of him as if he were back in law school—

but now he was determining the seating arrangements for the tickets the Rendell campaign had purchased for the NCAA Basketball Tournament eastern regionals at the Spectrum arena. They were being dispensed to various politicians and contributors as tokens of appreciation for their support, and because there were blocks of seats in two different sections, good ones in Section V near the end line, bad ones in Section B behind the court, the matter was fragile. To the average layman, a bad free seat at a highly prized sporting event was still a good deal, but to the average Philadelphia politician a bad seat was the greatest disgrace, a diss that would not be dismissed, and given the way Philadelphia politicians often voted on the basis of biorhythms, sheer malevolence, bad hair days, or whether or not Punxsatawney Phil had seen his shadow, one seating misstep by Cohen, much like a bomb squad expert cutting the wrong wire, might be fatal.

Businessman Lewis Katz, Democrat fund-raising juggernaut, true-blue Friend of Bill, and the mayor's biggest moneyman—any damn seat he wanted. State representative Dwight Evans, the most formidable threat to Rendell in the 1995 election—good seats. Hardy Williams, who had endorsed Rendell in 1991 but could make havoc with the group he headed, Blacks Networking for Progress—two good seats, four bad seats. State representative Mark Cohen, who had no clout and never would unless everyone else in the legislature died—bad seats. Ditto for state senator Vincent Hughes.

There was that Tuesday in April when a city councilman asked him to do something about the rowdy homeless people who were drinking and fighting beneath his open window in City Hall. Although it was hard to figure out just what Cohen's options were in this case—find another office for the councilman, shoot the offending homeless on sight, or maybe just walk two flights up and shut the window—Cohen was faultlessly politic and considered the situation seriously. But later that day, when a member of the mayor's staff began to complain about the absurdities of what she did for a living, Cohen stopped her short. "You think you have a bad life. You don't understand what I do." After he described it, she was speechless. *He* was right. He did have *a bad life*. And even if she had wanted to talk and commiserate, it wouldn't have mattered anyway, because Cohen had a meeting to attend about the budget in some dark and dreary high school auditorium.

Cohen may have felt beleaguered when another member of the city council called to make sure that a lawyer friend of his would be getting some legal work through the Parking Authority. ("It's a done deal," Cohen assured him.) He may have felt beleaguered when he called the police commissioner to see whether there was anything the department could do to locate the stolen car of someone who, in addition to being a victim of crime in the city, was also an old and influential friend of the mayor's. He may have felt beleaguered when, in response to questions by a city councilman about public use of City Hall bathrooms, he dutifully dashed off a memo that, while not exactly the stuff you would have expected from a former executive editor of the *Penn Law Review*, still showed a lucid analysis of the situation:

> We should *try* to have at least one bathroom open for the public on each floor of City Hall. (If possible, it would be great to have one men's room and one women's room.) Most importantly, I think we should have some clear signage at strategic locations throughout City Hall as to where the public can find an open bathroom.

After one particularly swirling day, Cohen mused aloud about checking into a psychiatric clinic. "You can't get phone calls. No mail. No visitors. What could be better?"

But it wasn't his style. And his blips of frustration were just that, infinitesimal bumps expressed privately and quickly, never publicly. And he reacted to the chaos not by succumbing to it but by somehow seeing whether he could conquer it, taking the puzzle and shaping it into a set of manageable pieces. To an astounding degree, he succeeded. And although it was true that he had become the ultimate javelin catcher for virtually every silly request, he was also depended on to do far more than that, not just the sublimely ridiculous but also the sublimely important—he was the keeper of the city's future on a day-to-day basis, fixated on everything, distracted by nothing.

He had done it with requests for tickets. He had done it with requests for parking spaces. He had done it with the five-year plan. And now the biggest question of all was being asked of Cohen: Could he do it with the unions?

And even if he could somehow do it with the unions, play his patented game of patience better than he had ever played it, on a bigger scale than he had ever played it, with hundreds of millions of dollars on the line, not to mention the very success of the administration, then what about the man who would ultimately have to pull the trigger? What about the mayor?

*   *   *

Labor negotiations in a major city were always tortured and tenuous, an unpredictable Crock-Pot-ful of ingredients ranging from race to politics to the courts to the media. But given the public pronouncements of Rendell from the very beginning—that this would be a different kind of negotiation, with concessions that went far beyond the normal fixation on wages—the stakes had already been driven beyond the outer reaches. Although Rendell had vainly tried to underplay the war of the unions in the blindly optimistic hope of reaching an amicable agreement, the assault against the city's four major unions was as remarkable as it was dangerous, a multipronged attack in which the city administration wanted to hold the line on wage increases, drastically decrease health and welfare benefits, reduce other time-honored benefits, and seek unprecedented change in the areas of management rights and work rules. On a practical level, the city was seeking labor savings of about $110 million, but more than just savings, it was also seeking a sweeping and fundamental change in the very way the city government conducted itself, a frank and startling acknowledgment that the city had made concessions to the unions so absurd and so politically motivated that it did not even have the right to unilaterally set schedules for its own workforce. As for the quality of service the public was getting from the unionized workforce, it seemed to be aptly summed up by a slight oversight over at the nursing home, where a dead body went undetected for four days because no one had bothered to look behind the curtain where it lay in repose. What happened or didn't happen in Philadelphia would also be a bellwether for cities everywhere, a crucial test of the ability of government to reverse a long trend of out-of-whack public-sector spending. Throughout the 1980s, the average rate of compensation for state and local government workers had increased more than four times the rate of compensation for comparable private sector jobs. In the private sector, the annual increase had been 3.4 percent, or $960 a year. In state and local government, the annual increase had been 14.6 percent, or $4,031. The anomaly was glaring in Philadelphia, where the taxpayer cost of employee compensation had more than doubled in the last ten years, from roughly $25,000 a year per employee to more than $50,000 a year.

There was something breathless about what the city administration was trying to accomplish, but there was danger, a real danger. As explained by Jim Sutton, president of District Council 33 of the American Federation of State, County, and Municipal Employees, the union representing most of the city's blue-collar workforce, *each* of the areas where Rendell was seeking significant change—wages, health benefits, other givebacks—would be grounds for a strike. But taken together, said Sutton, the seeds were there for an urban riot much like the one that had taken place just a few months earlier three thousand miles to the west in the aftermath of the Rodney King verdict. "You can have an L.A.," he said, and the impetus would be a white mayor trying to eviscerate a workforce that, in the case of Sutton's union, was primarily black.

The stark reality of what was at stake in the war with the unions was embodied by the black notebook that sat on a corner of Cohen's desk. It was barely noticeable in the right-angled piles that took up every inch of available lacquered surface. But unlike the other paper on Cohen's desk, which got read, processed, and filed just before the next avalanche hit the in box, the black notebook never moved. It had the title "Strike Contingency Plans," and the thick sheaf of confidential memos from department heads clearly depicted a city administration that was in the throes of war preparation and that, in the event of a strike at the stroke of midnight on June 30, would be in a state of war, simultaneously trying to keep the city running and warding off possible acts of sabotage and violence that could take place anywhere at any time. Among other precautions, the "Strike Contingency Plans" called for stockpiling a fourteen-day supply of toilet paper; backing up hard disks and systems software in case of computer sabotage; issuing nonstriking employees temporary ID cards that would be changed periodically to guard against enemy infiltration; changing locks on certain key buildings; providing security to fire department employees willing to cross picket lines under secret cover; providing police escorts for persons delivering certain key city documents, such as incoming revenue checks; assigning police officers from Narcotics, Highway Patrol, and the Marine Unit to the prisons to ward off riots; ensuring the availability of two jeeps equipped with snowplows to clear streets of trash; preparing secret contracts to handle removal of sewage sludge or, in the event that no contractor would touch such a job because of the attendant risks, arranging for the National Guard to truck the material.

II

All the material in the black notebook had been compiled by early June, on the obvious assumption that if there was no contract settlement by the June 30 deadline, there would be a strike. But as the deadline neared, the unions seemed in no rush to negotiate and instead seemed to derive a certain pleasure from making negotiating sessions as counterproductive as possible. On some occasions, the entire session seemed to be dominated by the question of where various members of the District Council 33 negotiating team should sit. Since the team was quite large and union protocol had a Kremlinology all its own, negotiators seemed to take forever to find the right seat. And once they were seated, they never seemed to have much to negotiate anyway since the unions were steadfastly refusing to take the city's bargaining stance seriously, and the city was steadfastly refusing to show any crack in that stance whatsoever, except for some minor concessions.

Other sessions degenerated into name-calling, with union negotiators livid and enraged and city negotiators mildly amused, as if they were watching a third-rate sitcom. "You assholes!!" Tom Cronin, the leader of the city's white-collar union, District Council 47, reportedly screamed at one such session at a Holiday Inn in the middle of June, less than two weeks from the contract's expiration date. The constant arrows from Rendell and Cohen in the media had gotten under his skin, particularly since every politician, when it came to election time, suckled the teats of organized labor with unabashed shamelessness, squeezing them for the honey of their support. "Fuck the Democrats!" screamed Cronin. "Fuck the Republicans!"

It was because of negotiating sessions such as these that Joseph Torsella, the deputy mayor for policy and planning and an integral member of the negotiating team, came to the conclusion that there would eventually be a strike. "I don't think there's any fundamental acceptance of the reality of the situation," he said. "They're talking to us, but they don't accept our contention about the fiscal situation." One of the unions, in its initial demand to the city, reportedly asked for an 18 percent wage increase—*in the first year of the contract.* When city negotiators tried to remind the union that the city was broke and was thinking more along the lines of no wage increase for the first year, the union did come back with a counterproposal: it would settle for 14 percent.

To city negotiators, the absurd flavor of the bargaining did signal some clear and calculated method in the unions' strategy. Workers might be ready to strike, but not when the contract expired at 12:01 A.M. on July 1. Instead, the unions were apparently hoping to hide beneath the umbrella of a state-mandated sixty-day fact-finding process. If such a process was in fact allowed by the Pennsylvania Labor Relations Board, it would effectively push back to August 25 the earliest deadline for a possible strike. It would also allow the unions to continue to work under the favorable terms of the existing contract. For the city administration, such a delay would mean the continued bleeding of money it did not have, $1 million to $2 million a week. It would also mean increasingly disquieting glances from Wall Street municipal-credit analysts, who would inevitably wonder whether the mayor, like virtually all mayors of Philadelphia before him, was just another paper tiger whose only real distinguishing characteristic was a great capacity for convincing bluster. Finally, it would have the effect of throwing Rendell's grand pronouncements about massive layoffs straight back at him.

If he was serious about laying off thousands of workers, then he could do it and in all likelihood watch a city under his stewardship ignite in unholy chaos, with every dire prediction in the "Strike Contingency" notebook—and dozens more that had not been predicted—becoming a reality. The public would support him for a while, following along with his rallying cry that short-term pain meant long-term gain, but as garbage piled up in stinking stacks and fights flared up on picket lines and the remaining city services barely functioned, how long could the public be expected to keep following him?

Beyond the tactic of delay, the unions' strategy seemed to hinge almost exclusively on political history and the inevitability that Rendell, in choosing an alternative to that grisly spectacle of chaos, would fall obediently into line and would do what every politician ultimately did: place his own survival above the survival of the city, avoid the hard choices, figure out a way to fall to his knees with enough spin and polish that no one would dwell too long on that stirring inaugural speech, and by using a legacy of phantom budgets, creative bookkeeping, carefully timed tax increases, and blame placed on previous mayors, give the unions much of what they wanted in a new contract. In the long-term, such a strategy would hasten the fall of the city by perpetuating the budgetary mess that made governance so untenable, but in the short term, which was the only time most American politicians ever lived by, it would avoid *Today*-show footage of striking workers in the City of Brotherly Love going for the throats of those trying to cross their picket lines.

And yet, despite what the union negotiators were expecting, Rendell's stomach showed an iron lining. Instead of buckling in the slightest, he seemed to be doing the very opposite, acting as if he were crazy enough to do all the things he said he would do if the unions did not accept the reality of the city's fiscal situation. And the city negotiators began to see a wonderful point of leverage in all this—the lunacy threshold, the absolute lunacy of the mayor in thinking he could take on the unions and survive to tell about it.

"There's no motivation like fear," said Kenneth Jarin, a lawyer in the city and a member of the negotiating team. "People are always more scared of someone they think is crazy than someone who is rational."

While Rendell worked the unions from the outside, Field General Cohen and high-ranking officers from the city negotiating team led a stealth campaign from the inside, planting mines and hurling Molotov cocktails in every conceivable place they could think of, performing like expert saboteurs in their camouflage of lusterless blue suits.

Of all the elements in the union negotiations, none was more important or more controversial than the health and welfare plan. Under a system that embodied the way cities all over the country had sold their souls to the municipal unions in return for peace and political support, the city of Philadelphia contributed an average of $475 a month per employee for health and welfare benefits. In comparison with the amount contributed in the private sector, that figure defied any rational economic explanation. Even more outrageous was the way in which the money was dispensed by the city: it went straight to the unions. The city had no rights of administration, no way of making sure that the money it doled out each month was being used solely for health and welfare benefits. And the distinct suspicion of the city negotiators was that although some portion of that $475 a month went for benefits, some portion of it also went for everything else besides benefits, such as patronage, consulting fees, and mortgages on various union-owned buildings.

On a Saturday morning in May, several members of the city negotiating team had sat in a law-firm conference room, their elbows leaning on a table so long and so heavily lacquered that it could have been used by a bowling league. There, in the corporate splendor of the clouds on the thirtieth floor, among portraits of lawyers and sycophantic proclamations, with an unblemished view looking west toward the massive stone of the Thirtieth Street Station, they pondered ways of outflanking the union enemy. Cohen was there, of course. So was Joe Torsella. And so was Alan Davis, who held the title of chief city negotiator. Wise and wonderfully laconic, Davis had a bespectacled, gnomelike physique that belied his long years of experience in the hand-to-hand combat of union wars. But he played the games of camouflage and subterfuge so well that one had to wonder whether underneath his button-down shirt, on the cusp of his shoulder, there wasn't a little tattoo in the shape of a smiling devil that said, "fuck collective bargaining."

Within the next several days, the city would formally propose to the unions a $332-per-employee cap on health and welfare benefits. Since such a proposal was nearly $145 less than the city's current contribution, it was a safe assumption that the union leaders would be sickened by the proposal, not because it was insufficient for health and welfare benefits for the rank and file (some health care providers, eager for the business, had already offered managed-care plans right around that figure) but because it would put a significant dent in the funding of these other activities and create serious cracks in the empire. After all, if a municipal union couldn't use health and welfare money for mortgages and patronage jobs, then how could it call itself a union?

Now Davis fretted over what the media coverage would be like when the city made its health-plan presentation to the unions. It would be made in private, but in the endless war being waged by both sides to win the hearts and minds of the public, leaks to the media were so fast and furious that keeping up with them was hard. In Davis's view, as in the view of the others at the long and lacquered table, the unions clearly had a pipeline to the city's newspapers, in particular to Kathy Sheehan of the *Daily News.* Unsmiling and sullen in a way that was impressive even for a reporter, Sheehan greeted every city pronouncement about the negotiations with deadened nonreaction. While most reporters seemed both dazed and dazzled in Cohen's presence when he went into one of his numbers riffs, Sheehan seemed quite uninterested in him, as if he were just some policy wonk with better than average stamina. She also did have good contacts within the unions. Earlier in the week the city had given the unions the wrong location for a negotiating session. It was a pure and simple accident, but a story about it had found its way into the *Daily News* under Sheehan's byline, told from the point of view of union outrage and insult.

"That's what you're dealing with," said Davis, and Cohen readily agreed.

"Anything we put in front of the unions will be in the newspapers the next day," he said, and the fear was obvious: the unions would be able to spin a story to the media about how the city's health-plan proposal was draconian, indecent, and an outrage to working men and women everywhere.

No one at the table thought there was a way to rub out Sheehan's machine-gun nest, but by using their own campaign of sabotage, they were confident they could render the bullets harmless. To counterbalance the unions' spin on the health plan, Davis felt it was important for the city's "propaganda machines" to get up and running as quickly as possible, weaving as many stories as possible about how a sizable portion of what the city contributed to the unions for health care did not *even go* to health care. It was one thing to pay for illnesses, but should the city also be paying for patronage?

"We will be prepared with whatever propaganda machines we have going—editorial boards—so that we win this thing publicly," said Davis. "We'll have to engage in media education here."

"I'm not sure I agree that the proper place is editorial boards," Cohen countered. Instead, he wondered whether the best way to neutralize a reporter such as Kathy Sheehan was by fanning the flames of various antagonisms that he felt existed, in effect pitting reporter against reporter by playing on their jealousies and egos. "There are reporters other than Kathy Sheehan we can go to. She is not particularly respected by her colleagues. Three *Daily News* reporters have independently come to me and have criticized her—and two from the *Inquirer*. If we want to play this game, one thing to do is sit down with these other reporters."

Someone then came up with a strategy that would be used throughout the war of the unions: when in doubt, douse a leak with another leak. As a result, it was suggested that Rendell write a heartfelt letter to city employees, giving his explanation of why health care benefits had to be cut. That letter could then be leaked to certain reporters in perfect sync with the unions' leak of the city's health-plan proposals and their claims of how outrageous they were, thus creating a veritable rainstorm of leaks and leaving reporters confused and conflicted about whose leak was the better leak.

"Sutton and Cronin will walk out and immediately call the papers, and there will be a story the next day," said Cohen of the two union leaders. "Can we send the letter the same day we meet with the unions and give it to the reporters that we want to?"

In the midst of discussion of the Rendell heartfelt-letter leak, another discussion quietly developed between Davis and Torsella, about the crazy-work-rules leak. City administration propagandists had assembled much of the material for this leak already, packaging it in the camouflage of a memorandum to the city negotiating team explaining why the city needed better management-initiative proposals. Written in exaggerated bureaucratese by midlevel officers Feeley and Michael Nadol, the cautious and stultifying three-page introduction served as the perfect smoke screen for what followed: a litany of outrageous work rules compiled not for the benefit of the city's negotiators, since they obviously knew all about these rules already, but as a document to be leaked to the media. It was marked CONFIDENTIAL at the top in underlined boldface type, not because it was meant to be confidential but because city propagandists knew that the very word creates an almost orgasmic effect among reporters.

Almost all the examples cited in the memo were powerful, but a few entered the realm of the twilight zone, including the one about the programmer for the Revenue Department who was dismissed by the city after his six-month probationary period because he repeatedly left work to play pinball and video games at local arcades. His union filed a grievance based on the theory that the employee's preference for arcade games was a gambling addiction and therefore should be treated as a handicap. After the time and expense of nearly three years of hearings, it was held that the city did in fact have the right to dismiss the employee on the grounds that playing pinball was not a handicap or a gambling addiction but something that shouldn't be done during work hours. Of course, after his separation from the Revenue Department, the employee went to work for the city's Board of Pensions and Retirement.

This example was sublime, but no more sublime than the difficulties faced by the city's Commerce Department, where the old joke of how many people it takes to change a lightbulb was apparently no joke at all. Because of union job classifications, the answer at Philadelphia International Airport was three: a building mechanic to remove the cover of the light panel, an electrician to actually replace the fluorescent-light fixture, and a custodian to clean up any dust or debris that might fall to the floor during the light-changing ritual. And the city's difficulties with lightbulbs may not have been any worse than the intricacies of cleaning various city walls. Custodians had no problems doing it, but only to shoulder level. Above the shoulder threshold, the job had to be done at increased pay by a category of workers called wall washers. If no wall washers were available, then custodians of course would do it, but at the extra pay accorded those with enough pride and skill to call themselves wall washers.

As a leak, the twenty-page memo was the equivalent of several direct torpedo hits on a submarine. The *Daily News* wrote about it. So did the *Inquirer*. Then, in the ultimate case of sabotage, *The Wall Street Journal* reprinted excerpts on its editorial page, and one could almost hear the unions, in their halfhearted defenses and denials, gurgle and sink to the bottom of the ocean.

III

Toward the end of June, members of the city negotiating team met privately with Rendell at his house in East Falls for a pivotal strategy meeting. At this point, the contract was only five days away from its June 30 expiration date, and everyone knew that there would be neither a settlement by that date nor a strike. The city may have been achieving a rout in the media war, but the unions, in their efforts to use delay as a weapon against the city, had also been successful. Despite Rendell's best private political wangling, it seemed clear that the Pennsylvania Labor Relations Board would in fact impose the sixty-day fact-finding period, thereby extending the terms of the current contract. Negotiations could continue during that period, but there could not be a strike, and the bleeding of the city's budget would continue. The imposition of fact-finding was a blow to the city, and the men who gathered at Rendell's house were hell-bent on besieging the unions from every conceivable angle.

The meeting took place in Rendell's family room. The mayor wore an aqua Lacoste shirt and gray running pants, and was eating Chinese food out of four different containers with such frantic and rapacious desire that it was difficult to know, from a purely medical standpoint, how food could travel that fast into the human body without doing severe harm. He was the only one eating, except for his dog, Woofie, who, lying on the floor next to him, took whatever morsels his master was willing to part with. The mayor graciously asked the others whether they were hungry, but given the appearance of things, they responded in a way that suggested they would rather go to their cars and drain the motor oil.

On a one-to-one basis with the unions, Rendell was as affable as ever, just a day earlier OK'ing the use of a platform at a union rally whose very purpose, as he himself put it, was to "beat up on Ed." "Why create ill will?"

said Rendell when the request was made. "It doesn't do shit." But privately he had vowed to "crush" the unions if he thought they were stalling on a settlement, and now it was clear that he meant it.

"The fact-finding was the Rubicon for me," he said. And this wasn't just a war of leaks now. In the war of the unions, no weaponry would be banned. The injection and heightening of racial divisiveness among the different unions, the purposeful pitting of union against union so that members of one would begin to hate members of another, the ceaseless ratcheting up of layoff notices, notices of the city's intent to privatize certain time-honored union functions—every conceivable piece of ammunition was being fed into the cannons now.

Technically there were four unions negotiating with the city. But in terms of negotiations, only two counted, the Fraternal Order of Police and District Council 33, which represented the city's blue-collar workforce. There was an obvious difference between the two unions in terms of the jobs their members performed. There was also a significant difference in the city's bargaining strategy toward each of them: District Council 33 had a right to strike, but under state law the police department did not. Instead, unresolved issues on a new contract for the police would be decided by arbitration. There was yet another distinct difference, not articulated but obvious, and as far as some city negotiators were concerned, it could prove a wonderful source of leverage—race.

The head of the FOP, the silver-maned and barrel-chested John Shaw, was whiter than white. So were most of his union's members. The mayor, of course, was white, and so were all the members of his negotiating team. Conversely, Sutton, the head of District Council 33, was black, and so was the vast majority of his union's members.

City negotiators assumed that such racial dynamics terrified District Council 33. And one of the keys, as they told the mayor that night, was to stoke those fears to the hilt—give District Council 33 the distinct impression that the mayor, a white mayor, was about to cut a favorable deal with a union head, a white union head, and with the police force, a predominantly white police force, and then take from District Council 33's hide, a predominantly black hide, whatever it didn't get in terms of givebacks from the police.

"They are afraid that you are going to cut a deal," Davis asserted. "You're white, and John Shaw is white. And [District Council] Thirty-three is black. They fear that they are going to lose their jobs to a cabal between you and John Shaw. It's a wonderful mind-set."

In the meantime, there was universal agreement that the machinery of layoff notices should start in earnest on all fronts, with all the notices leaked in various stages through the media to whip up as much hysteria and frenzy among the unions as possible. The strategy called not for just one layoff bomb, but a series of smaller ones, with different numbers of workers laid off each time, leaving virtually every worker in the city in dread and fear as to whether his name or her name would be included in the next round. "Think of all the leaks that come with this," said Davis. "You have all kinds of stages of pressure."

The machinery for contracting out union work had to start up as well— not just the little ticket items that the unions might not even care about very much but the big ticket items, the items that the unions had always considered sacrosanct. As a result, Davis urged the mayor to approve sending District Council 33 notification of the city's intent to contract out sanitation to private companies.

Sanitation?

To District Council 33, that was the same as challenging the existence of God. Of all union functions, none was more inviolable than sanitation, and the idea of a mayor even remotely challenging it, going after it, was just another example of the lunacy threshold. Was he willing to suffer the waves of physical confrontation that would inevitably sweep the city if the sanitation workers, virtually all of them black, found themselves put out of their jobs by a white mayor? On the other hand, if the mayor was serious about achieving fundamental change in the government regardless of the consequences, how could he give up a potential annual savings of as much as $30 million a year?

"I definitely think we should send it out," said Davis.

"There's no way we're going to do it," the mayor acknowledged, realizing full well that his nickname was Fast Eddie, not Crazy Eddie.

"But they don't know that," said Davis.

The mayor pondered Davis's comment for a moment. As he sat in his family room in his aqua Lacoste shirt and gray running pants, he found himself surrounded by some of the things in life he liked the very best— the razor-sharp minds of men completely loyal to him; exhausted cartons of food; his loyal dog, Woofie, at his feet after another fine meal. Without articulating it, he saw the beauty of what Davis was saying.

How could the unions predict his behavior? How could anyone predict his behavior even at this very moment, when in the midst of one of the most important meetings of his political career, with the future of the city balancing on the pinpoint of a pyramid, he mused aloud on the topic of death and concluded that "given his proclivities," his role model for such an exit was Nelson Rockefeller.

He told Davis to go ahead and send out the notice informing the union that its most precious commodity—garbage—was eventually going to be picked up by private hands.

IV

The following day the Pennsylvania Labor Relations Board approved the sixty-day period for fact-finding for the nonuniformed unions. Negotiations could continue, but there could not be a strike until the end of August at the earliest. True to the strategy that had been embraced at the meeting at the mayor's house, Cohen then spent the weekend hammering out a series of agreements for a new contract with FOP head Shaw. The agreements were minor, the kinds of concessions the city knew it would have to give up in arbitration anyway, but that wasn't the way they were cast to the media at a press conference the following Monday. The agreements were presented as major, and Shaw himself was depicted as a union man of reason and integrity and honor. The appearance of a white mayor and a white union leader standing together and congratulating each other on their ability to work with each other toward the common goal of a new contract was hardly subtle, and it was aimed directly at the black membership of District Council 33.

"I think they'll be scared to death," said Cohen.

But if they were scared, they had a funny way of displaying it. Several hours later as many as five thousand union members gathered at a massive rally on Dilworth Plaza in front of City Hall. The day was hot and sunny, lugubrious and slow, the way most summer days in the city were, but there was an edgy and excited mood to the crowd that transcended the heat. Union leaders spoke one after the other, none of them more powerfully than Jim Sutton.

Ed Rendell has shown that he has no respect for the labor movement! We intend to make him have respect! If he can't do anything else, he will hear this crowd, he will see around.

*We intend to fight with every ounce of strength that we have in our bod-
ies. And I say to you, Ed Rendell, if you think that L.A. had a bad time, mess
with District Council Thirty-three.*

*If you don't play by the rules, we will take whatever action we have to
take!*

Sutton was posturing, as all union leaders posture in the heat of battle
when playing to the rank and file, but there was something in his voice that
had never been there before. Rendell had always considered Sutton something of a soft heart when it came to union leaders, at one point half-
jokingly suggesting in private that he was going to have to teach Sutton to
"beat up on [Rendell] a little bit more" to make him seem more credible to
his own union. But as Sutton spoke now, his voice rising sharply over the
soup of the afternoon heat, it was clear he didn't need any training.

The crowd erupted, and in that moment the strength and the solidarity of
the unions seemed greater than they ever had before, coming together as a
potent force that would neither bend nor break under the city's artillery
shells and campaign of propaganda and injections of race, even if it meant
riots in the streets. Somehow, some way, Fast Eddie would be brought to
his knees, cowed and bloodied.

"No contract! No peace!" someone in the crowd yelled. Another voice
picked it up, and suddenly it became a rousing chorus:

No contract! No peace! No contract! No peace! No contract! No peace!

The chant continued as union workers blocked traffic and walked
around the nape of City Hall with their arms interlocked and their fists held
high.

No contract! No peace! No contract! No peace! No contract! No peace!

As the workers marched, another chant started up:

Fast Eddie! We are ready! Fast Eddie! We are ready!

As Rendell waited for an elevator on the second floor of City Hall, he
watched the rally making its slow circle. He just stared silently, without
giving his usual broadcaster-like commentary—one of those rare moments
when he seemed to have a need for privacy and introspection and the sort-

ing out of conflicting emotions. He wore a kind of weakly bemused smile, as if it were hard to imagine that he, a man who had spent so much of his life getting people to like him by coddling them and sucking up to them and suffering all fools gladly, had somehow managed to whip up such a frenzy of hate. He later claimed that the remarks and the chants didn't bother him at all, that they were all part of the war of the unions. But it wasn't true, and the look of Ed Rendell as he peered out that grimy window by the elevator was the look of a man trying bravely to remain calm, trying to be a politician and not a person and not take personally the attacks being heaped on him.

Fast Eddie! We are ready! Fast Eddie! We are ready!

As he lumbered onto the elevator, the chants of those below him reverberated and echoed.

Fast Eddie! We are ready! Fast Eddie! We are ready!

SEVEN

Crisis of Faith

I

Alan Davis had privately worried that it would happen, perhaps because
he was a seasoned fatalist with the wisdom of Merlin and the doe-eyed sadness of Marcel Marceau, but also perhaps because he knew better than anyone else in the city the delectable temptation to dance and deal. Fifty-five
years old, Davis had long been a keen observer of city labor negotiations,
and it was his unvarnished perception that mayor after mayor had consis-

tently traded long-term gains for short-term ones, economic issues always taking precedence over the non-economic ones, the ones that over time could truly change a city's destiny. He had no illusions about politics, and he understood the impulse that had guided other mayors. So why should Ed Rendell be any different, particularly when it seemed as if the war of the unions might drag on forever, past June now and into July, when most citizens had the wise sense to flee for the Jersey shore and the city had all the energy of a drooping eyelid, barely able to keep itself awake.

Davis's perception was based not just on observation but on active participation. As the city solicitor in the early 1980s under Mayor William J. Green, Davis had negotiated for the city in nasty labor disputes with the Philadelphia Federation of Teachers. It was also during the Green administration that nearly a thousand police officers and firefighters were laid off to close a budget deficit. "We traded work rules for economics in the early eighties, and I was ashamed of it," said Davis. It was an incomplete part of his agenda, and when Rendell asked him to serve as the city's chief labor negotiator, Davis, despite the comfort of his practice at Ballard Spahr that made him one of the most respected lawyers in the city, accepted the challenge. Although almost diminutive in appearance, he was hardly a lightweight. Labor negotiations with the schoolteachers had resulted in two strikes, and regional commuter-train lines went dark for four months when he represented the transit system. "I would like to make love, not war," he told an interviewer, but union leaders who dealt with him in the past could only figure that he had his fingers crossed when he said that.

Davis liked Rendell. He saw him as mayor the way many people saw Rendell as mayor regardless of whether they could articulate it or not—as a big kid having the time of his life. Absent the yellow feathers and beak, the mayor had become the political equivalent of Big Bird (they even had the same endearing waddle that comes with ample padding), and his comfort in who he was made him a willing participant in just about everything, except hammering a nail into a roof with one of those nail guns to put the finishing touches on a refurbished city recreation center. He'd climb a ladder to the roof, but they could forget about those noisy, nail-spitting guns, given his aversion to anything remotely mechanical, even a pen. "If I used a nail gun," said the mayor, "I would nail my ankles."

There were certain moments in the war with the unions that Rendell seemed to relish, like the time he walked from City Hall to his car and union members angrily showered him with copies of the city's proposed health plan. Sergeant Buchanico had urged the mayor to slip out by another exit, but Rendell was determined to forge ahead through the same exit he always used, and he was more than just determined—he welcomed the confrontation, particularly since it broke up the monotony of all those meetings. "It was kind of fun," he said in the car afterward, and he seemed so giddy at the thought of all those health-plan proposals being showered on his head like stale banana peels that he didn't get angry at the slow response of the car phone and passed up the usual ritual of banging it against the dashboard in frustration. But there were other moments that he did not relish, particularly the thought of a long and nasty strike in which he would be held up as a union buster and an absolute enemy of the common working man. Although Rendell himself had never been a common working man, he knew about the garment factories in New York because of his father. He knew what it was like to sew and stitch and do piece work while racing against production schedules. He respected and admired the skill of those who did it, and of all the things that later struck him about his father's funeral, it was the way some of those who had worked for Jesse Rendell came up to him and related what a fine and decent man his dad had been.

But the city was in crisis, and more than just in crisis, for Rendell had staked much of his campaign on a willingness to create a new type of government. Although the word was dangerous to use in any labor negotiations, there actually were some principles, and they centered on such issues as the city's right to lay off workers, a management-rights clause that would actually give the city greater latitude to set work schedules that might enhance productivity instead of hamper it, the right to contract out certain union work on the grounds that it could be done more cheaply and more efficiently privately, the enactment of a so-called zipper clause that would allow the city to "unzip" some of the more ridiculous and corrosive union practices of the past, and the right of the city to transfer workers from one job classification to another without endless hearings and grievance procedures. In most previous bargaining sessions, these issues, the so-called non-economic ones, had inevitably been discarded or watered down to the extent that they had no bite. They were difficult to quantify and had little sex appeal with a media far more interested in such classic economic issues as wage increases. But the Rendell administration, embracing a spirit of reform so sweeping it had been dubbed perestroika, had finally recognized the importance of these non-economic issues and how they could not be traded away if the city was ever to change, if services were ever to improve and government was ever to play more than a role of nominal caretaker and employer of last resort.

"The notion of taking control of the government and restructuring it for effectiveness was at the heart of our campaign platform," policy and planning head Torsella had written in a confidential memo to Rendell and Cohen several months earlier, arguing that these issues carry the same weight as economic ones.

Voters have the expectation that the Rendell administration will be a sustained exercise in remaking government; editorial boards, the national press, and many of our appointees share this expectation. The fate of the "non-economic issues" in the contract talks will be the first big test of our determination to stick with this agenda.

For well over a year, we have been lambasting the current contracts to anyone who would listen as representing the bargain with the devil made by past administrations: the giving-up of long-term rights for short-term financial relief. Now that we have convinced everyone, it is imperative that we not give anyone the opportunity to say that about the contracts *we* negotiate.

It was a fine memo, written with precision and thoughtfulness and a strong trace of the good-government piousness that Torsella—a true and earnest believer in the midst of crotchety wolves and coyotes—was known for. But it represented the ideals of government, a government that was proactive instead of reactive and one that determined its own fate instead of waiting for the latest kick in the teeth, so it really didn't represent government at all. Nor did it represent the reality—the reality of a mayor engaged in a showdown with the unions the likes of which had not been seen in any major city in decades, the reality of a mayor being increasingly enveloped in tourniquets of pressure that only intensified and increased with every hour and every day and every week.

Fast Eddie! We are ready! Fast Eddie! We are ready!

II

The first signs of what Alan Davis feared took place at the end of July at the Democratic National Convention in New York. Bill Clinton was about to accept the nomination for president, and since Rendell had been an early supporter of the Arkansas governor, it was presumably a heady time. But

Rendell was already exhausted to begin with, from the long days he worked throughout each week, and then he developed an infection in his elbow. When it came to doctors, the mayor had all the dignity of a child, convinced that the minute you saw one, you were guaranteed an amputation or inadvertent organ removal. He took great pride in the fact that he had virtually never missed a day of work due to illness in more than thirty years. Getting him to go to a doctor for a checkup or even for a life insurance exam was virtually hopeless. But when the lump on his elbow steadily grew to the size of a baseball and his arm swelled to the point where his wife, Midge, noted that he was rather ominously beginning to look like the Pillsbury dough boy, even he became scared and knew he had to do something. On a Thursday morning in July, he gave a press conference on South Broad Street, excitedly announcing the groundbreaking for a new theater that in fact wouldn't occur for at least another year. Then he was quietly driven a few blocks away, to Thomas Jefferson Hospital, for an examination. Afterward it was agreed that he needed to be hospitalized so the infection could be properly drained and cared for. He got out just in time for the convention, but the only way the doctors would let him attend was accompanied by a nurse, which was not only unsettling to Rendell but also somewhat humiliating, perhaps even worse than that moment at the 1980 convention when he addressed the floor to the interest of absolutely no one. After all, what other politician would be showing up at the convention with a woman who *really* was his nurse?

On a spiritual level, it was clear that the negotiations were taking their toll on the mayor. Once the smoke had lifted, he could see that the all-out offensive by the city had gained barely an inch of ground. Threatened layoffs, secret communiqués sent across enemy lines, legal appeals—none of it was working. During the sixty-day fact-finding period, the union was continuing to work under the existing contract, and a city that was on the edge of bankruptcy was losing roughly $2 million a week. In a sweet stealth strike all their own, the unions also had a little surprise in store for Rendell when he arrived at the convention in New York: a protest in his honor on Seventh Avenue that tied up rush-hour traffic. City workers carried signs labeling Rendell a REPUBLICRAT MAYOR and a member of the antiworker hall of fame, along with Frank Lorenzo, the former head of Continental Airlines. After the protest, they carried the signs into the convention itself in an attempt to embarrass the mayor in front of a national audience. Subsequently various national union leaders privately cornered Rendell at the convention. He later denied feeling any heat in the slightest and instead said he found all the protests amusing. But it was at the convention, according to Davis, that Rendell gave the union leaders an indication that in return for full concessions on health and welfare benefits, he would be amenable to wage increases of 10 percent over the life of the contract.

Ten percent?

It was a catastrophic statement, one that ran counter to every tenet of the negotiations. If the city was on the verge of bankruptcy, then why was the mayor committing it to such healthy wage increases? And if that was the mayor's private stance, then what about the stance of Alan Davis and the other members of the city negotiating team, who all along had been arguing that any wage increases in the life of the contract would be negligible at best? To the union leaders, the answer was clear: all the city's posturing over bankruptcy and no more money had been a bluff, the kind of transparent negotiating that always went on before a new contract was sniffed out. And every mayor in America had an epiphany in which he or she realized that choosing public considerations over political ones was just plain stupid if there was any interest in surviving beyond one lousy and meager term.

Davis forgave Rendell for what happened. He had known Rendell for thirty years, and he understood that the mayor had an almost compulsive need to be nice and generous. The mayor knew it too, lamenting once that his weakness for people was such that, "if I was a woman, I'd be pregnant all the time."

Whatever he told the national union leaders, it created a significant stumbling block in the negotiations. Rendell may have assumed that he was just musing in private, but national union leaders were far too experienced to let something like that remain informal. Almost as soon as he uttered "ten percent," according to Davis, they faxed the utterance all over the place, as if he had made an official contract offer. Davis thought there was a way to overcome it, in part by taunting the unions, by telling them yes, maybe they could have had wage increases totaling 10 percent, maybe they could have had a lot of things they desired—but that was before they had been dumb enough to stage their blockade of delay, before they had been stupid enough to try to hide under the cover of a fact-finding process that everyone knew was worthless.

But what happened next was much harder to forgive.

It happened toward the end of July, just a few days after the convention. Davis was on the phone with a labor mediator from the state. By coincidence, the chief negotiator for the blue-collar and white-collar unions, Deborah Willig, was in the mediator's office when Davis called. Davis and Willig didn't like each other, in part because they were adversaries in a volatile standoff, in part because their personalities seemed a toxic mix of worry beads and steel ball bearings—Davis quiet and whimsical with a soulful view of the city, Willig full of punch and vinegar, a lawyer who relished the opportunity to tweak Davis's nose whenever she got the opportunity, just to remind him that she was bigger and tougher than he would ever be. They got on the phone with each other, and it wasn't just a tweak that Willig was delivering but a hard taffy pull, to the point where Davis looked as misshapen as Cyrano de Bergerac.

"Don't you know what's going on?" asked Willig. "The mayor has agreed to a contract."

"I don't know what you're talking about," said Davis.

"Obviously you don't," gloated Willig. "And all of this stuff you're shoving down our throats—work rules—is all bullshit."

She then went on to say that as they were talking, Rendell and Cohen were in Washington putting the finishing touches on a contract agreement with Gerald McEntee, the national head of the American Federation of State, County, and Municipal Employees. It was a done deal, Willig was saying, and Alan Davis, the lead labor negotiator for the city, the man who knew more about labor than Samuel Gompers himself, Mr. Negotiations, *didn't even know about it.* Even worse, the source of the information was *Debbie Willig—Willig,* a name that after a while, if you said it enough times, really did begin to have a resemblance to *earwig.* As for all that stuff about changing the culture of city government and redefining it, Alan Davis could take all of it and shove it up his ass if Willig was right.

The mayor and his wonder boy had sold him out. Davis was stunned and also offended. He and the other members of the city negotiating team had been working for months. The hours had been long and the issues myriad and complicated, but they had been guided by their faith in a mayor who they believed not only grasped the importance of the principles at stake but also wanted to honor them. For Davis, these particular negotiations were not just exhausting. Given that his father had been a machinist and a union organizer in Philadelphia in the 1940s, they also created a personal conflict. A union lawyer involved in the negotiations had asked Davis how he could be involved in a scorched-earth war such as this one, in which the city seemed so intent on destroying every right and benefit that workers had built up over the years. Where were his heart and his sense of history?

Davis had replied that wage increases and benefits would be worthless if the city went bankrupt and thousands of workers had to be let go, and rather than taking away jobs, he was actually trying to save as many as possible. But the question gnawed at him, in particular because as a young boy in the city the nexus of life had always contained its share of civil servants, cops, and firefighters, who gave the neighborhood of Strawberry Mansion a history and character as intrinsic as the cracks in the pavement. As hard as he tried, he couldn't help but feel a little bit traitorous to what had made him all that he was as a husband and a father and a lawyer. But he had taken such a leading role in the negotiations because he thought it was right— and more than just right, crucial to the future of the city. If it was to have a future.

And now what the hell was going on in Washington with the mayor and Cohen, and why the hell hadn't he known about it until Earwig had lorded it over him? He had even seen Cohen the night before, at a funeral, and Cohen had obliquely mentioned that he and the mayor were going to be in Washington and were going to drop in on McEntee. But because of the casual way he had mentioned it, Davis naturally assumed it was a courtesy call on a national union leader, not a private negotiating session. But he was now convinced that the mayor and Cohen had been in McEntee's office not to pay a courtesy call but behind the back of Davis, behind the backs of the rest of the negotiating team, to work out a contract devoid of all the non-economic ingredients that were so essential. He called Cohen on the car phone, and he confirmed that he and the mayor had met with McEntee. "Here we go again," Davis said to himself, and regardless of whatever attempts Cohen made to mollify him and minimize the meeting, Davis didn't believe them. In fact, as much as it irked him, he was more inclined to believe Earwig than David Cohen.

Over his lifetime, Davis had watched the city that had spawned and formed him move steadily downward, the flesh and bone and stone of the neighborhood he had grown up in decalcify and putrefy until it had become what is commonly described as a bomb zone. Over his lifetime, he had watched the creeping hand of politics and self-interest spread its fingers over the city. And based on his personal experience in government, he had adopted a certain credo to help him stomach the reason things worked the way they did over and over again: *disillusionment is reality.*

He had watched the city retrench, and he had watched the shift of its labor pool from the country's most diverse to what he now described as an audience pool struggling to resurrect itself on the basis of tourism and culture. Over his lifetime, he had watched the city move from a series of urban-redevelopment projects that were risky and spectacular—the re-building of a city slum into Society Hill, the rebuilding of Center City—to a series of projects that were reminiscent of that scene in *The Third Man* in which Orson Welles notes that Switzerland's only lasting contribution was the cuckoo clock. As far as Davis could tell, the city's cuckoo clock was its convention center, not just the one here but those in dozens of cities that were hoping to reconstitute and remarket themselves on the basis of shiny, new block-long buildings dedicated to the preservation of free space for Shriners and software vendors and medical suppliers. A hundred years from now, would that be the city's most enduring contribution to urban culture, its lasting legacy? The convention center?

Despite such pessimism, Davis knew that in Rendell and Cohen lay the best hope for reversal or, if not reversal, maybe just a refreshing blip from the time line of decline. All new administrations in a government brought along a surge of hope. It was perhaps the most valuable feature of the mod-ern political structure—the excitement of rebirth that came from a new leader regardless of qualifications or expertise—and this administration had also brought along something else just as powerful—a sense of crisis.

For all Davis knew, he was overreacting. But maybe not, for Cohen's notes of the Washington meeting, taken in a small and tidy shorthand, re-vealed much discussion of wages and health and welfare benefits and vir-tually no discussion of the non-economic issues. And then something equally remarkable happened. According to Davis, the mayor apologized and reaffirmed his commitment not simply to the economic issues that would solve the city's problems in the short term but to the non-economic ones that if successfully won in the negotiations, would have lasting and enduring impact.

Davis later likened the whole episode to the mayor's having a major automobile accident in which miraculously no one had been killed. Davis thought the mayor realized that he would not be so lucky the next time he tried such a stunt, that he was fully aware now that next time on the wind-shield would be not only his blood and entrails, but the blood and entrails of the city as well.

III

In early August, a powerful group of national labor leaders descended on Philadelphia to meet privately with the mayor. They came to help and to make peace. That at least was the purpose of the meeting as it was conveyed to the media. But the labor leaders were really there to apply pressure once again, to warn the mayor of the repercussions if he continued to hold firm and fire away at the quality of the workforce in the hopes of moving public sentiment to his side. Given their collective might, they were hoping the mayor would succumb to the crack of their knuckles as they flexed their power. Spread comfortably around the table in the mayor's Cabinet Room, they talked in a way that oozed with affability, self-assurance, and just the slightest trace of condescension, as if to suggest that the mayor, a neophyte without any track record in the trenches, whose sum total of experience was exactly seven months, had no idea of what he was doing and had better learn quickly if he planned on having a political future beyond the backwater of some dying city that could lay claim in no particular order to Independence Hall, the Liberty Bell, Rocky, and the cheese steak.

By the time Rendell met with the labor leaders, in midafternoon, he looked drained and spent, as if the usual ruddiness of his features had been surgically sucked from him. In most instances in which he was clearly outnumbered, Rendell went right to his knees, disarming hair triggers of temper with charm, asking those gathered round him whether they wanted a soft drink and then running back himself to the little private alcove in between the Cabinet Room and his office to get it. The psychological impact of that was so enormous that people afterward, even if the meeting had gone totally contrary to what they wanted to hear, always remembered the graciousness of that glass of diet Coke.

But the mayor was in no mood for soft drinks.

Instead, he came into the meeting with that certain look on his face that he sometimes got, where the eyes were hard and slightly squinty and the teeth were gritted in between the lips. His body language lurched and jerked, the shift in his chair at the head of the table like the sudden capsizing of a ship, as if some internal war inside his body was being waged between Good Ed and Bad Ed, and he was trying very, very hard not to take everyone and everything in that room and fling it all out the window into the City Hall courtyard—the bodies, the little dumb mementos in the glass case, the coffee cups, the phone, every *goddamn motherfucking thing*. In the medical terminology of his office staff, who saw him in a way that no one else saw him, he was right on the border of what they generally diagnosed as a wig out. Wig outs had clear preliminary symptoms, usually accompanied by such statements as *"I am not an atom! I cannot split in two!"* when Marge Staton, his saintly secretary, called to tell him that his 3:00 P.M. and his 3:30 P.M. appointments were still in the waiting room even though it was now 4:00 P.M. But since wig outs were common and lasted for only a few minutes or so, no particular thought was given to either sedative or straitjacket, and they were treated in much the same vein as sudden changes in the weather.

The meeting began with one of the union leaders quietly asking the mayor whether Tom Cronin, the local head of the city's white-collar union, could sit in.

"This is just fucking outrageous."

Lynn Williams, the president of the United Steelworkers of America, who did most of the talking for the union delegation, asked the mayor to use his political contacts to get the state supreme court to hold off on rendering a decision about the legality of the fact-finding in return for a promise by the local unions to do some hard and earnest bargaining. Several weeks earlier, as a way of breaking the blockade, the city had filed an appeal with the supreme court to declare the fact-finding invalid. The supreme court had not yet ruled on the appeal, but the justices had agreed to hear the case, and that clearly was a bad omen for the unions.

"To be honest, I don't think the court will rule against us, and I won't take away one of our best weapons."

"You guys really don't want this thing to blow up, do you?" asked Williams.

"We don't want it, but we want a fair contract."

"Can't you think of some way of lightening this atmosphere?" asked Williams.

"I don't want to be a shit, and I don't want to be antilabor, but I can't grow hair, and I can't grow money."

Thomas Donahue, the national secretary-treasurer of the AFL-CIO, said the tenor of the city's propaganda offensive had made it clear to city workers that they were "not worth what [they're] getting."

"It's a fact of life."

To counter the claim that he was being too hard on the unions, he produced a copy of a recent District Council 33 newsletter and read aloud the quote that president Jim Sutton had given at the rally in June: *"I say to Ed*

Rendell, if you think that L.A. had a bad time, mess with District Council Thirty-three."

"Sticks and stones," Jay Mazur, president of the International Ladies' Garment Workers' Union, mimicked at the table in a singsong taunt, as if it were hard to believe that Rendell could be so thin-skinned over a silly little quote in which a local union leader had threatened a race riot.

Rendell made it clear, clearer than he had ever before made it publicly or privately, why he needed the concessions he was seeking from the unions, why raising taxes was the equivalent of placing a gun barrel flush against the city's forehead and pressing the trigger.

"We are losing our middle class, our working class, to other places. We have to increase our tax base, or we are finished. The city will become De-troit without the automobiles. I will suggest to you gentlemen that with the automobiles, Detroit is not a very pleasant place. Without the automobiles, it would be terrifying."

He also made it clear, clearer than he had ever before made it, that he would do what he thought he had to do regardless of the political conse-quences, regardless of the considerable clout the men surrounding him wielded in the Democratic party.

"I'm Jewish, so I don't have the slightest chance of national office. If I walk out of here voted out, I walk with my head held high because I've done the right thing."

Outside in the gloomy corridors of City Hall, the media lingered en masse, wanting to know whether some kind of conflagration had taken place. Rendell diplomatically called the meeting "helpful," then trudged back to his office. In private, without the need to posture and prance, he wasn't ashamed to admit to the toll that it all took sometimes. If the meet-ing with the national union leaders was all that had taken place this day, it would have been more than enough. But the whole day had been like that, an endless cycle in which every decision, regardless of the good faith in which he made it, carried threats that there would be hell to pay.

He was so exhausted that he seemed genuinely dispirited, showing per-haps the only emotion in his quiver of myriad emotions that he almost never displayed. "I make no judgments about my weeks," he told someone over the phone, the cheerful staccato turned hoarse and watery. "None of them are close enough to being good. I got threatened by six different sources today."

Several days earlier, in a moment of relief from the meetings stampede, he had mused about a new painting of the art museum that had been hung on the back wall of his office across from his desk. He knew that his wife, Midge, liked the picture, and because of his difficulties appreciating art (during a walking tour of a Picasso exhibit at the art museum, he was so loud that a patron, not knowing who he was and utterly frustrated by his banter, hissed at him to shut up), her seal of approval was seemingly enough for him. But the more he looked at the painting, the more unsure he felt about it. He definitely liked the frame, he was confident of that much, but he was clearly ambivalent about the clouds that had been painted in the foreground. He thought they gave the picture a drab look, and given his eternal optimism about the future of the city, not to mention the fact that he was the one who had to look at the picture all the time, he wished it had been painted to portray a sunny day. He asked the others in the room for advice, and the more he mused and talked about it and stared at it to make sure he hadn't missed something, the more perplexed and conflicted he became.

"Fuck it," the mayor finally said. "What do I know?"

EIGHT

Profiles in Courage

I

On the last Sunday in August, members of District Council 33 filed grimly into the aging interior of the Civic Center—a building whose last hurrah had come forty-four years earlier as the site of both the Republican and the Democratic National Conventions—and authorized a strike. District Council 47 of the American Federation of State, County, and Municipal Employees took the same action a day later, and the suspicion became

greater than ever that the two municipal unions were praying each night for
a stalemate in the city's ongoing contract talks with public school teachers
so they could all go on strike together. Several days later the mayor himself concluded that all hopes of a settlement were gone—*for everybody.* "It
looks like we'll have two strikes," said Rendell in that bemused voice he
got when it became abundantly clear that the apocalypse was at hand and
the only real intrigue left was in figuring where or how it could be worse
than already imagined.

The day was gray and drizzling, the city as monotonous as a flatland
prairie. The mayor's black Crown Victoria passed down South Broad on
the way to the Monti Funeral Home, where Rendell was to pay homage to
the memory of a police officer named Charles Knox, who had been killed
during a robbery at a Roy Rogers restaurant. Contrary to what others
thought, Rendell did have other city business besides the union negotiations—the business of offering vain words of encouragement to the officer's widow and nine-year-old son. Although he understood the protocol,
he also felt his appearance was inappropriate, an invasion of privacy that
only intensified the family's grief. Why should he be there? Just because
he was the mayor? It made no sense to him. "It must be so hard to go
through all this official shit," he said quietly in the car, staring out the window into the gloom. "A nine-year-old kid. What do you tell that kid as to
why he lost his father? How the fuck do you explain it? How do you tell
him the fairness of it all?"

The car pulled up alongside the funeral home, and for a brief moment
the phone wasn't ringing and there wasn't anyone scratching at the window wanting something. Rendell thought some more about that nine-year-
old boy, thought some more about what it must be like to have your father
taken away when there has been no time to prepare for it, no warning at all,
not even the time to say good-bye. "For whatever I'm good or bad, it's
mostly the reflection of what my father believed. He loved the seashore.
He loved sports. He loved politics.

"It's sad that I lost him when I was fourteen," said the mayor. He seemed
almost completely isolated at that moment, a man so totally at the whim of
public appetite and such a creation of it that he had lost his inner life long
ago. Given his innate gregariousness, it was hard to think of him as lonely,
and yet there were many moments when he seemed acutely so, a prisoner
of the performance of public life. He had a wife, and he had a child, but
on a daily basis he gave far more of his time to strangers than to them. It
wasn't selfishness but the nature of what he did, acting in front of people

he didn't even know on the dilapidated stage set of the city, focusing on them as if they were intimate confidants when in fact he had learned their names only moments beforehand.

"Where the fuck is Tucker?" he suddenly snarled to Sergeant Buchanico, as if slapping himself in the face. He came out of the car and was immediately surrounded by a sea of reporters in the gray and the drizzle, comforted by their presence and the obligation of their questions.

II

In large part through the masterful participation of Cohen, the teachers settled with the school district in the early part of September. As a result, the municipal unions' hope for mass chaos to be used as leverage in their dispute with the city went down several notches. But the unions still made their presence felt. Police reported roughly $10,000 of vandalism at the city's sewage treatment plant, and several days later an employee of the Water Department was surrounded by several militant union members, assaulted, and taken to the hospital for cuts on his forehead and under his eye.

In the middle of September, just as the mayor was boarding the Choo Choo Trolley at Broad and Walnut to kick off a new retail and restaurant promotion in the city called Wednesday Night Out, an unlikely visitor suddenly boarded the train. It was David Cohen, and the very fact that he had left his office and walked four blocks to see the mayor was significant. Cohen clutched the pages of something in his hands, and he slipped them to the mayor aboard the Choo Choo Trolley with that slightly devilish grin he inevitably wore when he had information that he knew everyone else coveted.

Two months earlier, in July, as a way of trying to break the unions' blockade of delay, the city had elected to make the appeal to the Pennsylvania Supreme Court challenging the fact-finding. When the idea of such an appeal had first been raised, various members of the city negotiating team were aghast. Placing your fate in the hands of the state's highest court was a little bit like playing Russian roulette with every chamber of the revolver loaded. Whatever happened, it could not possibly be pretty. As painstakingly chronicled over the years by the *Inquirer,* the court was a morass of internal politics, with temperaments so out of kilter that Sol Wachtler would have been considered a model of reserve. In succeeding months, one of its justices would actually be impeached.

There was just no way of knowing how the court would react to a case as explosive as this one, with the political forces of labor on one side and the city on the other. But there was genuine concern that actual legal considerations might be at the very bottom of the court's decision. "Once this petition is filed, a political process starts that is uncontrollable," a member of the negotiating team told the mayor. "You basically put [your] fate out of your control, because those animals will do anything. They're too powerful. It's like letting a tiger out of the cage."

Given the history of the court's conduct, this view made eminent sense. But as day after day ticked by and the negotiations continued to founder and the unions held as tight as Londoners during the Battle of Britain, Cohen came to the conclusion that the only way to break the vise of delay was with the court challenge.

In the tactical warfare of the city, this was a highly risky move, one that could do significant damage to the union front but could also explode within the city's own camp. If the supreme court granted the petition, the city would finally overcome the blockade of the fact-finding. More important, the way would be cleared for the city to declare contract negotiations at an impasse and unilaterally implement its latest offer, an offer that would naturally be enormously favorable to the city. Implementation would place the unions in a do-or-die situation. To combat the effects of implementation of a contract by the city, they would really have only two choices: take their chances on a strike and hope it would create havoc, or creep back to the table to discuss some sort of honorable surrender. On the other hand, a supreme court ruling against the city would give the unions an enormously important victory in the war and bog the negotiations down even more.

Now, on the Choo Choo Trolley, Rendell took the sheaf of papers from Cohen and saw the result of the gamble. Answers in legal opinions were sometimes difficult to find, a thicket of impenetrable citations and legalese that seemed to make the issues only more complicated and more fractious than ever. But here the answer was easy: the supreme court had ruled in favor of the city.

After seventy-seven days, the blockade of delay had finally been broken, and because of that, there was no other choice but for both sides to fire up their guns again in the war of the unions, this time to the point of no return. One way or another either the unions or the city administration would be leveled. Either there would be a strike the likes of which had never been seen in the history of the city, or there would be a contract with concessions the likes of which had never been seen in the history of the city.

Two days after the supreme court ruling, Rendell announced that the city and the unions had reached an impasse in negotiations. He was therefore laying out his "last, best offer" to the unions and giving them five days, until 5:00 P.M. on Wednesday, September 23, to accept it. If no settlement was reached by the deadline, Rendell announced, he would go ahead and implement the contract with the terms he had just laid out, terms that of course benefited the city in every way possible.

The announcement was a bombshell. Scurrying for cover, District Council 33 sought safety and refuge among the city's black politicians. In early September, a letter from a black politician had privately circulated demanding that the city negotiate in good faith, and according to Cohen, there was an implied threat of violence. The letter was a typical but masterful stroke of racial politics, clearly suggesting, without the slightest proof, that the mayor was trying to force the unions to accept a contract that was not only antiunion but also antiblack. Recognizing the enormous damage the letter could wreak, Cohen lobbied, with the considerable help of Council President Street, to get it killed. The lobbying was successful, but in return black elected officials placed their trust in the hands of Street to mediate a fair contract. Momentarily at least, it was hard to know whether Rendell and Cohen would have been much better off with the letter.

No other politician in the city, no other politician in the entire state, was like John Street. No other politician was more unpredictable in terms of mood. No other politician required more homage and subservience. No other politician had shown more pugilistic willingness during a fight with a fellow city councilman in the early 1980s.

Inside his inner office, accessible only by a buzzer (not even Rendell's inner office had a buzzer), there was a wall covered with memorabilia of Street's career. Most politicians, most people, used their walls as a place to display complimentary plaques and letters and clippings, little reminders of all the good they had done. John Street had covered his wall with just the opposite—negative clippings about him, negative letters, negative headlines. Some who had seen the wall said it served to remind Street of how far he had come. But to others, the Wall of Shame was a Rorschach of what motivated him—the ridicule of others, the lack of respect from others, and not simply getting mad or getting even but completely and totally obliterating those who had scorned him. And yet no other politician, with the exception of Cohen, was more dogged in trying to determine the gritty financial mechanics of what made the city work. And among blacks, no other politician was more willing to make decisions that might actually be good for the entire city, not just for the black neighborhoods.

Aware of the yin and the yang of John Street, Rendell and Cohen had played him like a precocious problem child right from the very beginning of the administration, a problem child capable of doing great good if coddled the right way, capable of doing great harm if he sensed even the slightest whiff of insult. Aware of his need for respect, of his need to be treated not simply as the city council president but as the chosen prince of government, they fed his ego constantly, caressing it and stroking it to the point where Rendell, whenever something good happened in the city, generally gave John Street credit regardless of whether or not he deserved it. Once a week the mayor held a private briefing with Street, or Council President Street as all but a select few were required to call him, and it was Rendell who trundled up the two flights of stone steps to Street's office and not Street who trundled down the steps to see Rendell. It was Rendell who waited dutifully as Street's secretary buzzed him in, Rendell who didn't seem to mind that about the only memento of levity on the Wall of Shame was a picture of the mayor himself on his hands and knees cleaning a City Hall bathroom. When public fanfare was made over the banning of parking on the apron surrounding City Hall, meaning that city council members who had parked their cars there would be allotted spots on the sidewalk instead, a city official received a call from Street's office requesting that one of the coveted spots go to a friend of his. "The city is not in the business of providing private citizens with authorized parking," said the memo to Cohen. "I would appreciate your resolving this matter with President Street before Mr. Gibson's car is ticketed and towed." In response to the memo, Cohen instructed the city official to "take no action at this point." When Street wanted tickets for a sporting event, Rendell worked the phones to get them as fast as he could. When Street became incensed by a series of editorials in the *Daily News* criticizing the conduct of the council, the mayor helped to arrange a meeting with two of the paper's top editors in an ostensible effort to clear the air. At the meeting, Rendell was largely silent, doing little to direct the meeting toward any constructive end. Street in the meantime yelled so much that Richard Aregood, the paper's editorial-page editor, later wrote a little note to the mayor saying, "Although I had been expecting a reasoned, if spirited conversation about the *Daily News*'s editorials, it was interesting to spend all that time being berated by a deranged asshole."

But then there was the other Street. As council president, he had done a remarkable job of keeping the rest of the council in line, a task as formidable as that of a grade school teacher presiding over a classroom of hyperactive students, all of whom had forgotten to take their Ritalin. In the battles over the budget, council members, instead of making life miserable for the mayor, as was their historical inclination, had offered virtually no resistance. They had also stayed out of the fractious atmosphere of the union negotiations. As a result, when Street entered the war, in effect acting as a go-between for District Council 33 and the administration, there was cause for hope.

Two days before the September 23 deadline for settlement set by the mayor, Sutton and Street reportedly met at Street's house and actually seemed close to hammering out an agreement. But once Sutton returned to his own camp, the agreement unraveled, and the demands of the unions suddenly spiked again like an uncontrollable fever. A day before the deadline, both Cohen and Alan Davis became convinced that Sutton, simply to save face with his union, would have to take a strike and then hope that his workers would beg to return to work given the general economic climate.

That night, after an elaborate shell game played to keep the media from finding out the chosen location, a lengthy negotiating session was held between the unions and the city. The following morning, seven and a half hours before the mayor's deadline, the unions sent a proposal to Cohen. He perused it briefly and took note of some of the demands, such as wage increases of 8 percent over the life of the contract and $76 million in payments to the health and welfare fund. He then organized a little pool among the city negotiators to see who could come the closest to guessing the accumulated deficit such a proposal would create in the budget at the end of five years. (The correct answer was $340 million.)

"I've always asked you this question, and you've always evaded the answer," said Rendell to Cohen. "What are they thinking?"

"It is not susceptible to an answer," said Cohen.

As the hours to the deadline wound down, the pressure on Rendell was incalculable. Regardless of the tough talk over the past several months, he wanted a settlement, not a strike, but now more than ever he was prepared for the worst. On the phone with an investment adviser from Pittsburgh, he was all too aware of what had recently happened there—acts of violence and horrific headlines as the result of a contentious newspaper strike. "I think the strike will be violent, and that will be bad for the city. Of course, you had your violence. It subsides, doesn't it?"

Alternating between rage and an uncharacteristic twilight calm, he reacted to the pressures of the job the way he usually did, by going after those who were the most helpless and posed the least resistance. An innocent tailor was cursed with having to measure him for white tie and tails for a wedding. Scurrying in tow like a terrified mouse, he somehow managed to measure Rendell's massive shoulders and inseam as the mayor gritted his teeth, slapped his hands, and stomped about the room. Away from the tailor, Rendell regained his composure, particularly when the reporter Scott Simon followed him around for a little while in preparation for a segment on the *Today* show.

"I've often wondered over the past several years why one with a promising future would want to be mayor?" Simon asked from the backseat of the mayor's car.

As the car made a slow loop around City Hall, Rendell talked convincingly about the challenges of the job. He talked about how utterly bored he would be as a governor or a senator. He talked about how a mayor of a big city was always in the thick of the action. It was the perfect sound-bite answer, until he added one more thought. "I gotta tell you, I'm not sure how much of a promising future I had. If I hadn't won this election, this would have been it."

Simon gave a little gulping laugh and chose another line of questioning. So much for the mayor as sacrificial angel on behalf of the urban time bomb.

At 2:00 P.M., with three hours to go before the deadline, Cohen got a revised proposal from the unions so drastically different from the one he had received earlier that it suddenly reduced the accumulated deficit by $140 million. The abrupt turnaround by the unions was mystifying, but there was hope among the city negotiators that a settlement could still be reached.

"It's not over yet," said Davis.

"God only knows where we are," said Cohen.

At 3:30 P.M., chief union negotiator Willig called Cohen's office to speak to Davis. Asked for his reaction to the day's initial union offer,

Davis was ravenously eager to comply, like a prisoner getting his first meal after a prolonged hunger strike.

"I can start from the top. We don't like the wages. We don't like the health care. When you're talking about scheduling, transfers, working down, classification—all of that are things that we want and we need—there's none of that in there." He hung up, and his smile fell over the stone of City Hall like a meteor shower. "It's conversations like that that make the whole six months worth it."

At 4:07 P.M., fifty-three minutes before the deadline, Ginnie Lehoe, Cohen's secretary, who worked almost as methodically as he did, typed up a letter from Davis to Sutton officially notifying him of the city's rejection of the union's proposals:

> In light of the continuing impasse, we hereby reaffirm our offer of Sept. 18, as the city's last and best offer, which, if not accepted, will be implemented today at 5:00 P.M.
>
> During the past several days, informal discussions have been conducted through intermediaries. Regrettably, such discussions have failed to resolve the impasse.

At 4:17 P.M., forty-three minutes before the deadline, Rendell called Street for one last update.

"There's no chance, right?"

"They want to set something up."

"When? We got forty-five minutes."

III

Rendell seemed calm after he made his decision. But he knew that the contract he was implementing was so favorable to the city that it would inevitably back the unions into a desperate corner. Sensing his vulnerability, an aide to the mayor told him that articles and television news shows all over the country were depicting him as a hero for having the courage to face the unions head-on. He was clearly the new political flavor of the month at *The Wall Street Journal*. The *Chicago Tribune* had been in town. So had *U.S. News and World Report,* and many others would follow. But in the face of an ugly strike, those clips would be of little consolation.

The mordant sound of "The Battle Hymn of the Republic" being played on a flute emanated from the City Hall courtyard through the open window of the mayor's office. Of all the sounds from the courtyard, it was the only one that carried into the office, as if there were a certain destiny to it. The musician played the same song every day, so lonely in the pierce of its notes that it evoked one of two reactions—a desire to fling oneself into the courtyard or a desire to take the flute and break it over the head of the musician playing it. Rendell did neither. Instead, he tried to be as upbeat as possible. Speaking over the phone to Cohen, he fantasized about the possibility of a prolonged strike, during which he could temporarily dump the mayor's job, get out of that teak-lined prison where everyone was trying to hold him hostage for something, and just go around the city collecting garbage. "Just think, if we had a three-week strike, I wouldn't have to do any real work. I wouldn't have to see any community groups. I wouldn't have to go to any meetings. I wouldn't have to give any speeches. It would be fabulous!

"Fuck it, I'm ready."

The following night, Rendell and Street got on the phone to each other and went through the elaborate choreography of the mayor begrudgingly giving in on two outstanding issues: one involving the use of prison inmates for volunteer work and the other an agreement to notify the union of the intent to contract out any work that cost more than $10,000. Rendell was convincing in expressing his reluctance, in showing how much it killed him to give up on these two issues. It was vintage Rendell, and it was also a vintage bit of Rendell acting. Before the call, the mayor and the city council president had agreed to give up on these issues. But they also assumed that Sutton and Willig would be listening to the conversation, since Street was calling from the union camp. The mayor and the council president went through the charade to give Sutton the opportunity to report to his union membership that he had faced down the mayor on these two pivotal issues. So close did the mayor and Street feel to a settlement, a settlement that would be incredible for the city, that one of their primary worries had become how they could make Sutton look like a union president who had shown some backbone and not like a union president who had flung away his membership. They knew he needed victories, something he could take back to the executive board as a show of toughness, and they were trying to feed them to him. Along the same lines, the mayor also agreed to a union request that former labor secretary Ray Marshall come to Philadelphia, go through the transparent act of bringing the two sides together, and then proclaim the contract a fair one. The way the plan would work, according to city negotiators, was that Marshall would meet with the mayor for a grand total of five minutes, but his presence in the city would give Sutton further strength with his executive board.

Despite the flurry, there was still no settlement by Friday. During the previous three nights, Cohen had slept a total of three hours, but he seemed utterly unaffected by the deprivation. As he told someone over the phone, "Actually I don't feel too bad."

Despite the sense of optimism that everyone on the city side felt, Cohen was still the ultimate realist. "There's actually a lot that's agreed to," he told the mayor. "The problem is they are so unhappy with what they've agreed to, moving a comma at this point is enough to make them throw up their hands and say the hell with it."

Early that afternoon, Rendell, Cohen, and Street convened around the table in the mayor's office. Street was hunched over the table, clearly luxuriating in his role as go-between for the city and the unions, the perfect man in the middle. "I like this shit," he said at one point, sounding like the Robert Duvall character in *Apocalypse Now* waxing enthusiastic over the smell of napalm in the morning. Expansive in private in a way that he almost never was in public, he told a story about his son, how he had lost count of the number of laps in a track-meet relay and so had stopped in the middle. The more he exposed his son's utter confusion, the happier he became, and by the end, tears of laughter were running down his face. He told another story about the city councilman named David Cohen, admitting that he didn't have the heart to yell at him since he was old and somewhat frail. "I don't want to be responsible for him having a heart attack," said Street, and he continued in his unique vein.

"I did that once."

Rendell and Cohen nodded.

Through the open window came the sound of "Amazing Grace" from the courtyard flutist.

"Fuck him!"

Street was referring to Tom Cronin, the head of District Council 47.

"He's a piece of shit."

Rendell and Cohen nodded.

Street was angry with Cronin for his general bombast as well as for blasting proposed efforts by Street and Rendell to reform the city's charter. Street said he had once worn the same style straw hat that Cronin fancied but then gave it up when someone from a distance mistook him for the union leader. Now he was reveling in the fact that Cronin, as head of a major union in the city, was being virtually shut out of the negotiations. "Crone Pain-in is being subjected to a humiliation that is completely justified," said Street.

"He's getting paid back for shit that he did."

Rendell and Cohen nodded.

Street estimated that there were still nineteen issues the unions and the city had not resolved. But he was supremely confident they could be resolved. "There is no way this thing shouldn't be done today," he said.

Cohen showed the same sense of urgency, born not out of confidence but out of a feeling that it was only a matter of time before the unions would wake up to the reality of what they were doing. "We really should aim to get it done today. The longer it sits, the worse it smells."

"What?" asked Street.

"This deal."

And quite clearly there were some within the unions who were the embodiment of Cohen's very fears. The day of implementation of the city's final offer, Rendell had sent a letter to all city employees, outlining the administration's position on the negotiations. The letter was humane and decent, expressing sadness and regret that the negotiations had escalated to such a point. Several days later his office received a message for the mayor that had been scribbled in raw and stilted print on the back of one of the letters:

> You are punk pussy jew racist who should be killed the way Hitler broiled Jews in his ovens. What goes around, comes around. You better get extra body guards to watch that fat jew ass, but even that won't stop armor piercing bullets.

IV

Ten days later the unions and the city were *still* negotiating, still attempting to effect the terms of a surrender. Progress was being made, but it was slow and inchlike, fraught with paranoia and suspicion—not to mention that from a union perspective this contract, if actually agreed to, would likely go down as the worst ever in terms of public-employee bargaining. Or as Cohen told the mayor in one of his status updates on the union's approach, "This is half my labor negotiations. This person can't meet with that person. We have to talk about that issue, but not with this person." Every time a settlement seemed within reach, the union backtracked or stalled or came up with a totally different proposal snatched from the mists, and city negotiators became convinced that the strategy of the unions was exactly the same as it had been since the end of June—to stall and obfuscate and pray for some sort of natural disaster that might kill Rendell and Cohen and Davis and all the rest of those bastards.

It got so bizarre that the union lawyers did not even show up for the hearing on their request for an injunction against implementation of the city's final offer. Their absence made no sense to Rendell, and he, like virtually everyone else, was growing frazzled. "Part of me says if they're not serious about [the court case], go on strike and get the fucker over with." But inch by inch, progress had been made, to the point where there was confidence that the economic issues had largely been settled. Under the tentatively agreed upon new four-year contract, there would be no wage increases in the first two years, a 2 percent increase in the third year, and a 3 percent increase in the fourth year; a contribution of $360 a month per employee to the health and welfare fund; and an up-front lump-sum payment of $39 million to District Council 33. All in all it was a remarkably favorable deal for the city, close to what had been asked for initially, and in past negotiations it would have been cause for celebration. But the commitment that Rendell had made to Alan Davis and the rest of the negotiation team over the summer had stood, and the non-economic issues, instead of being given away, were still being negotiated with ferocity. Among the myriad of issues, significant differences still existed over the city's right to lay off workers as well as the city's right to contract out work.

On Monday, October 5, there loomed a new deadline, this one set by the unions: a strike deadline of 12:01 A.M. Tuesday, October 6, if there was no settlement.

Negotiations between the two sides went on all day Monday and deep into the night, but movement was still painfully slow. Hours would pass, and a few meager sentences of contract language would pass between the two sides. Then hours would pass again. During the marathon session, which had actually begun the day before, on Sunday, Cohen watched as the Vikings made a remarkable comeback against the Bears. While members of the media scurried about the Holiday Inn Midtown to capture what they believed to be a tense and taut drama, city negotiators played hearts or caught up on magazines they hadn't been able to get to at home or read *The Long Goodbye* by Raymond Chandler or bonded together as if at a bad frat party without girls, kegs, or stale potato chips. What the city proposed was rejected by the unions. What the unions proposed was rejected by the city.

"I'm inclined to think they don't know what the hell they're doing," said Joe Torsella about the unions, and like others, he was leaning more and more to the view that there would still be a strike.

The mayor himself vacillated. Early Monday morning his mood was good, and with typical optimism, he still thought there was a fifty-fifty chance of a settlement. But as the hours ticked by and the updates from Cohen, while not entirely grim, also indicated that no real progress was being made on the remaining issues, he began to prepare for the worst and take steps to place the city on alert. A flyer had been circulated among city employees, telling them to congregate that night for a rally at Veterans Stadium, where the Eagles were playing the Dallas Cowboys on *Monday Night Football,* and to the mayor that only meant trouble. He met with Deputy Police Commissioner Seamon and told him to have police at all electrical and communication receptacles in the area of the stadium to guard against sabotage, as well as a dozen tow trucks in the area to be ready to counter any union attempt to play havoc with the traffic. "They should have the right to demonstrate," said Rendell of the union workers, "but it should not be anywhere near ingresses or egresses. The last thing we want is anything near a bloodbath."

"Any possibility of a settlement?" asked Seamon.

"Yeah, there's a possibility, but it's the kind of thing that won't happen until a minute before the deadline. There's all sorts of possibilities for violence before then."

Questions were also raised about the accessibility of City Hall to various groups that had scheduled events in the Reception Room. A German American group had conveyed word that it was coming on Tuesday regardless of what was going on outside in terms of protests and picketers, but an Italian American group had no plans to be anywhere near the building—a chain of events that the mayor found utterly predictable.

"If they're Germans, I would take them *seriously,*" said Rendell. "The Italians canceled, proving once again that they're lovers, not fighters."

Several hours later, in the afternoon, Cohen returned once again from the bargaining war room at the Holiday Inn and had little new to report. A press conference had been scheduled for 5:00 P.M., and as the two were going over what Rendell should say, Cohen was handed a walkie-talkie by Sergeant Buchanico, presumably to use once the strike was on. He looked at it with total puzzlement, as if it were a foreign object, and Rendell immediately understood the source of Cohen's apprehension. "Don't you know Jews don't know how to work instruments like that," consoled the mayor. "It's impossible. It's not in our background."

The sound of the clock atop the City Hall tower struck 5:00 as Rendell paced back and forth in his office by himself. He was taking deep breaths as he mouthed aloud what he would say at the press conference, making sure to remember Cohen's admonitions about not saying anything about the status of the negotiations (it was so hard to remember *everything* David told him to do sometimes), pacing behind the desk, then back and forth across the Oriental carpet, then to the edge of the round table—no jokes, no temper tantrums, no asides, just the grim reality that a strike, a goddamn strike, was about to hit the city.

Rendell, Cohen, and press secretary Feeley left the mayor's office and walked down the hall to the press conference, wing-tipped gunfighters in their dark suits. "There is a possibility that as of midnight tonight there will be a strike," said the mayor with both hands on the podium at the front of the Reception Room. He was calm and somber, reflecting not simply the tenuousness of the situation but also a genuine sadness about who would lose the most and suffer the most. "What we're fighting for here are the poorest ten or fifteen percent, because they simply have no alternative. Those who have the money to leave Philadelphia will." And then, like virtually everyone else in the city, he could do nothing else but wait.

On the phone with Cohen a couple of hours later, he told him to convey a message to Sutton "to settle this fucking thing," particularly after hearing that a mere 150 union protesters had showed up at Veterans Stadium even though the game was on national television. "If that's the best they can do, they should settle." He sat down to watch the game on the set in the console in the middle of the office while doing paperwork, proclaiming with gusto and enthusiasm "This baby is over!" when the Eagles forged ahead to a quick 7–0 lead, only to proclaim "Oops, that changes the whole complexion" minutes later, when the Dallas Cowboys' Michael Irvin broke off a long gain on a reception. He then went out to the game, sitting in the first row of the mayor's box with a plate piled high with chicken wings and macaroni salad that was immaculate by the time he left to return to the office forty-five minutes later. In moments of stress and anxiousness, the mayor liked nothing better than to eat and eat mightily—spaghetti,

popcorn, vats of ice cream. He wasn't at that precipice when he left the
game, but on his way back he called directory assistance for the number of
the White Castle on South Broad, to make sure it was still open. The connection wasn't great, and the operator hung up on him, making clear that
in the eyes of the phone company it didn't really matter whether you were
the mayor or a major felon, but he got to White Castle anyway and ordered
a ten-pack to go as a kind of reserve measure.

A half hour later, back in his office watching the game, he had eaten six
of the burgers and was yelling "We get the ball! We get the ball!" as the
Eagles recovered a Dallas fumble. Fifteen minutes later, at 11:15 P.M.,
forty-five minutes before the strike deadline and now eating a pear, he attempted to reach Cohen on his beeper. When Cohen didn't respond right
away, he thought something might be going on, a glimmer of hope. But he
was wrong. The strike had started.

At five minutes past midnight, Rendell watched on television as the
Channel 6 news showed union protesters shouting "Rendell, go to hell!" in
a unison so wobbly and thin that Rendell himself laughed. At the same
time Cohen was calling: Sutton wanted to talk.

At 12:15 A.M., while Rendell held an impromptu press conference as a ruse
to occupy the media, Sutton and Street quietly slipped into his office. The
mayor and Cohen arrived fifteen minutes later, and the four men sat at the
round table in the office. By prior agreement, Rendell played the good cop
and Cohen the bad one, which had the effect of making the mayor's assurances to Sutton all the more holy and sacrosanct. When Rendell said he
was willing to soften some of the language on management-rights issues,
Cohen balked, but Rendell, as if on cue, quietly overruled him anyway.
When it came to the issue of contracting out labor, the mayor promised not
"to jam it down people's throats." He gave the same assurances on layoffs.
But although he was willing to give some ground in these and other areas,
he did not back down or waver on his basic contentions that the city must
have the right to manage its workforce and that the unions must be held to
some standard of accountability. "I'm not going to fuck you, I'm not going
to lie to you," he told Sutton, but "you gotta give us the right to manage."

There was no yelling or histrionics during the meeting. Sutton, a decent and reasonable man, spent much of the time listening, and when he
spoke, he was so quiet and self-effacing that he sounded like he was in
church, whispering delicately to get someone's attention halfway down the
pew. He had walked into the meeting looking frail and furtive, his crane-

like features almost crumpled. When he left, at 2:20 A.M., he didn't look much better. He was in an almost impossible situation, with the sway of public opinion, so masterfully shaped by Rendell, overwhelmingly against the unions.

At 2:50 A.M., Sutton called the mayor on behalf of District Council 47 and asked for a $5.7-million lump-sum payment. The mayor agreed to it. At 4:00 A.M., after fielding one more update call, Rendell made a little nest for himself in the middle of the Oriental carpet with some pillows that had been brought from home. He slept on and off until 7:00 A.M., when Cohen called with that schoolmarmish voice he sometimes got when he sensed that the mayor, contrary to Cohen's specific instructions, had said more to the media during the course of the night than Cohen felt wise or appropriate. Rendell took a shower and put on a new white shirt, which one of his staffers crinkled a bit so it would look suitably rumpled, and purposely did not shave to add to the effect that he described as "not quite cinema verité." He removed the little nest of pillows that he had slept on, but then he put it back, knowing that reporters would undoubtedly want to see it for their inevitable reconstructions.

By 8:00 A.M., the board of District Council 33 was meeting to accept or reject the proposed contract. "The longer this goes on, the more worried I become," Rendell said a half hour later. But he was still in a good mood, still fantasizing about the tone he would use at the press conference announcing a contract settlement and how, regardless of the impulse, he would not gloat. But as minute after minute and then hour after hour ticked by, he became increasingly agitated. "Eleven fucking o'clock," he muttered from his office, and then he yelled at no one in particular, "Let's get it on!"

At noon, he received word from Cohen that the union bargaining agents were going crazy over the layoff and contracting-out provisions. "If they vote this down, there is no more negotiation!" he told Cohen. "We have bent over backward—bent over backward."

Five minutes later he received word that the union was balking at the potential use of prison parolees to perform city labor and at changes in the disability provisions that would cut down on the ability of workers to double-dip. "The only thing disability hurts is the fucking slackers," he yelled over the phone. "There is no decent worker that has anything to worry about."

Seven minutes later he spoke with Cohen again. *"Let's do the fucking thing, let's do it! Let's get on with the strike, and let's see what happens! That's life! That's life in the big city!"*

Eight minutes later he received reports that an elderly man had been pushed to the pavement and injured by pickets outside City Hall while police at the scene had done nothing. In the Cabinet Room, he watched a tape of the incident supplied to him by one of the local television stations, and he expressed his reaction to a police inspector. *"I want them fired! Terrific performance by the Philadelphia Police Department! I want everybody who was out there fired! Did the Philadelphia Police take a dive because of the unions? This is fucking unbelievable! Is this America we are in? This is not supposed to happen to citizens of Philadelphia! We all pick our noses instead of being at the site! What the fuck are we doing? How the fuck did they not see that? I want them down here in forty-five minutes! This is a despicable performance by the Philadelphia PD! God fucking Christ!"*

He said he wanted to see the top echelons of the police department as soon as possible. They arrived sheepishly in his office with the circumspection of cat burglars, hoping and praying not to be noticed, and sat for the most part in utter silence as the mayor paced behind his desk in a blind and teetering rage that went far beyond the diagnosis of wig out, approaching something otherworldly.

"These guys don't do a bloody fucking thing! They don't do shit, and I want them fired! I want them fired so the message gets out that no one in the police department takes a dive!"

One of the police officials tried to explain that no one had witnessed the incident.

"Oh wonderful, oh wonderful! What were they doing? Were they involved in street theater? Were they feeding the homeless? What the fuck were they doing? Fire them!"

Another police official tried once again to explain the circumstances of the situation.

Rendell took his chair and slammed it into the desk with all his might. And then, for the first time since learning of the incident, his voice lowered to a decibel level that if not quite reasonable, was somewhere close to it. And suddenly his mood changed, from livid to almost beseeching. "Maybe the city isn't worth saving? Is there anybody else out there who cares but me? Is there anybody else? Am I just spitting into the wind? I don't like having people call me names and dumping garbage on my lawn. If this is what my police officers do, why don't I just fold?"

An hour later, at 2:30 P.M., he sat quietly at the desk of one of his secretaries in the outer office, spent and exhausted, still dwelling on the incident with the police, still waiting for a moment that seemed destined never to come, when he received word of something surreal. At first, when Kevin Feeley told him, he didn't believe it, so he did what he always did when he needed certification.

"Is it true?" he asked Cohen over the phone, sounding both incredulous and slightly dazed, as if the whole thing were some prank.

Ed Rendell didn't jump up and down when he received confirmation of a tentative settlement in the war of the unions. He didn't hoot or holler or slap anyone on the back or break open a bottle of champagne. He didn't hug his schedulers or his secretaries or do a jig or stand on his head. He smiled from ear to ear, but there was something strangely muted in his behavior. Like most men defined by drive and the constant taste of action, he saw life as a matter of hopscotching from one crisis to another, and as soon as one hurdle was overcome, it almost instantaneously lost its sex appeal. The war of the unions was over, and now a new problem was gnawing at him, driving him berserk and causing him to mutter obscenities with passion and gusto: how to get to that epic football tilt between Penn Charter and Episcopal in time to see his son play, particularly if he had to go down to the Holiday Inn and play kissy face with Sutton and somehow make him look like a proud union warrior when the exact opposite was the case.

It was solely on the basis of a bluff that the city had taken the initial steps to contract out certain portions of the sanitation work performed by Sutton's union. As the city negotiators had so openly discussed during that meeting at the mayor's house, they had no intention of doing it. But the idea apparently terrified Sutton, in large measure because it was the support of the sanitation workers that had elevated him to his position as president of the union. Toward that end, as a secret part of the negotiations, Rendell wrote a confidential letter vowing never to contract out sanitation during the life of the contract. From Sutton's perspective, the letter had to be secret. If news of it got out, thousands of union members who were not in sanitation would go haywire at the way they had been sacrificed. From the city's perspective, the loss in potential savings from that concession was $30 million a year, not to mention the likelihood of improved efficiency in the one city service that affected everyone. But when someone later asked Cohen what the city got from the unions in return for the sanitation provision, his answer was both brief and blunt: "Everything."

The four-year contract contained no wage increases for the first two years and then minimal ones of 2 percent in the third year and 3 percent in the fourth. The health benefit was reduced to $360 a month per employee. The city for the first time would be allowed representation on the board of trustees that administered the unions' health and welfare programs, thereby giving it access to all books and records. Just as important were the sweeping and unprecedented changes in other areas. The city now had the right to contract out work under certain conditions as well as the right to lay off workers in certain instances. Specific past practices and work rules that restricted the city's ability to monitor performance and improve productivity were eliminated. The number of paid holidays was reduced from fourteen to ten. Double-dip disability pensions, in which a retired city employee could receive two disability pensions for the same injury, were eliminated. Overall, the city would save an estimated $79 million in the first year of the contract alone and $374 million over its four-year duration. By any measure, it was a remarkable contract, a nationwide model for what a city government could do under the right conditions of crisis.

Somehow the mayor was able to avoid the Holiday Inn, and forty-five minutes later he was at a playing field on the leafy edge of the William Penn Charter School on School House Lane, dressed in the blue suit that he had worn for the past thirty-four hours and the white button-down shirt that had been expertly crinkled to make him look disheveled. He should have been exulting in the greatest political victory of his career. He was on the verge of becoming a nationally recognized hero, with publications from near and far about to lavish praise on him as the new guru of municipal government, the mayor who knew how to reinvent the American city. During the game, as word of the settlement was broadcast over radio and television, people came up to him and congratulated him. He accepted their compliments with typical graciousness and self-effacement, minimizing his role and minimizing the extent to which the city had crushed the unions. Cohen had played a remarkable part. So had John Street in his role as intermediary, confounding his severest critics. But it was the mayor who always had been at the greatest risk in the absence of a settlement.

Quietly, as much as he could given who he was and what was happening, he inched away from everyone else. His shoes grew soiled from the dirt of the field, his gaze fixed and focused as he watched his son. In that sliver of peace and privacy before the inevitable press conference and the million and one questions from the media, before he trudged back up to the stage of politics and public life, he seemed more happy and tranquil than he had in months, luxuriating in what it was like, if only for a precious gulp of minutes, to have an existence in which the only important matter at hand was not the city, not the endless pondering of its fate, but a son playing football.

V

Alan Davis hadn't known Rendell and Cohen particularly well at the beginning of the whole saga. His impression of Rendell from their long-ago days together at the district attorney's office was of a man who was not particularly serious, and his impression of Cohen, based on their days together at Ballard Spahr, was of a cheerful workaholic who functioned masterfully as sidekick, assistant, and briefcase carrier to the firm's head of litigation. But the two had surprised him, showing dimensions and hues that he could not have predicted, thus creating one of those rare and glorious moments when political life, instead of lowering men and women to the muck of the occasion, had done the opposite. Far from buckling, the mayor, who could still be remarkably nonserious, had shown remarkable strength and resilience. And while Davis had been aware of Cohen's ability to synthesize huge hunks of information, he was stunned by his fearless comfort in the stinky halls of city politics.

As Davis sat in his forty-fifth-floor office at Ballard Spahr, the city expanded before him—the statuesque presence of the art museum, the slow bend of the Schuylkill River between bridges and plumes of cloud and smoke, the gray eminence of City Hall, the once mighty waterfront of the Delaware, with its slow trickle of ships and cargo haulers. Philadelphia never looked better than it did from up here, undulating and unfolding with history and strength as far as the eye could see—river, bridge, home, office, factory, and the crisscrossing veins of a thousand streets.

He knew that if he stared through those magnificent windows for too long, he would begin to realize how much of it was an illusion, an egg whose yolk had turned foul and muddy. He knew that the city was struggling mightily to reshape and redefine itself, to create a new skin for itself, and he knew that the effort, regardless of the intentions, might well be in vain. Avenue of the Arts, the convention center, casino gambling, Fun City, Fat City, Entertainment City, Restaurant City, the ultimate audience pool—it all rang hollow to him, particularly in a city as historically embedded in the no-frills grit of work and output and production as this one.

But the glow of the union negotiations was still with him. No one could have predicted an outcome such as this. Within the confines of government, a profound difference could still be made, and perhaps the most valuable lesson Alan Davis had learned was that he was wrong: disillusionment did not always have to be reality.

Bread and Circuses

NINE

Tidbits of Urban Wisdom

I

During those tumultuous months of 1992, Linda Morrison had watched the war of the unions with more than just a citizen's curiosity. Over the course of her lifetime, she had thought about the nature and the function of government in the city to a greater degree than most social and political scientists who were paid to. It was her passion and pursuit—poring over Charles Murray's words about the evils of welfare and its legitimization of illegitimate children, clipping articles from *Forbes* about liberalism and how the road to hell is paved with good intentions, reading Jane Jacobs's *The Death and Life of Great American Cities* so many times that she could virtually recite her favorite passages.

She had sharp and pungent ideas, but she was also practical, and the combination was intriguing to local politicians looking for a spark: in 1991, she worked as an issues director for a Republican mayoral candidate whose acclaimed ideas for reform were often the work of Linda's position papers; before that she worked for a city councilman whose *Wall Street Journal* piece about government in Philadelphia, printed in the form of an open letter to Mikhail Gorbachev and remarkable for its clever insight, had been largely Linda's creation:

> Dear Mr. Gorbachev,
> Your economy is a shambles, everyone is afraid to lend money or to invest in your People's Republic, government-run services are costly and inefficient, your streets are filled with potholes, there is political turmoil and anyone who can leave your workers' paradise is packing their bags. I sympathize—we have the same situation here in Philadelphia. . . .

The keenness of Linda's intellect and her considerable gift for writing had garnered praise and attention, but perhaps her most remarkable quality was an ability to become incensed about government with spontaneous combustion. She had come to the conclusion, based not only on what she read but also on her own personal experiences, that no surgery, short of something radical and untested, would be enough. A liposuction on the budget, a chin tuck on city services—even a full face-lift would do no good if the internal organs were on the precipice of failure. Won over long ago by their animus and their spirit, she had a feeling for cities that could bring her to tears. She saw that spirit being willfully destroyed, not by fate and the inevitability of a social shift from rural to urban to suburban but by programs and policies that made no sense. "Camden is dead. Detroit is dead. Newark is dead," said Linda Morrison as if she were talking about relatives who had been eaten away by a cancer that could have been cured. "And what scares me is that Philadelphia is on the verge. It could go either way."

Intrigued by what Rendell was trying to accomplish, she went to work for the administration during the war of the unions and helped shape the strategy of the attack. On the surface, it was a completely incongruous match. There was nothing that she and the mayor seemed to agree on in the slightest, whether it was notions of tourism, notions of the city's history and how to market it effectively (she liked it the way it was, pure and clean and unadorned; he had a colonial Williamsburg vision filled with costumed characters and battle reenactments), or the fundamental role that government should play in people's lives.

She was a Libertarian, a firm believer in the principle that government should exist only to the extent that it ensures the personal responsibility of the individual, and sometimes she uttered her political affiliation with pride, and sometimes she uttered it as if she had some communicable disease. But if she didn't believe in the system as it currently existed, she did believe in working within the parameters of the existing bureaucracy, however frustrating, to try to achieve change. She didn't advertise her Libertarian allegiance or try to convert others to her way of thinking. Even so, after going to work for Rendell, rumors did swirl around her. Or as one frightened city bureaucrat put it to another, "Did you know that Linda Morrison used to be a librarian?"

There were some in the city who saw her as savvy and visionary and admired the freshness and the provocative zeal of her ideas. Why was government in the business of building and subsidizing convention centers? Why was government in the business of giving money to people through welfare when all it seemed to do in so many cases was strip them of their incentive to work and encourage them to have children who they could not care for regardless of the honorableness of their intentions? Why was government in the transportation business or the public housing business or the health business or the school business when its track record in all these spheres had been one of abysmal failure? There were others who ultimately began to see Linda Morrison as a nut, a loose cannon who didn't understand anything about the true role of government as provider and protector and employer and edifice builder and economic developer and necessary regulator. But Linda really didn't care what others thought. Everywhere she looked when it came to government, she saw not simply the typical twin engines of bloat and waste but the perpetuation of a culture of dependence similar to a protection racket in which taxpayers are constantly being asked to subsidize an elite group of monopolistic institutions that are incompetent, above accountability, and have as their only successes employment and patronage mills for politicians. The open letter to Gorbachev in *The Wall Street Journal* referred to sanitation, the schools, and mass transit as Philadelphia's "urban collective farms." The letter argued for the privatization of these three services, but far more important, it spoke about what these functions, and others like it, represented:

> We used to understand the benefits of liberty here in Phila-delphia. As I walk to my office in City Hall, I pass an old red brick building with a bell in front of it. There are always scores of tourists—many from your part of the world—waiting in line to go inside this building and touch the bell. They are just dis-covering something that many in Philadelphia have forgotten. Not only is liberty right. Liberty works.
>
> If events over there get you down, I invite you to come to Philadelphia and touch the Liberty Bell with me. What it stands for may help both of us solve our common problem.

When Ed Rendell ran for mayor in 1991, despite his get-tough talk, she saw him as a typical liberal Democrat, which meant that she really didn't see him at all. She spit out the term "liberal Democrat" so that it came out sounding vaguely like "liverwurst," and as far as she was concerned, the contribution of liberal Democrats to the country was a legacy of more wel-fare, more public housing, more taxes, more economic-development boon-doggles, more subsidized transportation, and more unworkable schools. Instead, she worked for a Republican candidate named Sam Katz in the mayoral race. A successful businessman, Katz did not win the nomination of his party, but he had innovative ideas about how to get the city on its feet again, and the position papers that Linda produced were a source of admi-ration in the Rendell campaign.

In the spring of 1992, just as the war of the unions was heating up, Linda wrote a letter to a member of the Rendell administration suggesting that the city use the privatization of union work as a tool for achieving signifi-cant savings in the budget and as leverage in negotiations with the unions. The contents of the letter found their way to David Cohen, who was impressed.

She started out in a volunteer capacity. Then she ultimately became the director of the city's competitive contracting program, which put her in the maelstrom of the city's efforts to begin the delicate and controversial process of contracting out work that had been the domain of the city's unions. There was something refreshingly exuberant about her that con-trasted with the hangdog caution that could be seen in the people she worked with. With her straw-colored hair and her vintage Midwestern face, oval and ruddy as if it were still feeling the effects of a winter cold snap, she was utterly lacking in the dead-eyed look that most lifelong bureaucrats invariably acquire after a while. She spoke English, not bureaucratese. She laughed sometimes. She approached the whole issue of privatization with exuberance, even *excitement*. She also seemed to have been seized by something else, a sense of personal urgency that went beyond politics and personal philosophy. As she and the others sat around the table in David Cohen's office, taking careful notes on what to privatize and what not to privatize, insulated by the loud scream of an air conditioner that shut out most other sounds, they were running out of time. Out there *was* the city, and while there were thousands who were trapped and had no choice, there were also thousands who did have a choice and weren't feeling like citizens of the city at all, but like endangered species.

II

Linda did what she did out of love, love of the city.

Born in Peoria, where her father had worked for Caterpillar, she spent her growing-up years in a series of suburbs and towns and ended up going to high school in Clintonville, Wisconsin. Linda went through a diet of piano lessons and ballet lessons, but when she looked for places to actually enjoy such culture, there were none. Life in Clintonville, a town of five thousand so far north that it was even north of Green Bay, was particularly insufferable to her. She longed for the city, any city. She won a National Merit Letter of Commendation and could have had her pick of colleges around the country. But her parents wanted her close by, so as a compromise she chose the University of Wisconsin in Milwaukee because it was situated in the state's largest city. She left after a year and headed east to school, to study dance. A year later, in 1969, she headed for her version of the promised land—a crotchety apartment in the East Village five blocks east of the Fillmore East. She loved New York. The stimulation was greater than even she could have imagined—the Feast of San Gennaro, the Cyclone roller coaster at Coney Island at 2:00 A.M., the clubs that stayed open till dawn. She later moved to Forest Hills, Queens, and became an executive for a division of International Telephone and Telegraph involved in the export business.

After eight years, she returned to Milwaukee and went back to the University of Wisconsin to get a degree in business. She also opened a restaurant near the campus. Her father had been a political curmudgeon to begin with, but it was through the running of the restaurant that Linda began to evolve a political philosophy of less being more. The regulations heaped on her by various government agencies, not to mention the taxes, made the difficult job of running a business almost impossible. She couldn't help but think that government, instead of nurturing the notion of personal responsibility, had become an impediment to it. Instead of being praised for her initiative, she was being treated as a pariah, she thought. But if Milwaukee was the incubator for new ideas, she also hated every single minute of being back there, particularly since she had no sustaining interest in what she described as the troika of "beer, brats, and bowling." In 1981, she received her degree, and two years later she headed back to New York and what she thought would this time be a place in the promised land for good.

Linda came to Philadelphia the way nearly everybody came to Philadelphia, because it was on the way to someplace else. She knew about the Liberty Bell and Independence Hall, in large part because she had seen them once on some geeky trip with her class at Clintonville High. But as she and a friend who was settling there drove through the city on a summer day in 1983, making a meandering loop from Rittenhouse Square to South Philadelphia, feasting on cheese steaks and Italian ices, she was smitten by what she saw. People were sitting on steps, kids were playing in the street, neighborhoods were still intact and had not been savaged by the permanent scars of expressways providing easy access for the diaspora to the suburbs.

Hanging out the window of the car, Linda Morrison took in a city that still had scale and rhythms, a place that was charming not because it was trying to be cute and charming, like some mugging child actor, but because of its very lack of artifice and contrivance. New York was New York, electric, wonderful, intoxicating. But so much of New York was like living in the grouts of a water well, where one became thankful for the thinnest thread of space and fresh air. It had also become outrageously expensive. Philadelphia was a city with a sense of proportion and humanity and humility that New York would never have.

There were three books that Linda had largely depended on to figure out the mysteries of life. One was *Free to Choose* by Milton and Rose Friedman, another was *Atlas Shrugged* by Ayn Rand, and the third was Jacobs's *The Death and Life of Great American Cities*. Linda had always wondered whether there was some way of describing the unique draw and pulse of the city, but she had never seen it successfully articulated until she read Jacobs's book:

Under the seeming disorder of the old city, wherever the old city is working successfully, is a marvelous order for maintaining the safety of the streets and the freedom of the city. . . . This order is all composed of movement and change, and although it is life, not art, we may fancifully call it the art form of the city and liken it to the dance— not to a simple-minded precision dance with everyone kicking up at the same time, twirling in unison and bowing off en masse, but to an intricate ballet in which the individual dancers and ensembles all have distinctive parts which miraculously reinforce each other and compose an orderly whole. The ballet of the good city sidewalk never repeats itself from place to place, and in any one place is always replete with new improvisations.

To Linda, who settled in a neighborhood of the city called Fairmount, about a dozen blocks north of City Hall, that was it, exactly it—a sidewalk ballet with new impromptu performances every hour, reawakening the senses with an unpredictability that became its very guarantee. In her own way, she became a one-person convention and visitors' bureau for city life, extolling its virtues to anyone who would listen. She found a *New Yorker* cartoon showing a highway with a stream of cars passing under a sign marked LEAVING THE CITY and only one car passing under a sign marked STAYING IN THE CITY. Linda took the cartoon and jiggered it so the one lonely car was driving under a sign marked LEAVING PHILADELPHIA and the steady stream was passing under a sign marked NO INTENTION OF LEAVING PHILADELPHIA. It wasn't accurate of course. The city, like most cities, had been steadily losing chunks of population by the hundreds of thousands since 1960. But she hung the cartoon right inside her front door, framing it with a mat as red as a fire engine so people couldn't help but see it. "I had a thing about living in cities," she later said. "I wasn't born and bred here. I actively chose it because I actively liked it. It was a kind of defiant statement to have it hanging in my house." She felt a similar surge of pride and commitment in 1987, when she left Fairmount after roughly four years and moved to a neighborhood south of City Hall called Queen Village.

"Great cities are not like towns, only larger," Jacobs had written. "They are not like suburbs, only denser. They differ from towns and suburbs in basic ways, and one of these is that cities are, by definition, full of strangers."

Linda clung to that description, to that idea of the city being celebrated, and not endlessly condemned, for the very qualities that make it different from other physical places in American life. She later bracketed that section in a copy of the book that she gave to someone, to make sure that if he read nothing else, he would at least read that. She did not bracket the following paragraph, but it had just as much meaning:

> *The bedrock attribute of a successful city district is that a person must feel personally safe and secure on the street among all these strangers. He must not feel automatically menaced by them. A city district that fails in this respect also does badly in other ways and lays up for itself, and for its city at large, mountain on mountain of trouble.*

III

In 1990, Linda and her husband of two years, Jon Morrison, learned something wholly new about city life: when someone is stabbed near an artery, the blood doesn't flow evenly but spurts in syncopation to the beats of the heart.

They were in Queen Village when they discovered this fact, a "tidbit of urban wisdom" as Linda later called it. In 1990, the neighborhood was still going through a healthy period of growth. It was gentrified enough to appeal to a professional, two-income couple like the Morrisons but not gentrified enough to be just another "yuppie barracks," in the words of Jon Morrison. There were dozens of restaurants within walking distance, from the sensory overload of the Italian Market to the eclecticism of South Street, the wonders of South Street Souvlaki, and a particularly good Italian restaurant at Ninth and Catharine called Longano, where under a glitter-pasted ceiling the owners addressed you by your last name and the waiters called you "hon" or "sweetheart." If you liked to walk, and the Morrisons liked to walk, Queen Village was a wonderful, ever-changing maze with delicious surprises no matter how well you thought you knew it—street next to alcove next to alleyway without some conscious attempt to turn it into the Main Street of Disneyland, factory next to row house next to candy store because that's what made sense at the time. As far as they could tell, there was only one troubling aspect to it—three decrepit high-rise buildings that loomed in the sky like diseased redwoods, so completely out of scale and out of character in the neighborhood that it was hard to believe they had been put there as anything but some form of punishment and condemnation. They were part of a massive public housing project known as Southwark Plaza, and as far the Morrisons were concerned, they symbolized everything that was wrong not only with public housing but with government policy as it applied to the American city.

The Morrisons knew about Southwark Plaza when they settled together in Queen Village. But the essential character of the neighborhood overrode any concerns they had, particularly since Linda had already lived there for three years and felt familiar with it. The house they decided on, at 327 Queen Street, was irresistible anyway, a three-story row house with a red brick façade. The shutters and front door had been painted a mustardy yellow, but that was easy enough to fix with a coat of new paint. In back was an ample yard, and that was a major attraction as well. The view from there wasn't much: a narrow alleyway called Kauffman Street and across Kauffman a low-slung interconnecting series of drab and slightly grayish apartments. But in the excitement of purchasing their first house together and thinking about all the time they would spend together in that wonderful backyard, they paid little attention to what lay beyond the sliver of the alley.

Tired and exhilarated that first night in their new home, with boxes spread everywhere, they managed to find some clean sheets and throw them onto a mattress. They fell asleep—until they were awakened at 2:00 A.M. by the sound of screams coming through the sliding glass of the bedroom window. They rushed to see what was happening, and they saw a man stumbling down the alleyway of Kauffman Street. They heard his screams—*"Dad, you killed me, Dad, you killed me"*— and as they watched him step and stumble, they saw how the blood did not flow evenly from the stab wound, as one perhaps might have thought it would, but gushed out in syncopation to the beats of his heart.

The Morrisons tried to tell themselves that what had happened was the kind of isolated and horrific crime that just happens sometimes—and what good were the bragging rights of living in the city if you didn't have at least one tale of horror from the urban war zone to tell your suburban friends? But the wave of incidents emanating from the area of that drab, grayish-looking apartment complex across the sliver of Kauffman Street did not cease. Every week, it seemed, as Jon Morrison played in the backyard with the dog or did some planting, a police car would whiz down the alley responding to some call or other. Every night, it seemed, kids were playing and screaming and yelling, unsupervised, until 1:00 or 2:00 A.M. Linda herself began to call the police on a regular basis, asking them to do something about the noise. In response, she received an unannounced visit from a member of the city's Commission on Human Relations, who suggested that the problem was not with the parents, many of them single mothers, but with Linda and her own intolerance.

Feeling both desperate and angry, Linda Morrison made a determined effort to find out who owned the complex, and she was told that it was a so-called Section 8 apartment complex. Under the Section 8 program, administered by the federal government's Department of Housing and Urban Development, tenants contributed a portion of their monthly income in rent to a private landlord. What gap existed between the payment by the tenant and the actual market value of the rent was subsidized by HUD. Linda discovered the name of the agent for the Kauffman Street complex. She called several times trying to find out the name of the owner, but the agent refused to divulge the information and finally just told her to "fuck off." The forces of Kauffman Street overwhelmed Linda and her husband. They tried asking the parents to supervise their children, to keep them from screaming and yelling at all hours of the night, but more often than not they were met by amused half stares, as if such a request were not only impossible to comply with but also comical. The screams and yells continued, the only respite coming when it rained.

Linda and Jon Morrison began to feel surrounded, the glower of the Southwark high-rises on one side, the chaos of the Kauffman Street complex on the other. They literally went underground, particularly in the summer, burrowing into the basement to escape the noise, outfitting it with rugs and a television set and a couch. The yard, the very reason for buying the home, became unusable. They didn't want to be outside, not if it meant staring into Kauffman Street, not if it meant hearing the wail of another police siren. Through her contacts in the city, Linda had a friend in the upper echelons of the police department. Analytical by nature, she asked him to do a computer search of all the calls that the police had made in the area of the Kauffman Street complex. She found out that there had been more than ninety calls to the complex in one year, for such offenses as drug overdoses, fights, domestic disturbances, noise, gunfire, and several shootings. The police actually asked whether they could use the Morrisons' third-floor deck off the master bedroom to conduct surveillance of the complex because of its perfect vantage point. But not wanting to turn their house into a precinct, they said no. In the meantime, their car, an old Toyota, was stolen.

They went to community-association meetings in an attempt to change the situation somehow, and they were outspoken in their views. Political correctness was not part of their style, particularly when it came not only to the Kauffman Street complex but to an issue of far greater controversy within the Queen Village neighborhood: what to do about the high-rises of Southwark.

IV

In a way, the saga of Southwark was so predictable that mustering outrage about it was almost hard. Like similar high-rises in every city in America, Southwark wasn't some towering symbol or metaphor for public housing but was the typical embodiment of it. If Southwark stood out at all, if there was anything that distinguished the complex, it was in the color of those three twenty-five-story towers—a clammy, sickly yellow the human skin gets from chronic fever and stale air.

Public housing hadn't always been the festering sore that it was in 1992. When the first public-housing act was passed, in 1937, in the throes of the Depression, it was never intended to establish a form of permanent housing at all but was meant to provide temporary shelter for those requiring assistance until their income stabilized. While promoting many of the New Deal entitlements and other social programs, President Franklin Roosevelt himself recognized the danger of creating a permanent class of persons dependent on government. "Continued dependence upon relief induces a spiritual and moral disintegration fundamentally destructive to the national fiber," said Roosevelt in his State of the Union Address to Congress in 1935. "To dole out relief in this way is to administer a narcotic, a subtle destroyer of the human spirit. . . . We must preserve not only the bodies of the unemployed from destitution but also their self-respect, their self-reliance and courage and determination."

Public housing ultimately did evolve into a form of permanent shelter for many of those who lived in it. But into the late 1950s, it had neither the physical dilapidation nor the overwhelming preponderance of single mothers on welfare that it has had in the 1990s. According to a study of nineteen public-housing developments in Philadelphia in 1959, 63 percent of their residents were married, 58 percent were employed, and only 18 percent were receiving public assistance. The specter of so-called manless families was a problem then, but it was thought to be a solvable one. In fact, the local agency that administered public housing in the city, the Philadelphia Housing Authority, was the first in the nation to establish a social service division to deal with the issue.

Southwark itself opened in 1963 and for a short period of time was actually sought out as a desirable place to live. But by the 1970s, the quality of life in public-housing towers was beginning to fissure, and not just because of the inherent flaw of a structure designed to pack the greatest number of the poorest people into the least space possible. The second great migration of blacks from the rural South to the urban North, in the post–World War II era, put housing, any type of housing, at a premium. Various standards for rental properties that had existed in the past, such as prompt evictions and careful screening of tenants, were discarded. More and more, public housing became the very thing it was never supposed to be, the housing of "last resort" for those too poor to afford anything else.

By the early 1990s, Southwark had become a dilapidated horror. Two of the three high-rises were closed, and $48.5 million was earmarked for renovation, although many housing experts thought the whole concept of high-rise housing projects was fatally flawed regardless of how much money was spent on it. The questionable folly of rebuilding Southwark then turned into possible fraud in the winter of 1992, when it was discovered that the Philadelphia Housing Authority, after spending at least $6 million of the $48.5 million in renovation money, still did not have any usable architectural drawings. As for actual refurbishments, new windows had been installed in the three high-rise buildings. But the practical effect of that was blunted somewhat by the subsequent discovery that the windows did not meet specifications and had been improperly installed.

One didn't have to be a social scientist or an expert in public housing to understand a place like Southwark. Any adult, regardless of education—or any child, for that matter—could look at those towers and their utterly incongruous setting and see the malarial color that had infected them and know that they had been doomed to failure from the very beginning, casting a potentially fatal effect not only on those who were sentenced to live there but also on those who lived anywhere close to them. Anyone walking through the corridors of the one high-rise that was still open, 90 percent of whose residents were single mothers and their children, didn't need a PhD to realize that unless the social conditions inside such a place changed, no amount of money spent to rebuild and refurbish it would ever make a lasting difference. There were poor people in the city who desperately needed housing, but not like this.

Linda Morrison began to hate Southwark as much as she hated the Kauffman Street complex. She wasn't surprised in the least by the revelations of wasteful spending since her suspicion all along was that the rebuilding had more to do with feeding the ravenous appetites of the "poverty industry"— the architects and contractors and social service agencies, all of whom would be the greatest direct beneficiaries of whatever sums of millions were poured back in. Meanwhile, taxpayers and the urban poor, regardless of what they thought of each other, ended up as the ones who invariably benefited the least.

The planned rebuilding did strike her as financially nonsensical, given that the average cost of rehabilitating each of the seven-hundred-odd units in Southwark, roughly $65,000, was significantly more than the average cost of a home in the city. Beyond the cost, Linda saw Southwark as a monument of social-policy failure, the very thing that predictably happens when government assumes the role of provider.

She adored Queen Village, but more and more she began to relate to it like a widow going through the stages of grief—denial, heartbreak, anger, acceptance that what she loved had been irrevocably lost. She could still walk through its narrow blocks and alleyways and feel the city in her heart, but more and more she began to feel a certain coldness.

The Morrisons now had a son, named Ian. He was born in August of 1991, and that only added to their feelings of fear and insecurity in the neighborhood. To protect themselves, they bought a gun, and they went out to a firing range to practice shooting. The target could be set from far away but Linda had no interest in the delicacy of sharpshooting. She knew what the gun was for—self-protection and self-defense. She asked that the target be brought into close range, between six and eight feet away.

Blam! Blam! Blam! Blam! Blam! Blam!

She fired off the six rounds from the .38-caliber Smith & Wesson Model

10 without the slightest flinch, decimating the target, the smoke and the smell of gunpowder soaking the air.

"That's all I want to know how to do," she said.

By the spring of 1992, around the time Linda had decided to become involved in the war of the unions, she and her husband had run out of solutions. They were tired of living in a state of siege, tired of holing up in the basement, tired of walking out of a restaurant and scanning the street in all directions, tired of that horrible sense of being on guard all the time. "We felt there was no civilized way to solve the problem," said Jon Morrison as he later looked back on it. "If it were some sort of business or industry that was a nuisance, you could imagine legal ways to solve it. This was a problem without a handle on it."

They put their house up for sale, and on a Saturday night in the spring of 1992 they received further lessons on the rhythms of the human heart.

It was the night before an open house for prospective home buyers, and they had spent part of that day getting everything clean and shiny. They were asleep, just as they had been that very first night in 1990 when the exhilaration and giddiness of moving—sheets thrown happily over a mattress—had given way to terror. They heard screams, just as they had that very first night. But the victim was a woman this time, not a man. She had been shot, not stabbed, and she was staggering down Queen Street, the imprints of blood on the smooth stone of the sidewalk forming an orderly trail as delicate as a cat's paws, down a marble cornerstone and a black metal railing and an oval flower pot. The woman was a neighbor of the Morrisons, and she had been shot and mugged on her way home. She made it to her house, her blood splashing on the bottom two steps. Then she was carried to Linda and Jon's house, the blood splashing onto their steps as well. A pillow and a comforter were fetched for her to use until the ambulance came.

That Sunday morning, Linda worked diligently to cleanse her front steps of blood. At a certain point, the steps, like everything else—the shutters, the slight angle of the roof, the small symmetrical windows, the brick façade—embodied exactly what Linda had wanted in a house in the city. But now the splash of blood on those steps, seeping into the indentations and cracks, seemed only appropriate, as did Linda's efforts to clean it. Part of her efforts was an act of purification, but part was something far more practical: with an open house scheduled for that afternoon, it would be difficult to explain to prospective home buyers how part of the hidden charm of the neighborhood was those unexpected moments when a neighbor started bleeding on your front steps after getting shot. That was Linda's personal "tidbit of urban wisdom." Others who moved in would have to discover it on their own.

So after cleaning her own front steps of blood, Linda did what was only natural under the circumstances: she washed her neighbor's white steps of blood as well.

During the July Fourth weekend in 1992, Linda and Jon Morrison and baby Ian left Queen Village for good. They had no agreement of sale for their home, but they didn't care anymore. They made a deal with the person carrying the mortgage to take the house back. In return, he got all the equity and all the improvements, so the loss to the Morrisons was somewhere around $20,000. But they didn't care about that either. They dreaded the prospect of spending another summer holed up in the basement. Certainly in their short span of time in Queen Village they had witnessed some catastrophic crimes. But it was the little incidents, repeated over and over day after day, that had been even more wearing, "a hundred little things" as Linda called them—a broken window, a fight, a car alarm suddenly wailing into the night. None of these things made the news. None of them was particularly dramatic. But their buildup only reinforced, as Linda put it, the "chaos and self-destruction" of those living around her.

The bitter irony of leaving on July Fourth weekend could not have been lost on her. Of all the occasions and celebrations in Philadelphia, she liked July Fourth the best, and whenever she could, she went to Independence Hall on that day. She loved the perfect scale of the building, human and graceful and simple. She loved what it said about the nature of government, and she couldn't help but compare it with the federal buildings that now surrounded it, the courthouse and the IRS frowning and imposing and humorless like something out of the Stalin era. She reveled in the swell of the music and the reenactments at Independence Hall. She loved hearing the rereading of the Declaration of Independence.

We hold these Truths to be self-evident, that all Men are created equal, that they are endowed by their Creator with certain unalienable Rights, that among these are Life, Liberty, and the Pursuit of Happiness—That to secure these Rights, Governments are instituted among Men, deriving their just Powers from the Consent of the Governed....

Every time Linda read the words of the Declaration, it seemed impossible to square them with what the country had become and the kind of government that had been created, a government that instead of ensuring liberty ensured dependence, a government that instead of fostering a sense of individual responsibility had created a group of people addicted to the handouts of welfare and public housing and everything else. There were some who might have argued that Linda and Jon Morrison were simply paying the price of life in the big city. But the Morrisons refused to accept that. And they were convinced that what had happened to them wasn't the price of life in the city but the price of a certain type of government.

In 1990, Linda and Jon had bought a house in Queen Village because it was the fulfillment of a dream—to live in a house in a real neighborhood in a real city. On that first weekend in July in 1992, as she and her husband placed their belongings in boxes and fled to a house in the suburbs, Linda Morrison mourned the loss of that dream.

V

As the competitive-contracting coordinator for the city, Linda continued to perform with typical gusto and enthusiasm. In the aftermath of its stunning victory in the war of the unions in October of 1992, the Rendell administration continued serious pursuit of various privatization initiatives. This buoyed Linda even more since she had assumed that as soon as the war of the unions was over, the concept of privatization would disappear. Instead, it seemed likely that just as a start the security-guard functions at the art museum would be privatized. So would the union functions at the city nursing home and the maintenance functions at City Hall. Progress was being made, and Linda couldn't help but wonder whether Rendell really was on the cusp of something amazing. Perhaps she had been wrong about him all along. Perhaps he really wasn't a liberal Democrat, but underneath the creased suits and the herky-jerky carnival-barker exterior was a new kind of urban mayor altogether who was truly willing to pursue the tough steps that had to be taken if cities were somehow to stay alive.

In December 1992, the *Inquirer*'s Donald Kimelman wrote a column questioning the wisdom of rebuilding Southwark, particularly in terms of its impact on the Queen Village neighborhood. Morrison read the column with keen interest and several weeks later wrote a three-page memo to

David Cohen, outlining her and her husband's personal experiences there. Unlike most memos David Cohen received, so laden with the arcane script of bureaucratese that they read like the tract of some secret religious sect, this particular one was different:

> Last June, my husband and I made the decision to abandon our house near Southwark, and we fled the area in July. In doing so, we lost everything—all our equity in the house, all the improvements we made, all the neighborhood friends we had. . . .
>
> Besides all the money we lost, being run out of my City neighborhood makes me very sad. I consider myself a City-loving, hard-boiled urban person, used to putting up with a lot and tolerant of many things. But we had complained to every government agency you can think of for relief, and we finally realized that the vested interests in these projects take precedence over *endangered species like ourselves:* ordinary City people who work, respect others and their property and are good neighbors. But we escaped with our sanity and our lives, and we feel lucky for that.
>
> I think the last straw for us was scrubbing the coagulated blood of our neighbor off our steps one Sunday morning after she had been shot the night before by a Southwark resident. That and the terrifying thought that only about 120 units are occupied now in Southwark's 700 unit capacity. Imagine the neighborhood when Southwark is renovated and filled again!
>
> Almost everyone agrees that hundreds of bored, jobless, low-self-esteem women with fatherless, unsupervised children concentrated in high-rise public housing is an unworkable concept. Why are we proceeding with the madness of spending $70,000+ per unit fixing Southwark so it soon can become a larger and more menacing ghetto, when the average sales price of a decent home in Philadelphia is less than $40,000? The argument that "the federal government is giving us the money to spend like this, so we must" is ridiculous. If they bought us a rope with a noose, would we hang ourselves with it?
>
> The renovation of Southwark will be bad for the tenants, bad for the neighbors and bad for the taxpayers. The only people it will be good for are the poverty industry special interests who expect to cash in.
>
> The Mayor's office can use the influence you have locally and in Washington to put a stop to the madness of Southwark. . . . There are a lot of nice, decent people of all races and ethnic groups still holding on

in Queen Village, Pennsport and the South Street area, but no one speaks for them. These are the kind of people the City desperately needs to keep to remain viable.

It's too late for me, but I hope you will speak for them.

Since neither Cohen nor the mayor ever responded to what she wrote, she had no idea what they thought, if they thought anything at all. The administration was aware of the dilemma of Southwark, and there was basic agreement that such a high concentration of poor families wasn't good for anyone. But beyond plans to spend several million to tear down several low-rise buildings that were part of the project, there was no master plan. Between the city's financial crisis and the war of the unions, the fractious issue of public housing, a problem that had to be dealt with politically, not socially, had received little more than a reactive response from either Rendell or Cohen. But public housing was also one of those issues that could not be deflated or even well camouflaged. It would inevitably explode again during the course of Rendell's term, not just once but several times.

Linda didn't seem terribly surprised by the lack of a direct response to her memo. Rendell and Cohen were, after all, busy men running a government that was still in chaos. And beyond the immediate crises that greeted them every day, there was always something to attend to, given the very nature of politics—a request for zoo tickets, a request for a transfer for a favored policeman, or the ire of a major fund-raiser who called Rendell on his private line and without even bothering to say hello jumped all over the mayor for taking city legal work away from a certain local law firm; rather than hang up or tell the fund-raiser that his private line was for emergencies, the mayor hemmed and hawed and became visibly nervous, as if this were a dire emergency, and gave repeated assurances that the law firm would be made whole.

The house the Morrisons rented in Bala Cynwyd, a well-heeled suburb just beyond the western border of the city, had a short-term lease; they would stay there long enough to figure out what to do next. As a place to live temporarily, Bala Cynwyd was perfectly acceptable. The home was near public transportation. It was leafy and quiet. Given what they had been through in Queen Village, it was both an escape and a refuge. They were thankful for that, but Bala Cynwyd was absent even the faintest signs of sidewalk ballet. "It's very quiet," said Linda one wintry day in 1993. "It's very peaceful. It's green, and I hate it. You walk down the street, and you don't see one thing that's interesting." But it wasn't fair to blame Bala

Cynwyd for that. After all, it was exactly what it wanted to be. "It's a suburb."

Once a week she and her husband talked about moving back into the city—if they could find a neighborhood that wouldn't subject them to the same horrible surprises that had unfolded in Queen Village. Certainly if Linda was going to continue working for the city, she needed to live in the city anyway. But the decision was wrenching, and the trade-offs in both directions were enormous—the deadened placidity of the suburbs with its assurance of peace versus the ever changing texture of the city, where fear could gloss over everything. "We've been so burned [by living in the city]," Linda admitted that wintry day in 1993. "It's like having a love affair. You're afraid to go back into it."

And yet despite all that Linda Morrison had been through, she also knew that she was still very much in love.

TEN

Getting Paid

I

GOOD MORNING, LADIES AND GENTLEMEN OF THE JURY . . .

On a cold Thursday morning at the end of January in 1993, around the time Linda Morrison wondered whether there was still a place in the city where one could feel safe, Assistant District Attorney Mike McGovern was back in that space between the rows of spectators and the judge's bench, spinning a new story of his city to a mostly empty courtroom.

He had moved to a courtroom on the sixth floor of City Hall to tell the story of *Commonwealth v. Carlton Bennett and Giovanni Reed,* the story of a twenty-one-year-old and an eighteen-year-old accused of being part of a trio that had robbed and killed a twenty-two-year-old man. The third member of the trio, Dwayne Bennett, had pleaded guilty to first-degree murder the day before.

A heater hissed in the corner, and the windows were speckled with grime, and the courtroom seemed weighted down by something beyond the creep of age. Each gesture—the practiced innocence of the defendants with their heads turned toward the floor, the shrug of a police officer in a chair waiting to testify, the judge taking off his glasses and rubbing his eyes, the court-appointed defense attorneys earnestly scrutinizing pictures of the crime scene—had been scripted and played out a thousand times before.

McGovern refused to succumb to the stupor. He placed his hands gently on the front railing of the jury box as he gave his opening statement, lifting himself up on the balls of his feet for emphasis. He was calm and clear, letting the story he was reciting do most of the emotional work for him. He likened his opening statements to a jury to telling his children a story, but with one major difference: when he told his children a story, he wanted to soothe them and help them go to sleep; when he told these particular listeners this story, he wanted them to go home with nightmares.

THERE WAS A YOUNG MAN BY THE NAME OF ROBERT JANKE. HE WAS TWENTY-TWO YEARS OLD. HE LIVED IN CONNECTICUT. HE GRADU-ATED FROM THE UNIVERSITY OF CONNECTICUT IN 1991 AND DECIDED TO COME TO PHILADELPHIA TO GO TO THE UNIVERSITY OF PENNSYL-VANIA MEDICAL SCHOOL TO BE A DOCTOR. HE WASN'T VERY FAMIL-IAR WITH PHILADELPHIA. HE WAS NEW TO THE TOWN, EAGER ABOUT HIS FUTURE.

Virtually unheard of for a lawyer, McGovern could boast of having a job that was both professionally and personally satisfying. But it also exacted a price. The intensity of what he saw, the "heart of darkness" as he called it, had made him appreciate the preciousness of life more than ever. As a prosecutor in the city, he knew how ephemeral life could be, how an innocent act, something incidental and random, could result in something tragic. "In a way, you appreciate the beauty of life more," he said once. "In a terrible way, you are part of a select group of people who have a full understanding of man's inhumanity to man and the depths of that cruelty."

THERE ARE SIX MEN WALKING AROUND CENTER CITY WITH GUNS LOOKING TO ROB PEOPLE. TWO OF THEM ARE IN THIS COURTROOM

RIGHT NOW. GIOVANNI REED IN THE BLACK SHIRT AND CARLTON
BENNETT IN THE STRIPED SHIRT. THEY'RE LOOKING FOR A VICTIM;
THEY ARE LOOKING FOR PREY, SOMEONE, AS THEIR EXPRESSION IS "TO
GET PAID."

Earlier that fall, McGovern had traveled nearly two hundred miles up-
state on a special assignment, to assist the Tioga County prosecutor's office in a double homicide in which a husband and wife had been killed over
a dispute involving payment for marijuana. In the city, the case would have
been routine, relegated to a few paragraphs in the newspapers and hardly
high profile. But in Tioga County, it was the first murder in nearly a
decade. The district attorney was newly elected and scared of losing, and
McGovern couldn't help but feel a little bit like Gary Cooper in *High
Noon,* riding into the little town of Wellsboro to "slam-dunk" one of the
defendants accused of the murders. Tioga County is on the New York border and home of the Grand Canyon area of Pennsylvania. McGovern liked
the open space, and he was fascinated by the degree to which the ritual of
deer hunting influenced the local culture. As he drank in the brilliant fo-
liage and traveled in a leisurely arc from Bellefonte to Wellsboro, he became intrigued by the idea of living in such a region. He wasn't sure he
could do it, but at least he got a taste of what it would be like to live somewhere so different from what he was used to. Whether he intended it or not,
he was also forced to confront the emotional toll of his job, the kind of person that he had to be in order to do what he did.

He approached the murder case in Tioga County the same way he approached a murder case in Philadelphia. His outrage over the crime, his
hardened nastiness in regard to the defendant, filled the gentle wings of the
courthouse. The Tioga County district attorney watched McGovern in admiration and fascination. When a jury returned a verdict of first-degree
murder, he told McGovern that justice had been served, but he thought the
defendant pathetic and dim-witted, drawn into the crime by a manipulative
codefendant. Although he admired McGovern's aggressiveness, he wasn't
sure he could replicate it.

"You're nasty, and I think your aggressiveness may be important to
winning this trial, but you can have it because it takes too much out of
you," the district attorney told him at one point.

"I was sent here because you need a nasty guy," McGovern countered,
and he pointed to the pictures of the crime scene, in which two people had

been left dead. "Look at these pictures. Four people were in here, two people left alive, and two people were in this condition. Anybody who's capable of leaving a home in this condition is disgusting and evil."

The trail of carnage, especially in sleepy Tioga County, was beyond belief—the husband shot dead first, and then his pregnant wife, first in the meat of the arm and then in the head as she was fleeing for her life.

But when McGovern came back to the cramped quarters of his office on the seventh floor of the district attorney's office, brown case files piled upon brown case files, white pages of transcripts upon white pages of transcripts, each containing a tale of murder worse than the next, he thought about the conversation he had had in Tioga County, and there were no easy answers. "I know I'm good at what I do," he said. "You want to be a whole person, but you wonder if you've lost pieces of yourself." He had no innocence about the city anymore—how could he, in a world mediated by murder?—and he couldn't help but wonder whether he might be different if he left the district attorney's office and did something else. "Do you regain some of your lost innocence? Do you regain some of the desensitized nerve endings that have been covered over with rhinoceros plating? Do they regenerate?

"Is it like a guy smoking cigarettes? Once you quit, do your lungs become pink again?"

He had been at a golf tournament when a member of his foursome brought up a murder case that McGovern was prosecuting. He began to talk about it, and another member asked him to stop. "That was the first person I've met in a long time who was not dying to talk about murder," said McGovern. "Anywhere else I go, it's 'Mike, tell me a nightmare.' "

Nearly 80 percent of the defendants he tried were black, and given the absolute zealousness with which he performed his job—each act of violence taken as a personal affront—there were some who wondered whether his gusto was born of something other than professional dedication. "You really like putting young nigger boys in the electric chair, don't you?" a defense attorney once asked him after a guilty verdict.

"No," said McGovern, bristling at the insult, "but I wouldn't mind putting you in the electric chair."

Far from liking it, he couldn't help but be disturbed by the endless cycle of it. "When you see young black men routinely capable of numbing hostility, you just say to yourself, 'Why is this?' "

The temptation to be racist was enormous, but he fought it, and he also refused to temper his style because to do so would have been the antithesis of who he was and why he did what he did, and he knew no other way than the full-throttle way—to walk into that courtroom as if it were the penultimate arena in which questions of life and death were settled. "I'm not out to get a notch on my belt," he said. "If they're not guilty, I can live with the verdict." But the converse of that—that a guilty man might go free, might walk out of the arena of that courtroom and go home and pull a beer out of the fridge and a cigarette out of his breast pocket and lay his feet up on the sofa and give a little self-satisfied laugh—gnawed at him.

He thought about all these issues, and considering the financial constraints he would labor under as long as he worked for the city, he increasingly began to think that he had no choice but to leave. At the $70,000 mark, his salary had gone as high as it was going to go, and with a thirteen-year-old daughter on her way to Catholic high school the following fall at a cost of roughly $6,000, he needed either to make more money or to take out a second mortgage on his house. "Am I leaving for the wrong reasons?" he asked. "Should I stay? I'm really good at what I do. What happens if the next case comes to someone who is not as good as me, and he gets mismatched, and the guy walks?"

But in the arena of Courtroom 653, in the case of *Commonwealth v. Carlton Bennett and Giovanni Reed,* there wasn't the remotest scent of self-doubt.

You are going to find out that Robert Janke died.

After Robert Janke's graduation from the University of Connecticut, where he was on the dean's list, he entered a postbaccalaureate program at Penn in the summer of 1991 in preparation for medical school. "I simply ask for a chance, and promise that you won't be disappointed," he had written in his application for admission. He had been an Eagle Scout, an altar boy, and a newsboy. He had been the chairman of the local drive for the Cystic Fibrosis Foundation. He had worked with the severely retarded at a local hospital. He was one of those kids who seemed too good to be true because he was too good to be true, with a rare sense of duty.

He goes to his apartment, no way of getting in. He goes to a pay phone. He gets on the pay phone. He is stranded at Sev-

ENTEENTH AND SOUTH IN THE MIDDLE OF THE NIGHT, ON A PAY
PHONE AT THE CORNER.

There were six altogether when they started out from their homes at
4:00 A.M., Dwayne and Carlton and Gee and Tyrone and Richard and
Wanny. They had three guns between them, passing them back and forth
like a child's toys so that each would get the thrill of feeling the barrel
tucked inside their waistband. Dwayne Bennett, a twenty-year-old unemployed high school dropout, was the one most keen on "getting paid,"
street vernacular for robbing someone, or what McGovern described as the
urban equivalent of a hunter roaming for deer. They walked up from Fif-
teenth Street, then over to Sixteenth and Fitzwater, then up to Sixteenth
and JFK in the shadow of City Hall.

They sat for a little bit in the concrete park on JFK, and Tyrone went to
use a pay phone to call his girlfriend and let her know what he was up to
at 4:30 A.M., in case she was wondering. He told her who he was running
with, and she said to him, "You don't need to be hanging with them, you're
only going to be getting in trouble." They hung out at the park for a little
bit longer, but they didn't find any deer, so they went over to the Wawa
Food Market on Eighteenth and JFK, then down Eighteenth to Market, and
then down Eighteenth toward Chestnut.

Dwayne thought about robbing a cab driver he saw and spoke to him for
a little bit and asked him what time it was, but his instincts advised him
against it. They walked over to Rittenhouse Square, and Dwayne was
walking around the square looking really hard to get paid, but it was right
around 5:00 A.M. now, and he wasn't finding anyone, and he was getting
frustrated, and he said *"fuck it"* in a loud enough voice that several others
heard it. They split up, Tyrone and Richard and Wanny in one group,
Dwayne Bennett and Carlton Bennett and Gee—Giovanni—Reed, in the
other. Dwayne and Carlton and Giovanni walked down Eighteenth to
Eighteenth and Lombard, over by Graduate Hospital, then cut down Lombard to Seventeenth, and then started walking down Seventeenth over to
South on their way home. The sun was coming up over the dark brown of
the row houses, and they sure didn't have a lot to show for it. That's when
they saw the white guy in front of Ray's Cleaners using the pay phone, and
Dwayne, knowing he had found what he was looking for, wasn't saying
"fuck it" anymore but realized he had finally found his deer. He and Carlton and Giovanni watched as the white guy got off the phone and settled

on the steps of an abandoned grocery at Seventeenth and South, apparently waiting for someone.

DWAYNE BENNETT PRODUCED A HANDGUN AND BEGAN BRANDISH-ING IT, POKING IT IN MR. JANKE'S FACE, HIS CHEST; MR. GIOVANNI REED AND MR. CARLTON BENNETT STOOD ON EITHER SIDE.

Robert Janke had finished his shift at T.G.I. Friday's on Ben Franklin Parkway at 2:00 A.M. He had gone to a party at Ninth and Spruce, then to an after-hours hall on the Penn campus at Thirty-ninth and Chestnut. A friend named Liz Mahoney had offered him a ride home around 5:30 A.M., and he had gladly taken it. She had dropped him off at his apartment on Seventeenth, right near the corner of Seventeenth and South, and almost as soon as she left, he realized that he had done something stupid: he had left the gym bag containing his keys in the trunk of her car.

He found a pay phone in front of Ray's Cleaners, called the hall where they had been, and left Liz a message that he needed his keys. Then he sat in front of the abandoned grocery store at Seventeenth and South to wait for her.

"MOVE IT, MOTHERFUCKER, MOVE IT!"

Dwayne and Carlton and Gee had the deer in their sights now, sitting on the steps of that abandoned grocery store. Gee whipped out his gun, a .38 long, and cocked it. Dwayne grabbed Janke by the shirt and took the gun. Carlton was armed too, with a .22 short, a silver revolver with a white handle. Dwayne poked Janke in the back with the .38, and Carlton and Giovanni locked their arms around him and held him by the wrists as they directed him down Seventeenth toward Kater.

TWO MEN HELD HIM IN ON EITHER SIDE WHILE THE THIRD MAN WALKED AROUND CUSSING AT HIM, DERIDING HIM, SCARING HIM TO DEATH, POINTING THE GUN, SAYING "WHAT HAVE YOU GOT? WHAT HAVE YOU GOT? GIVE IT UP."

Dwayne got ahold of Robert Janke's wallet and saw there was only five bucks in it.

"I know you got more than that in there," he said.

"No, no," Janke pleaded. "I don't have any money. I don't have any money."

Dwayne could see Janke was scared. There was some brief discussion between him and Carlton about what to do with him now that he could identify them. Carlton suggested that Dwayne cap him. It seemed like a good idea. Why not?

He held the gun a little bit to the back of the right temple, flush against the head, like an execution. There was no resistance.

As Mr. Giovanni Reed stood on one side and Mr. Carlton Bennett on the other side, Mr. Dwayne Bennett walked behind Robert Janke, his face facing toward him, took the gun, and put it up to Mr. Janke's right temple, right up against his head, thirty-eight-caliber gun, and pulled the trigger.

Dwayne Bennett felt the body of the hunted go limp, and he gently laid it to the ground before he and Giovanni and Carlton ran away, back into the maw of the neighborhood. There was some inevitable discussion of the murder, and Dwayne, when he wasn't telling people to shut up about it, also seemed irritated by the reactions of others, particularly those who asked whether it weighed on his conscience, placing the rounded edge of that .38 barrel flush against the flesh of the temple so that it was touching like the soft graze of a kiss, squeezing on the trigger as the sun was coming up.

"I shot him. So what?" he said. And if the police got wind of it and started asking questions about it, Dwayne said he would tell them what happened without a lawyer, which is exactly what he did. He voluntarily gave himself up to the police a week later. He made no attempt to mitigate the crime or even lie about it, as if he really didn't care what happened to him. A life on the streets with no job and no future, or a life in prison—what exactly was the better choice? In his statement to the homicide detectives, he expressed what for him, at least, might have been the equivalent of a guilty conscience: "I only shot him once."

Carlton Bennett was arrested the same day as Dwayne Bennett, and Giovanni Reed two days after that. A day before his scheduled trial in January 1993, Dwayne pleaded guilty to first-degree murder. That left Carlton Bennett and Giovanni Reed as the remaining defendants. McGovern offered them twenty-five to fifty for a plea, but they said no and decided to take their chances and watched intently as McGovern told his story step by step and phrase by phrase in that oversize courtroom with its grimy windows and high ceiling, asking the jury to conclude, as he long ago had concluded, what the outcome of this trial should be.

I ASK YOU TO COME INTO THE TRIAL AND RENDER YOUR OATH AND RENDER A VERDICT ACCORDING TO THE EVIDENCE, SO HELP YOU GOD, AND I ASK YOU TO RENDER THE VERDICT THAT JUSTICE DEMANDS, AND THAT IS TO FIND THESE TWO YOUNG MEN GUILTY OF MURDER.

He guided them carefully through an array of witnesses, some favorable, some not so favorable, particularly in terms of pinpointing the exact location of Carlton Bennett and Giovanni Reed in relation to the victim. Two of those who testified had been part of the group of six that had all gone out together that August night, and their testimony, while not necessarily favorable to the defendants, lacked precision. Richard King wasn't in the group that had confronted Janke, but he had been nearby, and he had seen something. He said the two defendants were inches away from Janke, but then on cross-examination, he said they were several feet away. Tyrone Mackey had seen something as well. When McGovern prepped him at lunch right before he was to take the witness stand, he completely reversed his original statement to the police and now said the defendants had been some fifteen feet away from the victim. McGovern got into Mackey's face and stayed there with that scary and schizophrenic street look and warned him that he would be under oath and he had better tell the truth.

"I don't get paid enough to get fooled by clowns," he said back in the courtroom, as if he had just been thrown a brushback by some punk minor league pitcher. When Mackey testified, he dropped the fifteen-foot assertion and said the two defendants had been close to Janke that night.

McGovern's neck got stiff and started to throb, and the more he looked at the jury, the more it began to worry him, particularly since Philadelphia juries by their nature were wild and unpredictable. But he had the testimony of a nurse named Lorraine Hill, who had witnessed the killing from across the street while on her way to work and was resolute in her recollection that Carlton Bennett and Giovanni Reed had locked their arms in Janke's own arms and moved him down the path of his execution.

McGovern ended his presentation of the evidence with testimony from the assistant medical examiner. He did it on purpose, to remind the jury that ultimately this case wasn't about Carlton Bennett or Giovanni Reed but about the person who had died that night.

The assistant medical examiner spoke in the cold flatness of a trained professional, reducing the once vibrant life of Robert Janke to a series of forensic findings, anatomical blips across a report:

SIX FOOT THREE INCHES TALL, WEIGHT 179 POUNDS, SINGLE WHITE MALE, 22 YEARS OLD, DIED 8-11-91 AT JEFFERSON HOSPITAL AT 1:35 P.M. OF GUNSHOT WOUND OF THE RIGHT TEMPLE, BLACK POW-DER BURNS ON THE FACE, A PORTION OF BONE SHOT OUT OF THE HEAD, THE PATH OF THE BULLET THROUGH THE SOFT TISSUE AND SKULL OF THE RIGHT TEMPLE, THE RIGHT FRONTAL-TEMPORAL-PARIETAL BRAIN, THE ORBITAL PLATE, AND THEN EXITING FROM THE MEDIAL ASPECT OF THE ORBIT OF THE LEFT EYE.

McGovern asked the assistant medical examiner what the chances of survival were from an injury such as this.

"His chances of survival from this wound were zero."

"Thank you very much."

After five days, the jurors retired to deliberate. They reached a verdict in two hours and fifty minutes. "Should I bring my crying towel?" asked McGovern over the phone when he was told that the jury had come in. He ran his fingers through his hair, and as he threw on his coat and got ready to walk back over to the court from his office, he was supremely confident that the jury would convict on robbery and conspiracy charges. But he wasn't nearly so certain about the charges of murder, and he knew they hinged on whether or not the jury had believed Lorraine Hill. "There is enough humility in me that says, 'You should win, McGovern.' I hate losing so much that it scares the shit out of me. Those kids held him and watched the expression on his face when he was being tor-tured and tormented like taking the wings off a fly before he was killed. Are they going to be out hanging around tomorrow?" But he wasn't about to convey such doubt publicly. As word passed through the tiny cubicles of the homicide wing of the district attorney's office that a verdict in the Janke case had been reached, McGovern's Port Richmond bravado was as tight as a guitar string. "When I lose, I'll let you know, because that's news."

McGovern walked back to court. He listened as the judge asked the fore-man to rise and read the verdict.

Carlton Bennett, fat and slow-footed, wearing the same green pants and green striped shirt that he had worn the first day of the trial, went first.

On the charge of robbery:

Guilty.

On the charge of criminal conspiracy:

Guilty.

On the charge of second-degree murder:

Guilty.

Giovanni Reed, all of sixteen years old at the time of the killing, went next.

Guilty of robbery.

Guilty of criminal conspiracy.

Guilty of second-degree murder.

Mike McGovern knew that he was in a perpetual tug-of-war over living in the city, the pull of loving it endlessly tempered and tested by the financial rigors of a city wage tax and tuition for private schools. He knew that barring some miracle, he would be switching jobs in several months. But at the moment of those guilty verdicts and the sentence of life that they carried, it was hard for him to think of any feeling better than this one. Standing in that cavernous courtroom, accepting congratulations, he did what he always did after a trial: he marked the file, writing the word *guilty* next to the charges with a flourish.

"See how neat and pretty it is," he said as he left the courtroom and stepped outside into the yellowish haze of the hallway.

But for some, even those with a personal stake in the outcome, the sight of those fat and slow-footed defendants going off to prison for the rest of their lives wasn't a source of celebration but was a source of sorrow. "There are no winners," said Robert Janke's aunt, Lucinda Janke, when a reporter asked her for her reactions to the verdict. "Four young men will never be the same. Bobby was killed, and three others will spend their lives in prison without parole. I'm satisfied the system worked, but I wish I weren't here. It's just very sad."

There would never be any sufficient explanation of why Dwayne Bennett had pulled the trigger that August day as the sun was coming up. McGovern described him as a great white shark, with those deadened eyes that made no differentiation between right and wrong, good and evil. His attitude seemed unfathomable, unless perhaps you were part of the same environment of vacant houses and public high-rises and dishwater jobs that had yielded him. Then perhaps it was possible if not to understand the motivations of Dwayne Bennett, at least to see the effects of hopelessness on others. McGovern got on the narrow elevator, deservedly flush with his success. He pressed the button for the ground floor and rode past the second floor, past the mayor's office, where all that same week in January 1993 a pivotal institution of the city—one ostensibly designed to serve those in the greatest need, those who were black and poor and shared backgrounds similar to Dwayne Bennett and Carlton Bennett and Giovanni Reed without committing crimes—was in its usual throes of politically engineered chaos.

II

In a political career stretching back to the mid-1970s, it was an astounding concession for Ed Rendell to make. But never in his life, not during two terms as district attorney, not in his runs for governor and mayor, had he ever heard a yelling match between two public officials as long as this one.

Ostensibly the screaming had to do with the future of public housing in the city and the age-old mess of the agency in charge of it, the Philadelphia Housing Authority, but it really had to do with the things that invariably guided such institutions—political ego, contradictory agendas, and the bottomless differences of race. Lucien Blackwell, formerly a city councilman and now a congressman, was the screamer. Michael Smerconish, regional administrator for the federal Department of Housing and Urban Development, who had jurisdiction over the Philadelphia Housing Authority, was the screamee. But midway through the session, roles reversed. The federal official became screamer. The congressman became screamee. And then at a certain point, they said to hell with it and became simultaneous screamers, both men screaming so loud, with such sustained intensity, that not a word of what they said was remotely decipherable.

It was a comical, slightly pathetic sight, these two grown men yelling at the top of their lungs, not even directly at each other but through the wonders of a speaker phone, since the federal official was in the mayor's office and the congressman more than a hundred miles away, in Washington. It made the whole spectacle even more surreal, the federal official in his crisp white shirt and presidential cuff links, yelling into a little plastic box on top of the desk in the mayor's office as if it were alive, the congressman yelling back with such force and velocity that the little plastic box seemed to skitter across the desk every time the scratchy racket of his voice sounded.

"It's amazing we get anything done," Rendell whispered to a visitor midway through, and then he just shook his head and rolled his eyes and stared rather forlornly at the little plastic box, as if it were hard to believe that something so small, which never worked particularly well during a *local call,* could be responsible for so much noise *long-distance.* But in the long and sorry history of the Philadelphia Housing Authority, which controlled more than twenty-two thousand units of public housing in the city and served as landlord to more than eighty thousand tenants, the interchange between the federal official and the congressman came as close as anything to clear and constructive dialogue.

Public housing once provided safe, comfortable housing for people in need. Today high-rise public housing is a threat to the health and safety of its inhabitants and a cause of blight in its host communities.

To undo the tragic deterioration of these communities requires that we face up to the harsh realities of the present situation and adopt bold new initiatives to end the cruel and inhuman conditions that exist.

No one who knew anything at all about public housing in the city would have taken much issue with that statement. It was a succinct summation of what public housing had become in the city, and other than the fact that it had been written *fourteen years earlier,* in 1979, it was still hard to quibble with, except perhaps that its depiction had proved overly optimistic. By the early 1980s, roughly 10 percent of the housing authority's units stood vacant, even though more than twelve thousand families were on the authority's waiting list. By 1992, the vacancy rate at the housing authority, the fourth largest in the country, had climbed to 20 percent while the waiting list had grown to at least thirteen thousand applicants. The Department of Housing and Urban Development, which oversees public housing in the country, had set a standard of thirty days in which to reoccupy a vacant unit. The Philadelphia Housing Authority, not content with that, had set a standard in its own handbook of seven working days. But the reality turned out to be slightly longer than that, somewhere close to sixteen hundred days, or approximately four and a half years.

In his first year of office, Rendell had concentrated on the city's financial condition and the union negotiations, but public housing had inserted itself on his agenda anyway, without waiting for an appointment. In February of 1992, Smerconish, in his capacity as HUD's regional administrator and eager to establish himself as bold and aggressive, froze millions in federal funds earmarked for the rebuilding of Southwark, the high-rise public-housing project that had played such a pivotal role in driving Linda Morrison out of Queen Village.

About a month after that, a draft audit of the housing authority by HUD showed conditions that were shocking even to those who had already assumed the worst: in a random inspection of eighty-seven units, eighty-six had failed HUD's standards for safe and sanitary housing. Each unit inspected averaged eleven violations. Infestations of roaches were common. So were tub and sink faucets that would not shut off. One unit had twenty-nine violations, including a rotting subfloor in the kitchen, a second-floor bedroom ceiling that had caved in because of leaks in the plumbing, and large holes in the living room walls. The inspectors doing the audit declared the unit uninhabitable, but because of the limited availability of decent housing in the city, that wasn't the case. Instead, a household of five slept in one bedroom.

The audit presumably did not include units that the mayor himself talked about, where sewage and excrement came through the sink. Nor did it include unit 3C of the Cambridge Plaza high-rise on North Tenth Street, where the radiators raged with such heat 365 days a year that Gaynell Gillespie could put a pot of water on top of them and literally boil eggs. Gaynell lived in the three-bedroom unit with her seven children. She was well aware of the dangers of those radiators, and over and over again she asked maintenance people to come and fix them before something horrible happened.

Six of her children were old enough to stay away from them; they understood why the windows were open and why the fans were blowing in the dead of winter, but her youngest child, Adam, was too young to grasp such incongruities. He was a little bit over a year old, just learning how to walk, and, when she heard his screams from one of the bedrooms and smelled the odor of sizzling hair, she knew what had happened. She ran to the bedroom and grabbed him, but it was too late—his head was jammed between the radiator and the control knob. There was a burn in an oblong shape from right below the earlobe to the jawline, and whole pieces of his skin looked as if they had been ripped off. She prayed and she called 911, and when the doctor at the hospital fixed him up, he told Gaynell Gillespie that if she had found her son a second later, he would have been glued to that radiator, the flesh of the baby's skin melded with a boiling chunk of metal in a public-housing high-rise in the city. She spoke with other tenants, and they too had stories to tell of scaldings, including that of one girl whose lobe had been melted. She once again begged the maintenance people to do something, but, she said, she was told she was lucky to have heat. It was only when she appeared at a public meeting and told her story in the presence of a reporter for the *Inquirer* that something was finally done. "I sat home and waited and waited," she said. "They didn't take it seriously about my baby's face. If they could have been there when he screamed."

Maintenance workers put wrappers of insulation around the pipes and new plastic knobs on the radiators, but the one in the bedroom that had burned her son still raged, and in the dead of winter she still had a fan on to stifle the heat.

As awful as it was, her story didn't appear to be isolated, for the audit depicted an institution that had, at the very least, a lackadaisical attitude toward those it was supposed to serve and, at the very worst, outright contempt for them. Maintenance work orders that should have been completed within a week were still outstanding forty-five days later. Millions of dollars in rent that should have been collected from tenants, thereby solidifying the authority's financial condition, was simply ignored. On the other hand, the audit found that the authority had nearly five hundred more employees than it should have had according to recommended staffing patterns, a strong indication of the degree to which the authority existed not for the housing needs of its tenants but for the patronage needs of local politicians. In one two-year period, while the authority's uncollected rents rose by $2 million and operating reserves declined by $5.4 million, its board saw fit to award bonuses of $82,000 to senior staff members for their performance. The audit did not specify who exactly received the bonuses, and finding out might have proved an unfathomable pursuit anyway, since the authority had no less than forty-nine directors, deputy executive directors, deputy and assistant directors, division directors, and executive assistants.

The HUD audit was as scorching an indictment of a public institution as any in America. The Philadelphia Housing Authority was the ultimate quagmire, drowning those who stepped into it regardless of the purity or the impurity of their intentions. Ed Rendell also knew that this was hardly an issue of public urgency. The eighty thousand tenants who lived in public housing in the city were by and large invisible, holed up inside monoliths of hopelessness, treated with scorn. "The general public doesn't care at all about the housing authority," said Rendell at one point. "Because it serves only poor people, it has no constituency." But with the results of the audit, he knew he had to do something. Michael Smerconish knew it too.

Both knew that the authority provided a perfect Harvard Business School case study of why public institutions fail—because they are guided not by efficiency or accountability but by power, patronage, webs of impenetrable bureaucracy, and racial politics. Both knew that the driving force behind the authority had not been the needs of the tenants but had been the needs of the feudal kingdoms that existed. Both knew that major decisions affecting PHA, particularly those involving personnel, required the OK of certain politicians, as if they were major shareholders of a private corporation with access to an enormous number of proxies. Both knew of the potential for corruption in free-flowing contracts. Both knew the degree to which the question of race swirled through everything, since the vast majority of those living in public housing in the city were black. Both knew, because they were white, that anything they did, regardless of how much managerial sense it made, was likely to be treated with suspicion and contempt and accusations of racism. These ideas, more than mere suspicions, were vividly expressed in a remarkably candid letter that the mayor received from John Paone, the executive director of the housing authority until he left under fire in the spring of 1992.

Under the umbrella of confidentiality, Paone's letter told a sordid tale of the forces that controlled a public institution supported by taxpayers' money, a system of spoils in which three groups—tenant leaders, employees, and politicians—were guided by complete self-interest. The tenant leaders, Paone wrote, formed

> your shadow government. In other words, continue to maintain a plantation society type organization where the tenant groups really ran the show in the developments and kept the peace. In return, they expected certain perks, jobs for relatives and friends, transfers to better developments, trips to conferences etc. I found out early on that you didn't have to have leadership qualities or even abilities to be part of the top management at PHA, you just needed the political savvy to stay on the right side of the tenants and their political allies.

Race, Paone wrote, was used as an effective cudgel:

> Another factor to take into consideration is that 95 percent of all PHA tenants are Afro-American, they have been able to use

racism as a weapon against successive administrations that
have been predominantly white and, thus have been able to
frustrate reform. This is not to say you can't have a white Executive Director, but you must have a minority Board Chairman
and a significant number of minority senior staff members, including a minority Chief of Staff.

The employees of the authority, wrote Paone,

have sought protection from the tenant groups or politicians to
maintain their jobs because they see that the tenant groups and
politicians have power and influence. Their loyalty is to the tenant leaders and to politicians, not the PHA administration. . . .
Over the years, the tenant groups and the tenant leaders have established their own system of patronage and coerced the various PHA administrations to support it.

As for the influence of politicians, Paone was equally blunt.

Let's make no bones about it, PHA has been a political
dumping ground for every inept political crony in this town for
the past twenty-five years. It has served as a retirement home
for former city/state officials and their relatives who needed
some place to go to finish out their careers. No one's hand is
clean here, everyone dumped on PHA; the tenants, the Board,
various city administrations. . . .

In a private meeting in 1992 with Smerconish shortly after the federal
audit was released internally, the mayor framed the authority in a startlingly blunt way: "The two things that have driven PHA over the past
three or four years have been patronage and the black issue. Many of the
blacks [hired] are incompetent. Many of the white contractors absolutely
fuck the tenants and skimp on everything because they know there's no
oversight." Rendell understood the suspicions of black politicians in the
city in regard to whites coming in and trying to run the authority. But incompetence was incompetence regardless of skin color, and in the crisis
seizing the authority, he made it clear that there was no time for racial politics. "All of us have to be conscious of the black issue, but it can't be the
tail that wags the dog."

Shortly after that meeting, in May 1992, the federal government took over the housing authority on the grounds that it was in "flagrant substantial default of its obligation . . . to provide decent, safe, and sanitary dwellings." It was a stunning act, the largest takeover of a public-housing authority in the history of the federal government, and for a one-year period, HUD assumed control of all the authority's functions, including hiring, firing, and daily management. The appointed board that had run the authority in the past was still there, but only in an advisory capacity.

True to what Smerconish and Rendell had spoken about privately, a plan was put into effect to reorganize the authority, fire the worst managers, and hire the best managers available on the basis of merit. But the urgency for change that had seized the authority, based on the idea that an institution sustained by $200 million a year in taxpayers' money had some accountability to those taxpayers, quickly sank in the all too familiar racial flogging that had already made effective management nearly impossible. Tenant leaders claimed that the hiring process was racially biased against blacks, and in January of 1993 the accusations were so intense and furious that a memo was faxed to Cohen listing those who had been hired at the authority as part of the reorganization. The list did not give any insight into their qualifications, what they could do or could not do, their strengths and weaknesses and sources of expertise. Instead, next to each name were two rows: one listed the person's race, and the other listed his or her sex.

It was the issue of race that had set the stage for the memorable exchange between Smerconish and Congressman Blackwell. Tenant leaders in particular were incensed by the firing of two individuals they had supported, so they did what came naturally to them: they ran to the congressman. And the congressman went to the mayor and waved the race card in front of him like a gigantic Fourth of July flag.

"Someone has given the appearance, even inadvertently racial, that we're letting go of Afro-Americans while hiring Caucasians" came Blackwell's squawky voice over the speaker phone. As a result, both he and City Council President Street wanted the hiring process stopped.

Smerconish balked. For more than a decade, every politician in the city had clamored for radical change at the authority, and now that it was happening, why was it necessary to go through this? It wasn't possible to please everyone in a purge such as this, and the process had already been the subject of a federal court challenge and had been deemed fair and reasonable. The two people in question weren't let go because of racism. They were let go because they were no longer found qualified for their jobs, and the person presiding over the process, the special master appointed by HUD to run the authority in the aftermath of the takeover, was himself black. Halting the process, even temporarily, would smack of the political favoritism and meddling that had made the agency such a hopeless morass. In addition, tenant leaders themselves had said repeatedly that the authority needed to be reshaped.

In trying to make his point with Blackwell, Smerconish used the analogy of the person who repeatedly says that it's time to clean up Congress, just as long as his favorite congressman goes unscathed. "Throw the bums out, but not my congressman."

Rendell rolled his eyes. He knew that of all the analogies that could have been uttered at that precise moment, using the infinite variety of words in the English language, this *was* the very worst.

"Why'd you say Congress?" snapped Blackwell over the phone.

The screaming of Blackwell and Smerconish just got louder and louder. Blackwell said that a mistake had been made in letting Smerconish, a Republican appointee under George Bush, stay on now that a Democrat was in the White House.

"I'm not backing off!" screamed Smerconish. *"If you don't believe I deserve to be here, have me terminated!"*

"I know we made a mistake when we asked you to stay on!" the congressman screamed back.

"Any racial charge is not going to get landed on my doorstep!" Smerconish screamed back.

"I'm the reason that he's there! I'm the reason that he's there!" the congressman screamed back.

Ever the conciliator, Rendell suggested that a meeting be held in the city in several days to resolve the hiring dispute. He mentioned the names of those who should be present but omitted Blackwell's.

"Why would you meet with them and not me?" snapped Blackwell. "I'm the congressman!"

Rendell gently said he assumed that Blackwell would be in Washington and therefore unavailable.

Blackwell, still firmly on the side of the tenant leaders, hung up in a huff, and Rendell, initially at least, offered an idea on how to proceed: "My thought is to machine-gun them all."

He said he had every belief that the right decisions had been made in the reorganization process. But in subsequent days, he shifted and ultimately threw his weight behind a moratorium on it. Terrified of creating any fissure in the fragile coalition that he had established with the city's black politicians and aware that one false move could land him a black challenger in 1995, when his term ended, he wavered. And he did the same later in the week when the two finalists for the post of executive director of the authority were interviewed.

From one standpoint, Rendell could understand the threatened feelings of the tenant leaders and the threatened feelings of the black politicians. He knew the history of race in the city, how blacks had been all but disfranchised until the early 1980s, when the city had elected its first black mayor. From another standpoint, he could see the tender cheek of a baby, jagged and permanently scarred by a radiator that never, ever shut off, not in the dead of winter, not in the heat of the summer. He could walk into the Cambridge Plaza high-rise where that baby lived and go past the concrete of the dimly lit lobby, where urine had soaked into the corners. He could feel the chill of riding up an elevator that had become the perfect setting for robberies and walk past the filthy stairwells and the green walls covered with graffiti. He could enter an apartment that was dark and impervious to light and walk into one of the bedrooms and find kids splayed across a bed like winter coats, barely paying attention to a television sitcom, trapped inside because their mother was too scared to let them play outside. He would know he had no choice but to do whatever was necessary regardless of politics, regardless of anything, to help that mother.

The two finalists for the executive director's job had been chosen after a long and exhaustive search. One of them, Benjamin Quattlebaum, was the executive director of the Camden, New Jersey, Housing Authority. The other, David Gilmore, was executive director of the San Francisco Housing Authority. In terms of credentials and experience, Gilmore was clearly the better choice. But the credentials that were not on paper—Gilmore was white and Quattlebaum black—became as much a part of the selection process as anything else, although they were never made part of the public dialogue.

Michael Smerconish had unusual poise for someone his age. Although only thirty, he rarely stammered in front of politicians, and he had held his own in the screaming match with Congressman Blackwell, except that his white dress shirt had turned soggy with sweat. Meeting in private with the mayor to discuss the housing-authority job, he made it clear that Gilmore was a far better candidate, not only in terms of experience but in his ability to handle the rough waters of public-housing politics. But there was also a problem, and that's when he began to stammer a little bit. "The biggest thing against him," he said, and then he paused, as if scanning the mayor's office to make sure no one was hiding behind one of the plants, "he's white. The tenants will go bat shit if it's Gilmore. They can live with Quattlebaum."

Rendell interviewed Gilmore later that afternoon and seemed more sold on him than ever and said the job of executive director was his if he wanted it, regardless of whatever pressure was mounted by black politicians or tenant leaders. "Fuck it," he said. "We just can't be chickens."

Gilmore's tenure in San Francisco had not been unblemished. A HUD audit had questioned whether the authority's self-evaluation had been inflated. But under Gilmore's tenure, the San Francisco Housing Authority had been removed from HUD's infamous troubled list, and the *San Francisco Examiner* noted in an editorial that Gilmore has "brought the troubled agency into the black, he has pared the vacancy rate down to less than 1 percent, helped reduce the crime rate and improved the authority's relationship with the feds."

"It's hard to refute that *Examiner* editorial," Rendell noted, and he also got assurances from several HUD officials in Washington, who promised to say complimentary things about Gilmore if contacted by the local media.

But several days later Rendell wavered once again, in part because of a concern that Gilmore might be too headstrong for his own good, but in larger part because of the politics of race. It was relayed to him that Council President Street was very concerned about his picking a white executive director, given all the recent controversy over the reorganization of the authority and the reaction that tenant leaders would have to such a choice. The mayor's gung-ho endorsement of Gilmore suddenly became lukewarm, and Gilmore, twisting in the wind, withdrew from consideration. That left Quattlebaum, who was deemed too inexperienced for a job as difficult as this one. So that left no one, the agency as fraught with politics and infighting as it had ever been, the lives of the residents continuing to suffer. An interim executive director was chosen, but he was just that, an interim executive director. By the end of March 1993, the housing authority was still in disarray. The vaunted reorganization had ground to a halt, and in the past year the vacancy rate had climbed from 20 to 25 percent.

From the darkness of apartment 3C in Cambridge Plaza, Gaynell Gillespie couldn't begin to sort out all the Byzantine politics of the housing authority. No one could, not even those who worked there. But she intuitively knew what it represented. "To me, the city is goin' haywire," she said.

"The city is goin', I don't know, it's letting down a lot of young people to me. They look at us, they don't respect grown-ups, and why should they?"

The issue of the housing authority would not disappear. In the coming months, Ed Rendell would have to deal with it again, in ways that he had never dreamed of when he took the oath of mayor, and the impulse to run from it would be stronger than ever. But in May of 1993, as a gray and drab winter gave way to a kind and gentle spring, the mayor's focus drifted to other issues.

The circus wasn't coming to town, but the president of the United States was.

ELEVEN

Urban Sacrifice

I

The air transport carrying the president would be on the tarmac of the Philadelphia International Airport in less than an hour, but members of the mayor's staff had already been emotionally depleted by the mercurial changes in plans that were a feature of the Clinton presidency and by the way in which these changes were communicated—by advance people who greeted everyone with frozen smiles of superiority and stiffness.

In the preceding twelve years, Ronald Reagan and George Bush had visited the city on several occasions. They had known where they wanted to go, who should be on the tarmac to greet them when they arrived, who should be in the little row of chairs behind them on the podium when they gave their speeches, which contributors they had to acknowledge to keep the pump primed. For Clinton's staff, the simplest decision became a crisis of indecision, with everyone but the president scurrying about below. The president will go here. No, scratch that. The president will now go here. No, scratch that. No, the president will go back to where you suggested he go in the first place. Start planning for it. And that's final. Until you hear from us otherwise. The president wants this person on the podium. No, forget that person. Well, maybe that person is OK after all. No, maybe not.

By the time of the appointed visit, certain members of the mayor's staff were cursing, swearing, and showing total exasperation with the changing dictates. They were also nervous and excited. After all, a visit by the president, however torturous it was to plan for, was still an important event. Only one member of the mayor's staff rose above the swirl of chaos and seemed oblivious to the Secret Service requirement that the shades in his office be drawn as a security precaution against snipers. He didn't find it the least bit noteworthy when the trained dog sniffed his office for explosive devices. Instead, he sat at his desk, working the phones, reading documents, not looking up at the person who was there for a meeting with him.

"I'll keep talking while you keep not listening," she said.

He still didn't look up.

When Sergeant Buchanico came in afterward and asked whether he was going to the airport to meet the president, his answer was a flat no, as if the very idea of the question—leave his office to greet the president?—were preposterous. Who did the president think he was? The president?

"All I want to do is get some work done," said David Cohen, in the hope that he might be able to take at least one day off during the upcoming Memorial Day weekend. "And it doesn't even have to be contiguous."

Sergeant Buchanico looked at him in understandable puzzlement. What the hell was a contiguous day off? What the hell wasn't a contiguous day off?

"That means a half day Saturday and a half day Sunday."

Buchanico just got up and left. What possible use was there in trying to understand?

* * *

Across the hallway, Mayor Rendell *was* going to the airport to meet the president. It was a matter of protocol, but it was also more important than that. As the motorcade made its way to City Hall, where the president would give a speech, Rendell would have twenty minutes of precious private time in which to bring up the issues that he believed were of the utmost importance to the city and the ways in which the federal government could help realize that agenda. The list was potentially endless, and everybody had an idea of how best to maximize the time. Even if the route of the motorcade had been from Philadelphia, Pennsylvania, to Philadelphia, Mississippi, Rendell could have kept on going. But in the modern era of politics, where photo ops and sound bites fed to the masses set the standard, twenty minutes of private time with the president was a millennium, and the mayor had to be judicious.

The weeks preceding the president's visit had been particularly grim and unremitting, even for the city. The Senate had killed a jobs bill President Clinton had proposed, meaning a loss to the city of as much as $70 million. The failure of the bill in the Senate came in the wake of news that the city had lost 17,700 jobs in the previous year. On top of that, there was a report by the National Association of Realtors that housing prices had dropped more precipitously in the metropolitan area than in any other region of the country in the past year—by 9 percent. And on top of that, there was a report that seven million square feet of office space in Center City was vacant. Ten entire buildings had been mothballed, and the vacancy rate in the downtown area was at its highest in nearly fifteen years.

As if in response to the grim economic news, the city expressed dissatisfaction, not with the intensity of the wrenching days after the death of Robbie Burns in Kensington but in ways that were chilling in their lawlessness. At the beginning of May, on a quiet Sunday, a man named Santiago Pineda, tired of the drug dealers in his neighborhood, tried to chase them from the front of his home on North Eighth and Pike. As a result of this act of protecting his family and his neighborhood, Pineda was ambushed, shot twice, and beaten.

Six days later four juveniles robbed a man over on Torresdale. There was nothing unusual in that, but then, after fighting over who was going to share in the meager spoils, they went back to their victim several minutes later, realized he was intoxicated, and sensed an opportunity: they poured some clear liquid over him, set his hair on fire, and then ran off laughing as the flames quickly spread to his head and shoulders. The coup de grâce—the lighting of the first match—said the police, was administered by a fourteen-year-old.

A day after that, Mother's Day, Rendell spent the bulk of his time in Newark testifying before the federal government's Base Closure and Re-alignment Commission, the same commission that had made the decision to close the navy yard. Rendell was there to fend off yet another potential round of military-installation closures in the city that had been recommended by the Pentagon and would mean the loss of an additional ten thousand jobs. "I understand the need to reduce the [federal] deficit," he told the commission. "In sixteen months, we have eliminated a four-hundred-and-fifty-million-dollar deficit. But the city of Philadelphia will lose more jobs than forty-seven states. This would cut us off at the knees at a time when we're just getting on our feet."

There would be no word on the fate of those jobs until the end of June, but twelve days after Rendell's Mother's Day testimony, the city was told that construction of a proposed $200-million General Services Administration building had been canceled. The news made Rendell livid. Not only would the construction project have been an enormous boon for the moribund building and trades industries, but the cancellation also raised the question of whether the city, beyond the obstacles it already faced, was being willfully pushed closer and closer to a state of impotence. It wasn't a matter of complete extinction because there would always be a downtown. Given the building boom of the 1980s, there would be enough skyscrapers to last until well into the twenty-first century. There would be quaint shops along Walnut and a renaissance of restaurants and the newly constructed Pennsylvania Convention Center and jaunty shuttle buses painted purple to take conventioneers to the city's favored attractions and men and women in uniform cleaning the streets. Mayors everywhere, sensing the changing tide of the economics of cities and seizing on tourism and entertainment dollars from conventioneers and suburbanites as the new solution, had restocked their downtowns so they never looked better. But it was often deceptive, a brocade curtain hiding a crumbling stage set.

Publicly Ed Rendell always exuded hope. Privately he anguished over his ability to effect the massive change needed to resurrect the city. He always wondered whether all anyone could do was supply hope in the way casinos pumped in oxygen to keep weary gamblers awake and stimulated during the wee hours of the morning.

In anticipation of the official opening of the Pennsylvania Convention

Center the following month, the city was planning an eleven-day extravaganza called *Welcome America!* Leading up to Independence Day, it would
be replete with laser shows, fireworks displays, giant hoagies, and visits by
both President Clinton and Vice President Gore. "I feel like the Roman
emperor," Rendell said during a planning session. "I can't give decent city
services. I want to close [city] health centers, and I want to cut back on
[city] library hours, and here I am giving bread and circuses to the people."

II

The mayor arrived at the airport tarmac to await the president, and he was
well aware of the machinations that had taken place in preparation for the
visit, the constant changes in locations and itinerary like something out of
Mission: Impossible. "What a fiasco!" he whispered, but he was in a buoyant mood. Only an hour earlier, shining his shoes at his desk, he had
seemed quite nervous, not about what he was going to say to the president—he seemed quite secure about that—but about what he was going to
say at a wedding he had agreed to officiate at right before meeting the
president. Fortunately the bride had cried in joy, and the mayor of course
had started getting weepy too, just like a damn bridesmaid, and the whole
thing had been beautiful, and as he stood on the hot asphalt waiting for a
personal séance with the most powerful leader in the world, he seemed
positively aglow.

Some of his aides had thought he should push the issue of the navy yard,
pressing the president on what the federal government could do to ease its
transition from a massive defense installation to an industrial and economic center, particularly since word was out that Mercedes was shopping
around for a site for its first U.S. plant. But rather than fog the president's
head with a myriad of issues, Rendell thought it was better to focus on one
issue, the base closures recommended by the Pentagon, which would cost
the city nearly ten thousand jobs.

For the ride from the airport back to the city, he slid into the limo, where
he and the president, as he later put it, "bullshitted" for three or four minutes. Then he spent the remaining seventeen minutes on the base closures.
He pointed out that with the Pentagon's proposal, the city would lose more
jobs than just about any other place in the country. He showed Clinton a
copy of an executive order issued by President Carter, noting that urban
areas should be favored by the federal government in cases of consolida-

tion or relocation. He knew these arguments carried some weight, but not the weight that mattered the most, so he gave Clinton two sets of numbers:

Two point nine, four, and thirty-one.

Nine, twenty-five, and seventy-four.

The numbers seemed cryptic, one of those silly logic games the object of which is to figure out what each set had in common. The first set, Rendell explained, was for Cumberland County, Pennsylvania, where the jobs would go under the proposed relocation and consolidation plan: 2.9 percent was the unemployment rate; 4 percent was the poverty rate; and 31 percent was Clinton's share of the votes in the presidential election. The second set was for Philadelphia: 9 percent was the unemployment rate; 25 percent was the poverty rate; and 74 percent was Clinton's share of the votes in the presidential election.

Clinton laughed.

If there was another politician in the country who would make an appeal to the president this way, it was hard to know who it was.

What Ed Rendell didn't say was that in working so desperately to keep his city afloat, he wasn't simply fighting the effects of a stingy Congress or the effects of the Reagan-Bush years, when the incidence of poverty in America's cities had multiplied. He was also fighting one hundred years of history and federal policy that had willed his city and other cities like it into such a condition that the best he could do, the best any mayor could do, was beg from a speeding motorcade and depend on the strength of his charisma.

III

It was a map, and it lay buried and folded in a musty box of documents in the National Archives in Washington, untouched at this point except by a smattering of scholars driven enough to find it. It was color coded in shades of green and blue and yellow and red, and it was marked with the letters *A, B, C,* and *D* to correspond to the colors. It had held up well, and the colors looked as good now as they had in 1937, when a team of appraisers had spread over the city, quietly doing their work for the federal government. The map had divided the city into about twenty-five different sections, each section delineated by boundary marks, each section given a particular color and grade, depending on the appraisers' determinations.

The map was easy to read, even down to the street names. The appraisers had done their work well. It was hard to believe that in this map, in the careful and deliberate choice of colors and grades for each section of the city, like the inverse of a secret treasure, lay startling evidence of the seeds of the city's destruction.

But it was true, for the map, along with the other documents in that box, provided shocking insights into the reason the American city had seemed destined to fail as far back as the 1930s and the way the federal government, in terms that were blatant, racist, and unsanitized, had aided and abetted that destruction while opening up the floodgates of the suburbs.

> *Location well-protected against encroachment . . .*
> *Lower part of section is threatened with Italian expansion. . . .*
> *Colored forcing way in some spots . . .*
> *Influx of Jewish has discounted values. . . .*
> *High grade Americans. Professional and Executives . . .*

These terse descriptions of Philadelphia had been typed succinctly across the neighborhood survey form, NS Form 8, without a single note of shock or regret. Headings such as "Negro," "Infiltration of," and "Foreign Born" were all part of the standard criteria to determine the level of risk in granting a mortgage. The more "Negro" there was, the more "Infiltration of" there was, the more "Foreign Born" there was, the less chance someone living in a particular neighborhood would get a mortgage.

These survey forms and assessments, which in turn formed the basis for the color-coordinated map of the city, had been prepared by a federal agency called the Home Owners' Loan Corporation. In the plethora of programs started by President Roosevelt in the New Deal era, it was hardly the most noteworthy. But as pointed out by Kenneth T. Jackson in his remarkable book *Crabgrass Frontier,* HOLC ended up affecting every facet of American life, from the future shape of cities to the future shape of suburbs to the blockade that kept minorities from the American dream of home ownership.

Signed into law by Roosevelt in June 1933, HOLC refinanced tens of thousands of mortgages that were in danger of default because of the Depression. But the real value of HOLC, Jackson wrote in his book, a history of the suburbanization of the United States, was the way it "introduced, perfected and proved in practice the feasibility" of the modern mortgage. In the 1920s, a mortgage had an average life of five to ten years and then was subject to renewal. With the advent of HOLC, mortgages were extended to twenty years, and the payments were fully amortized. But as a precaution, the federal agency established exhaustive appraisal procedures to determine which areas of a city or suburb were more suitable for lending than others. Metropolitan areas all over the country were analyzed, including Philadelphia. The resulting maps may have looked clean and almost lovely with their different colors, but they were often brutal in their findings when it came to the future of the cities.

"First Grade" areas, which were marked by the color green and the letter *A*, signified areas of a city that were well planned, virtually free of blacks and what HOLC appraisers referred to as "foreign-born white," and therefore ripe for mortgage funds in the maximum amount available.

"Second Grade" areas, which were marked by the color blue and the letter *B*, signified areas of a city that were still good but were beginning to fade around the edges a little bit. Mortgage lenders in these areas were advised to make loans 10 to 15 percent below the maximum limit.

"Third Grade" areas, which were marked by the color yellow and the letter *C*, were characterized, according to HOLC literature, by "age, obsolescence, and change of style; expiring restrictions or lack of them; infiltration of a lower grade population. . . ." Mortgage lenders in these areas were advised to be very careful in making any loans.

"Fourth Grade" areas, which were marked by the color red and the letter *D*, were characterized by "detrimental influences in a pronounced degree, undesirable population or an infiltration of it." Mortgage lenders in these areas might well refuse to make loans altogether.

For a city like Philadelphia, not only were the HOLC surveys devastating, but they also told an enormous amount about what the federal government privately thought of big cities (the surveys themselves, because of their inflammatory nature, were confidential). Philadelphia had older housing stock to begin with, and HOLC surveyors saw considerable risk in investing in much of it, particularly given what they saw as the combustible elements of blacks and foreign-born whites. Of the thirteen neighborhoods in the Philadelphia metropolitan area that received first-grade, or A, designations, none had a black presence. Only one had a foreign-born presence, but it was "nominal," according to the survey form—as if you could hear the appraisers' sighs of relief. In all, less than 5 percent of the total population of the city received first-grade designations and were therefore adorned with the vaunted color green.

The bulk of the city received fourth-grade designations and was therefore awash in red on the survey map. South Philadelphia, right below the central business district, was painted red. So was North Philadelphia, right above the central business district. So was Kensington, home of the city's greatest manufacturing plants. So was much of West Philadelphia and southwest Philadelphia.

HOLC appraisers had this to say about an area of the city somewhat bloodlessly designated D18, a large swath of South Philadelphia, as an explanation for why it had received the lowest grade and been painted red: "No great demand for property in this section at any time. Many Negro families doubled up. Section has been slowly deteriorating for years. Italians are slowly driving Negroes out." Section D6, in North Philadelphia, was dismissed because of what surveyors listed under "detrimental influences": "Heavy concentration of Negro—properties in poor condition." Section D13, also in North Philadelphia, was painted red not simply because of "nominal Negro population" but also because of "concentration of Jewish in Northern part." Section C14, in West Philadelphia, fared slightly better, receiving not the lowest designation but the second lowest. But appraisers were hardly optimistic since "infiltration of Jewish into area have depressed values." Section C15, in southwest Philadelphia, was considered risky as well, said the surveyors, because of "Negro encroachment from south and east."

If the HOLC appraisers damned the city, they delighted in the suburbs that ringed it, not simply because of the amount of undeveloped land there, but also because of the ethnic and racial purity. Virtually every suburban area that was appraised received a first- or second-grade designation. Rydal and Meadow Brook were praised because of residents the HOLC appraisers termed "high grade Americans." The area comprising Brookline, Oakmont, South Ardmore, and Lanerach received high praise as well because its inhabitants were "all Americans." Under the heading "Favorable Features," the surveyors noted both "good transportation" to the city and "no colored." The areas of Devon, Berwyn, and Dalesford were also praised because of the quality of their so-called Americans. So was Haverford—and Ridley Park, and Rosemont, and Springfield, and Villanova, and Wayne, and Paoli, and Newtown Square, and Lansdowne, and East Lansdowne.

When suburban areas did not fare quite as well in the eyes of the appraisers, the reasons could be traced to the familiar concerns: Roslyn Station and Willow Grove had a "mixed population"; the area comprising Jenkintown, Wyncote, and Glenside had small pockets of "Negro settlements."

The irrevocable legacy of HOLC, Jackson and other historians have noted, lies in its appraisal system and the way in which it was copied and modeled by the greatest tool of housing ever developed, the Federal Housing Administration. By insuring long-term mortgages from private lenders, the FHA made home ownership more accessible than ever. Buoyed by the guarantee of the federal government, lenders were willing to shave more interest points off mortgages than ever before, amortize payments over twenty-five or even thirty years, and require a down payment of only 10 percent. The FHA, founded in 1934, was intended to help revive the nation's dormant housing industry during the New Deal. But the ultimate influence of the FHA and its housing cousin, the Veterans Administration, went far beyond that, making the dream of home ownership available to millions of middle-class Americans, just as long as it was a dream that largely confined itself to the suburbs and not to the older cities.

From its inception, wrote Mark I. Gelfand in *A Nation of Cities,* the FHA "red-lined [a term that presumably came from the color coordinates of the HOLC survey maps] vast areas of the inner cities, refusing to insure mortgages where the neighborhoods were blighted or susceptible to blight. This action practically guaranteed that these districts would deteriorate still further and drag cities down with them."

The FHA took a keen dislike to rental housing, which was predominant in cities. It disliked the construction of multifamily units, which were also predominant in cities, and it discouraged the use of loans for home repair. Its underwriting manual, as one social critic cited by Gelfand put it, "read like a chapter from Hitler's Nuremberg laws." Among some of its more established practices were the issuance of insurance only if steps were taken to minimize adverse influences, racial zoning, and tacit approval of restrictive covenants.

From 1934 to 1972, the percentage of families owning homes in the United States increased from 44 percent to 63 percent. The majority of these families lived in the suburbs and never would have realized the dream of home ownership without the policies of the federal government. The majority of these homeowners weren't born in the suburbs. As census data clearly show, they moved by the millions from cities that had been all but written off by the federal government in terms of the lasting viability of residential investment.

There was something ironic about the seeds of the cities' destruction being planted in the era of the New Deal, since Roosevelt was the first U.S. president to pay any deliberate attention to cities whatsoever. But much of what Roosevelt did was enact entitlement programs and dispense federal aid to keep cities from the brink of collapse and insolvency. He had little direct interest in the social viability of cities and even less love for them, and he did what he did because he needed the urban vote and the influence of urban legislators if he was going to push the New Deal through Congress. Like the vast majority of Americans, he found cities dirty and grimy and far too big for their own good. As he said in a speech in 1937 dedicating the Bonneville Dam in the Pacific Northwest: "Today many people are beginning to realize that there is inherent weakness in cities which become too large for their times and inherent strength in a wider geographical distribution of population."

In the 1950s, despite considerable downtown renewal, ten of the country's fifteen largest municipalities lost population, and the percentage of people living in central cities in metropolitan areas dropped from 59 percent to 51 percent. Since the beginning of the Republic, the '50s marked the first decade in which cities lost a significant share of their population, and this trend would only accelerate. In the age of the automobile, the only physical impediment to the suburbs' domination was an effective way of getting to them from the city, and President Eisenhower took care of that in 1956, with the passage of the Highway Act, which created a forty-one-thousand-mile highway system that eviscerated city after city while making exodus to the suburbs easier than ever. City planners actually welcomed the expressway system because they thought it would hasten the return of shoppers downtown, but they were wrong, underestimating the degree to which Americans would embrace the flat and predictable flow of the suburban shopping mall and the antipathy that Americans have always had for the city, not to mention the degree to which cities were already beginning to buckle.

"More and more of the old cities will show population declines," Professor Raymond Vernon of Harvard had told a Senate subcommittee not in 1989 or 1979 or 1969 but in 1959. "More and more, they will be the repositories of those who are prepared to live in obsolescent housing—the lower income groups and the older citizens of the country."

Vernon predicted a loss of retail jobs as population sagged and a loss of manufacturing jobs as businesses looked for newer and more spacious sites in the suburbs. He also predicted a growth in downtown development because of the desirable location and the desirable address for the elite. Vernon shrewdly predicted that such residential areas as Boston's Back Bay and Philadelphia's Rittenhouse Square and New York's Upper East

Side would thrive and represent city life at its finest. But it was all an illusion. "We must recognize that this kind of activity is limited to a minuscule portion of the old cities and will remain so limited," Vernon told the subcommittee.

Out beyond the central business district, in the endless miles of built-up neighborhoods that some of us call the "grey areas," the rot goes on unchecked.

As Vernon described it, the rot included hundreds of square miles of space filled with "worn-out housing and outmoded factories which promise to be more and more neglected and underused in the decades ahead." Given the magnitude of the problem, the forces of private markets would not be able to stem the rot, Vernon said. Nor would cities themselves, in light of tax bases that were already shrinking. "Some of these city areas, built at high densities for a horse-trolley era, should probably be redesigned for fewer people and more open space. But in how many cities could officials initiate and finance such a move?" The window of opportunity for a reversal was already narrow, and he urged the federal government to do something proactive, to help shape the future destiny of its cities before it was too late and a two-tiered America set in for good.

Richardson Dilworth, the mayor of Philadelphia in 1959, testifying before the same subcommittee on behalf of the U.S. Conference of Mayors, advocated federal assistance, not in the familiar terms of urban aid and entitlement programs, but in something far more lasting and socially meaningful. He argued for the establishment of a single government for each of the nation's metropolitan areas, in which a chief executive would have true jurisdiction not only over the city but also over the suburbs ringing it. Such a form of government, Dilworth felt, would unite the city and its suburbs instead of dividing them along social and racial lines. "We cannot continue to set up one class against another," he said. "That is being done today with the cities against the suburbs. We have to work out some program for the proper allocation of our industry, and . . . every mayor of a big city would feel that actually there should be one government—one local government—for every great metropolitan area and that this hodgepodge of governments creates conflicts, creates an enormous manner of additional problems, and leads to the inefficient, terrible tax burdens and makes it difficult to have any proper development in the area to meet the problems of democracy."

The words of Vernon and Dilworth were prescient and bold. As it turned out, the men were not exaggerating at all. But given the federal attitude that had existed about cities at least as far back as the 1930s, their words were doomed to collect dust on some urban-studies shelf.

With the exception of the popular mythology of small-town girl and small-town boy making it big in the starry glitter of New York, cities had always held a place in American culture that was tenuous at best and reviled at worst. "Enthusiasm for the American city has not been typical or predominant in our intellectual history. Fear has been the more common reaction," wrote Morton and Lucia White in *The Intellectual Versus the City.* "We have no persistent or pervasive tradition of romantic attachment to the city in our literature or in our philosophy, nothing like the Greek attachment to the *polis* or the French writer's affection for Paris." In examining the writings of Jefferson, Hawthorne, Emerson, Thoreau, Melville, and Poe, the Whites found what they called an "anti-urban roar," particularly since American cities, unlike the great capitals of Europe, were first and foremost belching creatures of commerce.

"The city is doomed," said Henry Ford, advancing the antiurban rhetoric. "We shall solve the city problem by leaving the city."

Lewis Mumford, America's great urban and social critic, in his 1938 book, *The Culture of Cities,* described big cities as on the verge of becoming "cemeteries for the dead," built up without any human dimension and only to keep pace with population expansion and industrialization. "Forms of social life that the wisest no longer understood, the more ignorant were prepared to build. Or rather: the ignorant were completely unprepared, but that did not prevent the building," wrote Mumford.

But cities were not simply condemned because they were big or ill tuned for the industrial expansion that had seized them. What *was* wonderful and exciting about them—the spontaneity, the togetherness of community, the creativity that comes from getting along and not getting along, the endless characters populating the streets, the chaos—never found a natural place in the American soul. The frontier spirit that was so intrinsic to the psyche of the country, the creed of individualism and ruggedness and privacy, of staking out your own piece of land and building your own house, hardly lent itself to the culture and spirit of the city. In 1890, when the Census Bureau determined that the western frontier no longer existed, that ideal of individualism was more difficult to satisfy. But the spirit of privacy, of having a separate space, exhibited itself through the patterns of settlement. In Europe, it was the cities that were valued and the suburbs that were devalued. It was the city that was a desirable place to live and the suburbs that were a drab and undesirable place to live. It was the city that was the source of life, and the idea of being close to one another was not rejected but assumed. In the United States, the opposite prevailed. A man could no longer move his family west in search of his own private homestead. But at the very least, he could go ten or fifteen miles in any direction outside the city limits and find his own house on a tidy plot of land.

"Throughout America's history we have always looked fondly on the small town as a well-spring of our moral virtues," said MIT political science professor Robert T. Wood in a speech he delivered in 1959. "We have always believed in the sturdy yeoman. And we have always regarded the city as a real villain in our melodramas of growth as a nation."

If the long-range goal of federal policy has always been to help cities grow and adapt to the ever changing dynamics of their populations, then federal policy has failed despite the goodness of its intentions. But if the long-range goal of federal policy has been the very opposite—to slowly and deliberately defrock cities, diminish their influence, and promote instead a distinct and separate suburban culture based on race and socioeconomics and privacy—then federal policy has been enormously successful.

"The lasting damage done by the national government was that it put its seal of approval on ethnic and racial discrimination and developed policies which had the result of the practical abandonment of large sections of older, industrial cities," wrote Kenneth Jackson. "The financial community saw blighted neighborhoods as physical evidence of the melting-pot mistake. To them, cities were risky because of their heterogeneity, because of their attempt to bring various people together harmoniously. Such mixing, they believed, had but two consequences—the decline of both the human race and of property values."

As Ed Rendell rode in a limousine with the president of the United States, he had a choice of ways in which to reinforce the point of what federal policy had really done to the country's cities. He could point out, as he did so effectively, the inequity of taking jobs away from his own city, in which a quarter of the population was at the poverty level, and relocating them to an area in which 4 percent of the population was at the poverty level. As the motorcade made its way over I-95, he could have pointed to the navy yard and questioned the efficacy of silencing a place with 192 years of history and service to the country. To his left, he could have pointed out the malarial towers of Southwark and told the president how the federal government's answer to housing for the poor in the city, in the aftermath of slum removal (also known as Negro removal), had been these high-rise horrors that were doomed to fail. He could have mused aloud about what it meant that a federal Department of Agriculture had become a Cabinet-level department in 1889 whereas a federal Department of Housing and Urban Development had not been established until 1965.

Or he could have just given the president two maps: one would have been the map prepared by the federal HOLC appraisers in 1937, with its shades of green and blue and yellow and red; the other would have been a map of the city in 1993, similarly colored, showing the areas with the greatest loss of population and vacant housing. Holding the maps side by side, looking at them for several seconds, the president would have discovered what anyone else would have discovered: despite a span of fifty-five years and eleven months, they were virtually the same in terms of what they revealed; they were mirrors of each other.

North Philadelphia had been painted red by the HOLC appraisers, meaning it wasn't worth mortgage investment. In the forty years between 1950 and 1990, North Philadelphia had lost 53 percent of its population; it now had a vacancy rate of 17 percent and contained 11,512 abandoned residential structures. South Philadelphia had been painted the red of obsolescence by the HOLC appraisers. Subsequently, in the forty years between 1950 and 1990, South Philadelphia had lost 45 percent of its population; it now had a vacancy rate of 12 percent and contained 4,185 abandoned residential structures. West Philadelphia had been painted red by the HOLC appraisers. In the forty years between 1950 and 1990, West Philadelphia had lost 33 percent of its population; it now had a vacancy rate of 12 percent and contained 4,118 abandoned structures. Kensington had been painted red by the HOLC appraisers. In the forty years between 1950 and 1990, Kensington had lost 37 percent of its population; it now had a vacancy rate of 10 percent and contained 1,712 abandoned structures. Virtually all the suburbs favored by HOLC, on the other hand, ultimately grew into vibrant and steady residential areas.

Was it fate that had driven these cataclysmic changes? Or were they the result of the prophecies of those federal appraisers, who saw the city as doomed? In the outlines of those two maps, capable of being laid on top of each other like identical twins even though one was old and the other modern, the answer was apparent: by predicting the obsolescence of so much of the city, they had guaranteed it; by promoting the promised land of the suburbs, they had guaranteed it.

IV

In city after city, the changing dynamics of population coupled with a catastrophic loss in the industrial base made urban America more dependent on the federal government than ever before. But in the reality of politics, the reality in which money, public works projects, and certain policies flowed because they meant votes, the influence of cities in the national arena had never counted for less. Cities could deliver votes, but not in the way that had counted in the past, not in the way that had made Roosevelt and Kennedy and Johnson feel something of a political debt to them. Of all the facts that had been written about the 1992 presidential election, the one that was the most startling in what it revealed about the country—and was perhaps focused on the least—was that for the first time ever a majority of the country's voters lived in the suburbs.

In a piece in *The Atlantic Monthly* in July 1992 entitled "The Suburban Century Begins," William Schneider wrote that "urban America is facing extreme economic pressure and the loss of political influence. The cities feel neglected, and with good reason: they are the declining sector of American life."

Schneider's exhaustive analysis showed that in metropolitan areas around the country the huge margins of urban votes that had swept Democrats into office in the past could now be outmatched by the margins of suburban votes: "The urban base doesn't have enough votes anymore. The Democrats have to break into the suburbs by proving that they understand something they have never made an effort to understand in the past— namely, the values and priorities of suburban America."

The clout of America's cities was little more than a whisper in the rant of retirees and health care providers and failed savings and loans and those who wanted their personal and property taxes lowered. The obsession was with the middle class, the same middle class that had begun to empty out of the cities forty years earlier, thanks in no small measure to the incentives of the federal government. Cities weren't ignored in the conference rooms and offices of the nation's lawmakers in Washington. Instead, they were treated with the faint whiff of patronization; the mayors who represented them were patted on the head, promised careful thought on the subject, and then quietly whisked away. The attitude toward cities could be measured in urban policy—more precisely, what urban policy?—and it could be measured in reams of statistical and demographic data showing the mightiness of the suburbs.

For Ed Rendell, it could also be measured in the personal interactions of one day spent in Washington in May 1992. The riots in Los Angeles had occurred less than a month earlier, so there was now an impetus for Rendell and the nation's other big-city mayors to be there, beyond the usual hat-in-hand begging. The window of opportunity for cities had presumably never been opened wider, for the riots had given proof to the mayors' repeated warnings that it was only a matter of time before hopelessness and despair resulted in violence and lawlessness. In the reactive responses of Washington, riots were strangely good for cities; it was no accident that enough political support for a Department of Housing and Urban Development, which had been actively discussed and debated since the late 1950s, materialized only after the 1964 riots.

In a round of private meetings on that day in May, Rendell came face-to-face with the men who moved Washington, or who at least tried to move it despite the perpetual gridlock that now defined it—Bradley, Cranston, Dole, Danforth, Durenberger, Kasten, Kerry, Lautenberg, Moynihan, Mitchell. Just as important, he came face-to-face with the men behind the men, the chiefs of staff and deputy chiefs of staff who knew how to drive and push policy. He also came face-to-face with other big-city mayors—Ray Flynn of Boston, David Dinkins of New York, Maynard Jackson of Atlanta, among others. Without the media there to tamp the dialogue into meaningless pabulum, the talk was direct and unadulterated.

Ray Flynn talked about an altercation that had recently taken place at a Boston church in the aftermath of a drive-by shooting. Upset by the killing, nine gang leaders had paid their condolences by interrupting the funeral and stabbing one of the friends of the deceased. Despite a wave of national publicity, the city had remained calm. "We kept the lid on things," said Flynn, speaking with the humility of relief. "The business community congratulated us. I don't know how the hell we did it. Just by holding people's hands every day." But for how long could Boston escape? For how long could any city escape?

"Cities are beginning to come apart at the seams," said Flynn. "And it's not just Los Angeles. It could happen in Boston, Chicago, Philadelphia—any city. We don't want to talk about it, but it's evident."

"We use the term *underclass,*" said Jackson of Atlanta. "Under who? Under what? These are Americans digging into the garbage cans of our streets, living in the viaducts of our tunnels. I'm not just trying to get across the reality. I'm trying to get across the urgency. I don't think we have time to play around with this one. The issue is not, Can we keep the lid on? The issue is, When will the lid come off?"

"How in the hell can the Congress be talking about twenty-four, twenty-five billion dollars of aid in the Soviet Union and just about every other place in the world while our country is coming apart at the seams?" asked Dinkins.

The shared ground of their rhetoric, coupled with the sympathy of at least some of the senators they encountered, emboldened them. Under the umbrella of the U.S. Conference of Mayors, they agreed to ask for $35 billion in federal aid.

Rendell was hardly silent during the meetings. He too shared the fears of his fellow mayors. But the amount being requested seemed preposterous to him, not because the cities didn't deserve it but because he knew they would never get it, regardless of the impetus of the L.A. riots. He seemed more inclined to listen to the comments of Senator Bob Dole, who, unlike his colleagues, Democrat or Republican, saw little purpose in being obsequious with men who presided over something that the majority of Americans didn't care about. Given the nature of Washington politics, said Dole, there was a chance for the cities to get something, but the window was already closing. "We don't have a very long attention span. In my view, it's going to have to be done in the next thirty days. Even in the two weeks since L.A., there are already voters saying, 'What are we doing this for?' "

Rendell himself favored the tactics of compromise and conciliation that had worked so well in Philadelphia—not what should happen, but what could happen given the political reality. He advocated something far more modest than what the other mayors were asking for: $4 billion to $5 billion in urban aid, precisely what the Bush administration was giving Russia, and an extensive program of urban enterprise zones. The amount wasn't plucked from the air but contained a clever bit of political blackmail: if President Bush wasn't willing to give such aid to cities, then the message was clear that he cared more about Soviet citizens than he did about the citizens of his own country. "The hardest thing to understand is that we're not Washington bashers," said Rendell to Dole's deputy chief of staff, Jim Wittinghill, in the privacy of Dole's Senate office. "The frustration out there and the hopelessness out there is enormous. Of all the emotions out there, lack of hope is the most tantamount. If we don't do something about that, cities are going to burn.

"Everyone tells us there's no money. For S and Ls, we find money. For Russia, we find money. For space stations, we find money. It's very hard for us to hear there's no money."

Aware of how the suburban middle class ruled, he then posed the problem in a startlingly blunt way. "Even if you say, 'Screw the cities,' then you're going to have to pay a ton of police to encircle us and keep us in."

Jim Dyer, the president's deputy assistant for legislative affairs, sounded encouraging when he met with Rendell later that day. "I think there's a consensus between liberals and conservatives that we really ought to be trying to do something here." He actually seemed sympathetic to the plight of the cities, although the bookshelf of the office he was in, which included such notable titles as *The Homosexual Network* and *Abortion Providers,* made the moment seem slightly hollow.

Several weeks later Congress and the president did come to an agreement on an urban-aid package. It wasn't the $35 billion that the U.S. Conference of Mayors believed was necessary, nor was it the far more modest $4 billion to $5 billion advocated by Rendell. It was $1 billion, the majority of which would go to Los Angeles for riot relief and to Chicago for relief from a downtown flood. A $5 billion urban-aid package was then passed by the House over the summer, this one containing fifty enterprise zones. The amount to be spent was to be spread over six years. But as a compromise, only twenty-five of the enterprise zones would actually be in urban areas; the rest would be in rural ones. The bill, said *The New York Times* in an editorial, "spreads money too thinly, in an obvious attempt to buy support." But it didn't matter. Shortly after his loss to Clinton, Bush vetoed the bill.

As America's newest president, Clinton might be different, or he might not be. Rendell was enormously fond of him personally, and the president at least talked about cities as if they had a place somewhere in American society. But Clinton was still subject to the rigors of a Congress focused on the suburban middle class, and although he seemed inclined to test the theory of enterprise zones in a way that was bold and might actually accomplish something, there was no national mandate for a far-reaching urban policy. Cities were not rioting, despite Maynard Jackson's prediction. Their neighborhoods were just continuing to fall apart, the schism between the poor who lived in the cities and the wealthy who lived in the hidden fringes, in palatial hills and gated communities, wider than ever. What a mayor could gain for his city, if he or she could gain anything, seemed largely dependent on the rapport established with the president. Appeals and fiery, impassioned rhetoric about America's moral imperative to save its cities seemed out of touch. To the contrary, the history of federal policy, with the exception of Lyndon Johnson's Great Society days of the middle 1960s, had proved that America felt no such moral imperative whatsoever. The best a mayor could hope for were stopgaps to staunch the bleeding every now and then—a conversation with the president not about saving the city, but about saving something within it.

At the end of June 1993, a month after Rendell made his pitch to the president to save those ten thousand defense jobs, the mayor gathered with a hundred politicians, workers, and reporters around an eighteen-inch television set in the City Hall Reception Room. They were there to witness live on C-SPAN the Base Closure and Realignment Commission's decision on the fate of those jobs, and it was an eerie moment, reminiscent of the one when the commission had decided to eliminate more than seventy-five hundred jobs at the navy yard.

The commission voted, and as had been the case in the fate of the navy yard, the decisions handed down were unanimous:

Naval Aviation Supply Office—2,416 jobs: to remain open.

Defense Industrial Supply Center—1,872 jobs: to remain open.

Naval Air Technical Services Facility—200 jobs: to remain open.

Defense Personnel Support Center—3,956 jobs: to remain open.

Not all 10,000 jobs had been saved, but 8,444 had been, and every politician and every worker who had gathered around that television set knew whom to thank: the mayor of the city, grinning from ear to ear. He had no direct proof, but he was convinced that his pitch to the president had made a significant difference in the outcome of the decision.

In a series of wonderful crescendos, it was yet another wonderful crescendo, another defying of the odds, and in the back of his mind, Ed Rendell wondered whether maybe, just maybe, there *was* a chance for something stunning and everlasting. *Fuck* the federal government. *Fuck* those bureaucrats whose contempt for cities could barely be concealed by the smarmy glint of their smiles. *Fuck* those senators whose idea of urban hardship was a lumpy pillow at the Four Seasons. He and his city would do it alone, if only they got just the slightest push of help every now and then, if only there wasn't some issue they could not control, if only confetti would fall from the sky forever.

TWELVE

The Last Sermon

I

Cohen had gotten there early and, wielding a cellular phone with balletic fluidity, had the situation fully assessed and ready for briefing by the time Rendell arrived.

"Who are the protesters?" asked the mayor as he gazed up the street. He had already seen hundreds of them during his term, but these demonstrators, given the uncharacteristic gentility with which they conducted themselves (one of their signs read, LET THEM EAT CAKE. MARIE ANTOINETTE 1798.), seemed as if they had just been brought up from the minor leagues. They were certainly not of the same caliber as the group of disabled citizens who, upset by the mayor's refusal to spend tens of millions of dollars the city did not have on federally mandated curb cuts, had slithered off their wheelchairs right outside his office and then peed into little bottles they carried with them, thus making their removal by the police not only politically incorrect but rather messy.

"We got FOP [the police union] on the left," said Cohen. "We got homeless right in front. We got Uhuru on the right."

"Who's Uhuru?" asked the mayor.

"No one," said Cohen. "They just want publicity."

The mayor seemed satisfied. Even the protesters were in wonderful alignment today, adding a spot of good-spirited democracy in action to the painstakingly orchestrated proceedings, and off Rendell went to make small talk with Vice President Gore in the waning moments before the dedication of the city's new convention center. To some, like Linda Morrison, it was just a building, and a particularly wasteful building at that, built at a taxpayer cost of $522 million and subsidized by taxpayers in terms of operating costs and bond debt for years to come. But many others were hailing it as a new and wonderful dawn in the life of the city, the cornerstone of economic revival.

"It's more than just a convention center," said the vice president to the brimming crowd that had gathered outside. "It's a building block for the revitalization of Philadelphia. It's the kind of revitalization President Clinton is trying to bring about for America."

At 11:28 A.M. on a sun-drenched Saturday at the end of June in 1993, the vice president tugged on a red ribbon to officially open the building. Fireworks shot into the sky, and like the opening of a jack-in-the-box, a high school marching band burst through a set of doors in hats and uniforms.

The scene bore inevitable comparison with another moment in the life of the city when a high-ranking public official had used the occasion of a grand opening as a symbol of something greater. Like Gore, he too had spoken on a stage filled with politicians and other dignitaries. He too had been surrounded by the swell of jaunty music. But unlike Gore, he had spoken not of hopeful revitalization, because the very suggestion of such vulnerability seemed unimaginable, but of a strength and a might the likes of which had left an entire world envious.

The city was still feeling the might of the consolidation that had made it the largest city in physical size in the entire world, drawing into its boundaries the ring of suburbs desperate for its superior services. Its population had continued to boom and thrive with no end in sight, a growth of 21 percent, or some 140,000 persons, in the six years alone since the last census was taken. New homes of vintage row-house style were being built at the rate of 6,000 a year to handle the constant influx, and with 9,000 manufactories in the city employing nearly 150,000 people, the work was always plentiful. It was a proud boast of the city that its working class was better housed than that of any other city in the world, and it was a boast that appeared to have merit, since nearly half its 130,000 dwellings had been built specifically for laborers. The waterfront thrived, with twenty-one shipping docks, twenty-three piers, and 2,000 men employed just in the daily shipment of 30,000 tons of coal. About a mile away, near Broad and Spring Garden, another 3,000 were employed at Baldwin Locomotive. The thoroughfare of Market Street was home to John Wanamaker, believed to be the largest and most complete clothing store in the entire world. Eight different railway lines fed into the city. There were twenty-seven daily and weekly newspapers and 34,000 rooms in which to bathe while reading those papers, most of which supplied hot water.

The appointed day started off rainy and cloudy. But the sun broke through by the early morning. Six new hotels with nearly 5,000 rooms had been built expressly for the occasion, and crowds by the tens of thousands arrived at the newly built depots of the Reading and Pennsylvania Railroads. They came from Boston and New York and Baltimore and Washington and Harrisburg and Pittsburgh, but they also came from Germany and France and India and Turkey and Ireland and Japan and China, crowding the grounds with their eclectic attire, and the words of official greeting put them in a mood to celebrate.

One hundred years ago our country was new and but partially settled. Our necessities have compelled us to chiefly expend our means and time in felling forests, subduing prairies, building dwellings, factories, ships, docks, warehouses, roads, canals, and machinery. Most of our schools, churches, libraries, and asylums have been established within an hundred years. Burdened by these great primal works of necessity, which could not be delayed, we yet have done what this Exhibition will show in the direction of rivaling older and more advanced nations in law, medicine, and theology; in science, literature, philosophy, and the fine arts. Whilst proud of what we have done, we regret that we have not done more. Our achievements have been great enough, however, to acknowledge superior merit wherever found.

"I declare the International Exhibition now open," pronounced President Ulysses Grant from the stage that had been set up in between the Main Building and Memorial Hall. It was now somewhere close to noon on May 10, 1876, and all threat of rain had disappeared for good. The flag of the United States rose up the Main Building, the largest building in the world, with a length of nearly a third of a mile, and the flags of foreign countries rose up on the other buildings. The perfect ovals of glass for the windows had come from the country's two greatest centers of glass-making, Pittsburgh and Wheeling, West Virginia. Fountains shot cologne-scented water into the air, and a chorus and an orchestra blasted out Handel's "Hallelujah" chorus to the accompaniment of a newly built pipe organ containing 2,704 pipes and made by the great Boston firm of Hook and Hastings. A procession of four thousand, which included the president, the emperor of Brazil, and members of the U.S. Senate, the House of Representatives, the Supreme Court, and the Cabinet, passed through the Main Building into Machinery Hall. The president and the emperor approached the platform on which was displayed an elaborate engine designed by George H. Corliss of Rhode Island—forty feet high with fourteen hundred units of horsepower, a fifty-six-ton flywheel, and twenty tubular boilers. They touched a designated lever, the flywheel turned and cranked to generate power, and within that hall five miles of machinery came to life.

The Centennial International Exhibition of 1876 had officially begun, and in the buildings spread across 236 acres in Fairmount Park in the city of Philadelphia lay example after example of the magnificence of America and the magnificence of the industrial city, a revolution in the very nature of work and mass production—an automatic shingle maker capable of making twenty-five thousand shingles in a single day; a machine for bending the stout wooden beams of ships; a ditchdigger that could dig eight cubic yards of earth per minute, or as much as a man could dig in a single day; a wallpaper machine capable of printing a roll in fifteen different colors; an envelope maker that could cut, fold, and gum 120 envelopes per minute; a machine for the manufacture of rubber-soled shoes; a cork maker that cut corks of various sizes; a tack maker that churned out four hundred tacks per minute; an automatic nail cutter.

The power loom of the United States Corset Company attracted considerable attention. So did the power looms of John Bromley and Sons of Philadelphia, capable of running off thirty-five yards of carpeting a day. So did the machine of the Pyramid Pin Company of New Haven that could

stick 180,000 pins into paper in a single day. The fully automatic elevator
was introduced here. So was the telephone as a tool for commercial use.
Another display highlighted perhaps the country's most valuable social
contribution to the rest of the world—the public school system.

"All were at work," a chronicler of the time wrote of that moment after
President Grant and Emperor Pedro II of Brazil had set the great Corliss
engine in motion. "The looms weaving their varied fabrics, the printing
presses throwing off their sheets like huge snow flakes, and pumps, lathes,
drills, hammers, and the wilderness of machinery, which you see around
you, were humming, pounding, whirring, and clattering, a grand chorus
and tribute to their unsceptered monarch.

"Industry."

One hundred and seventeen years later, in the summer of 1993, it seemed
incongruous for a convention center, even one as beautiful as this, to be the
savior of the city. It seemed incongruous for the Workshop of the World to
fashion a totally new wardrobe as the Host of the World, for the sound of
factory machinery to be replaced by the sound of small talk around an exhibition booth, for the row houses that had gone up to house those factory
workers to be replaced by the pink polish of convention hotels to house the
American Society of Hematology and the National Solid Waste Management Association, for the spiritual solace of men and women coming home
from a hard day's work knowing that the labor of their hands had made
something to be replaced by men and women coming home from a hard
day's work hoping that the flawlessness of their drinks and meals had
pleased conventioneers from Peoria and Fargo in sufficient measure for a
generous tip.

The Pennsylvania Convention Center in all likelihood was not the ultimate answer, and it might well turn out to be the taxpayer boondoggle that
Linda Morrison feared. The service jobs it might generate in hotels and
restaurants and stores would be of little use to someone like Jim Mangan,
who had spent the bulk of his career as a ship welder, unless he reached the
point of utter desperation in his search for a job. There was something
painfully ironic about a city that had forged its reputation on producing
nearly everything there was to produce now trying to reforge its reputation
by serving as a gracious and convivial host.

But Rendell had neither the time nor the inclination to ponder such disparities. He dwelled little on the industrial history of the city, perhaps because it augered so badly for the present. Staring with dewy eyes at empty

factories or dreaming of the day when cargo vessels would once again ply the waterfront was a worthless pursuit. In talking about the city's budget problems, he said it would be wonderful to give deserving programs all the money that was desired—just as it would be wonderful for him to wear his hair in an Elvis pompadour. But the truth was he didn't have the money, he didn't have the hair, and the city no longer had anything remotely resembling an industrial base. In the absence of a miracle, the city had no choice but to focus on what it did have—health care, banking and legal services, tourism—the familiar anchors of the so-called service economy.

He seized on the opening of the convention center with full force, and he transformed it from just an opening into an event of enormous psychic significance, as pivotal in its own way as the era of growth that had been ushered in by the Centennial Exhibition. He believed in tourism not necessarily because it was the best answer but because it was quite literally the only one, and he envisioned a quadrangular nexus—the convention center; a Disneyesque repackaging of the city's history, with battle reenactments and costumed Franklins, Washingtons, and Jeffersons helpfully giving tourists directions; the Avenue of the Arts along Broad Street, with its orchestra and its concert and theater halls; and riverboat gambling.

He was at his indefatigable best, furiously dishing out bread and circuses better than any emperor. Over the course of the Welcome America! celebration highlighting both the opening of the convention center and a visit by President Clinton on July Fourth to award the city's Liberty Medal to Nelson Mandela and F. W. de Klerk, he went to no less than fifty-two events. His enthusiasm was like that of a child celebrating a birthday over and over and over and blowing out the candles with more determined gusto each time. He was the mayor, and he was expected to be at events such as these, but his presence had taken on star proportions in the city.

The night before the convention-center opening, at an elaborate black-tie dinner, he entered the center's huge exhibition hall with the vice president, and it was he who received the louder ovation. "That's what happens when you don't raise taxes," he quipped with his usual self-effacement, but that wasn't why the guests were clapping. So often disheveled, to the point where an untidy appearance seemed to be part of the act of being mayor, tonight he looked resplendent in black tie. Every detail of the event, from menu to who sat where, had been personally planned by the mayor, and this wasn't mere obsession. He wanted the night to be perfect and memorable, as fine a bread and circus as he could possibly conjure up. "I think cities are run by the perception about them and the mood people have and

the feel people have about them almost more than the substance," he said
to the *Inquirer*'s Matt Purdy. He knew that with hope, however precarious
its foundation, there was the possibility of a miracle. He knew that without
hope there was the possibility of nothing. Pragmatically he could fix the
budget and take on the unions and talk a number of businesses thinking of
leaving for the suburbs into staying, but the most awesome power he could
unleash on the city was as simple as it was elusive—belief.

After Vice President Gore spoke at the dedication of the convention center and after the marching band burst through a set of doors, people on
nearby rooftops showered the politicians and the other dignitaries on the
stage with confetti. They were startled at first; then a confetti food fight
erupted. The mayor was drenched, and the mayor's wife, Midge, found
herself engaged in such heated *mano a mano* confetti warfare with the city
controller that she seemed perfectly willing to leap several rows of seats in
order to shove some of the stuff down his shirt. The frozen smiles of decorum gave way to laughter, real laughter, and in that moment the convention center didn't look like a mere building at all but appeared to be the true
beginning of the economic resurgence that Ed Rendell had promised was
on its way.

II

The next day, a balmy churchgoing Sunday, the spirit of a woman named
Fifi Mazzccua, as strong a spirit as there was in the desert of North Philadelphia, received yet another blow: today was Robin's last sermon.

To the million and a half people who lived in the city, this meant
nothing, particularly in the midst of the front-page giddiness over the convention center. But to the loyal handful who went each Sunday to Cookman United Methodist Church, putting away tears and tragedies and the
onslaught of obliteration to find solace in its stone and brick, the loss was
immeasurable. And as strong as Fifi was, as resolute as she had been in the
face of tragedies that had left a son in prison for murder and a grandson
dead in a shoot-out in the streets, given the rigors of days spent taking care
of four great-grandchildren under the age of seven, despite diabetes and di-
verticulitis and complications from a hernia, how much more could she
take?

"He's been there spiritually, physically, moneywise, foodwise, because
he literally had to feed us," said Fifi of Reverend Robin Hynicka, or Robin,

as she and just about everyone else called him. "I hate the fact that he's leaving. I cried. I got angry. I wanted to hit someone, anyone."

Sixty-one years old, short and sweetly plump, unabashed about wearing a shirt that said in bold letters on the front, WANTED: SUGAR DADDY WITH CONDO ON THE BEACH AND EXOTIC SPORTS CARS, Fifi had a face with the varied expressions of a summer storm. Kindness, mirth, the drains of sadness and memory, they moved over her rapidly, the hues changing like the shift of the clouds. Her voice had a similar quality. When she was feeling good, she said "hi, honey" as if it were the opening lines of a '40s swing song, melodious and rich and full of smoky heart. When she felt stress, worrying about everything to the point of exhaustion, she spoke in a trembling whisper. She was smart and savvy, and she saw the changes that had taken place from generation to generation, with the traditional concept of family more fractured than ever. She had raised her children; she had raised some of her children's children; now she was raising some of her children's children's children. "It's just a vicious cycle," she said in one of those moments when she seemed too tired even to move.

She had been born in 1932 in the grips of the Depression and grew up on Olive Street near Front and Fairmount in a section of the city called Northern Liberties, the daughter of Henry Sigler, who worked for the Pennsylvania Railroad and was called Big Henry, and Susie Mae Sigler. The neighborhood was a true melting pot. Skin color and ethnic background didn't matter, nor did one's income, since everybody's was just about the same. Rents were cheap, about eight dollars a month, and houses were small and humble, and Fifi remembered sleeping six to a bed sometimes. But no one seemed to care. As the Depression lifted, the fathers and uncles worked as longshoremen along the thriving wharves, and no one bothered to lock their doors. When it got hot during the summer, too hot to sleep indoors, everybody just piled quilts and army blankets on top of the sidewalk and slept outside. For fun, they went to the movies over at the Four Paws or took the train after church on Sundays to a park or snuck down through Slop Alley to the wharves where the men were unloading the produce and grabbed anything that had fallen off the trucks. "That was like our whole kingdom," said Fifi of Olive Street. "We didn't need anybody else."

She was living now in a different part of the city, but it wouldn't have mattered anyway, for the days of Olive Street were gone forever. The city had changed so much since then—in the way blacks and whites got along; in the way the young were yielded up in casual sacrifice; in the way crime and drugs owned the streets, providing temptation for those who wanted to take part and showing no remorse for those who wanted to stay away. Fifi had been affected by all of it, and sometimes she hardly had the strength to get out of bed in the morning. But she did, and her devotion to Cookman and to Robin Hynicka was one of the prime motivations. Robin restored her faith in religion after the Baptists had squeezed it out of her by one too many offertories. He taught her what it truly means to love God and offered support and advised her on the intricacies of matriarchy, trying to make her understand that her greatest gift—compassion—must somehow be tempered with an understanding of the stresses that it also produced. And now he was leaving, moving on after fifteen years to a better job within the hierarchy of the ministry. But as far as Fifi was concerned, he was leaving her behind.

"He called personally and told me, and I said, 'Robin, why, why you? Is it something we've done?' "

She had first met him five years earlier, in the midst of planning a funeral for her grandson Keith. Since Keith's father was in prison for murder (he had been there for much of Keith's life), the responsibility for burial was left primarily to her, and in looking for a church, she discovered Robin and Cookman United. The church was just a few blocks from her home, around the corner, past Huntingdon and then two blocks up Twelfth Street in the desert of North Philadelphia, on the fringes of a section the police had appropriately named the Badlands because of its daily propensity for drugs and death. When she was younger, taking care of children and grandchildren by herself, she had walked to Cookman and had found some blessed relief in the quiet of its stone steps, but other than going to the basement to drop off various kids for day care, she had never been inside. She had gone instead to a Baptist church a couple of blocks away, where, like the wheel-of-fortune game at the casinos, you could get a five-dollar blessing, a ten-dollar blessing, or even one for twenty if you were feeling particularly lucky. That didn't seem right to Fifi—to let the gas bill go so you could get a blessing for twenty bucks, particularly since there didn't seem to be a heck of a lot of difference between any of the varieties anyway. She turned away from the church and did not find a suitable replacement until, out of necessity, she needed one to bury her grandson.

When she went to Robin and asked whether she could hold the funeral at his church, he agreed under one condition: "I will let you have the funeral here, but I will not glorify his death."

She readily abided by that because she was not one to romanticize the killings over drugs and money that were routinely taking place around her, nor would she make excuses for them. She had loved Keith, as she loved the myriad of those who came under her crowded roof and beckoned for her help, but she also knew that he was living on borrowed time, with no one there to control him. Shortly before he died, he had bought a cross, and Fifi figured he had gone out and purchased it because he knew he was going to die, because he was irrevocably consumed by the fatal self-definition with guns and drugs that had already claimed the lives of so many young black men. She saw his temper, and she also saw the way he invariably chose to deal with it—with the barrel of a revolver.

Keith was killed in a gun battle over drugs and money in December 1988 on North Carlisle Street, not far from where she lived. He fired seven times and was shot at five times. He was hit in the throat, and blood gushed from his face like water from a running faucet, and he fell on the sidewalk next to a boarded-up home and a pile of trash. In the horrid spray of bullets, his eleven-year-old sister, Renee, got caught in the cross fire and suffered a bullet wound in the hip. Keith was rushed to the hospital, but the doctor said there were just too many bullet holes to do the patchwork necessary to keep him alive. He was seventeen when he died, which in the lifeblood of the desert of North Philadelphia was hardly exceptional. Some died older and some died younger, but they seemed to be dying all the time from illnesses everyone was familiar with but no one ever cured—hopelessness, inferior education, the sight of streets that had been left to putrefy, the ephemeral glitter of dealing drugs.

"They sell drugs around here like candy, like ice cream," a Baptist preacher told the police reporter for the *Inquirer*. "Nobody wants to do anything about it."

Keith's murder had been the 350th to take place in Philadelphia that year. Ninety were related to drugs, according to the police.

Fifi could have succumbed to the obliteration. Her neighborhood at best was vainly struggling to keep from drowning altogether. Right across the street from the solid stone of Cookman United, down the long finger of Twelfth Street in an unbroken line, lay the sockets of one vacant house after another. Several blocks from the church, on Lehigh, red graffiti snaked its way up dirty white columns of the local branch of the public library, making it look more like a shanty whorehouse than a place to read books. A little bit farther down, jags of barbed wire protected the little Mobil Mart. Her own street, Huntingdon, teetered according to the state of the drug trade. Two homes across the street had been abandoned. Cars got stolen, and the sound of gunfire filled the air with such regularity that few turned their heads to see where it was coming from. People young and old walked up and down the street hooked on crack, leaving their little vials behind on the sidewalk, and one of the great-grandchildren that Fifi took care of would play with the little containers the next day as if they were marbles. Dice games filled the monotony of the afternoons. Young teenage boys stopped Fifi on her way to church and tried to give her a few dollars to pray for them, as if they knew they were already dead. Young girls, twelve, thirteen, and fourteen, dressed up in skimpy clothes and sequins sold three-dollar blow jobs for hits of crack underneath the bridge at Thirteenth and Cumberland, high heels and cheap perfume amid trash and muddy puddles. Fifi knew what the drugs did to them—how they looked in the mirror and saw something different and beautiful, someone they thought was worth something. She used to get on them, beg and plead with them to stop. But not anymore. After a while, it wasn't worth it because it never seemed to do any good. "Now I just pray to God to forgive them," said Fifi.

Then there were the older women, translucent apparitions at the age of thirty-five, with gaunt bodies and glassy eyes, flesh on the bone like bare patches of meat, stumbling to a well-known crack house for just another hit. "Why do you go over there?" she sometimes asked them.

"Well, Miss Fifi, I just need a little hit. I just got to cope."

But as much as she could, she chose not to dwell on it, for the drug of hopelessness was more addictive than anything else, and she fought instead to cauterize the wound.

She had lived on Huntingdon Street since 1969 and in the same row house on the street since 1972. It belonged to the Philadelphia Housing Authority, a scattered-site unit, in the bland parlance of public-housing lingo, and she rented it for $179 a month. Even though she had had to wait eight years for a kitchen sink, she loved the house. It had become hers, a place to put things, and with the considerable help of her extended family she had amassed some strong and sturdy possessions—the couch, a comfy armchair, a dining room set. Like *Pee-wee's Playhouse,* the place was impossibly cluttered, thanks to Fifi's love of flea-market bargains. She once bought a fish tank for three dollars. It then took another seven to get it to work, so it really didn't turn out to be much of a bargain after all. But she loved staring at those fish. In her role as Mama and Grandma and Great-grandma and court of last resort to those who were both devoted to and utterly dependent on her, the slow shuffle of those fish through the water soothed her and was worth every penny. To be a fish in a fish tank in the desert of North Philadelphia—now that was a good life.

She still loved the street on which she lived, despite the social and physical changes. When she had moved to it, blacks and whites were still living there. People would get out their brooms for an equal mixture of gossip and sweeping. The uniform row houses had a well-scrubbed look, and none of them was vacant. But then a perpetual shadow formed over this part of the city. First it was the loss of factory jobs. Then it was the loss of population. Then it was the ceaseless onslaught of crack. "The older people have died out," said Fifi, and those few who were left were often too scared to sweep and gossip anymore. "You're in your house behind closed doors, scared to come to the windows or anything." As much as she could, she refused to tolerate it, once chasing after a drug dealer with a machete.

People on the block, in a kind and admiring way, called her the crazy lady.

It was after the funeral that Fifi began to go to Cookman United every Sunday, and it wasn't long before Robin became her spiritual soul mate. She confided in him, told him things that she could tell no one else. However strong the spirit, being in your sixties and taking care of four great-grandchildren under the age of seven was hellish. Their parents loved Fifi desperately and gave her financial support. But sometimes they treated her like the live-in sitter. They knew that she would take care of the kids, and when they got frustrated with their own lives and told the kids to shut up because they were crying or got in trouble and went off to jail, they knew that Fifi would take over. "You can see why I have a nervous condition," said Fifi, and the demands placed on her, even though she had a job as a cook and companion to an elderly man who lived over in East Falls, were endless—the laundry in the basement that always needed to be washed, so much of it that Fifi used a shopping cart to get it from the washer to the dryer; the toys that filled the living room floor like weeds and always needed to be put away; the school programs and after-school programs that had to be arranged; the bouts of bed-wetting and hyperactivity; the different requests for breakfast. Budda, at six the oldest of the great-grandchildren, wanted Pop-Tarts and oatmeal. Three-year-old Kalih wanted a cheese sandwich. Three-year-old Susette wanted peanut butter and jelly. Two-year-old Tonya wanted cereal. Every day it was like that.

Every single day.

She loved the kids more than anything else. They sustained her and filled her with laughter when she was feeling pinned and desperate. But they also drove her crazy sometimes, the nonstop energy of them. She became strict, but they were always one step ahead of her. "I lay down rules," said Fifi. "It's like laying down spaghetti."

She talked about the pain she felt for her son Tony, a smart and decent man trapped in prison for life for a stupid and impulsive grudge killing. She talked about the pain she felt for Tony's three boys, so clearly affected by a father whose attempts at parenting from behind the gray walls of prison, his pleadings that they not follow his path, were of no use at all. Keith was dead before he was old enough to vote, and the other two boys, Cochise and Gino, had also gotten on the treadmill of crime and jail. Gino, the oldest, was in a detention center on a federal firearms charge, and agents from the federal Bureau of Alcohol, Tobacco, and Firearms were passing pictures of Cochise around the neighborhood as they searched for him.

She also talked of the pride she felt for Posquale, the one grandson who seemed determined not to lose himself to the streets. He was going to the Community College of Philadelphia to get a degree and hoped to go into business for himself as a caterer. He felt he owed it to Fifi not to follow the same path taken by some of her other grandchildren, and he was striving to make good on that debt. She had raised him from birth until age eleven, and she had given him the "strong hand" of love and stability and discipline that all children need. He had had his bouts with selling drugs and playing dice, and he had risen above them. He was working to get ahead, and he was making steady and impressive progress, but his aversion to birth control had made him the father of eleven children out of wedlock, according to his own account, all but one of them by different mothers. Three of the children died of medical complications as tiny infants, but that still left eight children to raise. Fifi wasn't sure that all the children really were his, and Posquale himself had questions about three of them. But he knew that word was out in the neighborhood that he was a good man to peg as a father because of his reputation for not running out. So he provided for all of them, by his own means and also with the help of public assistance. He was proud of the fact that he had been taken to court only once for failure to provide child support, and on weekends he frequently had all the children together. He loved them, but he also acknowledged that he would have done it differently had he been given the opportunity. "If I had a chance to go back and fix all my problems, I wouldn't have any kids," said Posquale. "I would have learned about the condom."

The more Fifi got to know Robin, the more she depended on him. When he said he was getting married, she didn't understand it. How could he? How could he do this? What was wrong with him? "I kept asking, 'Robin, why do you need a wife? We cook for you, we clean for you.' "

Robin tried to explain to her that it was about more than just cleaning and cooking.

Fifi sort of understood. She grew to accept the change in his marital status. She embraced Robin's wife as she embraced Robin. And Robin was still there for her, to revel in her laughter and give sympathy during her bouts of pain and dispense practical advice when she began to sob from exhaustion and frayed nerves—custody hearings, doctors' appointments, shopping, sandwich making, after-school pickups, so many piles of laundry that it had begun to smell, calls from prison, calls from jail, calls for money, calls for help. "Sometimes you feel like an octopus putting tentacles out," said Fifi. But then the sobbing would pass, and the spirit would take over, prompted by a Mario Lanza song on the radio where she worked or a particularly good sermon or the Can-Can sale at Shop Rite or a flea-market spectacular or something the great-grandkids said.

"I'm gonna tell Grandma you were kissin' all the girls today."

"I wasn't kissin' all the girls. They were kissin' me."

In addition to her salary, she also received financial assistance from various family members. Money was tight, but there was enough to go around, and she lived frugally, using supermarket coupons with almost surgical precision and ferreting out bargains no matter how remotely tucked away they were in the mile-long aisles—cans of soup, frozen bags of corn on the cob, precooked Chinese dinners, cartons of iced tea.

Robin knew she was a remarkable woman, unlike any other he had ever met. And she believed he was equally remarkable, a true miracle who had taken the disintegrating shell of Cookman United and saved it from extinction.

III

The original charter of the church dated back to 1881, and in celebration of its dedication a decade later on the last Sabbath of May, 1,333 people swelled through its doors. The original building was destroyed by fire in 1925, but the structure was quickly rebuilt, and its interior of solid wood and straight lines served a congregation of whites who lived and worked in the neighborhood. Attendance numbered regularly in the hundreds until the end of the 1950s, when many of the members left the neighborhood for the suburbs. The church reflected the job loss and population loss that had seized North Philadelphia, and by the time Robin Hynicka arrived as a missioner in 1978, it was barely there at all. Robin was a graduate of Albright College in Reading who had grown up on a farm in Lancaster County, the son of a plant manager for RCA. With a master's degree fresh from the divinity school at Duke University, he was twenty-four at the time and unprepared for what lay ahead. He drove down Lehigh Avenue with his mother and brother and pulled up to the house next to the church where he would be staying. It was unrenovated and dilapidated, with a bathtub in the front room. That first Sunday he preached to five people, two adults and three children, and the biggest issue facing him when he delivered his sermon was whether to stand at the pulpit or on the church floor.

He was a white in an area of the city that was black, and he knew he needed the divine intervention of God to build trust and ease natural suspicions. He liked basketball, and he joined a neighborhood team called the Smokers. The coach put him in, and he was the only white on the court. It was the championship game, he got fouled, and although he had been a fine athlete in college, he had never been more nervous than he was at this moment, and he prayed to God in a style that the Duke Divinity School had probably not taught him—"Please God, please let me make this shot"— and then the wind started to blow, and the hoop began to shake, and he threw up the shot.

It hit one side of the rim.

God was answering him.

It hit the other side of the rim.

God was still answering him.

He closed his eyes.

God was *still* answering him.

It went in.

Shortly afterward, he accidentally locked himself out of his house. He had to walk through some of the roughest parts of the city to get another set of keys, and he made it to within three or four blocks of where he needed to go when he saw a group of black kids standing on the corner. He couldn't avoid them, and he felt instantly afraid and automatically as-

sumed that they wanted to rob him or shoot him or just mess with him a little bit when one of them said, "Hey Robin." The kid had recognized him
from the basketball game, and in that moment Robin understood that the
problem was not what those black kids on the corner felt but what he felt.
"My reason for being afraid was based on my own racism. They had done
nothing. There were no weapons visible. There was no verbal abuse."

It was a pivotal point of self-awareness, one that he remembered as he
began the long and improbable task of rebuilding the congregation.
Prophecies about human nature were risky and self-defeating, and he
quickly found that those who he thought would support him the most supported him the least and those who he thought would support him the least
supported him the most. There was no grand scheme or master plan, just
the sweat of labor and dedication. The neighborhood, which was bad when
he got there, only got worse, thinning out the desert even more. The
Botany 500 plant, several blocks up the street from the church, at Broad
and Lehigh, closed, and the ravages of crack set in in an epidemic every
bit as corrosive as the earlier tuberculosis scares. Eventually a cure had
been found for tuberculosis, but the cures for crack—decent jobs, decent
schools, decent places to live—were further away than ever, and Robin
knew that every family in the community in which he served had been affected. Families that were struggling to remain stable came unglued.
Grandmothers became baby-sitters for husbandless daughters who roamed
the streets like the living dead. Once-beautiful women turned to prostitu-
tion. A faithful churchgoer on her deathbed whispered to Robin, not asking for salvation but announcing that her fourteen-year-old granddaughter
was pregnant. A mother he knew was beaten so badly by her son for five
dollars that she was put on life support and eventually died.

But with help from what Robin called the mothers of the church, women
like Fifi and Ester Potts and Ellen Arttaway, the congregation slowly grew.
There was an irrepressible spirit, and the church served as its focal point.
The congregation never came close to the numbers that had sustained it
in the 1920s and '30s and '40s, but by the time Robin decided to take the
next step in his life, it numbered 108, more than twenty times the number
that had shown up that very first time.

He had the soul of a man of the cloth, but he still had the competitive ferocity of the wide receiver he had been in high school and college. He was
long and lean, and he didn't like being screwed with. When he witnessed
a purse snatching near the church, he ran and tackled the guy and ended up
with a huge gash in his head that required thirteen stitches. When someone

stole his favorite jacket, the one with the leather sleeves, from the wall rack in his office, he embarked on a high-speed chase for two blocks, all the way to the Broad Street subway line. He never found the perpetrator, but at least he was able to retrieve his wallet, which had been left on top of a token dispenser. His parents thought he was crazy to be doing what he was doing, but he kept on despite his own bouts of self-doubt. He wondered whether the church was really relevant, whether anything could really be relevant in the mess of the desert out there. But he also realized that the role of the church wasn't necessarily to save but was to offer peace and refuge. "That's what I provided as a person; that's what the church provided," he said at one point. "I provided a step every week out of the chaos. I was available."

In his life, Robin could remember books that were so touching and so real that he had avoided reading the final chapter for as long as possible so they would never end. He had done that with *To Kill a Mockingbird,* and he was doing it now, at the end of June 1993, in saying good-bye to Cookman. "We're trying to avoid the last several pages of this book," he said a week before his last sermon, and his normally cluttered office had now been filled with the smell of cardboard moving boxes. The once-crammed bookshelf was empty; all that was left were the Holy Bible and *The Life of Christ* between faded covers.

His new job, as executive director of the Frankford Group Ministry, would involve far more administration than his job at Cookman had, and he seemed to welcome that. But the bonds he had forged, the strength and the intimacy of them, were unlike anything he could have imagined. He had come to Cookman as a young pragmatist. Fifteen years later, he was leaving as a true believer in the miracles of the human spirit.

In the days before the last sermon, his mind traveled. Sitting late one night in the pharmacology lab at Penn, where his wife, Weslia, a PhD candidate, was doing an experiment, his mind raced back five years and then ten years and then fifteen—to the house next door to the church with the bathtub in the front room, to the providential foul shot that became a rite of acceptance, to his fear of those boys on the corner that exposed his own vein of racism and wrongful expectation. He knew that going to the Frankford Group Ministry was a good move. There was infinitely more responsibility in the job, and there was the challenge of supervising a staff. But there was always the question of what would happen to those he was leaving behind. His constant accessibility at Cookman, he admitted, had been a weakness as well as a strength. He always had this sense that he was picking up the pieces, constantly picking up the pieces. But it was hard to imagine what life for someone like Fifi would have been like without him. Truly he had been her heart. When she hugged him, she just felt secure, and in the desert of North Philadelphia, in the context of her life, that was a sacred feeling.

Robin's final service on the last Sunday in June began with the singing of "Sweet, Sweet Spirit." He stood in a white frock with his hands on either side of the pulpit, as if slightly steadying himself, but he looked comfortable and serene. The church itself was not crowded. Many of the pews were empty, but that only gave the moment a greater sense of intimacy, a true gathering of friends. The sound of a crying toddler echoed from the dimly lit wood, but no one seemed to mind, and through the opened slats in the stained-glass windows came the sound of the city—sirens, car alarms, honking horns. Muggy chunks of heat pushed through the windows, and the congregants gently cooled themselves with little off-white fans courtesy of Baker's Funeral Home.

The children's choir got up to sing, dedicating their songs to Robin. There were only four members, but they sang with such off-key gusto that their spirit was utterly infectious, their voices loud and shrill and easily carrying to the height of the massive vaulted ceiling.

I will serve thee . . . Because I love thee . . .

Robin spoke next, his voice slightly quavering. There had been a celebration at the church in his honor the day before, and although the emotional aspects of it had been wrenching, it was nothing compared with this.

"I knew that today would be harder than yesterday, to stand here for the last time," he said, and he spoke about the tone of the previous celebration, how "not a word was mentioned about race, because race has no place. We built a bond of trust early on, and that bond of trust carried us through fifteen years together.

"I love you all from the bottom of my heart and will always remember this time as a time of great strength, of great creativity. I'll remember where I first learned about those things, at Cookman Church, Twelfth and Lehigh, in your arms."

Through the church came cries of "amen," and then the adult choir went to the pulpit to sing. There were six in this group, and in the middle, like a tamped-down version of the Statue of Liberty, was Fifi, singing with gusto, joyfully undaunted by her occasional off-key notes. Though she had risen at 6:00 A.M., between getting the great-grands ready for Sunday school and making sure everyone got fed in the chaos of the kitchen, she had been late for the service. But it didn't matter now. She had dreaded this moment when she would have to say good-bye, but she fought back her emotions and lost herself in the rousing song, swaying, smiling that smile that could cut through the thickest wall, dressed gloriously in a white top and black skirt.

You ought to take the time out to praise the Lord . . .

Robin spoke again, this time to give his sermon. He hadn't written it out because he knew that this was a moment when the spirit had to take over. Whatever he said—whatever words floated into his mind as he stood on the pulpit now would be the right ones.

I grew up here. I learned some things here I never would have learned any-where else. I don't know how many furnaces I learned to fix. I don't know how many cars I learned to hot-wire—when someone stole 'em, we stole 'em back. I don't know in how many households I was able to receive nour-ishment. I don't know how many lives touched my life.
You have taught me to believe in miracles.

Despite the emotion of the occasion, he told those gathered that this was not the end of anything at all.

Today is not a day God has brought us to say "It's over, it's fin-ished." Today is a day God has brought us to say "It's new, it's a begin-ning." Are you ready?

His refrain of hope was appropriate, but in that simple church built for another time and another era, it was hard to know just what would happen. For nearly thirty years, the church had been on uncertain ground, recently nursed back to life a slow step at a time. Now in this moment of good-bye, it seemed more fragile than ever. A successor was in place, but the post would be part-time.

Inside there was still peace and serenity, but outside life went on as al-ways. If you were born here in the 1960s and lived here still, you were a witness, every single day of your life until you died, to an environment that had only deteriorated. Under such conditions, as if watching the creep of cancer through every pore and every tissue, why wouldn't you turn to crack? Why wouldn't you become pregnant? Why wouldn't you father as many children as you could? Why wouldn't you pick up a gun? Why wouldn't you want to die?

Robin ended his sermon with the parable of the eagle who thought he was a chicken, lost and confused, unaware of his strength, until he found his proper path.

My friends, you are now all eagles. You will soar with God. You will keep your eyes on the sun. You are wonderful.
God loves you. So do I.

After the sermon, Robin invited the congregants to the altar to reaffirm their devotion to God. They came and knelt, and Robin slowly went down the row with tears in his eyes, hugging each of them, clasping their hands.

A mile away, in the heart of Center City, lay a glistening convention center that had been dedicated the day before, a shiny and no-expense-spared Mecca for the out-of-towners who would start flocking there from all over the world with their disposable dollars to spend. But here there was no convention center. There was only the faith of those somehow strong enough to have it still.

The choir sang one final time, the words lingering there.

At the cross, at the cross, where I first saw the light, and the burden of my heart rolled away . . .

One by one the congregants filed out of the pews in the dim light and said their good-byes, first to Robin's wife, Weslia, and then to Robin himself. Fifi lightheartedly promised Weslia that she was going to send her a tape of her singing. Then she reached up to hug Robin, and he reached down to hug her. "God bless you," he whispered, and she closed her eyes, and her hug became a little bit tighter. Then she and her daughter made their way back home along Twelfth Street, walking slowly and side by side in their Sunday finest, past the litter-strewn gutter, past the sealed-up homes that had long ago been left for dead, past the clump of teenage boys rumbling with a pair of dice in the early-afternoon light, farther into the desert of North Philadelphia.

THIRTEEN

Hot Dog Day

I

It started with a clatter of noises on the City Hall apron, not the familiar garble of protest through a bullhorn with bad sound but something different and more curious. Even Cohen couldn't resist, so he turned and peered through the grime of his office window. Down below he saw someone he most definitely recognized lightly wrestling with a six-foot mascot known as Smiley, and then he heard a voice as familiar to him as his own loudly saying something, the very same voice that in the very same week had helped structure the successful sale of more than $500 million in bonds on behalf of the city.

"I, Edward G. Rendell, mayor of the city of Philadelphia, do hereby proclaim July 23, 1993, as Hot Dog Day."

Cohen was rattled, his legendary focus momentarily broken by the sight of a man, the mayor actually, wrestling with a mascot in the shape of a very pink pig, and when he fielded his next phone call, he couldn't help but dwell on what had just taken place, as if he had just had a vision: *"I hear Ed's voice, and there he is, reading a proclamation with a six-foot pig next to him. The mayor of the fifth largest city in the country is reading a proclamation about a hot dog with a six-foot pig jostling him. Yesterday he sold five hundred million dollars of bonds. Today he's being jostled by a six-foot pig. When he takes off the jacket, I say, 'What is he going to do now?' And then he puts on a hat and apron, and he's suddenly surrounded by all these kids in little yellow caps. I am stunned. That's all I can say."*

In return for the appearance, a company called Hatfield Quality Meats had agreed to contribute $5,000 to the city's Recreation Department, so there was a cause and an effect of such behavior, but even Rendell wondered whether he had gone past the threshold.

"The things that I will do for five thousand dollars," he later lamented.

In the afterglow of the success of the Welcome America! celebration and the convention-center opening during the summer of 1993, such actions increasingly defined the mayor. He hated the tag of supersalesman, this notion of him as some amalgam of Deepak Chopra and Lou Costello, the big-city mayor who never saw a pool opening or a groundbreaking he could resist. He liked to think of himself as sober and serious, a statesman with maybe a few strange moments here and there. But he never stopped pumping on behalf of the city.

In recent months, he had worked mightily to raise the nearly $80 million that was needed to build a new orchestra hall in the city. When he heard that fashion magnate Sidney Kimmel was good for $10 million, he figured he could extract another $7 million or $8 million out of him if there was an agreement to name the hall after him. Some, particularly those in the sainted community of the orchestra, might balk at the notion of something called the Kimmel Concert Hall. What kind of artistic ring did that have? But not Rendell, not if it meant getting the damn thing built. "Short of a Nazi, I don't care if it's named after Garfield the Cat."

Obsessed with making the city as appealing as possible to first-time visitors, he worked on a plan whereby taxi and limousine drivers would automatically take visitors downtown from the airport on Interstate 95 instead of the Schuylkill Expressway, thereby avoiding the smelly jangle of oil refineries and the junkyards that were bound to terrify. When he wasn't appearing somewhere or trying to sell someone on something, he was attending to the egos of fragile politicians—like a scene in *E-R,* there in rumpled suit and tie attending to an always full waiting room of easily bruised and insecure egos. A state senator was pushing a candidate for the state supreme court. Could Ed maybe make a few calls for a fund-raiser? A congressman was running for reelection. Could Ed maybe make a few calls for a fund-raiser?

"When it comes to kissing political rear ends, I'm pretty good at it. I didn't know that I would have to be a major fund-raiser for people."

In the midst of the daily cacophony, he made the calls.

"Has anybody hit you for Vince Fumo's guy, Russ Nigro? If you can send me a thousand dollars for him . . ."

"You may hate him, and I don't think you do, but I need a thousand dollars for Lu Blackwell for Congress."

He considered the calls demeaning and a waste of valuable time, not because people wouldn't cough up what he asked of them ("It's scary how no one says no," Rendell himself remarked) but because there was so much else to do. But if he didn't make the calls, he knew what might happen—projects and votes that he needed backing on suddenly disappearing into a stew of funk and hurt feelings, particularly since local politicians never, ever forgot. With each day crucial, he could not take the risk. But he also knew he was lucky enough not to have to worry about the day-to-day management of the city.

"My advice, if anybody wants to be the mayor of a big city, is to get yourself a David Cohen. Because another David Cohen doesn't exist, get yourself three people you can depend on to run the day-to-day affairs. . . . I love analyzing memos. That's why I read and analyze them from midnight to two-thirty in the morning. Where do I have the time during the working day to turn off the phone and really think? It's very hard. I really do envy David."

"He envies me?" asked Cohen several days later, peering up momentarily from the pages of some dense and turgid memo that only David Cohen could love. "Good God."

It was a typically self-effacing response, but it was deceptive. Cohen was affable to everyone, and he returned all phone calls personally and promptly whether it was a United States senator or to use the mayor's own term of art, a "smack-ass." But behind the exterior lay the soul of a bounty hunter. He reveled in his role as the clearinghouse of all information at City Hall. Nothing went on without him knowing about it first. And if someone tried to circumvent that, Cohen would discover the source. He or she could run to the deepest crevice of the Grand Canyon, and there a hundred yards behind, in drab blue suit on a mule, would be Cohen with that cheerful smile on his face.

Several years earlier, in the midst of the budget crisis, somone had leaked a report to the press questioning the city's fiscal recovery. The release of the information bothered him, but what really got to him was the leak. He considered it an act of defiance, and he wasn't about to let it go unchecked.

He privately drew up a list of the city officials who would soon be getting another confidential report on the city's financial health. At the bottom of each page, in tiny type, was the seemingly innocuous phrase, "The numbers contained in this report were prepared by departments and have not been independently verified." No one in the history of city reports had ever paid attention to this phrase, until this moment. He took his distribution list and matched each name with a piece of the phrase so that the list looked like this:

Rendell	The
Cohen	num
Mullin	bers
Masch	con
Harris	tained

He matched up thirty-eight names this way. Based on his master list, he went to the same page in each report and faintly underlined different bits of the phrase. That way, when a reporter came swaggering into his office with a copy of the report, Cohen would innocuously ask to see it. He would give some excuse to turn to the "code" page, and depending on which piece of the phrase at the bottom had been underlined, would know exactly who was the source of the leak. If "The" was underlined, it was Rendell. If "bers" was underlined, it was city finance director Stephen Mullin. If "con" was underlined, it was city budget director Michael Masch. And so on.

"That will work, don't you think?" he innocently said, as if he had just made up a grocery list, and then he secreted it away.

Some politicians called Cohen the real mayor and the one you wanted to see to get the real answers, not the visceral off-the-cuff ones that the other mayor sometimes gave. There was some truth to that, because Rendell's immediate instinct was to leap from the heart, to promise something and assure someone of something regardless of the reality of it, not out of some motive of nefarious political manipulation but because he hated to displease anyone. His absence of malice was totally at odds with public life. He hated being called Mayor or Mr. Mayor but insisted on Ed. He hated being surrounded by members of his security detail—as if he deserved some special protection. He hated firing anyone, regardless of how poorly he or she had performed, because he could feel the horror of what it must be like to lose a job in the current economic climate.

But even he sensed that there were times when he might be going too far. At the end of certain meetings, right at the moment when everyone was brimming and smiling because the mayor had said exactly what they all wanted to hear, he issued what appeared to be a benign caveat: before uncorking the champagne bottles, it might be a good idea just to walk across the hall and "check with David." When they did, Cohen would sit ever so slightly slumped in one of the chairs at the round table in his office and make it clear to those assembled that they were stark raving mad to think what was being proposed had any prayer.

When Cohen wanted to stop using campaign funds to pay a worker who he felt didn't have enough to do, Rendell felt pain and anguish. He reluctantly decided that the worker should do something else but found a job for him in the private sector and gave him a personal check so he might be able to finish college. While Cohen's mind whirred and clicked with perfect focus in preparation for a budget address, Rendell stared out the window of the hotel room they were in, with its view of the magnificent fountain of Logan Circle and the solid stone of the Cathedral of Saints Peter and Paul and a homeless man wrapped in rags like a mummy, and he said aloud, "Every day I see people out of work, just desperate."

Neither man threatened the territory of the other, and each did what the other could not possibly do. After nearly two years in the full-throttle ride of the four-year term, their duet was still harmonious, their passion for the city punctuated by just the right high notes of how absurd it all was sometimes.

"That was interesting," said Cohen after a typical meeting, "and totally useless."

"Like most meetings," said the mayor.

"No," said Cohen. "Most meetings aren't interesting."

Like the wife that all men dream of but so very few have, Cohen perceived his whole role as making life easier for the mayor, even when he was admonishing him to keep his mouth shut, as he frequently did ("You should now assume that a reporter will be present for everything you do unless you're talking to Midge in the bedroom"). He posed no threat, and his loyalty, like that of a palace guard, was absolute. Like a well-meaning but sometimes careless husband, Rendell promised not to repeat the mistakes of the past ("You tell me what to say, and I'll be good") and paid Cohen the ultimate compliment: "As you get to know him, he becomes better. For most people, it's just the opposite. You like them a lot, and [then] it's all downhill."

Rendell had little patience for the numbing detail that was the sustenance of Cohen's life. Cohen, in turn, had just as little interest in the mayor's glorious and deliberate willingness to be foolish. Cohen seemed impervious to it, although there were times, like this day in July, when the mayor wrestling with a pink mascot pig captured even his attention.

The mayor himself seemed quite giddy afterward, and when he discovered later that afternoon that the new issue of *Philadelphia Magazine* had quoted him as saying "Your magazine sucks the big wong," he barely seemed bothered. Most politicians, even if the quote had been correct, would have denied it to their dying day, but not Rendell. "Anybody who knows me knows that it has the ring of truth, so I'm cooked. If I had said 'Your magazine eats shit,' I could have denied it."

Such irreverence was a part of him that had been there and always would be. There were moments when he overstepped, the irreverence dissolving into a mixture of crudity and cruelty that went far beyond the bounds expected of normal adulthood. But he often said what he said and did what he did as a way of releasing tension and momentarily focusing on something other than what lay ahead—his private mechanism for granting himself reprieve. To be the mayor of an American city meant facing potential tragedy twenty-four hours a day. But to be an effective mayor also meant willfully avoiding that very thought as much as possible. Optimism and hope were not luxuries but requisites, elements for sustaining sanity in the job. When one problem ebbed for a little bit, another one inevitably rose in its place, and in the summer of 1993, just as the glow of the convention-center opening began to wear off, the continued nemesis of public housing appeared again, with renewed vengeance.

II

In May of 1993, when the Department of Housing and Urban Development ended its one-year takeover of the Philadelphia Housing Authority, there was general agreement about the impact of the federal government's intervention: virtually every barometer of performance indicated that conditions had worsened, supplying ample support for Linda Morrison's adage that anytime government tries to make something better, the exact inverse occurs. The vacancy rate in the public-housing units had risen from 20 to 25 percent. The backlog of repair requests had increased as well, and the top three positions at PHA were unfilled. The five members of the housing-authority board celebrated their return to power with a meeting filled with all the glories of the good old days—yelling, dissent, acrimony, resentment, name-calling.

More and more, pressure mounted for Rendell to go beyond his behind-the-scenes maneuvering and take direct control of the agency, to do something besides cower behind the big brother of HUD when the waters got rough or cave in to the black politicians. "Now that the city has regained control of PHA, it is clear who has the main responsibility for seeing that the agency fulfills its mission," said the *Inquirer* in an editorial at the end of May. "It's Mayor Rendell." Rendell took pleasure in newspaper editorials, because they gave him an instant reason to grind his teeth and clap his hands in his best *Exorcist* style. He knew that making himself accountable for the agency was the quickest form of political suicide and would result in a trail of bludgeoned corpses. And those who had been through the horror had already warned him to be very, very careful. "You must know that PHA is like a bottomless pit filled with quicksand," John Paone had written to the mayor the previous year. "Everyone who comes in contact with the agency gets sucked in. The more you try to change it, the deeper you get pulled in until you become mired in the mess itself."

It seemed far better to get criticized in the sanctimonious who-gives-a-shit soup of an *Inquirer* editorial than to assume any real responsibility. But then something terrible happened. No less a political figure than Henry Cisneros, the secretary of HUD, personally asked the mayor to assume direct control of the agency by becoming its chairman of the board. For eighteen months, the machinations of the authority had been a considerable source of trouble. Complaints from tenant leaders were becoming legion, and even worse, the coverage by the *Inquirer* had been exhaustive and relentless. Almost as soon as a story hit the presses, it was faxed to HUD officials in Washington, and they examined each one under a microscope. Public housing in Philadelphia wasn't merely a social problem. Now it was a political one, a public relations disaster unfolding daily at one of the largest public-housing authorities in the country.

The idea of being chairman and being directly responsible for the housing authority was bad enough for Rendell. But having to sit there like a choir boy during those three-hour yelling fests that passed for meetings—the very thought of it, as he sat at his desk in his underwear one day, changing back into his suit after the annual City-Suburbs softball game, made him slightly sick. And in that instant, he seemed to long for the more carefree days of just a few weeks earlier, when he had sat at the round table in his office mapping out a softball team made up entirely of local mascots.

"At second base, Captain Sewer. At first, the Textile Ram. At shortstop, Barney Buttery. Third sack, Drexel Dragon. Here's my outfield. Hot Shot in right, the Phanatic in center, and the Smiling Porker in left."

Rendell first met privately with Cisneros at the end of August 1993, and it was then that the plan for the newest resurrection of public housing was put forth, an unprecedented partnership of federal and local government in which Rendell would become chairman of the housing-authority board, Council President Street would become vice chairman, and John White Jr., a black former city councilman, would become executive director. The selection of White had already been cleared with the constituency that created the most terror, the black female tenant leaders, so that took care of one potential problem. Like Rendell, Street was admirably risking political stock by getting involved, but because he was black, he would be insulated from instant hate and disrespect. Rendell's installation as chairman, on the other hand, was potentially apocalyptic. At least one tenant leader, when told of the possibility by officials in Washington, had responded with anti-Semitic references.

When the mayor met with Cisneros, his basic question was blunt: in return for his going on the board, what extra measures would HUD take on behalf of the housing authority? How could he sell his presence to those who were already inclined to hate him? Rendell wanted a series of specific commitments from the federal agency that would free up millions of dollars for modernization and demolition. That way he could at least bring something real to the table, not just the usual round of hollow commitments.

On a Monday toward the end of August, Cohen spoke with the HUD assistant secretary for Public and Indian Housing, Joseph Shuldiner, who promised to forward a written document with the commitments that Rendell sought. Two days later, on Wednesday, after considerable cajoling, HUD officials reluctantly faxed a copy of their proposed commitment, but it was vague and wishy-washy and, in Cohen's words, "garbage."

In the meantime, Cisneros had scheduled a press conference for Friday in Philadelphia, but Cohen's instinct was to try to get it canceled. There were too many loose ends and too many unanswered questions. The city's role in the partnership was precarious at best. Without written assurances from HUD on how it would actually improve public housing in the city and what specific programs it would support, Rendell really was beginning a death march. In the ultimate game of political chicken, Cohen was convinced that HUD was trying to shove an unsatisfactory agreement down the city's throat. But then the little wheels whirred and clicked.

He knew what a big-city mayor was like since he worked for one, and he assumed that Cisneros, himself a former big-city mayor, was true to type—impulsive, aggressive, and slightly starry-eyed when it came to headlines. He could sense how feverishly Cisneros wanted Rendell to do this. If Rendell said yes and entered into the kind of historic federal-local partnership that Cisneros envisioned, the splash of publicity would be impressive. Rendell would look bold, but Cisneros would look even bolder, like a true visionary who really wanted to do something novel about public housing. The more Cohen thought about it, the more he realized how great the Cisneros plan was, not necessarily in terms of what it meant for public housing but as a means of leverage for the city to get exactly what it wanted. He sensed need, desperate need, and he knew that whenever there is need, there is behind it the divine lusciousness of weakness. Eagerness, Cohen had realized long ago, was the Achilles' heel of an opponent. A man who was eager was a man who could be had, particularly by a man who didn't seem the least bit eager.

Based on his knowledge of every arcane detail (although he also knew that there was no such thing as an arcane detail), he made a series of assumptions as precise as chess moves in a strategy of checkmate. He knew that Cisneros badly wanted to make the announcement in two days, on Friday, particularly since there was the threat of a newspaper strike—after all, a major announcement during a strike was like the proverbial tree falling in the proverbial forest: if there were no headlines, has something actually happened? He also knew that Cisneros had no openings in his schedule for the next two weeks other than the one on Friday. He knew that HUD officials had already talked about the plan with various tenant leaders and legislators and members of the labor unions and that many of them were walking time bombs of gossip and press leaks, making it that much harder to put the plan on hold suddenly. He knew that HUD officials had already scheduled meetings with the editorial boards of the *Inquirer* and the *Daily News* for Friday, thereby digging themselves in even deeper. Finally, he knew that because Cisneros would be in Des Moines on Thursday, his ability to get directly involved in some crisis negotiation over the agreement was limited at best.

It was time to strike.

On Wednesday night, Cohen and several other city officials wrote out a list of eleven items that they wanted from HUD on behalf of the housing authority as part of the written agreement. Specific and detailed, the items ran well into the tens of millions of dollars—the ultimate wish list.

Cohen then worked all night preparing his own version of the agreement with all eleven items incorporated. He patiently waited until Thursday afternoon, by which time Cisneros was safely trapped in Des Moines and the scheduled press conference in Philadelphia was roughly twenty-four hours away. Then he faxed his version of the agreement, fifteen dense, single-spaced pages, to Assistant HUD Secretary Shuldiner, employing an old negotiating trick he had learned as a lawyer: always get the opposition to work off *your* draft, not theirs. He waited a little bit, then, at 5:00 P.M., with the scheduled press conference now *less than* twenty-four hours away, calmly gave Shuldiner the following message: the mayor is unwilling to proceed because there has been no response to the proposed agreement that was faxed. The response wasn't instantaneous; Cohen assumed that Cisneros was getting a panicked phone call in Des Moines saying that the mayor of Philadelphia was threatening to walk unless the city got exactly what it wanted. Shortly afterward the phone in Cohen's office rang. HUD, with the exception of some minor changes, had agreed to Cohen's version.

The next day, Henry Cisneros came to Philadelphia bright and brimming with anticipation of the 3:00 P.M. press conference that he had so sorely wanted.

"I think this is a national model, and this is the best hope we have together for really making a difference with public housing in Philadelphia," said Cisneros in announcing the unprecedented partnership. He also gave high praise to the mayor for his willingness to serve as chairman of the board. "I cannot say how powerful it is, how important it is, that the mayor would accept this kind of commitment. Most mayors run the other way in public housing. It's like 'Wall 'em up, it's someone else's responsibility' and never touch it.''

"I didn't want to be here," Rendell admitted. But he was, and if there was any solace, it was, as he put it privately, the degree to which the city had pulled a fine bit of "extortion" with the federal government.

Given the dynamic of racial politics in the city, the specter of a white mayor presiding over the drowning public housing authority, unable to provide a virtually all-black constituency with the barest of essentials, would be irresistible to those who hoped he would falter. One could almost hear the sound of State Representative Dwight Evans, the most likely black candidate to mount a challenge against the mayor in his bid for re-election in 1995, doing a little precampaign jig and pirouette. Could anything be more divine than those board meetings, with Rendell smack in the middle as the ultimate political piñata? Even Rendell, already thinking about reelection, could see the horrible ramifications. "If we haven't improved things, can you imagine that as a campaign issue? I'll get *banged* on it."

But the mayor, contrary to all the warnings, felt a sense of responsibility that reached beyond the narrow sphere of his own political dimensions. He heard the chorus of those who told him to walk away. He said that John Street, no less, understanding the potential for disaster, had privately suggested that the board be made up totally of tenants so that the board members would have no one to blame but themselves when things ground to a halt.

"Why *is* Ed doing this?" someone asked Cohen a moment before the announcement.

"There are two choices for Ed," Cohen replied. "One is to say 'This isn't going to work' and get as far away from PHA as he can. Just run from it. The other is to do what he is doing—'I can help, I'll lay my reputation on the line.' He's not a very professional politician. Most people would run."

There was the admirable motive of sacrifice, and there was also the pragmatic motive of politics beyond the walls of the city. Cohen felt that Rendell would say yes to Cisneros out of loyalty to the president. Given the way that cities now basically fended for themselves, competing desperately for whatever largesse the federal government did hand out, such loyalty might be useful, assuming the president was even aware of it.

As it turned out, the president did know about it, personally calling Rendell one day at the beginning of September to congratulate him. He seemed truly gratified by what Rendell had done, and his obvious appreciation could only enhance the city's position for the greatest federal handout of all—a highly coveted urban empowerment zone potentially worth hundreds of millions.

III

The two men had worked their wizardry again, political guts and guile melded into one, always several steps ahead. But success was not without its penalty.

Cohen, however much he enjoyed the legend of immaculate perfection, worried about the impact of his work on his wife and two children. As a lawyer, he had always worked inhuman hours, but in spite of his obsessive preoccupation with whatever case was at hand, there had been some breathing space. As chief of staff, he was barely ever at home, and even when he was home or out with the family, there was no respite. He would watch the local news or read the papers, and something would make him livid, and off he would go on a round of furious calls with reporters and editors, trying to get a headline changed or a beginning paragraph softened. He would be out at a school function with his kids, and his beeper would go off five times in an hour and a half, Rendell and Fumo and Street all calling like lost children looking for their lunch boxes. Rhonda and he would go to the movies, and someone would hand him a slip of paper, asking for a job. The family would go on trips, and in the car the kids would be silenced in the backseat so their father could conduct the business of the city over the car phone in the front. Wherever he went, it didn't matter. He was always in the glass box of work, a victim, albeit a willing one, of his own indispensability.

The effects of his constant absence were only intensified by the fact that one of his sons, eight-year-old Benjamin, had special needs as a result of the considerable complications at birth. He knew that Benjamin needed more attention than a normal child, not less, and now he was afraid that other children would ostracize him because of his differences. He was a remarkable child. He knew all the lottery numbers and could read at a seventh-grade level and was writing a fifteen-chapter book on penguins at the computer. But his social and physical skills were different from those of other children his age. "Other eight-year-olds want to play dodgeball and baseball, and Benjamin can't do that and will never be able to do that," said Cohen. "It tears at me, but it tears at Rhonda ten times worse." One night when he came home at 10:30, which was early for him, he found her crying. She was a highly regarded lawyer at Ballard Spahr, and he knew that the pressures of work and the pressures of home that she faced were enormous. But Cohen also knew he was of little help. "I'm never there, I can never be counted on," he confessed.

It was a rare personal admission, as close as he could come to a confession of failure about something, a segment of his life that he had let atrophy. There were many who thought Cohen reveled too much in his role as governmental gunslinger to ever consider leaving, and the pace at which he worked was as intense as it had been during those first days in January of 1992, when the beeper had gone berserk and he had 182 phone calls in one day. But every now and then he did harbor private doubts as to how long he could sustain it. "It's impossible to have an expectation of the unrelenting nature of it," he said. And when asked whether he truly liked what he did, he looked up from the perfectly arranged piles on his desk for a moment and laughed and shrugged his shoulders and went back to work. He had loved being a lawyer, in itself a strange and anomalous thing, but this was different. Very different. Every now and then, when another problem got dumped in his lap, when someone did something that was sloppy and incompetent and required his overhaul, there was just the slightest recognition that he might one day have to sever his ties to the mayor and return to his former life.

For Rendell, returning to his former life meant being out of elective office. He sometimes mused about what he would do once his tenure as mayor was over, at the end of 1995 if he failed to win reelection or at the end of the two-term limit. He threw out the possibility of running a foundation or maybe teaching or starting a business with his son or even doing a radio show. There were many who thought he would make a great baseball commissioner, but the reality of all that seemed unimaginable.

His wife, Midge, had seen the impact of those awful times in the 1980s when he had gotten whipped in two elections back-to-back, first in the Democratic primary for governor and then in the Democratic primary for mayor. He was adequate as a lawyer in private practice, but she likened his situation to that of a vocalist suddenly having his vocal chords removed after years of singing or being told to find a new way of breathing. The loss of politics in his life combined with those humiliating losses, not once but twice in succession—"to have everybody slap you in the face," as Midge described it—filled him with self-doubt. After the loss in the Democratic mayoral primary, he and Midge went away for a little bit, and he sat on the foot of the bed and talked about how worthless he was and what he was going to do now that he was a political failure. The littlest thing would go wrong, something as simple as not being able to find a sock, and off he would go into a paroxysm of feeling worthless. Jesse, still a young boy then, identified with his father thoroughly, and these moods caused Jesse's confidence to falter. "Jesse took it really hard," Midge remembered. "I had two kind of unhappy campers on my hands." Midge, a lawyer in a high-powered local firm, also had the considerable rigors of her own professional life to deal with. "I wasn't real happy," she confessed.

On a day-to-day basis, they were fine, but there was always this undercurrent of "walking on eggshells" as she put it, waiting for that moment when something would go wrong and there would be this invective of *"I'm worthless. I can't do anything right."* At those moments, she didn't know how to react to her husband. Sometimes she sympathized and told him he was being silly. Other times, many times, she told him to just grow up. Sometimes she agreed with him, as a kind of challenge. "It got to the point where I'm looking in the mirror going, 'OK, I tried this. I tried this, and I realized I couldn't change it. I couldn't alter his perception.' He was going to have to do it himself. It's like quitting smoking or something. So I kind of let it be, and I figured it would have to work itself out."

They went to California on vacation. Midge was playing golf while Ed and Jesse went to the beach. They had a board so Jesse could surf, and they were carrying a chair, and they had to walk an extra block, and Ed was getting frustrated with all this *goddamn equipment,* and then he started yelling at his son. Jesse was eight or nine at the time, and he just sat down and started crying uncontrollably. At dinner that night, Jesse just said to Midge in a way that was almost sheepish, "Mom, you should have been there today."

"It was an epiphany for Eddie," she remembered. "He said to himself in a way that I never could have and nobody ever could have, 'What am I doing to this kid?' This one event turned his whole life around. I will say to him to this day, 'You know, you changed your life.' And he did. He really did."

Midge was a counterpoint to her husband, organized and even-keeled. She didn't have his ebullience, but she also didn't have the flash point of temper that could make him truly terrifying, that sudden and unpredictable switch. He was also the mayor, captive of the city twenty-four hours a day, and the compromises were such that tears came to his eyes. But they were

tears of guilt, not tears of action. He might think there was another way for
him, but there wasn't. And it wasn't the power that seemed to make him
such an addict of politics—in fact, the least of its appeal was the power—
but the very juice of it, a constant source of energy for a man who had to
be plugged into something all the time.

"Eddie is not a controlled person in any way, shape, or form," said
Midge of her husband. "And that is one of the things that is amazing about
him. He is totally uncontrolled. He could never do the things he does if he
was controlled. He lets his vision go, and it's mind-bending. As far as it
goes in every direction."

Rendell and Cohen spent more time with each other than with their wives,
and they talked to each other more, and the results of that union, whatever
the personal impact, had been this unprecedented streak of success. "Think
about Ed," said Cohen. "From the time he entered the election for mayor
in 1990, virtually everything has gone his way. It's an unbelievably sustained period of time for anyone in the public eye."

Cohen tried to be humble about it. He knew how much was left to do,
and he knew the cunning nature of the city, its instinct for chaos in the middle of calm, the way it lurked and crept and then pounced. But watching
the two of them fill each other in day after day, one found it hard not to feel
a tiny bump in the heart and hear the whisper of something improbable.

"My God, they're going to do it. They're going to save the damn city."

Everything was going so well that it seemed as if fate itself had given in
to them. For the first time in six years, the city's budget actually had a sur-
plus. Because of the success of the union negotiations and other cost-
saving initiatives, the Rendell administration had eliminated a structural
deficit of almost $200 million—almost 10 percent of the entire operating
budget—without raising taxes. Even the Phillies, picked for ignominy in
1993, were making a march to the World Series with a group of crude and
burly players who scratched and spit like cavemen and were somehow lovable in their loathsome way. A trip to the Series would mean not only another psychic boost for the city but an extra kick of revenues from a
sold-out stadium and packed hotels and restaurants. Together in the
mayor's office, Rendell and Cohen watched game five of the National
League championship as the Phils battled the heavily favored Atlanta
Braves. The game was tight and went into extra innings with the score
knotted at 3–3. Center fielder Lenny Dykstra homered in the top of the
tenth to give the Phils a 4–3 lead. Reliever Larry Andersen then came in to

work the bottom of the tenth and gave the Phils the win when he struck out Ron Gant. It was a dramatic victory, and Rendell let out a loud and glorious whoop and seemed just about ready to start running around the office with arms lifted high in a personal victory lap. Cohen himself smiled. History would record that he at least did that. The pitch that Dykstra had sent soaring for the home run was clearly on his mind. Curve? Sinker? Fastball?

"That pitch cost us three hundred fifty thousand dollars."

It was an instant computation of how much the city would have to shell out in extra police security if indeed the Phillies eked out another win and took the National League pennant. The mayor laughed, but there was something hollow about it, and for a brief moment, as he shot a glance at this man next to him, it was hard to tell whether he was laughing because he thought David Cohen was funny or because he thought David Cohen was really quite mad.

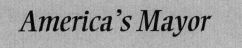

America's Mayor

FOURTEEN

"We Hardly Knew Ye"

I

The day after the president of the United States called to congratulate the mayor of the city for assuming control of the housing authority, Assistant District Attorney Mike McGovern was back in that space between the rows of spectators and the judge's bench, spinning yet another story of his city.

He was dressed in a crisp blue suit, and his contempt for the defendant

sitting at the table next to him, trying to act like some sweet-Jesus choir-
boy who was in court only because his spitball had broken a stained glass
window during silent prayer, was fierce. But with one slight variation:
Today, September 10, 1993, was his last day with the district attorney's
office.

He had submitted his resignation.

Earlier that summer, as he lay on the beach at Avalon on the Jersey
shore, figuring out his future, he knew it was time to leave. He was joining
a small firm in the city with two former prosecutors he knew and admired
professionally. The job change meant that he would be representing criminal defendants instead of prosecuting them. For someone who approached
the prosecutor's job with as much zeal as he did, this was a morally queasy
position to be in—knowing he might be the one to produce the self-
satisfied laugh of someone getting away with murder. He knew how much
he would miss that sense of being the white knight, depended on by the
victims' family members to act with vigilance and seek vindication. "It
makes you feel you really were a crusader for a good cause," he said, "and
it's hard to walk away from." The wall of his little office had been a testament to the work he did, covered with notes and letters of profuse thanks
for squeezing something good, something just, out of the horror of what
had happened. But economic reality dictated the move, and McGovern's
eternal competitiveness, the way his street folksiness hardened when challenged, made the transition more palatable.

But it was still odd to see his helter-skelter office, like a manager's office at a busy train station, stripped so bare, the notes and thank-you cards
gone, the pictures and mementos packed away, the brown cardboard cartons piled high with notes of testimony hauled into storage—the Sean
Daily case, which had defined him as a lawyer; the Will Taylor case, with
its wrenching window onto the racism of the city; the case of Robert Janke,
the young man who had died because of a misplaced set of house keys; the
case of Gilda Taylor, the former cocaine addict who was trying to scare her
sixteen-year-old son when the gun she was holding went off and who was
found by the police kneeling next to his bed, trying vainly to resuscitate
him, with blood all over her face and hands. As he recalled these and other
cases he had tried, he could once again feel the heart of darkness, the endless capacity of men and women for evil, vengeance, and sadness.

"Someone once said to me, 'You see things that no one else ever sees.'
I told him, 'Hey, I see things that no one else wants to see.' "

All that was left was a piece of paper taped to a beige file cabinet, a note that had been left by one of his colleagues: "Mikey, we hardly knew ye."

The final days had been bittersweet and conflicted. He still took notes on legal pads and scraps of paper, and he knew that the jazzy equipment lawyers fancied now, "candy" as he called it, the laptops and the cellular phones, was no substitute for a closing argument that went right to the jugular. In his office, packing up the few remaining items that were left, he remembered trying a case in which the defense attorney used a computer and a phone and a beeper that flashed lengthy messages. McGovern himself was equipped with a legal pad and a number 2 pencil, and the lawyer was cross-examining a witness and scoring points when McGovern heard a little murmur from the lawyer's back pocket. "Your phone is ringing," he said to break the momentum and allow the witness time to regroup. And of course there was no way he could have resisted what he said next. "If it's my wife, tell her I'm not here."

As he was packing, he came upon the first newspaper article to mention his name, a 1982 column in the *Daily News* by Pete Dexter, who went on to win the National Book Award for *Paris Trout*.

> *Todd White was smiling Friday. Common Pleas Judge John Meade had just turned him loose. Probation. Besides that, Judge Meade had thrown Assistant DA Mike McGovern out of the courtroom. McGovern hadn't wanted White turned loose. The reason for that was that White had just been convicted of robbery. He had gone into the home of a 57-year-old disabled minister in South Philadelphia, pistol-whipped him, taken $60, his television and his radio, and threatened to kill him if he told the police. . . . McGovern stood up to argue. Among other things, he said probation in this case was an outrage to the community. Meade instructed a sheriff's deputy to take him out of the courtroom. "That young man's problem," the judge said later, speaking of McGovern, "is that he's young. I was just saving him from being held in contempt of court."*

It had been a grand ride, hadn't it?

And it had been more than just obligation that had prompted McGovern to say in his resignation letter to District Attorney Lynne Abraham, "I regret that I shall not continue to be part of this fine Office and its noble and tireless pursuit of justice for the citizens of Philadelphia. I will cherish my

years as an Assistant District Attorney for a lifetime." But the other part of
the letter told the truth about why he was leaving. "Unfortunately, as my
children have grown so have my family's financial needs. Of course, this
growth requires one to make difficult choices."

The McGoverns' oldest child, Bridget, had just started ninth grade at
Nazareth Academy, and they had three younger children to worry about as
well. They had tried the public schools once, which seemed only reasonable since their tax dollars went to support them. Bridget had gone to
kindergarten at Comly Elementary, over on Byberry and Kelvin, but as
McGovern's wife, Mary Pat, recalled, the teacher was in her sixties, had a
heart problem, and often fell asleep because of the medication she was taking. She was replaced—but by revolving-door teachers. The school itself
was old and dirty, and the McGoverns became unwilling to consider
the public schools a viable option for any of their children. That meant
parochial schools, and that meant tuition costs that would only multiply as
each child reached school age. They weren't alone in this. Because of the
quality of the city's public school system and the reliance instead on private and parochial schools, Philadelphia had the lowest percentage of its
students attending public schools of the ten largest cities in the country.

It made the McGoverns, as it made so many thousands of others in the
swath of the middle class, subject to the illogic of city life. Because the
city's public schools were uniformly poor, they spent thousands on education that they would not have spent if they had lived in the suburbs. Compounding this, because McGovern lived in the city, his salary was subject
to a 4.96 percent city wage tax that he would not have had to pay if he had
lived and worked in the suburbs. In return for the additional taxes he paid
as a city resident, McGovern not only was unable to use the schools, but
he also received a level of service that was a shadow of what he would
have received in the suburbs.

Liberated now from such strictures, McGovern and his family could
move. They could cross the border. When Mary Pat tallied it up, the ledger
sheet of reasons to stay and reasons to leave was so lopsided that it was
hard to believe anyone within the spectrum of the middle class was still
left. Beyond sheer emotion, what exactly was the reason to stay?

Housing costs in the city were generally cheaper, and her husband had
a shorter commute than he would have had from some of the suburbs they
might have considered. She also knew that her husband might want to be
a judge someday, a position that required residence in the city.

On the negative side, there was the school dilemma, which by the time their son Michael went to high school, in the fall of 1995, would cost them about $15,000 in tuition. There was the wage tax dilemma. There was the car insurance dilemma, with rates in the city nearly twice as high as rates in the suburbs. There was the services dilemma, particularly when it came to such things as snow removal. There was the parking dilemma. There was the traffic dilemma. There was the surroundings dilemma. There was the safety dilemma.

All of that might have been somehow palatable, but what particularly disturbed Mary Pat was the indignity of it all. There were good things about city life, but the penalties were so onerous as to completely drown them out, as if over the years, city officials, through their tax policies and their school policies and their fiscal policies, were literally daring people to leave. It disturbed her that the middle class was given no incentive to stay while businesses and corporations, many of them rich and thriving, were given all sorts of incentives to stay—free land and tax abatements and low-interest loans. She understood the need to preserve jobs, but in the meantime, demographics showed that the middle-class family in the city was moving closer and closer to extinction. "They give businesses tax breaks and incentives to stay in the city all the time," she said. "But what about the average citizen?" You paid taxes for schools you couldn't use and for services that were often inferior, and after a while what joys you might derive from the city got lost in hardened disdain. "Why should I be loyal to the city?" she asked.

Mike McGovern's debate with his wife over leaving or staying would only intensify. But on his last day of work, he wasn't dwelling on that. He was just thinking of saying good-bye in some way that would do justice to all the emotions he felt. He stood in Courtroom 696 and found the room as effervescent as ever despite the usual accoutrements of sound-blasting air-conditioning and tired wooden chairs and limp brown shades hanging halfway down dirt-soaked windows.

Because the complete notes of testimony in the case at hand, *Commonwealth v. Edward Graziano,* were not available, defense attorney Jack Meyers wanted a thirty-day continuance. McGovern argued vociferously against it because he sorely wanted to end his career with a sentencing, particularly the sentencing of Graziano. He argued so vociferously, in fact, that the judge presiding over the case, Ricardo Jackson, had to tell him to shut up.

"Doesn't counsel understand that I'm talking?" said Jackson.

"I'm sorry, your honor," said McGovern sheepishly.

According to testimony at the trial, Graziano had killed a college student outside an after-hours club in an apparent dispute over the victim's girlfriend. Dominic Capocci was twenty when he died, his look of intimidation and menace that night amounting to shorts, a T-shirt, Air Nikes, and a Yankees cap turned backward. He was killed with a single bullet from Graziano's gun, which had been placed almost equidistant between the eyes, the bullet making a silver-dollar-size hole in the forehead and then exiting above the bill of the Yankees cap. The look on his face when he died wasn't terror but absolute shock, as if he couldn't believe what had just happened. He was a junior at La Salle University and worked at his family's sandwich shop.

Graziano had been talking with Capocci's girlfriend earlier in the evening and claimed that he pulled the gun he was carrying and fired accidentally in self-defense when Capocci and four of his friends surrounded him. But McGovern, during the trial, had called the shooting "totally unprovoked," and a jury supported him with a murder conviction.

Judge Jackson said the sentencing could proceed without the notes of testimony.

"It was one of the most vicious killings I've seen in my eight years as a homicide prosecutor, and I'm not just saying that to make a speech," said McGovern, dressed in his crisp blue suit. Pointing to the defendant, he said that Graziano, after shooting the victim in the forehead, then turned to the girlfriend and said, "There, take him home."

Suddenly from the grim soup of the courtroom came a voice. *"Fuck you, motherfucker. You don't know nothin'."* It belonged to the defendant, and McGovern turned red, the kind of deep red that anyone from the old neighborhood in Port Richmond would have recognized and immediately fled from in terror. But to the bitter end, he was a good and loyal prosecutor, and however much he wanted to make a rousing speech for his grand finale or just walk several feet and strangle the defendant himself, he knew, even without the benefit of a laptop, that this was the time for a different strategy. The defendant had just made the best speech of all.

"The Commonwealth rests, your honor," said McGovern abruptly, and he sat down.

"You have a smart-guy attitude, and you should spend your life in prison," said the judge. Just for good measure, he threw in ten extra years on two gun charges.

"I wanted that guy like meat!" McGovern snapped outside the courtroom, his face still red and glowing. But by the time he got back to the

homicide wing at the district attorney's office, he was exultant, his com-
bativeness there for the world to challenge. "I crushed my last one like a
grape!" he said to a colleague. Heading down the hallway back to his own
office, he muttered to himself those final, epic words of his life as a prosecutor in the city. *"Fuck you, motherfucker. You don't know nothin'.*

"I know one thing," said McGovern in the singsong taunt of a child.
"You're spending the rest of your life in jail."

To the very end, he was passionate and exultant. Maybe that was why,
as he had walked back to his office, he had been stopped by several people
who knew that this September day was his last and wanted to express their
regret. They liked McGovern personally, but it was more than that, for as
one of them told him as he grasped his hand, "The city's gonna miss you."

II

Several days later, still in September, as the mayor entered the sprawl of
the navy yard, he seemed on the edge of total eruption. Karen Lewis, one
of his saintly schedulers, was in the car with him, going over upcoming
events. She could sense the build up of a wig out but knew that sometimes
in moments such as these he was able to maintain his hold on rationality.
Lewis watched with patience, looking for some inkling: Dr. Jekyll today
or Mr. Hyde? Yin or Yang? Santa Claus or Scrooge? The answer came moments after he entered the yard.

"Fucking waste of time! Fucking waste of time! Fucking waste of time!"

The question of the mayor's mood had been adequately answered.

He most decidedly was unhappy to be going where he was going, to
board the aircraft carrier USS *John F. Kennedy* as it pushed up the
Delaware and into the navy yard for an extensive overhaul. Although his
outburst had to do with the endless burdens of overscheduling, this visit to
the yard, however brief, was a sad and bittersweet experience that didn't
help matters any.

About sixty-two hundred workers were still employed there, but the
massive facility, spread over some nine hundred acres, barely stirred. In
the absence of a miracle, its closure two years from now, on September 15,
1995, would be a monumental disaster for the mayor in terms of job loss
in the city. As added injury, the closure would also come during the heat
of his campaign for reelection.

The overhaul of the *Kennedy* did provide some reprieve. Some fifteen hundred to two thousand construction workers would be employed at any one time during the $500-million project. In addition, nine hotels and apartment houses had won low-bid contracts for housing crew members who would reside in Philadelphia during the overhaul. But this was the last hurrah.

The mayor's car stopped at a landing strip. Rendell looked out the window, his fury of a few moments ago replaced by a voice simultaneously forlorn and mortified. *"Look at that thing."*

It was a helicopter, a big, clattering, kick-ass navy transport helicopter, and it would take Rendell and the aides traveling with him to the *Kennedy*. He got out of the car and lumbered to the craft. He resignedly clambered on board, where he got strapped in and had to don a life jacket and protective gear for the head and ears. "What the fuck am I doing here?" he said, now laughing at the absurdity of it, aware of how bizarre he looked, with his gray suit pants sticking out of the life jacket and his head covered by plastic earmuffs. Even though he disliked heights, he seemed OK as the helicopter lifted, until he realized something else, and the voice of mortification returned. *"Aren't they going to close this door?"*

There was no door, at least no door that could be closed, and as the helicopter made its way toward the flight deck of the *Kennedy,* past the quiescence of the yard and its lines of mothballed ships, Rendell clutched the sides of the little bench he was sitting on with fanatic devotion. He talked incessantly even though no one, over the noise of the rotor blades and through the earmuffs, could hear a word except for a loud *whooohhh* when the helicopter made a sharp bank to the right in its final descent.

Once on board, the mayor seemed as if another person from within had taken him over. He passed out pretzels in the *Kennedy* control room, instructing crew members on the proper etiquette: "You eat these babies with mustard." He sat in the chair of the carrier's commanding officer, and eyeing a string of phones nearby, he asked, "Which one is for the president?" He saw that the chair had protective padding that he recognized from someplace else, and then it dawned on him—"Oh, you got taxi beads." He also conducted a spirited conversation with crew members on the authenticity of the Cher video in which she sings "If I Could Turn Back Time" on board a battleship, parenthetically noting that his son, Jesse, had changed the lyric to "Look at my firm backside."

Once safely back on the ground, he couldn't get the Cher song out of his mind and began to sing it to himself over and over, with his son's substituted lyric, of course. He described his visit to the *Kennedy* as "amusing, fun, but a total waste of time." It may have been, but passing out pretzels and making crew members laugh seemed far more constructive than viewing the parade of politicians falling over themselves in their attempts to suggest that the yard would somehow survive its closing date with new work. There was inspirational talk about creating a national maritime and industrial center, in which the yard, operating as a public-private partnership, would continue to compete for naval maintenance and repair work while becoming a focal point for the development of shipbuilding-related technologies. There was still talk of enticing Mercedes-Benz to build its new plant inside the yard. There was talk of getting new subway cars built there.

"The people at the shipyard should not be looking for jobs now," proclaimed Congressman Thomas Foglietta, who made sure he was on the flight deck of the *Kennedy* as well. "I have a lot of faith in that."

"This shipyard can move forward as a center of shipbuilding and maritime work and help point the way to rebuilding the maritime industry in the United States," proclaimed Senator Harris Wofford, even though most shipbuilding experts considered this an absurd fantasy.

"If they do their usual top-notch work on this ship, there will be more work to come," proclaimed Congressman Rob Andrews, whose district in southern New Jersey included a high percentage of shipyard workers.

As a shipyard worker himself, Jim Mangan listened to what the politicians had to say in this latest round and digested it and continued steadfastly not to believe a word of it. Ever since the yard had been slated for closure in 1991, it had been the same, a massive manipulation of the hearts and minds of workers for their political support, an immoral trade of false hopes for votes, and he refused to buy into it. The effect of such comments on the workers was both predictable and cruel. The yard was a swell of rumors, and Mangan saw worker after worker cling to what the politicians said as if it were Scripture. "They still feel there's some miracle around the corner," said Mangan. "They are still in denial—'We've got to do a good job [on the *Kennedy*] and then [the yard] will be saved.' "

Early in his career, Mangan had enjoyed watching when one of the massive carriers came into the yard. He vividly remembered the first one he saw, the *Saratoga*, amazed something that big could actually float. But when the *Kennedy* arrived on this clear September day in 1993, Mangan didn't even bother to watch. He felt no swell of feeling one way or another, except that it meant some work and probably some overtime, "the last gasp" as he put it, "the last chance to make money."

The yard really had been reduced to a whisper anyway, so the work was welcome. There had been little for welders to do, and Mangan had spent most of his time repairing welding cable or, in his own blunt words, "doing practically nothing." The shipyard was aware of the lull, and Mangan had been assigned to go down to the navy yard in Charleston, South Carolina, for thirty days at the end of the summer, but with six kids at home, he didn't know how he could possibly do it. Neither did his wife, Linda.

She was supportive of him in what he was going through as he faced the uncertainty of his future, and she did her best not to get nervous or in any way add pressure. When asked whether she was worried about what Jim would do if the yard closed, she said no without the slightest tic of reservation. After a year of volunteering, Linda now worked part-time as a classroom aide at nearby Smedley Elementary. It helped make ends meet, but she did it primarily to keep an eye on two of her children who went there and had come home with stories of fights. The school was small and overcrowded, and many of its students were reluctant refugees from the Catholic schools, there because their parents could no longer afford the tuition. She and Jim had discussed the idea of her working full-time. The pay would help, and so of course would the benefits if Jim decided to go into business for himself once he left the yard. But since the school district wasn't hiring, the issue was moot.

She had been terrified when Jim came home and told her the yard wanted him to go to Charleston, although she tried her best not to show it. She got headaches and had stomach problems. She worried about how she was going to take care of the kids by herself, but she also worried that if he didn't go, he would get into trouble and maybe even lose his job. Pocketing her fears, Linda got out a suitcase and bought him new clothes. Jim in turn made a reservation at a hotel in Charleston, figuring he had no choice. Then, on the day before he was supposed to go, he heard of six or seven others in the welding shop who were refusing the assignment. As an old union steward, he knew there was safety in numbers. He went into the backyard of the little home on Haworth and told Linda he wasn't going, even though in all probability that meant a five-day suspension, but she was relieved.

Jim was relieved too. He had not wanted to go in the first place, and if he had gone, he would have missed the birthday party for his daughter Cheryl. He was devoted to his wife and children, and he couldn't help but worry about the impact the loss of his job would have on them, not simply in terms of the enormous financial burden but also in terms of how they would think of him if he somehow failed in his role as the family provider. He still thought of running his own business, but it was a daunting prospect, and then he watched an episode of *60 Minutes* about Hewlett-Packard hiring software engineers from overseas, and that just added to his feeling vulnerable in the marketplace. "I was worried about competing with kids right out of college. Now I'll be competing with people from other countries."

He thought he at least had the underpinnings of the solid high school education he had received in the city. His children, as far as he could tell, didn't even have that, in part because of the quality of the education they received, and in part because of their own mercurial motivation. Because of the spread in their ages, they attended three public schools in the city, Smedley, Harding Middle School, and Frankford High, and Mangan wished he could be in all three of them simultaneously to try to figure out what really went on. Because Linda worked at Smedley, they at least had that base covered. But as far as he could tell with his older children, none of them had ever sufficiently grasped the basics, and this seemed most glaring in his daughter Michelle, who was a senior at Frankford. By her own admission, Michelle had never written a real term paper. The most she had done was an essay with a couple of paragraphs, and she admitted that she had no idea of how to write a letter requesting a job. She had difficulty with geometry and physics and had taken general physical science instead. She said she got a B in the course without ever taking the final, and her strongest impression of the teacher was that he spent part of each class doing push-ups with the football players. Perhaps her greatest achievement was in ceramics, evidence of which could be seen in the ten little pots neatly arrayed at the bottom of the entertainment unit in the Mangans' living room.

"You have to sell an awful lot of those pots to pay off a mortgage," said Mangan to his daughter.

"I'm getting better," said Michelle.

Cheryl, who was in the tenth grade at Frankford, reported a similar atmosphere. In ninth-grade biology, she said, everyone shared the homework and the tests, so "you didn't learn nothing." In algebra, she did not get a regular teacher until October, a not unusual feature of the chaos that marked the beginning of every school year. She didn't think the school was particularly dangerous, but most of the bathrooms had been locked after a group of students set fire to a schoolbag that had been left behind and threw it in a toilet.

It just seemed to Mangan that his two oldest children were learning in high school what he had learned in grade school, and it puzzled and concerned him. "I got a chip on my shoulder," he said. "I pay real estate taxes. That goes to the Philadelphia public schools, so let them educate my children." He knew from his own experience how competitive the job market was, even if you had a specific skill. But his kids seemed to have no conception of it, and instead of seeing them taught the basics of reading and writing, he saw them filling their days with what he termed Mickey Mouse projects—assignments for Black History Month and assignments to write about your ancestors, and Mangan knew that his children could barely write at all. He thought about Catholic school for his children, but given what was happening at the yard, there was no way he could even dream of paying for it. The *Kennedy* had come in, and that would keep the place going for a while, would give workers who were scared out of their wits the opportunity to deny the inevitable or just put it off. His daughter Michelle might have received a totally inadequate education, but she was smart enough in the fall of 1993 to ask her father the questions that counted most: "What's going to happen to these people when they close that place down? Where are all the jobs going to come from?"

"That's the question of the hour" was the only answer he could give.

The politicians were telling him he really had nothing to worry about. Foglietta, Wofford, Andrews, Specter—congressmen and senators alike claimed that good times were ahead for the navy yard now that the *Kennedy* had come in. They were sure of it. They guaranteed it. They promised it with the cameras running and the reporters scribbling. But what was the risk of supplying such mushroom clouds of false hope and delusion anyway? After all, they weren't the ones losing their jobs.

On the outside, Jim Mangan seemed remarkably calm and stoic, showing a true sense of courage on that humble and hearty red-brick block of Haworth. But on the inside, he felt something different. "I'm in turmoil. It just doesn't leak out."

FIFTEEN

Vision for the City

I

The meeting of the committee established by the mayor to develop a new vision for the city and usher Philadelphia into the next century quite naturally began early, so Linda Morrison was at the platform of the train station a little before 7:00 A.M. It was early in December 1993, and the slight chill of winter had just begun to set in.

She had made it to the station with a good five minutes to spare. The last-minute push of commuters up the narrow hill of Benezet Street hadn't begun yet, and those who had already reached the station were inside the little waiting room. Linda was outside on the platform listening to her Walkman, and that was a wonderful development. In her days of shell shock after Queen Village, she never would have done that. She would have stayed in the waiting room and caught the train just before it left so as not to linger on the platform any longer than necessary. Like many who had been victims of crime or witnesses to it, she wasn't about to take any chances, however improbable the odds. She had been mugged before in the city, and she had heard the scream of the stabbing outside her bedroom window on what was supposed to have been a first night of euphoria in a new home. After several months as refugees in the suburbs, she and her family had come back to the city, and they had picked their spot carefully. They were living now in a neighborhood called Chestnut Hill, in the north-west corner of the city. It was known for its tranquillity and its insulation, a privileged neighborhood where parents could let their kids roam on bikes and not consider themselves negligent or overly permissive. She was more relaxed than she had been in over a year, and when she arrived on the plat-form before the train chugged its way around the curve from the Gravers Lane Station, she didn't feel scared or apprehensive at all.

That isn't to say Linda wasn't agitated about something. When it came to the bureaucracy that she dealt with every day in her job, there was no inner peace. The initial burst of contracting out and other cost-cutting initiatives by the administration had been bold, but she worried about whether the momentum would be sustained now that the budget was in balance and the union negotiations were over.

In many ways, it seemed surprising, if not slightly comical, that she had ever been allowed to get anywhere near this committee to develop a new vision for the city, particularly when her first suggestion might be to get rid of City Hall altogether, its towering spine smack in the epicenter not only an impediment to the flow of traffic but also an unwanted monument to the almighty colossus of government. Although she commanded respect from various colleagues for her intellect, her dissatisfaction with even an im-proved status quo—the way she was always dashing off a memo to Cohen on why not try this and why not try that?—had never made her popular. Most managers in government, she had discovered in her job as the city's competitive contracting coordinator, had little interest in doing what her job title suggested should be done—improve the delivery of city services by contracting out various functions that could be performed better and more cheaply by the private sector. City managers still judged themselves by the size of their budget and the size of their workforce: the bigger the budget and the more people working for them, the better the job they were doing. If they reduced their spending or contracted a particular function out, it was usually because someone above them, most likely Cohen, put the fear of God into them and told them to do it. As a result, the idea of someone like Linda coming along and jauntily suggesting ways to cut their budget and their workforce did not make her subject to long embraces. Almost incredibly, she couldn't tell who was more resistant to contracting out, the unions whose functions would be taken away or the city managers who would presumably now be able to offer the public a better level of service.

But Linda persevered, in many ways developing a program from scratch, what she referred to as Linda's Handy-Dandy Checklist. When reporters came from out of town and pointed to Rendell as the next city messiah, contracting out was one of the miracles they cited. By the mayor's own estimate, which he presented at the prestigious Wriston Lecture of the Manhattan Institute in New York City in November 1993, fifteen different functions had been privatized, and fifteen more were on the drawing board, for a total savings of close to $35 million a year. "Privatization has not proven nearly as hard to do as everyone expected," said the mayor. "And it is more than just a money saver: in almost every case, we are delivering a better product to the citizens of Philadelphia." With an endorsement such as that, it was hard to believe that Linda had anything to be concerned about. But still she worried.

Her presence on the strategic plan committee made her even more ambivalent. She knew her views on government were different from those of the people she worked with, and she wasn't sure how her input could make even the slightest impact. But the chairman had urged her to take part, and then the mayor officially appointed her to it, writing her a letter in November emphatically stating the importance of the work she and the others would do in the coming months. "The city's Strategic Plan will establish the City's vision, develop action plans to make that vision a reality, and position the city for the year 2000," wrote the mayor.

From the letter at least, it sounded like a heady assignment, and Linda seemed to be a bit intrigued by it. Perhaps she could urge her fellow committee members to come up with a vision for the city that truly was different and far-reaching, not the same warmed-over bromides. Why not inject competition into everything, if it improved the delivery of services? Why not dismantle such bureaucracies as the city's public schools? Why not privatize them and make every teacher and every principal compete for his or her job—or at least offer vouchers? Why not markedly lower the city's wage tax and the business privilege tax and the net profits tax? The rote answer to these questions, she knew, was that it couldn't be done because of money or because the dictates of politics simply wouldn't allow it or because the unions were too powerful or because she was naïve and pie-in-the-sky and out of her mind.

It was true that the city depended on its wage and business-related taxes for more than $1 billion in yearly revenue, just as it was true that those same taxes had made the cost of doing business in Philadelphia higher than the cost of doing business in any other city in the country and had driven thousands of jobs away. It was true that privatizing the schools was impossible given the alchemy of unions and politics, and it was true that vouchers were fraught with difficult ramifications, but it was also true that no single factor contributed more to the middle-class exodus and the poor languishing behind than the horrendous Philadelphia public school system. She still loved the city, but she and her husband, like thousands of others, were right on the edge, and many of those thousands, tired of bad schools and demoralizing tax rates and the fear of crime, had already left.

In fact, since 1990, despite the wonders of Rendell and his almost universal acclaim, the city had lost more residents than any other city in the country, and the mayor knew exactly what that meant: the cancer in the pores of the city was still very much there.

Since her house was close to the train station, Linda could leave at 6:45 A.M. and still get there in plenty of time. She and her husband were renting a house just two blocks down the hill, on Benezet Street, and it hadn't taken them long to fall in love with their new surroundings. With roots going back to the 1700s, Chestnut Hill was still a gem of a place, a village within the city that many considered the last oasis of civility and— most important of all for Linda and her husband, Jon—the last oasis of safety. With its effortless sprinkling of $750,000 homes along streets that were quiet and fat with trees, with its main thoroughfare of Germantown Avenue, where precious antique stores looked in disdain upon the nouveau riche arrivals of The Gap and Banana Republic, Chestnut Hill had a reputation among many in the city as entitled, spoiled, and irreversibly snotty. Anytime a new store or restaurant tried to open, there was an immediate hue and cry among certain Chestnut Hill residents who were sure that the place was finally going to hell for good, that the end of refinement and the onslaught of riffraff were upon them. But the result of such eternal vigilance was a place unique not only in the city but in all of America, suburban in feel but not too suburban to be rendered androgynous, physically set off not only by the hill but also by a deep gorge that ran along the western boundary, a moat donated by God.

The street the Morrisons lived on was named after Anthony Benezet. Concerned about the pernicious effects of slavery in the middle 1700s, Benezet had spent twenty years conducting classes for Negroes from his home and also started a school for girls in Philadelphia so they could learn Latin and Greek as well as needlework. The street itself was an architectural wonder, admired by planners the world over for all that a city street should be and so often was not. Even in the coziness of Chestnut Hill, there was something uniquely inviting about Benezet Street. The side the Morrisons lived on contained a block-long row of three-story twin houses that had been built in the early 1900s in a style that was part colonial revival and part English Jacobean and had come out looking slightly gingerbready. On the other side were several long stone houses that had been split up into spacious and airy quadruplets. All the homes on the Morrisons' side had marvelous wooden porches that gave the street a community feel that was rare and blessed, a throwback to the days when everybody in the city, unafraid of crime and one another, had sat outside after dark and talked. On one porch, there might be a candlelight dinner. On another, the slow tune of a rocker to the reading of a magazine. On another, the frolic of children.

Emotionally and spiritually the Morrisons could not afford a repeat of what had happened in Queen Village. They had picked their newest location carefully, and during the seven months or so that they had been living in Chestnut Hill, they could not have been happier or more content. It had taken Linda little time at all to feel at home, to feel she was part of something special.

The train hadn't arrived yet when Linda walked down the platform to the vending machine and bought the *Inquirer*. As she did, she saw something, and she immediately knew what was happening, but for a split second she rejected the knowledge. This was *Chestnut Hill,* the city's last refuge. What was happening could not be happening. It just couldn't.

About twenty-five to thirty feet away, a man in a black jogging suit with the hood of the sweatshirt pulled over his head was quickly coming toward her. Before she knew it, she could feel the tip of something cold and blunt in her side, then at her head.

"Give me your purse, or I'll blow your head off."

She screamed, and there was a millisecond struggle as he pulled away the purse, the strap of which she had draped over her arm. Her briefcase, which hung by a strap from her shoulder, fell to the platform. He took off down the stairs and out of the station. She ran down an exit ramp in the op-posite direction because she knew there was a pay phone there, and she called the police.

As far as Linda was concerned, the police were inclined to do little. She had not been able to get a good look at the perpetrator because of the way he had drawn the hood of his sweatshirt so tightly around his face. But the ticket agent had seen him when, shortly before the incident, he had come into the little station booth and asked for a schedule. She suggested that the police might want to show the ticket agent some mug shots, and they did. Nine days later.

Linda walked home. Her husband was still there and gave her some cash since she no longer had any. She managed to get herself to the committee meeting, but she was late and felt obligated to give the other members, who were already deep at work on the city's future, an explanation for her tar-diness. "I'm sorry that I'm late for a meeting of the internal working group on creating a vision for the city for the year 2000," she told them. "But I was just mugged in one of the city's nice neighborhoods."

In the aftermath, a range of emotions ran through her—terror, anger, foolishness for having let herself be so vulnerable and not following the cardinal rules of the city. Because she had been mugged before, many of these feelings were sadly familiar. But one feeling was different: the hor-rible sense of loss, the realization that even in a community like Chestnut Hill, there was still no immunity from crime and there never would be un-less all the residents, instead of fighting the newest restaurant or chain store, decided to pool their money and build a fort.

"I just can't do this anymore. I just can't stay here anymore."
That's how Linda Morrison now felt.

II

The Christmas tree lighting ceremony in the City Hall courtyard, another new feature of city life ushered in by the Rendell administration, was spec-tacular, as always. City Hall itself was ablaze with thousands of tiny lights that had been painstakingly placed on its borders, making the massive structure actually look warm. The long expanse of the parkway, from Logan Circle to the foot of the art museum, had been lit up with twinkling snowflakes, paid for by the Legg Mason investment firm. It was a fact he kept in mind when he later called the city treasurer, Kathryn Engebretson, and said that such largesse really did deserve a little bit of city business ("Legg Mason did the snowflakes on the parkway, so we thought it would be nice to reward them immediately").

The ceremony itself, replete with appearances by Eric Lindros of the Philadelphia Flyers and Shawn Bradley of the Philadelphia 76ers, only added to the occasion. Even the church youth choir, singing the carols with a kind of James Brown subtlety, so that each word sounded like a bullet through glass—not "Joy to the world" but *"Joy!!!!!!!!!!!!!!!!!!!! to!!!!!!!!!!!!!!!!!!!! the!!!!!!!!!!!!!!!! world!!!!!!!!!!!!!!!!"*—prevented anyone from dozing off.

Rendell loved these occasions, and he may have particularly loved this one since a significant political scandal, the first real one the Rendell administration had faced, was being uncovered with fanaticism by the *Inquirer*. It had to do with a state senate race that under normal circumstances would have received barely more than obligatory coverage. But this one, between Republican Bruce Marks and Democrat William Stinson, had true statewide implications. Whichever party won it would retain control of the state senate in Harrisburg and the power of the state's budget purse strings. Given that Democrats outnumbered Republicans by two to one in the district, Stinson should have been the surefire winner. But he was such a bland and unremarkable candidate that panic set in, and several weeks before the election, Rendell sent private letters to his A-list of fundraisers, telling them that contributions to the Stinson campaign were far more important than contributions to the Democratic National Committee. "This is an urgent, top priority plea for you to give and/or raise as much money as possible for Bill Stinson's Senate campaign within the next week," wrote Rendell. "We need a minimum of $100,000 from the Rendell Finance Committee no later than next Monday. . . . I do not impose upon my friends often, but I need the help now. Please don't let me down."

Stinson won by a bare 463 votes out of the 40,000 that were cast, and the Democrats were immediately alleged to have stolen the election. The *Inquirer*, in an effort that ultimately included the efforts of forty-three reporters, turned the allegations into reality. The paper uncovered hundreds of cases in which voters, many of them Latinos, had been outrageously manipulated, talked into signing absentee ballots, which were obliquely described to them as a "new way to vote."

Ironically, it was Rendell's off-the-cuff comment that stoked the *Inquirer*'s curiosity and led to the relentless coverage. In its initial story on the troubling outcome of the November election, the paper cited cases of three dozen voters who apparently had been fraudulently induced to cast absentee votes for the Democratic ticket. Rendell threw down a gauntlet in response, declaring that no investigation of voter fraud would be merited unless the number of questionable ballots reached one hundred.

The mayor would have been better off simply putting a red bull's-eye on his backside and letting reporters take whacks with their little notebooks. Given such a challenge, it was little wonder the paper ultimately uncovered more than five hundred questionable ballots, as if saying to the mayor, "Is that enough, or should we go out and get some more?"

The stories were long and in some cases remarkably repetitive, feeding the angry belief of the mayor and others in the administration that the true goal of the paper was not public service but the personal aggrandizement of winning a Pulitzer. The story only intensified, to the point where a former public official and well-placed Democratic fund-raiser privately begged Cohen to get the mayor to convene a blue-ribbon panel to study possible reform of the election code, not because it would serve any constructive purpose but because it would help the *Inquirer* win the damn Pulitzer and thereby get the paper off the story.

"This is their Pulitzer application," said Tom Leonard, a former city controller, in a heated conversation with Cohen. "They're looking for governmental action." Leonard was savvy in his assessment on several levels: Pulitzers are often won on the basis of results and reforms, and Pulitzers were also the great sustenance of the *Inquirer,* with seventeen won between 1972 and 1990. His thinking apparently was that a blue-ribbon panel might be enough of a result to "sate" the paper. He even had a name in mind to head it, a former U.S. attorney well-known for righteousness, and he thought such a move would put Rendell, whose every word seemed only to inspire the paper even more, on the side of the angels. But Cohen rejected the idea because he thought it would look utterly transparent and also because he doubted it would in any way diminish the paper's coverage.

The election story beat on mercilessly, taking up huge chunks of the front page in December. But other than those working for the paper and a handful of those directly involved, there was always some question of how many others in the city truly cared about it to the insatiable degree that the *Inquirer* did—a scandal without a broad constituency. The mayor himself obviously didn't like the coverage. He found no public motive in what the *Inquirer* was doing; the fact that the paper had uncovered astounding examples of election fraud seemed of no moment to him. But at a certain point, he seemed resigned to the continued onslaught of it and to the worst of all possible fates: "Who the fuck cares if they win a Pulitzer anyway? The readers don't care." And given the condition of the city and the daily question of its ultimate survival, there were more important issues to become distraught over anyway.

The year 1993 was in its final day. The halfway mark of the administration had been reached—and far more than that in a psychological sense because portions of 1994 and 1995 would be occupied by the mayor's bid for reelection. The line on the graph of the administration had shown an unbroken upward movement since Rendell took office two years earlier. But in those last breaths of 1993 came the kind of news that would render any chart meaningless.

Without being given any clear right of appeal, the city was told that consolidations in the Internal Revenue Service would cost Philadelphia about 3,800 jobs over the next five years. The announcement was crushing, coming on top of the closings of such vintage Philadelphia businesses as Whitman's Chocolate, Mrs. Paul's Kitchens, and After Six. All told for the twelve-month period ending September 30, 1993, the city had lost an estimated 21,400 jobs. Under the IRS plan, Philadelphia would suffer enormously while other areas of the country, such as Ogden, Utah, would benefit greatly, a circumstance that once again cemented the view that the federal government's policy in its treatment of the cities wasn't simply one of benign neglect but was one of deliberate dismantlement. It wasn't just the loss of jobs that was crippling; it was the types of jobs—decent ones in the range of $20,000 a year that provided good benefits and didn't require an abundance of sophisticated skills, jobs that were perfect for thousands of city residents and impossible to replicate.

With an urgency in his voice that at times bordered on desperation, Rendell spoke by phone to the Democratic National Committee chairman David Wilhelm, asking him to arrange thirty minutes of time with the president and the vice president to discuss not only the IRS decision and the continuing crisis of the navy yard but also the crisis of America's cities: "We have let loose an absolutely ferocious school of piranhas in the name of reinventing government, and this school of piranhas eats indiscriminately, and they don't give two shits about America's cities. It's not just Philadelphia, David; it's all large urban centers. We are getting unintentionally screwed up the rear by the administration."

Moments later he spoke with Marcia Hale, in charge of intergovernmental affairs for the White House, and he said something to her that he never would have said in public because it would have undercut all the bread and circuses, all the confetti throwings and summer pool submergings and roof nailings and mascot fightings and menorah lightings and Mickey Mouse appearances that were, more than anything else, sustaining the city. There were times, many times, when the mayor postured to make a point, exaggerated because he thought exaggeration was the only way to make people understand, but this wasn't one of those times. Alone in his office he spoke from the place where he always spoke best and most clearly, from an unclouded heart.

"Putting aside my mayor's hat for a second, we're dying," he said over the phone. He was sitting at his conference table, leaning ever so slightly, with one hand pressed against the side of his head. As always, his left leg frantically pumped up and down, as if, by the very rhythmic frenzy of the action, he could just speed everything up, make everything happen that needed to happen. "We're dying," he repeated with a little more emphasis this time. "Forget all the good things I've done; Philadelphia is dying. It's happened a lot more slowly since I took office, but we're dying."

III

Several months later, at the end of March 1994, Rendell and Cohen found themselves on a Metroliner headed for Washington for a private meeting on the housing authority with HUD Secretary Cisneros. As they found seats in the dining car, the two men seemed relaxed and happy to be out of the chaos of City Hall. Cohen, who rarely accompanied the mayor on his forays to the nation's capital, had come armed with a briefcase full of paperwork that he hoped the two of them could get to during the train ride. Rendell didn't mind doing paperwork but seemed equally interested in the fat-free chocolate muffins he had bought at one of the little vending booths in the station just before the train pulled out. Despite their divergent styles, they had eerily assumed twinlike behavior in certain areas. Both had brought along brown-bag lunches for the ride, and even though they had ordered separately, both had gotten the same thing: Russian-dressing hoagies with a side of turkey.

They were in good moods for a variety of reasons. Despite their protests that the *Inquirer*'s coverage of the state senate race had been sensational and overheated, a federal judge had taken the unprecedented action of voiding the results of the election. But a few days before the train trip to

Washington, they had gotten wind of news that made them feel vindicated, and they could barely conceal their glee. The Pulitzers wouldn't be announced for another several weeks, but the initial judging, the worst-kept secret in all of America, had already taken place, and the *Inquirer* wasn't even a finalist. The paper's editors and reporters said repeatedly that a Pulitzer Prize had never motivated the coverage, but Rendell and Cohen reveled in what they were convinced was the paper's humiliation, particularly since the paper had built its reputation on winning journalism's most prestigious award. "I was significantly worried that [the judges] would be seduced by those thousands of column inches all saying the same thing," said Cohen. "It has restored my faith in the Pulitzer process."

"I am satisfied," said Rendell. "I think they worked incredibly hard to drive a story line and exaggerate and embellish."

Two days before the train ride, a profile of Rendell had appeared on the front page of the Sunday *Washington Post.* Long and mostly laudatory, it had certified Rendell as the great dragon slayer on behalf of the cities. He tried to be humble about it, moaning that he could never again show his face at a U.S. Conference of Mayors meeting without risking "assassination." But despite his efforts to minimize the story, the glow of it had clearly carried beyond that of the usual publicity fix. Four years earlier Rendell had been seen as a has-been politician trying to make a desperate comeback. Now he was a star, not just a star of the city but a national star, Vice President Gore's words about him forever committed to print in one of the nation's most prestigious papers: "America's mayor."

It was a crowning moment, and as the train sped past Wilmington and the two men laughed and joked and dipped their hoagies into their little vats of Russian dressing in perfect sync, it seemed hard to believe that any other single moment of the administration could be better than this one. In that rumpled suit, with that bemused look on his face, inviting everyone around him to try one of those fat-free chocolate muffins and see, *see,* how it tasted like the real thing, Ed Rendell *was* America's mayor.

But in between the moments of relaxed banter, Cohen continued to go through the contents of his briefcase, and he pulled out the results of a private citywide poll of voters. The poll documented Rendell's stunning popularity in the city, with a 76 percent approval rating. It also showed that a majority of those polled, 52 percent, thought conditions in the city were better than they had been a few years ago.

But the poll pointed out other trends as well, trends that were foreboding not only in terms of what Rendell had achieved but also in terms of what lay ahead for a city that was as divided as ever along class and economic lines, a city where the gap between the haves and the have-nots wasn't simply a gap but was perhaps an unbridgeable gulf. The poll also suggested that in running his administration like a Broadway musical, with a great series of showstoppers to make up for a bleak and depressing story, the mayor may have reached his peak.

A criticism of Rendell had always been that he was a downtown mayor driven by downtown interests to the virtual dismissal of the neighborhoods. He bristled at that, sending his critics vitriolic letters noting the millions upon millions that had been spent in the neighborhoods. He also argued that economic development, regardless of where it was located, meant jobs for people in the neighborhoods. He was right about that, but he also knew that it was perception that counted, and the poll showed that the vast majority of the electorate remained unconvinced about his commitment to the neighborhoods. "Voters overwhelmingly think you care 'mostly about the problems of downtown businessmen and Center City' (64 percent) instead of 'mostly about the problems facing average people in the neighborhoods' (28 percent)," the pollsters concluded. The number-one problem in the city, the poll showed, was fighting crime and drugs, and nearly 70 percent thought the mayor could be working "a lot harder" to try to solve it. The poll also showed that 50 percent believed that the mayor, after starting fast, was now slowing down.

From a political standpoint, the poll concluded that "there exist several weaknesses that a potential opponent could try to exploit next year." Dwight Evans, whose name had been whispered and repeated the most, was currently running for governor in the Democratic primary. Because he was black, no one gave him a ghost of a chance in a statewide election (it had once reportedly been uttered by political huckster James Carville that between the poles of Philadelphia to the east and Pittsburgh to the west lay Alabama). But Evans's showing in the primary would be an interesting barometer of his potential strength in a mayoral election, where the dynamics of race were very different and where blacks in past elections had constituted a majority of registered Democrats in the city.

From a practical standpoint, the poll was depressing proof of what demographers and other social scientists feared most about the city: its unabated evolution into a two-tiered place with a narrow crust of wealthy residents feeding off the downtown renaissance and an enormous swath of blacks and working-class whites struggling vainly to survive, a schism so strong that the pollsters had highlighted the following passage in italics:

*Examining just the overall numbers about the improved confidence of
the city ignores real concerns among black and less educated white
voters about the direction of the city. The enthusiastic feelings about
the improved Philadelphia are driven mainly by the optimism of better educated and upscale white voters.*

But in the euphoria of the moment for Ed Rendell, stemming from *The
Washington Post* piece and the approval ratings and the creamy Russian
dressing in ample supply in its plastic cups and the safe company of a brilliant man who had put loyalty to him above loyalty to a wife and children,
that schism didn't even seem to register, except perhaps as a potential political problem.

As the Metroliner pulled into Washington's Union Station right around
2:00 P.M., America's mayor was still soaring and would continue to soar.
At least for another hour.

Rendell and Cohen crammed themselves into the backseat of a taxi and
were on their way to HUD headquarters to see Cisneros when they pulled
out their cellular phones simultaneously to check in for messages. Cohen's
phone was sleek and black and was easily removed from his breast pocket.
The mayor's was gray and clunky and held together by a rubber band, and
it wobbled as it was brought forth from his brown valise.

"Hi, Annie," said the mayor.

"Hi, Yvonne," said Cohen.

The mayor was given a brief rundown of who had called. So was Cohen.
In the cab, neither man had any idea of the code-red crisis that was exploding 140 miles away in their own city. The *Daily News* had gotten hold
of a profile of the mayor that would shortly appear in *Philadelphia Magazine,* and by all accounts it was a heart stopper, not because the reporter had
taken potshots but because of what the mayor had said to the reporter—
stuff about spiky metal bras and what the reporter might be like in bed and
how the mayor and Clinton were alike in just a whole lot of ways beyond
being Democrats and married to lawyers.

The writer of the *Philadelphia Magazine* article, Lisa DePaulo, had previously produced stories with sexual twists to them. In 1991, she had done
a story for the magazine about the Republican mayoral candidate Sam
Katz, much of which dealt with accusations of sexual harassment. It was
merciless, and Cohen not only remembered it vividly but also had kept it
in his office as if never to forget it. He had warned the mayor of the reper-

cussions of letting DePaulo spend the day with him on a trip to New York, describing her as "treacherous," and a "bitch." But the mayor hadn't listened. So Cohen had gotten Tom Leonard to go with the mayor and De-Paulo as a chaperone. But that clearly hadn't done much good.

The meeting with Cisneros went flawlessly. "Congratulations on the Sunday piece" were Cisneros's first words to the mayor. The Cabinet secretary praised the mayor and the other officials there, in particular Council President Street, for taking on the responsibility of the housing authority. City officials had come armed with a list of needs that they wanted HUD to honor, and Cisneros, because of the mayor's involvement, indicated that he would do his best to honor them, even if that meant granting the city special exemptions.

"Are you getting positive strokes with the press?" asked Cisneros.

"The principal reporter covering PHA [for *The Philadelphia Inquirer*] went to *The New York Times* two and a half months ago and hasn't been replaced," said Rendell. "The other principal reporter got transferred."

"There wasn't enough bad news," said Cisneros. "That's good."

Actually there was.

At several points during the meeting, Cohen abruptly left to answer phone messages to his beeper. It seemed rude, even for the always-fixated Cohen, to just get up and walk out while a member of the president's cabinet was literally in mid-sentence. But one of the messages had come from press secretary Feeley, and the news he had could not wait for later.

The second the meeting was over, Cohen was on the phone in the outer office trying to do damage control, trying to figure out what to do about a story in which the writer, while in many ways complimentary to the mayor, had also come up with passages such as the following:

> *It is equally hard to imagine Mayor Giuliani sitting in a car with a female reporter and casually mentioning, as Ed Rendell did with me on a rather fascinating ride back home, in the presence of Frank the driver and prominent Philly lawyer Tom Leonard, one of Ed's best friends, that he heard "something very interesting" about me. Then proceeding to tell me, in raw and alliterative terms, how he presumes I am in bed. All of which he says I "should find flattering."*
>
> *How does one respond to such a thing?*

Of course that was no longer DePaulo's problem.

The Metroliner ride back to Philadelphia wasn't nearly as jaunty and cheerful as the ride from there, which now seemed as if it had taken place months ago. Rendell, with Cohen at his side, called DePaulo. He told her he had meant no offense by his comments and asked her whether in fact she had been offended. She said she was not, which in the minds of Rendell and Cohen became an important point. Back in Philadelphia, while Rendell muttered to members of his office staff, "I can't fucking believe I agreed to do this," Cohen took over completely, standing behind his desk with the reserve of a fighter pilot. He was as intense as he had ever been, but he didn't seem particularly surprised to be handling a crisis such as this one. Rumors of intemperate sexual behavior by the mayor had been so frequent over the years that the entire populace of the city seemed to consider his womanizing a foregone conclusion even though not a single word had ever been written about it before. To a certain degree, what seemed most amazing about the episode was that it was the first of its kind to surface publicly in nearly two and a half years.

When Nicole Weisensee of the *Daily News* called to ask about the magazine piece, Cohen said he hadn't seen it yet, using the ignorance-is-bliss tactic, when of course he had just read it. He also said he was doing the speaking because the mayor was still in Washington, which wasn't true either. His instincts told him that anything the mayor might say without him there as censor and radar detector, would only lead to greater disaster. "No good can come of it, only a lot of harm," he said to the mayor, who had come into his office ashen faced, with that furtive look of a child who knows that yes, it was he who lit the match that burned the house down.

Most of the mayor's intemperate comments had been made on the limousine ride home from New York. Rendell's idea was to get in touch with the driver, who he thought would certify that DePaulo "gave as good as she got" and that the whole atmosphere was one of levity and laughter. "He would have buried her," said Rendell with an upbeat tick in his voice, but Cohen knew it was a terrible idea. There are times when the best antidote to a story is to discredit the reporter, but this wasn't one of them.

"Is there no sign that the *Inquirer* is doing anything?" the mayor asked. So far at least, the answer was no, and that was good news because the basic rule of thumb of the administration was that if a story appeared in the tabloid *Daily News* and did not appear in the *Inquirer,* then it really hadn't appeared at all.

The *Daily News* put the story on the front page the next day, and everyone in City Hall knew this was just the beginning. Columnists and radio reporters who had not been seen in months were beginning to swarm like smiling killer bees. Privately DePaulo became a clear target of the administration's wrath, and the venom was repellent and disgusting, not to mention totally unwarranted. At least one administration official referred to her as Miss Slut Ball, and another speculated as to how many cocks she had sucked to advance her career. But in public, at Cohen's paramilitary directives, contriteness was the rule of the day. Rendell was about to give a press conference on an unrelated subject, but undoubtedly the matter of the profile would come up. Cohen told him, "You're going to have to handle questions on this."

"Yeah, absolutely," said Rendell.

"They're going to do it a hundred times, and you're going to have to do it lightly. And at some point, walk away with a smile on your face. I suspect they're hoping to see you explode."

"Yeah, absolutely."

The press conference was a masterpiece. Not only did Rendell follow Cohen's directions precisely, but he expressed them in a remarkable way, with just the right blend of humility and strength. "I am what I am," he told the throng of reporters. "Again, I'm not perfect. I do like to joke around and kid around. This job is a crusher. It's a high-pressure job. I do certain things to have fun and release the tension.

"If I felt this would have been offensive to the reporter, I never would have done it. . . . Let me repeat, I've never intentionally, or with great negligence, done something to offend someone."

He walked back to his office with that slow shuffle he used when he was either tired or wondering what on earth it was that had possessed him to go into politics, besides the romance of listening to the 1952 Democratic National Convention over the radio with his father. What was astounding about the magazine episode wasn't necessarily what he had said but the poor judgment that had gotten him into the predicament in the first place. Why had he not heeded the warnings of those who had told him that this would be the inevitable result of letting DePaulo spend the day with him? Why would he make such comments to a reporter? Why would he display such a dangerous level of trust?

"My most terrible character flaw is that I like people tremendously," he said in the privacy of his office once the press conference was over. "I have this boundless optimism that I can get people to like me, and I like people to like me." For a man who had spent much of his life in power, it was a strangely insecure comment. He said he considered DePaulo a friend, someone he occasionally saw at parties and gossiped with about who was sleeping with whom. In the rarefied atmosphere in which he dwelled, a world of obsequiousness and attention from others and snatches of life in half-hour meeting slots, that was how he found friendship—on the run during a moment of down time, there to fill his momentary craving to be something else besides the mayor. Given the abnormality of the life he led as a politician, it was hard at times not to feel almost sorry for him—a man for whom everything was a fleeting and tangential moment, whether it was an afternoon with his son or a stunning victory in the union negotiations, a man who simultaneously could be the most popular on the face of the planet and also seem like the loneliest.

His wife, Midge, was hurt and upset by what he had said to DePaulo. She was also embarrassed. The timing, coming just after she had been sworn in as a district court judge, could not have been worse. She knew her husband could be immature and say things to people that just weren't appropriate. He had called her during the infamous limousine ride, and she had heard lots of laughter in the background. It had indicated to her then that everyone was having a good time, and it suggested now that the reporter had hardly been mistreated. But she could tell it was one of those moments when her husband was getting wound up, moving into that space where he would say whatever he wanted without regard for the propriety of it. But she wasn't angry with him for what he had said. "I didn't feel our relationship was threatened," she said later. "I mean I kind of understood it. It's horrible to say, but I did. But hell, being married to him for twenty-three years—I would hope I would understand it. I mean it was a little beyond the pale than I might have thought," said Midge Rendell. "But I'm sure without me he does a lot of things beyond the pale."

IV

The next month, in April of 1994, Linda Morrison sent yet another memo to Cohen. But this one had nothing to do with fixing the city or improving it. Only three paragraphs long, its message was direct and uncharacteristically flat, as if she just didn't care anymore.

As far as she was concerned, her fears had become a reality, and she was doing little more than, as she put it, "rearranging the deck chairs on the *Titanic*." She needed backing in her daily battles with department heads and agency heads. She needed support, and it was clear to her that she wasn't getting it anymore but instead was being ridiculed. On one occasion, she had suggested that the city Parking Authority, long a scourge in terms of inefficiency and patronage, make arrangements to sell two of its garages to a private company. Since the authority did not own the land underneath the garages, the deal was a complicated one, but the company still had said it was interested, and it had handled similar transactions before. Cohen had been livid, however, and had sent a memo not simply to Linda but to several others stating that the suggestion was impossible and ridiculous. If these two garages were going to be sold, Cohen wrote, then the city might as well sell other properties it didn't own, such as the White House, the Pennsylvania Turnpike, and the Mirage casino in Las Vegas.

Upset, Linda had met with Cohen privately and had asked him point-blank whether he would like her to quit. He had said no and had even praised the contracting out of city work as one of the success stories of the administration. Taking him at his word, Linda had subsequently written him a memo condemning the proposed expenditure of nearly $300,000 by the Water Department to hire a consultant to study the contracting out of one of its functions since the department had its own division of planning and research that had already spent $1.2 million in salaries and overtime. "They don't get it," she wrote of the department. "How can we make them get it, so I don't have a chronic case of combat fatigue?" The memo, because of its strong wording, was obviously meant to be private. But Cohen, for reasons that Linda never understood, gave it to the head of the Water Department and to several managers.

"I propose that I end my employment here before the end of May," Linda wrote to Cohen in telling him of her resignation.

Six days later Cohen sent out a memo to various members of the administration, saying that the days of contracting out were pretty much over anyway. The initiative had run its course. The mayor was able to tout it at speeches in New York to the admiration of fiscal conservatives, and the savings that it had generated, in excess of $35 million, were considered sufficient, particularly since the budget was in balance. "I am concerned that we not become the pariahs of city government," he wrote. "We may be putting too much emphasis on our relentless pursuit of additional contracting out initiatives."

Cohen conceded that he and Linda had fundamental differences. He viewed contracting out not necessarily as a way of reducing the role of government but as a way of forcing the unions, through the very threat of contracting out, to become more efficient and more competitive. Linda, he felt, because of her fervent desire to reduce the role of government as much as possible, wanted to contract out virtually everything. He described her as an idealogue, but he also said he had been pleased by the quality of her work.

Linda believed that the words of Cohen's memo were directed at her. She wasn't shocked by them or terribly surprised by them. She was a pariah of the bureaucracy because that's what she thought she had to be to change the culture of the bureaucracy. And while she found it palatable to be a pariah with support, she found it impossible to be one without support. When she wrote her last memo to Cohen, she didn't elaborate on her emotions, on how sad she felt that the opportunity for change that the mayor had after the union negotiations—incredible and wholesale change as an entire city lay at his feet—had drifted from his fingers. Maybe she was too much of an ideologue. Maybe she should have been more tactful. Maybe she didn't understand the rigors of politics. But it didn't matter now anyway.

"On the one hand, I admire him and he has a lot of courage, and he's the best mayor the city has ever had," said Linda. "Unfortunately, that's not good enough."

SIXTEEN

"Inappropriate Conduct"

I

For the first time since he and Rendell had taken office two and a half years earlier, even Cohen acknowledged in the spring of 1994 that a lull had been reached, an uncharacteristic groping for the next shot of optimism, and the whispers were everywhere that the mayor, once thought to be invincible, would be seriously challenged in his run for reelection.

The underbelly of disfranchisement that existed in the city's neighborhoods, particularly in its black ones, seemed to have ripened, and some of those closest to the mayor thought this alienation could be transformed into empowerment if the right candidate came along and was able to deliver the message that America's mayor cared a lot more about the rest of America than he cared about his own city. There was a feeling that all the national press Rendell had received, most recently a profile in *The New York Times Magazine* several weeks earlier that included the usual recitation of urban miracles accomplished, only reinforced the image of a leader, a rumpled Nero, endlessly fiddling with national reporters while the city continued to teeter.

Cohen was confident that the surge in momentum would once again reassert itself, but even he seemed weary, particularly as deals that had been in the works for months and in some cases years—a new sports arena, a plan to have the outdated Civic Center razed and turned into a billion-dollar hospital complex—wore on at a painstakingly slow pace, on again, off again, on again, off again. "I don't think I can take it anymore," he said, once again acknowledging that however steady he seemed to the outside world, he was not impervious to the pressures of the job. He had a propensity for the melodrama of self-flagellation, and because he never got distracted, it was hard to conceive that he would one day jettison it all. But the swirl of the chaos, the needs and the demands of the city, had only intensified.

A lawsuit for wrongful dismissal filed by the former inspector general of the housing authority contained charges that the mayor had refused to support him in efforts to clean up the troubled agency. The search for a new school superintendent was turning into a quiet racial war even though the white candidate was by any standards far better than the black one. People were coming into the office and whispering about the emotional instability of certain elected officials. Beyond the usual suspects, even reporters were coming into the office and asking for jobs. The mayor's schedule was so crammed with trivial events that Cohen himself, when asked about a particular event that seemed nonsensical, just shrugged.

The care and feeding of City Council President Street continued to be a full-time job in itself. Contrary to their initial impressions, both Cohen and the mayor had developed a tremendous respect for Street. His capacity for work was rivaled only by theirs, and he had proved himself far more reasonable and more dedicated to the common good of the city than they, or anyone else in government for that matter, ever would have imagined. But fearful that he would blow at any moment like Vesuvius because of some perceived show of disrespect, they still doted on him. The previous month, as the city was putting together its application to the federal government for an urban empowerment zone, the mayor had been reluctant to include a census tract that Street wanted. Rendell became almost terrified that the omission would offend the city council president. He also knew that Street was having a fund-raiser at the time, so he told Cohen to have the Rendell campaign immediately cut a check. It was perfectly legal, but like all contributions, its intent went beyond pure largesse. "Ten," said the mayor to Cohen, meaning $10,000. "That should be some assuagement." The gesture of the campaign contribution went hand in hand with the strategy for handling the city council president that they had adopted from the very beginning, a strategy that went beyond zoo tickets and football tickets. It also meant putting his name right underneath the mayor's at the construction site of the new Marriott Hotel ("He'll like that," Cohen had said to the mayor), supporting at one point a $1-million Urban Development Action Grant to the wife of a friend of his for a performing arts center that the mayor himself knew was a complete waste ("They'd be better off taking the money and handing it out in thousand-dollar bills," quipped the mayor, and ultimately the grant was never dispensed), and mollifying him during some flap involving the vending activities of his brother Milton by personally inviting him to a meeting with Willie Mays ("John loved it!" the mayor said to Cohen). The campaign contribution might work, but it seemed inevitable that down the road something else would be needed.

There had been other periods like these during the administration, but never one as intensely dark as this. The news pouring forth in May only heightened the uncertainty of the direction in which the city was headed and continued to raise questions about whether the Rendell administration was now about change or the mere perception of it.

Examining just the overall numbers about the improved confidence of the city ignores real concerns among black and less educated white voters about the direction of the city. The enthusiastic feelings about the improved Philadelphia are driven mainly by the optimism of better educated and upscale white voters.

That passage in italics, which had seemed so innocuous in the glory of the last-hurrah train ride to Washington in March, now seemed increasingly like a prophecy come true. An effort to reform the city's charter, which Rendell had vocally favored, had gone down in a smashing defeat. His arguments that a reformed charter would only enhance the performance of the government had been resoundingly rejected, especially and surprisingly by a coalition of blacks and working-class whites. The gubernatorial primaries had been held at the same time as the charter vote, and the most significant news wasn't the showing of the winners but the performance by Dwight Evans. Despite being black in a state that boasted the largest number of National Rifle Association members after Texas, he had finished second in the Democratic primary. This was a strong showing, and it only added to the swell of rumors that Evans would not only challenge the mayor for reelection next year but would also pose a true test.

The mayor, by his own admission, spent the majority of his time on economic development. No company was too small to escape his exuberant sales pitch. Without the direct intervention of the mayor, the city's rate of job loss would have been far more catastrophic than it already had been. But despite meeting after meeting, the attraction of new businesses, whether a second major convention hotel or discount stores or fancy chain restaurants, was proving remarkably difficult. At one point, Rendell was so desperate for another large hotel that he promised the considerable carrot of a riverboat-gambling license to whoever built it. But once the questionable legality of such an incentive was pointed out to him, not to mention the fact that the state had never even legalized gambling, he quietly withdrew the promise.

Beyond the tightly controlled curtain of the downtown, a city once known for its neighborhoods was increasingly becoming a patchwork of vacant lots. In a radical shift of policy caused by population loss and acceptance of the hard fact that there was no longer any point in trying to save or rehabilitate blighted housing, acre after acre of the city was being leveled. Now the hope was that one day a less dense, more suburban style of housing could be built on this land. Every week the city's Department of Licenses and Inspections demolished twenty-five "imminently dangerous" houses, corner stores, and factories. In areas where the blight was still small and self-contained, the city put up false fronts like Wild West stage sets, so the neighborhoods would at least appear to be intact.

At the southern end of the city, the navy yard, despite the continued foot stomping by area politicians, moved ever closer to its death. Toward the end of May, the U.S. Supreme Court threw out the suit that had been filed by Senator Specter challenging the process the navy had used to determine the yard's closure. This meant, as Rendell pointed out privately, that nearly three years had been wasted on a lawsuit that had always been destined to go nowhere, regardless of Specter's self-serving rhetoric. It also made more important than ever the need for a coordinated strategy for deciding what to do with the yard once it closed a year and a half from now. But despite their writing petulant letters to one another and holding meaningless press conferences, area politicians seemed to share no consensus. Instead, they continued to advance pie-in-the-sky schemes—such as using the yard to turn Russian ships into scrap metal—that did nothing but once again inflate the false hopes of those who worked there.

The initial idea, floated by Republican congressman Curt Weldon, received front-page treatment in the press, particularly when Weldon said it could generate between two thousand and three thousand jobs and keep the yard busy for at least another decade. The Russians, desperate to raise hard currency by selling off war matériel, were receptive to the proposal, and Weldon, whose district in Delaware County was filled with shipyard workers, was quoted as saying, "What a day it will be when the first Russian aircraft carrier, the *Kiev,* is towed up the Delaware." Democrat congressman Thomas Foglietta seized the idea as well, perhaps because he truly believed in it or maybe because his Philadelphia district comprised the yard. The city hired the consulting firm of Day and Zimmerman to study the proposal, and a consultant concluded that 2,000 was the accurate number of jobs, give or take about 1,865. In addition, Day and Zimmerman concluded, the effect of creating those 134 jobs would be a net loss of $16 million in the first year. Various proponents of the proposal asked the mayor to get the consultant to revise the findings, making them more optimistic. The mayor concluded that such fiddling would look "sleazy and awful," and the idea finally faded away, understood as being totally unworkable. In the meantime, the city's top official in charge of the navy yard conversion said that the Russian-ship-scrapping idea, in addition to being utterly foolish, cost the city six months, time that should have been spent focusing on the realities of the future of the yard and those who worked there.

All these issues were swirling in the middle of May 1994, and the idiosyncrasies of the mayor's behavior only added to the atmosphere of flux. In the private sanctum of his office, the mayor passed through so many different moods so quickly that it was hard for anyone, much less him, to keep track of them. He could be utterly calm at a meeting with his schedulers, then suddenly be set off by the news of an appearance that he did not want to make, or by the realization of a time conflict and bang his fist on the table and grit his teeth and hiss. He could be perfectly calm over the phone, then hang up and start yelling, "Son of a bitch! Fucking son of a bitch!" Like most politicians, he had that turn-it-on, turn-it-off capacity to be enraged in private and the very next moment, once the camera lights came on, bubbly and effervescent. He himself admitted that he "acted" in his job 90 percent of the time, and it was no surprise to anyone who knew him that only one take had been needed for him to play a cameo role in the movie *Philadelphia.* Since he was playing the role of a mayor, it was pretty easy, he said, but the director, Jonathan Demme, was still stunned and claimed he couldn't remember the last time he had filmed anything in one take.

The mayor normally was able to separate his public and private behaviors and not let one spill into the other—until the end of May, when he felt fully besieged. As much as things had gone right with the city, something was always about to go wrong. Someone was always criticizing or complaining or trying to incite, and with the exception of his bathroom, from which the mayor could make private calls, there was no zone of privacy.

Earlier in the year, at the city's St. Patrick's Day Parade, demonstrators from the fire department were there, screaming at him and protesting because of the outcome of the union negotiations and other efforts to cut the department's budget. Rendell never looked at them, and he refused to give them the satisfaction of thinking that they might be getting to him, creeping under his skin. He acted as he always did—warm, ebullient, funny— but they *were* getting to him, and when fifty people were screaming at him and hating him and condemning him for actions that he had taken for the greater good of the city, it did him little good to tell himself quietly that he was the most popular politician in the state.

He knew better than anyone else how politics worked, the persona and the aura of the job subsuming everything else. People saw him as the mayor, always the mayor, never as a man who might have brushes with insecurity and sadness and even frailty. He wasn't being thin-skinned in confessing that the demonstrators had upset him; he was being human, and it was in moments such as these that he wondered whether the standards for politicians were just impossible to ever fully meet. He knew the eternal fickleness of voters, in which the line between adoration and loathing could hinge on a missed garbage pickup or an overzealous meter maid or a poor job of snow removal. By its nature, living in the city was at best a moody, manic-depressive experience with aggravations sometimes clashing with the force of atomic particles. He knew it was the basic nature of voters to be on the lookout for someone else who could do the job better. Or as he put it one day in his office, "If they had a choice between Jesus, Moses, and Muhammad, fifty percent would say, 'Can't we get someone else?' "

He also had wondered whether the smart thing to do politically was cash in on his success with the city, quit, and run for governor at the beginning of 1994. He had taken on the unions and successfully balanced the city's budget, and he knew that he would never have a greater and more unblemished story to tell than that of his first two years. "From a political standpoint, I'm doing absolutely the wrong thing by not running for governor," he said. "Clearly I will never be as strong and popular as I am now. I will never have a greater story to tell."

And he was right.

It was hard to know what had put the mayor in the foul mood that clearly engulfed him that day in May of 1994. It may have been the search for a new school superintendent, which continued to be mired in the misery of racial politics. It may have been the wrongful-dismissal suit that had been filed against the housing authority. Or it may have been the crisis of the moment, an endless dispute over the construction of permanent housing for the homeless in a neighborhood of the city that, in some quarters at least, was violently opposed to it. Rendell insisted that he was in favor of the project, but every action the city had taken, to the point where a federal judge had found it in violation of the federal Fair Housing Act, ran counter to that claim. Now there were reports that $15 million in federal funds for the homeless might be denied if the dispute was not resolved.

Around 6:00 P.M. on that day, *Inquirer* reporter Amy Rosenberg waited outside the mayor's office in the second-floor hallway of City Hall to ask him about the threatened cut-off of federal funds. It was a serious and important story, and there was nothing remotely exceptional about her waiting for the mayor in the hallway. Reporters had done it thousands of times before.

Rendell came into the hallway looking ashen. With her deadline fast approaching, Rosenberg walked alongside him and started to ask questions. Normally he would have stopped, and given that he was on his way to a reception around the corner in celebration of public displays of art in City Hall, he could hardly claim that he was late for an important event. He kept on walking, and he seemed all right—until a particular question was asked. Suddenly and impulsively he threw out his arm and grabbed the reporter in the area of her neck and shoulders as they continued to walk, almost as if he were putting her in a vise. The look on his face, inches from hers, was a lock-jawed grimace, and he spit out his words as he muttered at least one obscenity. He looked terrifying.

Rosenberg was understandably scared and shaken—the gesture, in its impulsiveness and underlying menace, *was* frightening. The mayor let go after several seconds, and then instantly blended into the crowd at the reception as if he had no idea of what he had just done, shaking hands, posing for pictures, putting an arm around people's shoulders with bearlike gentleness. Rosenberg in the meantime sought out press secretary Feeley and told him she was thinking of filing a police report detailing the incident. She did not, and the paper itself was mercifully kind the next day in its reporting of what had taken place. When Feeley asked the mayor for his version, he said he was "stunned" that he had offended her. But he apologized the next day, and he also received a letter about the incident from the *Inquirer*'s city editor, David Tucker:

> Thank you for apologizing to Amy Rosenberg today for having grabbed her neck yesterday afternoon in reaction to questions she was asking you in City Hall. While we appreciate your apology, I feel obliged to make clear that we regard it as inappropriate to manhandle any reporter, even amid the pressures of public life that can produce tension and exasperation. We regard it as absolutely inappropriate to grab an individual's neck, whatever the provocation.

Five days later the mayor sent Tucker a response in which he said, "I agree with your letter. Touching a reporter is inexcusable and inappropriate no matter what the circumstances." He claimed that he was in no way trying to intimidate Rosenberg and was "just trying to get her to focus and listen to what I was saying.

"Nevertheless," the mayor concluded, "it was totally inappropriate conduct and it will not be repeated."

In the midst of what was already taking place, the incident only added to the spiral. Over at the *Daily News,* questions about the mayor seemed to be intensifying. It wasn't the mayor's behavior that had turned the paper's staff into doubters but a more fundamental sense that the administration—behind the façade of its great public relations machine and the optimistic shtick of the mayor opening those great canisters of oxygen day after day—had in no significant way altered the city. A meeting of the paper's City Hall bureau and its top editors had been held, and the message was clear that the administration had been treated far too lightly. The mayor loathed the charge that he had turned his back on the city or was interested only in the economic development of the downtown. He knew that the appellation of America's mayor was becoming a noose, and he rightfully pointed out that he had not sought out any of the national reporters who had written about him. Trying to accommodate them—the Joe Kleins and the Jacob Weisbergs who sat in his office like creepy Buddhas for a couple of hours in some meek attempt to capture the mayor up close and personal— was a pain in the ass, he said. He argued steadfastly that he was more than the convention-center mayor or the tourism mayor or the riverboat-gambling mayor or the Avenue of the Arts mayor. And yet on the night of the last day of June, his actions were so clouded and seemingly contrary that even his most loyal partisans wondered what had possessed him, as if every political and personal instinct born to him had somehow disintegrated. Psychological interpretations are always dangerous, but now it seemed as if—for whatever reason—Rendell were willfully pushing himself out onto the edge, daring someone to seize the disfranchised masses of the city and challenge him for the right to be mayor.

II

It was a shooting in a city in which shootings occurred all the time, and the power of it lay in its capacity to evoke emotions of outrage and sadness that went beyond race and class and socioeconomics, one of those acts, almost always an act of violence in the city, that galvanize and for the briefest of moments make people everywhere realize the degree to which the place they are in, an American place, has gone berserk.

Michelle Cutner, whose destiny was to be six years old in a place that had no destiny, was walking home from school with her mother. They stopped at a variety store to buy potato chips and soda. Michelle left the store while her mother, Elizabeth, paid for the purchases, and that's when the shooting started, and Elizabeth Cutner, with the reflexes of all adults in a neighborhood such as this, gathered the children in the store around her. Outside on Twentieth Street, a fifteen-year-old named Jerome Whitaker had a gun. He was angry, and he may have been looking for revenge, but neither of these motives mattered anyway, his reflexes being the same as Elizabeth Cutner's inside the variety store, all of them ingrained, all part of the culture in which they lived.

Jerome Whitaker started firing in the blossom of the afternoon, as kids all over the neighborhood were walking home from school. He was shooting at a car, as if that somehow made it all right, and he was shooting because he himself had been hit in a drive-by shooting the month before and probably felt like a victim too. But none of that mattered either because one of the bullets missed its mark or ricocheted off the car he was firing at, and a neighbor ran into the variety store and told Elizabeth Cutner that her six-year-old daughter had been shot, and she ran out of the store and saw her daughter on the sidewalk and said, "Oh God!" and "My baby!" and that didn't matter either because the little girl was lying there with blood pouring out of her side and her eyes open, and Michelle knew, as much as a six-year-old girl can know about such things, that she was dying.

Neighbors wept, and reporters perceptively noted that right near the patch of blood where Michelle Cutner was killed were the familiar red and blue caps of crack vials. The police bemoaned the easy access to guns, and one resident, between sobs, said, "Why? That's all you can say—why? It don't make no sense."

The night after the killing a neighborhood meeting was held at the Varick Memorial AME Zion Church at Nineteenth and Catharine Streets to grapple with the problems that had infected the neighborhood. It was pouring outside, and the falling rain only oppressed the streets even more, robbing them of what little crevices of life and light there might have been. It wasn't refreshing, as a summer rainstorm could sometimes be, but cold and harsh to the touch, the sidewalks spotted with puddles almost instantly. The church inside was cavernous and slightly musty smelling. A chandelier with naked bulbs hung limply from the ceiling, and an American flag stood in the front in a tired salute. A coat of paint would have helped, but there was also an atmosphere of survival to the place, with beams of dark wood crisscrossing the ceiling in a sturdy patchwork, as well as a sense of delicate beauty, with feathery hues of browns and beiges and blues in the slender panels of the stained-glass windows. The beat of the rain against the roof seemed almost reassuring, and the two hundred people who were there, mostly blacks but also a smattering of whites, fanned themselves with little fans courtesy of the Andrew W. Nix Jr. funeral home. Since the meeting had been well publicized, a host of representatives of the city were there to give the appearance of concern, and at one point there were so many introductions that the meeting began to resemble a celebrity softball game.

A spirit of feeling left out and forgotten emanated from the rows of the pews, but there was no contentiousness. There was blame for the system, but there was also self-blame. There was a plea, not for handouts or magical cures but for the simple tools to stay alive and have their children stay alive—without constant fear.

Someone in the audience wanted to know how a twenty-four-hour-a-day crack house could exist in the neighborhood in the shadow of a police station. The police captain present almost comically blamed the court system, as if the police played no role whatsoever in preventing crime, and he also noted that the seventeenth district had been rather busy, with a total of eight people shot over the last six days. But when he spoke of the need for curfews, many in the audience applauded. A woman asked what she should do outside the school when there were problems, and a representative of the city gave her his business card, as if that would be an effective antidote in the next round of drive-by shootings.

In the midst of it all, a man named Rotan Lee spoke. He was the head of the Philadelphia Board of Education, and he was there at the meeting because Michelle Cutner had been killed on her way home from school, and he wanted to announce to those gathered that the school would be kept open this summer so kids would have someplace to go. But he had more to say than just that, and the target of his passion was obvious.

This is more than about convention centers and Avenue of the Arts. This is more than riverboat gambling and Delaware Avenue. The question is, What good is the beautification of the city if the streets are not safe? What good is making Philadelphia the number-one city if young African American men and women have nothing to do in the summer but kill each other? Just as you have to step to a sixteen-year-old who is disrespectful of you, you have to step to a politician who is dissing you!

Lee's comments received applause, the loudest applause that night. He had seized on something, and in the tired canvas of that church something fluttered and then came alive, the need palpable, the resilience palpable, and the strength palpable—if someone were only there to unleash it. It sounded like a campaign speech, the very speech that a challenger would use to cut away at the Achilles' heel of the mayor, and its effectiveness was only heightened by the fact that the mayor was nowhere in sight.

After two hours or so, those who remained went outside and formed a vigil. They did not march. They did not chant. They just walked side by side in a slim line to the block where Michelle Cutner had died. The rain had let up, but the gloom of the neighborhood, its hermetic loneliness, made the walk like a wade through the fog of a weird and faraway place that bore no link to anything around it, a Wild West outpost in various stages of disintegration. "I've been fightin' this twenty-five years and nothin'," said a man to the person next to him. "You know what I call that—a forgotten neighborhood."

They walked over the shards of glass that had filled in the cracks of the sidewalk like pebbles. They walked past the corpses of houses that were as much a part of the landscape as the street signs. They walked past fences that were tilting under the weight of overgrown bushes. The procession went by the precise spot where Michelle Cutner had been shot, marked now by a small bouquet of flowers lying on a patch of red.

"The blood was so thick even the rain ain't wash it away," said a girl in the humble procession.

They came to the corner of Twentieth and Carpenter, near the little variety store where Michelle Cutner had bought the potato chips with her mother. The streetlamps cast an orange and sickly light that made everything seem infected, and as far as the eye could see, grim lines of row houses ran down the street until they disappeared in the darkness. They looked like tombstones, but it didn't matter. A giant circle was formed, and the mourners held hands, and a prayer was uttered, and a plea was made. It came from Anthony Yates, whose five-year-old son, Marcus, had been killed six years earlier in the cross fire of a drug war.

"This is not Beirut," he said.

"This is not Vietnam," he said.

"This is Philadelphia."

Rendell had known about the meeting at the church; he had elected not to go because of a belief that such meetings inevitably dissolved into accusations that he wasn't doing enough. He also thought there was really nothing that could be done anyway, unless the social problems underlying such shootings were somehow solved. "If I had a thousand more police, don't you think this would have happened? Of course it would have.

"The only thing that will prevent this is to execute some of these people. If they catch whoever did it, I hope we execute 'em," he said, strangely unaware, despite the avalanche of media coverage, that the perpetrator had been arrested and that the shooting, as horrible as it was, most likely did not involve the kind of premeditation required for the death penalty. He said he had planned to send the police commissioner to the meeting (he didn't go either) and that the other problem he had, the real problem, was his schedule. The Welcome America! celebration that had been such a hit last year when the convention center opened was in its second season.

It was true that his schedule, as usual, was crammed to the brim. The Hoagie Day celebration, featuring a fifteen-hundred-foot hoagie courtesy of a convenience-store chain, was kicking off at 5:45 P.M. And after that was a performance by Chubby Checker. And after that was the Summer Mummers Parade. And after that was the flick of the switch to light up a new thirteen-foot neon hot dog.

That night, Oxman, the mayor's brilliant political strategist and adviser, turned on the local news. What he saw was coverage of the mayor joyfully attending Hoagie Day on the apron of City Hall juxtaposed with coverage of the community meeting at the Varick Memorial AME Zion Church, where humble blacks spoke of crime and drugs and the senseless death of a six-year-old. Oxman, like others in the administration, had been quietly concerned by the contrast between what he called the Good Ed, who had existed up until the opening of the convention center and was focused and sharp and responsive to the needs of everyone, and the Bad Ed of the period that followed, who was less focused and more susceptible to hubris. Oxman, of course, was intimately familiar with the poll that cited Rendell as a downtown mayor. As he watched the news, he imagined the type of ad that it would make in a political campaign—a mayor more interested in hoagies than black neighborhoods where six-year-olds were dying. He became convinced that with the right black candidate and a million dollars in the bank, he himself could fashion the right campaign to beat the mayor in next year's primary. He wouldn't do it, of course, because he was absolutely loyal to Rendell and knew his capacities for leadership better than anyone else. But he also knew this: for all the mayor's popularity, he was not invincible.

Cohen also privately admitted that the juxtaposition of events on the news that night was horrendous. Acutely aware of the increasing chorus of complaints that the mayor was turning his back on entire swaths of the city, he did what he always had done. He buried himself in the facts. He conducted his own analysis of the mayor's schedule for May and June. He determined that of the six hundred items on the mayor's schedule, 34 percent were spent on "Center City" issues and 24 percent on "neighborhood" issues, and the vast majority of the rest, on government business. But based on his analysis, Cohen also concluded, with vintage precision, that many of the meetings in the Center City category really should have been in the neighborhoods category since they involved neighborhood issues even though they took place in Center City. Even without these corrections, Cohen noted in a lengthy memo, Rendell's neighborhood commitment was "hardly de minimis," since he was still making almost two and a half neighborhood appearances a day.

Cohen concluded that the real problem lay not with the mayor's spending too little time in the neighborhoods but with the way in which the television news media covered him, which was a result of their basic sloth. "I believe this perception is largely inaccurate and is primarily the product of the laziness of television," Cohen wrote, noting that a television crew had an easier time covering the mayor in Center City than it had covering him out in the neighborhoods somewhere. The solution: begin to ration the number of Center City appearances on the mayor's public schedule that were announced to the news media. "If the press wants to see EGR or talk to him, we should make them go to the neighborhoods."

III

Six weeks after the death of Michelle Cutner, the phone rang in the home of Fifi Mazzccua on Huntingdon Street. She had just gotten home from work, and she picked it up and answered it. She listened for a little bit, and then she dropped the receiver and let it fall to the floor because she couldn't believe what was happening—

In recent months, as she neared her sixty-second birthday, her eyes seemed more tired than ever and the weariness that had come from the cycle of taking care of children and grandchildren and great-grandchildren seized her with increasing frequency. She had begun to feel the edges of mortality in a way that she had never felt them before. She hoped that her grandson Posquale would stay in the community college and stick to his catering business and not fall into the trap of drugs and petty crime that had claimed the life of one grandson. She hoped that she would not die before her great-grandchildren were old enough to take care of themselves, for she was fearful that they would be split up and not looked after properly. But the prayer that had become the most fervent lately and the one she knew was the most distant and the most remote was to live to see her son Tony walk out of prison, not for the funeral of another son killed on the streets but because he was free.

One day together beyond the prison waiting room, with the green walls and the overbearing smells of grease from the hamburgers and hot dogs dispensed through the vending machines; one day when she didn't have to hug him and cry on his shoulder under the naked lights while guards sat in high chairs like plantation owners and other inmates hugged and kissed and secretly groped their wives and girlfriends and little children played at their feet on the floor; one day when she didn't have to empty her pockets and walk through the metal detector and have her body run over with some pronged device that tested for drug residue; one day, just like she told him whenever she saw him.

"One day, baby, you'll see, one day."

Was it too much to ask, dear Lord? Was it too much to ask to answer this one prayer, just this one. Please, dear Lord, *please*! For once, just for once, couldn't you just say something and give an answer?

She felt that she was running out of time, and as the summer days of 1994 turned hot and thick and nasty, life in the desert of North Philadelphia wasn't getting any easier. Robin had left the church, and the new reverend who was there, Donna Jones, had proved a wonderful replacement. But she was there only part-time, and something was always happening in Fifi's life, something for which she always needed counseling and support. Tony's remaining two sons, Gino and Cochise, the ones who were still alive after Keith had been shot down, were in jail, and she felt some relief about that because she at least knew where they were. Another grandson, Bundino, was hanging around with thugs who liked to snatch pocketbooks, and she had walloped him good for that one and was trying to get him locked up in the belief that he too would be safer in jail. Her granddaughter Fifi had been in an institute in Augusta, Georgia, since the end of May for treatment of incurable bronchial asthma. The great-grandchildren were the great-grandchildren, feral yet touching at times, like when they asked her to smell their breath so they could prove to her that they had brushed their teeth. She loved them to death, and she believed that taking care of them was what kept her going. But they could also be, as Fifi put it, "a pain in the keister—I'm not gonna lie about it."

And then there was Tony. He had been in prison for sixteen years for a murder that in today's climate would have merited little more than a shrug. But unless some miracle happened, he was destined to be in prison the rest of his life because that was his sentence. In the state of Pennsylvania there was no automatic parole eligibility for a life sentence, according to a spokesman for the state board of pardons. He needed a new trial, which seemed a remote possibility given the number of appeals that had already been rejected, or he needed a commutation of his sentence by the governor, which would make him eligible for parole.

For sixteen years, Fifi had been writing to governors of the state, asking them to grant her wish. For sixteen years, she had gathered money together and hired lawyers to handle appeals, some of whom had done things and some of whom, as far as she could tell, hadn't done a damn thing except take her money. For sixteen years, she had thought about why this had happened to her and her son and how this had happened and how, on the basis of faith, it would right itself.

During those same sixteen years, Tony had had time to examine carefully the pages of his own life. He knew what had happened to his three boys, how one was dead and the other two constantly in the skirts of trouble, and as he told his mother, "I missed my children's life. That's probably why they're in jail." He knew what it was like to hear through the prison grapevine that his son had died, shot down in the streets, and not be able to do anything about it except hope that the prison officials would at least let him view the casket. He knew what it was like to sit in his eight-foot by twelve-foot cell in B block, equipped with its bed and cabinet and radiator and sink and toilet and combination TV–radio–cassette player, and ponder the likelihood that regardless of what he hoped and prayed for and regardless of what his mother hoped and prayed for, this was where he was going to die.

He had pondered other things in prison, and as he weighed their consequences, and thought about what he had seen over those endless years, he felt himself gripped by something, his own edges of fate and mortality. His mother insisted that he had been unfairly convicted, and a journalist met with him to hear the story of what had happened that night of August 28, 1976, the night that had landed him in prison for the rest of his life. In his appeals and briefs and testimony in court, he had insisted that he had been the victim of a vendetta against him. The journalist assumed that this was the story he would tell again now, tell it so well based on all those briefs he had painstakingly written and all that fantasy he had fed himself all these years. Tony talked about the first lawyer he had, who told him he could get him ten to twenty on a guilty plea and how offended he was by that, how much it pissed him off, this lawyer telling him to cop a plea without even hearing the facts. The journalist assumed that the interview would be a continued litany of outrage and woe, of how the system had screwed him, of how his lawyers had screwed him, of how he was in prison for a crime he hadn't committed.

"But I did," said Tony Mazzccua in a prison interview room, with its hard wooden chairs and peeling walls. For a brief second, the din outside in the visiting room went silent.

"I did."

After sixteen years, he had decided to tell a different story of what happened that night, a story that resembled the truth of what happened, particularly when matched with the facts that were already available in the public record. Not even his mother knew what had gone on that night. She had asked him once at the very beginning whether he had done the shooting, and he had said no, and that had been enough for her, as it would be for any mother trying so desperately to save her son. She had held bake sales and parties to raise money for his appeals, and the tragedy of what he would say now was that if he had told that story to a lawyer sixteen years ago, he might not have been where he was now, in prison for the rest of his life. He would have taken the plea of ten to twenty if it had been offered. If he had still insisted on going to trial, a lawyer could have argued a case of self-defense and mitigating circumstances that would not have gotten him off but might have resulted in a conviction on manslaughter instead of first-degree murder. There wouldn't have been any guarantee, but by not telling the truth on the witness stand, one thing was certain: he had *guaranteed* himself life imprisonment. His contradictory story was utterly transparent. And he knew that.

The facts of what happened that night, as Tony Mazzccua told them in the prison interview room, were straightforward and plausible, unlike the story he had told the jury. Every Friday and Saturday night, Tony and his brother-in-law George Butts would play cards, and they were at a local speakeasy buying some wine when they saw a man they both hated. He was referred to in the court records only as Danny, although Tony of course knew his full name. The man had had a relationship with Tony's sister, and when she broke the relationship off, Danny and George Butts got into a fight, and Butts had his neck so severely slashed that it required nearly 175 stitches. Tony and Butts had been looking for Danny, and the tension was obvious when they saw him at the speakeasy.

"We wanted to get this guy," said Tony Mazzccua in the prison interview room. His intent, he said, was to hurt him, not kill him, just as Danny had hurt his brother-in-law. Maybe shoot him in the leg or maybe even in the butt because it would be comical and humiliating and something he would remember every time he sat down. Tony was also depending on what he called the law of the ghetto. The year was 1976, and the Philadelphia police force, under the direction of Mayor Frank Rizzo, had made clear that its only interest in blacks in the city was to beat the bejesus out of them to extract confessions. Police were a rare sight in the neighborhood, and the underlying assumption was that as long as you took care of what you needed to take care of in the neighborhood—shot someone, stabbed someone, beat someone—no one in authority gave a rat's ass.

Tony got a shotgun. Then he and George Butts went looking for Danny and found him in the doorway of an apartment building. "We thought we were going to surprise him," said Tony in the prison interview room, "and we got surprised." Danny had the door open a crack, and Tony, as he later related in court, said he saw him with a gun. So he walked past a little bit. He wheeled and fired, and simultaneously a burst of shots came toward Tony from the apartment and also from the corner. As Tony fired, he saw another man near the apartment doorway. His name was Bernard Redding.

Tony said he had no idea whom he had shot or not shot, but he did know one thing: he had been shot right below the ankle. In the time it took for George Butts to throw Tony into a car, his shoe had filled with blood. He was seriously wounded. He went to his mother's house, and it was then that he made up a story about being with her and getting accosted and then shot by five kids walking down the street. He was taken to Temple University Hospital, and the next day he was visited by police officers and placed under arrest for the murder of Bernard Redding.

His mother pleaded with him to listen to the lawyer and take a plea. But headstrong and uncomfortable with the string of attorneys he ended up with, he decided instead to try to beat the system in a jury trial, and he told a story that made no sense, and he was eviscerated in masterly fashion by the prosecution. He said that Danny had shot him for no reason. When asked why he hadn't filed a complaint against Danny, he referred to the law of the ghetto. Despite eyewitness testimony to the contrary, he claimed he was unarmed, an innocent bystander. The story was only contradicted further by testimony indicating that he originally had told the police he had been shot by the five hoodlums. The thrust of his testimony was totally self-incriminating, a textbook example of why defendants, ninety-nine times out of a hundred, should never get anywhere near the witness stand.

The absolute waste of what happened that August night was apparent even to the judge, who had no choice under the law but to sentence Tony

Mazzccua to life. Common Pleas Judge Theodore Smith noted that Tony
had no criminal record to speak of. He noted that he had an IQ of 115,
which would have qualified him for officer candidate school in World
War II. He urged him to get his GED and maybe take some college courses
as well once he got into the swing of things. He told him to get some
psychotherapy, learn to think things out instead of acting so impulsively.
Then he wished him "good luck," as if he were going on an exotic voyage,
and sent him to prison.

It could be strenuously argued that Tony Mazzccua had more than paid
for what he had done. He had spent sixteen years in prison for a crime that
in today's world of urban violence would have merited two paragraphs in
the newspapers. On one of the days that Fifi came to visit him, a man was
sentenced to eight to twenty years for beating his one-year-old son to death
because the child hadn't learned to walk yet and the man had grown tired
of him "acting like a baby." In another case the same day, a couple was
sentenced to four to ten years for nearly starving their seven-month-old son
to death. In the sad spectrum of violence, was Tony Mazzccua's crime
anywhere near as egregious as these? And didn't his admission of the
crime after all these years reveal something important about his soul and
his character?

In the late 1970s, when Tony Mazzccua was sentenced to life, it was not
uncommon for the governor, Democrat Milton Shapp, to commute life
sentences to sentences of life with the eligibility of parole. He did it 254
times. But after that, such commutations became rarer and rarer. The
next governor, Republican Richard Thornburgh, granted only seven. The
state's governor in 1994, Democrat Robert Casey, had granted twenty-
four. If Republican congressman Tom Ridge, with conservative ideas
about the criminal justice system, succeeded Casey in January of 1995, as
many thought he would, there was a likelihood that no life sentences would
be commuted during the next term.

In the absence of an answer by the Lord to Fifi's prayers, the cycle of
Tony's life seemed likely to continue. For the rest of his mother's life,
Tony would see her amid the din and the greasy smell of a prison visiting
room. For the rest of his life, he would communicate with his children by
phone or letter or visits once they got out of jail. He kept up with them as
best he could, and when he communicated with them, he apologized for
what he was. He held himself up as an example of what their lives must not
become—lives of potential ruined by the millisecond of gratification that

comes from violence. But the cycle of life was too firmly in place. His wife turned to crack, and his sons ran wild, and the middle one, Keith, had died in a shoot-out at seventeen. And it seemed only fitting that Tony should learn intimate details of Keith's death not from Fifi or other family members but from the lips of someone he had never laid eyes on before.

But since they were doing time together—the father whose son had been killed and the young man who had killed him—meeting each other was just a matter of working out cell-block logistics.

Tony was on A block when he got word through the prison grapevine that Terrell Moore was in B block, serving his sentence for killing Keith. Tony heard that he was scared, and Tony himself didn't know what he would do if they met. He could feel the old hostility rising as he thought about this "little motherfucker" who had killed his son, but he also knew that he had to see him, so he passed the word through a go-between.

"You tell this young brother I don't care what he do, where he go, he's gonna have to see me. He's gonna have to see me now, or he's gonna have to see me later."

Tony was at the end of the sanitation shop, where inmates pick up supplies, when there was a knock on the door. He had never seen his son's killer before, but he knew it was he as soon as he saw him. Other inmates cleared away, and Tony and Terrell Moore spoke privately.

"Why'd you shoot my son?" were the first words he asked him.

Moore tried to explain what happened, how there had been a fight and then a shoot-out in which Moore himself had been injured in the leg and shot in the chest but didn't die because he was wearing a bulletproof vest.

"What about my daughter?" Tony wanted to know. "How could you have also shot my daughter, my daughter Renee. My God, she was only eleven."

He said he hadn't.

What did he mean he hadn't? Then who the hell had?

Your son, Moore gently told him. Your own son. As he was falling backward to his death, his upper body filled with bullets, one of the guns he was carrying had gone off, and the bullet hit her.

"You telling me my son shot my daughter?"

"Yes, Mr. Mazzccua."

Tony had never heard that before, and it was shocking to hear it now from this man who was half his age. He felt a burst of anger. But then a sense of calm came over him. And when he looked at Terrell Moore, he saw someone who was scared and frightened and much like the young man he had been when he had gone to prison so long ago. And Tony was thankful for the way he felt.

He asked him whether he had any children, and he said that he did, a little daughter, and Tony asked him, "Don't you want to be with your daughter?" He said yes, and Tony shared with him how old his children were when he left the streets to come to prison and the devastating impact of that on all of them. He felt no hostility anymore toward the young man in front of him. He felt sympathy and a sense of paternalism, and he urged him to break the cycle. "I'm doing life for what I did," said Tony. "You got another chance to make something out of your life. You got a little girl out there, you got a woman who cares about you."

And after that, after they spoke for those forty minutes, he never saw him again.

Tony went back to the routine of his cell block, and the killer of his son went back to the routine of his.

At least once a month and sometimes more, if she could arrange the transportation, Fifi went to visit Tony. The first few years she felt apprehensive all the way up and then cried all the way back. But after a while the rhythm of acceptance set in, and the trip became an automatic part of her life, just like taking care of children and grandchildren and great-grandchildren. Up Henry Avenue and then over to Ridge Avenue until it turned into Ridge Pike. Then into the gray-water town of Graterford. When she had the time, she stopped at the Stroehmann factory to get some bread on the cheap, and when her parents were alive and visiting with her, they always went to the smorgasbord at the Collegeville Inn. Sometimes, when they had taken Germantown Pike instead of Ridge, her father would proudly show her the tracks of the railroad that he had built.

She had dressed beautifully on this particular day when she went to see her son, as if to conceal from him the worries and the responsibilities that weighed her down. "You look great!" he said, and she acknowledged that she had not only done up her hair but she had also put her teeth in. They hugged each other, and he called her Mommy. The severity of the rules of prison visiting had increased and decreased over the years and had recently become quite spartan. There was a time when you could pull chairs around to play pinochle, but that wasn't allowed anymore, so Tony and Fifi sat side by side in a long row of sagging chairs with greasy arms. She bought him the food he liked from the vending machine, and they talked idly and comfortably for two hours, and it was hard to believe that this was the way they had been forced to talk for all those years, under the glare of guards and over the noise of other inmates and against the green grime of those walls. Their love truly did flow like a river, unyielding and undying, mother to son and son to mother. He privately worried about how tired she looked, and she privately worried about how some gray was beginning to show around his temples. She dreamed of cooking him a meal. He dreamed of taking her on a cruise. He worried that she would die while he was still in prison, and she worried that she would die before God answered her and he was set free.

"Keep the faith," he said when it was time for her to leave, and he bent to give her a hug, one of the two he was allowed during visitation, a brief one at the beginning, another brief one right at the very end.

"I'll try," she said as tears formed in her eyes.

Then he stayed where he was, and she lumbered out through the visitor's room and back up the stairs.

The stairs were steep, and there was a little elevator attached to the railing for those who were handicapped. Fifi sighed and laughed and looked at those stairs as if she were scaling Everest and told a guard that the next time she came, she was going to go the proper way, in that little elevator. Then she looked at the stairs, and she did what she always did. She took hold of the railing and climbed them.

Fifi ran around the corner on that August day in 1994 after she dropped the phone. She saw the crumpled fence and the car that had smashed into it and all the blood. There had been a terrible crash that made for front-page news even in the desert of North Philadelphia, where there seemed no room for new horrors. A man apparently under the influence of cocaine had been driving his car like a madman five minutes before noon. He sped through a stop sign at Eleventh Street, went over the curb, struck the steps of an empty corner store, and swerved back into the street for half a block. Then he mounted the sidewalk again, ran over a signpost and crushed a woman who was six months pregnant and her three-year-old son against a fence.

The three-year-old would survive, and so miraculously would the baby. But the woman, named Kim Armstrong, would not. She was twenty-four years old, and Fifi knew her well. Sometime earlier Kim had given birth to a son. His name was Taheem, and his father was Tony's son Keith. Now both his parents were dead, his father killed in a shoot-out over drugs, his mother killed by a driver out of his mind because of them.

A few weeks earlier Fifi had asked aloud whether the cycle would ever stop.

"Sometimes I wonder, What more, what more, what more?" she said.

Now she knew the answer.

On the last Friday in August of 1994, people in the neighborhood gathered at the Cookman Church in the aftermath of Kim Armstrong's death. The issues they discussed were much the same as the ones that had been raised at the community meeting that had taken place at the end of June in the aftermath of the death of six-year-old Michelle Cutner. Black men talked about the need to regain control of the neighborhood. A police sergeant said drug activity in the neighborhood was so intense that there was at least one arrest a day. He urged people to call the police, and when people in the audience said there was little point in calling the police because the police never came, he meekly responded that for every call that did go out over the police radio, someone "eventually" responded.

Fifi was there. Her daughter was there because she had been the meeting's organizer. So were about fifty other people who just wanted some semblance of law to be brought back to their community. The mayor sent along an aide who, within the privacy of Rendell's office, existed largely to serve as a willing target at those moments when the mayor felt like ridiculing someone. His presence at meetings was virtually a sign of their unimportance.

"I just left the mayor," said the aide, who arrived an hour and a half late. "He very, very much wanted to be here."

SEVENTEEN

Don't Mess with Ed

I

Everywhere Rendell and Cohen went, he seemed to be behind them, out there in the shadows. Just when they figured they had shaken him, out-witted him for good and put him off the trail, there he was, the glint of his badge just barely visible in the summer sun.

They had given him the mayor's contributors' list when he had run for governor, which was like going to the wine cellar and handing over the rarest bottle of Mouton Rothschild coveted during the war. They figured he would accept it in the spirit in which it was intended, part gift, part buy-out, but there he was. They called their best fund-raising lieutenants to the long table in the Cabinet Room, held the political equivalent of a Mafia war summit, then sent these grim and powerful soldiers on a do-or-die mission to raise so much money from every law firm, bank, investment house, and business that no one, no one, would dare risk a challenge.

By the middle of the summer of 1994, the Rendell campaign had $1.7 million sitting in various bank accounts. And yet there he was, inscrutable, impossible to read, refusing to go away, the sweet speculation of rumor only making him stronger.

There had been a time during the spring when Cohen had become utterly convinced that State Representative Dwight Evans would run for mayor. He had seen him in Harrisburg during negotiations for the state budget. Evans was angry in a way that shocked Cohen, and had suggested that there was no true commitment to minorities in the city. The process of budget negotiations in Harrisburg, the endless horse-trading and behind-the-back deals that the petty men who called themselves legislators mistook for power, was always exhausting, and Cohen thought Evans's private outburst was partially a reaction to that atmosphere. But Cohen thought something else was driving Evans, something he couldn't blame him for at all. The state capital of Harrisburg was a miserable place, not only because the town was an ugly and crummy backwater but also because of the absolutely corrosive attitude that most legislators bore toward the city. Cohen himself saw it when a legislator whom he had never met before expressed his admiration for the mayor this way: "He's done a helluva better job than the nigger you had in there before."

By the middle of the summer, Cohen wasn't so sure what Evans would do, but he did know this, just as the mayor's political strategist, Neil Oxman, had known it the night his client the mayor shared a giant hoagie instead of the pain over the death of a six-year-old: given the racial breakdown of the Democratic party in the city, Evans would be a credible and formidable challenger to the mayor if he decided to run. They had known it from the very first day of the administration, and they knew it now.

As a state representative, Evans had served his district in the city loyally and well for thirteen years. Without shrillness and without the immediate instinct to hold a press conference or play racial politics publicly, he had become a leading advocate of the city's minority community and was particularly masterly at strong-arming the mayor in a way that was quietly effective. He wasn't flashy, and he might not have had the stamina for a citywide campaign against Rendell in a Democratic primary. The mayor's popularity was formidable, and his ability to raise money daunting. But Evans had something the mayor would never have: immediate access to the base of the city's minority vote. If Evans could get to those neighborhoods, if he could take the community that had humbly gathered in a church to mourn the death of six-year-old Michelle Cutner and a dozen other communities and seize upon their alienation, then the possibility of an upset wasn't some fantasy.

Like a hard-to-get date, Evans refused to clarify his intentions one way or another, and there was always something mercurial about him. But Rendell and Cohen were acutely aware of his presence and of the need to head him off. The Rendell administration came up with a plan, the Philadelphia Plan it was called, a way of showing that the mayor, beyond his own private feelings, did care about the neighborhoods and the minority residents of the city. The plan, to rehabilitate housing, had good intentions and was modeled after the public-private partnership that Jimmy Carter had devised in Atlanta. But since one of the motivations behind it was politics, the polish and the presentation of it bore little resemblance to the reality. In private, the mayor readily agreed with the assessment of the plan as a drop in the bucket that would do little unless the city was able to increase its jobs base, with casino gambling or a second convention hotel or maybe even some miracle at the navy yard that no one had even considered. But perception was paramount, and one of the debates over the plan had to do with choosing the maximally effective visual backdrop for the press conference—should it be bombed-out buildings or rehabilitated ones?

Rehabilitated homes won out, and the Philadelphia Plan was announced amid great fanfare on a picture-perfect day of clear blue skies. The governor was there. So was the mayor. So was Dwight Evans, and so were so many other politicians that someone must have spread the word that there were free umbrellas and tote bags for those who got there on time. So were representatives of the nine corporations that, under the terms of the plan, had made a commitment to contribute $250,000 a year for ten years to community-development corporations to develop and build new housing. Standing next to the mayor and the governor, they were preening and proud. Given the federal and state tax credits that existed for such neighborhood investment, the real out-of-pocket expense for these corporations, with aggregate assets running well into the tens of billions, was about $50,000 each per year, but that information wasn't highlighted.

The largesse of one of the participants, PNC Bank, was particularly notable. In its press release congratulating itself for its participation, the bank noted that "all companies should view community investment as an integral, not supplemental, part of their business." PNC was a good corporate citizen, but less than a year later it would inform the city that it was thinking of consolidating its back-office operations. The bulk of the jobs, about eight hundred of them, were already in Philadelphia, and the total number of jobs at stake was somewhere around twelve hundred. PNC would then sit back as the cities of Philadelphia and Camden fought for those jobs like rats fighting for the last piece of cheese. Camden, desperately trying to revive itself, wanted the jobs. Philadelphia, trying not to lose any more jobs than it already had, desperately wanted to keep them. Camden, buoyed by the pro-business policies of Governor Christine Todd Whitman, at one point offered an incentives package worth millions in low-interest loans and tax reductions. Philadelphia countered with its own multimillion-dollar package. Camden sweetened its offer. Philadelphia sweetened its offer, particularly after PNC wrote letters to state officials noting that the New Jersey proposal was $5 million better than the Philadelphia proposal and how nice it would be for the city or the state to rent two city office buildings that the bank was planning to vacate, thereby securing an income stream.

The mayor himself knew what was happening, how he was being forced into a horrible bidding war by a corporation that knew it had the city cornered. No big-city mayor anywhere could afford to let go of this many jobs, and during one phone call with PNC Bank Corporation chairman Thomas O'Brien, Rendell became livid. He wrote a letter of apology afterward, explaining, "It has been a tough week for the city and sometimes it seems that no matter how effective our administration is, it simply doesn't matter and we are nothing more than a very good doctor to a patient who is dying slowly but surely."

By the time it was over, Philadelphia would keep the jobs in the city, to the tune of various grants and loans that were worth, estimated conservatively, about three hundred times more than the first-year out-of-pocket commitment PNC had made to rebuilding a few homes as part of the Philadelphia Plan. None of that could have been known at the time of the press conference since it hadn't yet occurred. Instead, PNC, at the time of the press conference, had to be content with the business fees that it collected of nearly $170,000 a year from the city and the fees for various securities transactions that totaled more than $1 million over the past three years.

But none of that mattered on this flawless summer day. The swell of effusion for the plan was enormous. Dwight Evans himself spoke in favor of it and offered the mayor high praise, and that buoyed the mood of members of the mayor's staff because, they thought, if Evans was planning on becoming a challenger to the mayor, he sure wasn't sounding like one. The media was in full bloom, with the cameras clicking and the reporters taking notes, and when someone asked press secretary Feeley off the record whether the plan might actually work, he smiled through his *Risky Business* sunglasses and whispered what could have been the motto of modern-day politics: "It has absolutely no relevance."

What happened in private immediately after the press conference was a far better barometer of the mayor's commitment to the city's minority community than what happened during the press conference. As he returned to his car, he was surrounded by a group of girls in their early teens who insisted on taking him on a tour of the neighborhood. He obliged and started walking down Stella Street in his patented waddle. Three of the girls held his arm, and he didn't seem like the mayor at all but like a father out for a walk with his children. There was a simple earnestness to him, a mood reminiscent of that first year in office when he had shown a spontaneous and unyielding passion for his city. But that first year seemed almost dreamlike now.

The girls surrounding him talked nonstop, interrupting one another in their efforts to point out the severity of the problems in their neighborhood. As he walked down the street, other residents saw him and chimed in as well. A woman selling pretzels from her stoop asked him to do something about the stray cats that carried fleas. Another asked him to remove the debris that had been piled next to an abandoned house for almost a year. Another asked whether he could stave off eviction for her and her four children. Another pointed to a house on the corner and said it was becoming a drug den. A man in his twenties who was newly married asked him for a job. The young girls bobbing around him asked for a rec center and a swimming pool, as if he were the Pied Piper.

He listened to their problems, and he scribbled them down on a piece of paper inside a red folder. He walked up to people standing in doorways and introduced himself as "Ed, Ed Rendell," and he walked up onto porches. Every single need in that neighborhood was real, and Rendell himself knew that without jobs, without the reinvention of the city, there was little he could do. He could call someone to get rid of the debris and maybe even those pesky cats with the fleas, but he could not fix the fundamental flaws that existed.

History, attitude, the tides of federal policy, had transformed the country into a suburban nation, with the American city an appendage at worst and an entertainment satellite at best. And if the trends of population and race and class continued, this neighborhood and thousands of others like it across the urban landscape were doomed, and so were the people whose pity it was to live in them.

He kept on walking, writing furiously to keep up with the requests.

"We need a playground, something for us."

"Mr. Mayor, is it possible for us to find some type of work for us young guys just sittin' around here?"

"I don't want to be sellin' drugs."

"Don't forget about my phone call."

"Don't forget about my job."

"Bye, Mr. Ed Rendell."

He went back to his car and was immediately on the phone with various city officials to see what could be done. One of them had been at the Philadelphia Plan press conference and was ecstatic. "That was great!" she said, as if he had just appeared on the *Oprah Winfrey Show.*

"It was great," said the mayor in a muted voice, as if he were the only one there who understood the limitations of it. "I think some good can come out of it."

"That was nice!" she repeated. "You'll get a lot of great play out of that!"

He gave no response. Instead, he asked her whether there was any way of getting rid of all that debris one of the residents had complained about, and in that moment in the front seat of his car, surrounded by the fallen might of North Broad Street as he headed back to City Hall, trying to keep up with the list of complaints he had taken down in the red folder, he showed once again why an entire city had fallen in love with him.

He seemed at peace, but then the next meeting started, a frank discussion of the painful social reengineering that would have to take place because of the continued cancer of blight, a discussion of which blocks of the city to save and which blocks to tear down and how the various affected residents should be removed, like war refugees, to the neighborhoods that still had a chance of survival.

There was no lasting peace for Ed Rendell, just as there was no lasting peace in the city.

II

The foulness of mood, the scary unpredictability of where it would take him, whether impulsively upward or downward, showed up again several months later, in October. Dwight Evans was still in the shadows, refusing to dampen the speculation that he was going to run. In response to the threat, the mayor's schedule was more brutal than it had ever been, a wrenching amalgam of city business meetings, regular political appearances, and campaign activities all over the city that often started at 7:00 A.M. and did not end until 11:00 P.M. War-weary staffers could sense the hair trigger, could see the snarl and the flecks of foam around the corners of his mouth. He was doing too much, extending himself beyond all limits. People who worked for him knew what happened when he got like this—chairs thrown in his office, staffers grabbed in fury and frustration, emotions unleashed.

Within the stirrings of the cultural community in Philadelphia in the fall of 1994, there was considerable pride in and excitement over a new book by two professional women who worked in the city. The book was called *Sisters,* and it was, as its title suggested, a compilation of essays about sisters and photographs of sisters, the essays by Carol Saline, a senior editor at *Philadelphia Magazine,* and the photographs by Sharon Wohlmuth, a photographer for the *Inquirer.* It would eventually become a phenomenal success and would spend sixty-three weeks on the *New York Times* best-seller list. Among those profiled were the Masiejczyk sisters, Donna, Debbie, and Shirley. They were all Philadelphia police officers, and Debbie was on the mayor's security detail.

A party to celebrate the publication of the book was being sponsored on a Thursday night in October by *Philadelphia Magazine,* and it seemed only fitting for the mayor to make an appearance, given the inclusion of Debbie Sheeron (née Masiejczyk) in the book. Her family was going to be there, and she would be quite proud to have the mayor there. So, of course, would the authors. The event was added to Rendell's schedule, but he clearly did not want to do it.

When he got to the event, he kept muttering, "What the fuck am I doing here? What the fuck am I doing here?" He had seen Sharon Wohlmuth dozens of times before in her capacity as an *Inquirer* photographer, and that's what he apparently thought she was now, a goddamn motherfucking *Inquirer* photographer. He seemed to have no idea that this was a party in her and Saline's honor and had nothing to do with the *Inquirer.* He had no idea that she was one of the collaborators on *Sisters.* Wohlmuth herself felt honored and excited that he was there. Dressed elaborately in a Japanese jacket, she was about to thank him for coming when he looked at her with venom, clearly thinking she was there for the *Inquirer*—even though she was not carrying a camera.

"If you want to photograph me, you do it!" he snapped.

Wohlmuth was stunned by the comment. "Fuck you," she said, enraged and insulted that a crowning moment in her career and her life, the publication of a book that had taken nearly a decade to complete, had been so utterly belittled by a mayor who thought she was there to take his picture. This was her night, not his.

The incident should have ended there, but it did not.

The event was public, but it didn't matter to him. He lunged at her and grabbed her arm with such force that his hold caused the beginnings of a black-and-blue mark. He slightly tore her Japanese jacket and started dragging her along with him. Those who witnessed the incident said it was something far more than an example of the time-honored custom of a politician taking out his frustrations on a representative of the media; it was something shocking.

"It was so scary," Wohlmuth said later. "He attacked me."

And then he suddenly stopped, Wohlmuth recalled, and threw himself into a temper tantrum, acting as if what he had just done wasn't his responsibility at all, blaming the overworked people in his scheduling office, blaming everyone but himself. "I never know where I'm supposed to be!" he wailed. "I never know where I'm supposed to be!"

Wohlmuth found herself consoling him as a mother consoles a child, and in that moment she didn't see America's mayor. She saw someone who was pathetic.

Sergeant Buchanico, the head of the mayor's security detail, was having a drink with someone else from the mayor's office at a restaurant bar when he was beeped by Debbie Sheeron. She was driving the mayor that night, and she sounded upset, and he asked her what was wrong.

"He went off," she said of the mayor.

"What do you mean?" asked the sergeant.

"He went off," she repeated and reported what happened. She said that the mayor acknowledged that he shouldn't have lost his temper and that he thought some apology was appropriate, not an apology by him personally but by Debbie Sheeron on his behalf. Buchanico, who was better than anyone else in the entire city at patting down the hills of messes until they were minor speed bumps, went to Wohlmuth himself. The photographer was polite and dignified with Buchanico, but that wasn't the way she felt. The party had been ruined for her, and the mayor's lunge at her only added to the aftereffects of another event: about a week earlier she and her husband had been mugged at gunpoint near their home, in one of the most fashionable neighborhoods of the city.

Kevin Feeley, convinced that the mayor's schedule was subjecting him to intolerable stress, suggested to Cohen that more downtime be built into it. Cohen told Feeley that it was totally unnecessary. He said that the incident had not been nearly as bad as some had claimed. The biggest problem with it, Cohen said, were members of the mayor's staff who kept talking about it.

Cohen had been at the party that night, but not when the incident occurred. He got there about fifteen minutes later, talked to some people about what had happened, and said later that everyone described it as inconsequential and that even Wohlmuth's collaborator, Carol Saline, had joked about it. Saline and Cohen knew each other well: it was Saline who had written an early profile of Cohen that had started him on his ascent to mythic stature in the city. He had liked it so much that he had a framed copy in his office.

Hours after Cohen said that, Saline was at a book-signing party for *Sisters.* In the midst of it, she saw Cohen's deputy chief of staff, Ted Beitchman. Now, without Cohen present, her attitude toward the incident was anything but jocular. "Can't you get someone to talk to him?" she asked Beitchman about the mayor. She then gestured to Wohlmuth, who was signing books at a nearby table. "Because of her, we have kept this out of the press."

Debbie Sheeron was also at the party that night, and she spoke again about the incident—"Oh God, it was awful."

But all those sentiments were expressed privately. The incident was successfully kept out of the press. And it became abundantly clear that the mayor was being shielded by the impregnable wall of power that politicians have constructed around them as if it were their birthright. And this wall now was being reinforced by the loyalty so many people had to a man whose efforts on behalf of the city had been unparalleled.

Sharon Wohlmuth, of course, knew better than anyone else what had happened. She knew how a night in her life that should have been wonderful had been ruined. She got messages from *Daily News* reporters asking to interview her about what happened. But she too felt the conflict that others felt—abhorrence at the mayor's behavior but admiration for his efforts on behalf of the city. She thought Rendell had been a good mayor in a city that so badly needed a good mayor. She did not want to hurt his campaign for reelection. She did not want to hurt the city. So she refused to talk to any of the Philadelphia media, and the mayor's handlers, mortified by the thought that the incident might find its way into print, began to breathe a little bit easier. Feeley had sorely feared what he called the "drop, drop, drop" effect, in which the media, coupling this event with the one in which the mayor grabbed a reporter's neck and various rumored incidents, would inevitably write something. But it didn't happen.

Wohlmuth briefly thought Rendell might convey some personal apology in addition to sending out a member of his security detail to do the work for him. Several weeks after the incident she hadn't heard a word, not that it mattered at that point anyway.

"I don't even want an apology from that bastard."

III

Through the fall of 1994, the quiet and relentless march against the shadow candidacy of Dwight Evans continued. Money was raised by the fistful, not only from those who had been loyal to Rendell in the past but also from those who might at one point have considered giving money to Evans, thereby further squeezing the opponent's base of support. Rendell courted members of the city's black clergy with a vengeance in the hopes of gaining their endorsement, and given the way they had related to the mayor in the past, it seemed clear they were willing to listen.

At a meeting the previous February in the Cabinet Room, eighteen of the city's most powerful black ministers armed with a list of written demands had surrounded the mayor as he sat at the table. They knew how the game was played, for the first thing on their agenda was the statement that the "clergy here this morning is a cross section of denominations representing hundreds of thousands of voters." They said they expected the mayor's next appointments to both the Board of Education and the Zoning Board to come from their own list. They expressed their unequivocal support for the black police commissioner, Rich Neal (despite misspelling his last name), and made a point of telling the mayor that they had heard rumors that he was planning to fire him. They suggested that "serious attention be paid" to appointing an African American male as the superintendent of the city's public school system. At one point, Rendell left the room to get something, and right before he went back inside, he said with a chagrined smile on his face, "Being mayor means having the right to be held up—stick a gun in your ribs." He did his best to be conciliatory, and although the meeting was tense at times, the appropriateness of the mayor's responses to the demands was enough to induce the ministers to utter a little prayer at the end, giving thanks to "our mayor, our beloved mayor."

Rendell and his handlers also sought the endorsement of the *Philadelphia Tribune,* the city's black newspaper. Regardless of what his critics said, Rendell had done, within rigorous financial constraints, as much as any mayor could have done for the black neighborhoods of the city. Clearly Cohen hoped that would be enough to get the *Tribune*'s endorsement, and he blanched at the suggestion that he might have been trying to sweeten the pot just a little when he had helped the paper get approval over the summer for adequate press parking spaces on the street outside its offices. The two issues were completely separate, he said—even if he did file the thank-you letter from *Tribune* publisher Robert W. Bogle under "politics."

A series of secret focus-group sessions had been held in August to assess the mayor's performance, and they once again revealed the mayor's Achilles' heels: neighborhoods and crime. Rendell began to talk about crime more frequently, blasting judges, promising more police under the Omnibus Violent Crime Control and Prevention Act that had just been signed by the president. It was hard to know what effect any of the new rhetoric was having, and in the middle of November of 1994, in the space of forty minutes, it all became moot anyway.

The first calls started coming in to 911 operators around 10:00 P.M. and were responded to as if the desperation of them, the insistence that the police come because something horrible was happening, weren't a cause for action but were a cause for resentment. The undercurrent of the operators' attitude was so strong that the only explanation for it could be traced to the inevitability of race: the operators, most of whom were black, were clearly bristling at what they believed to be the pushiness of one white caller after another, as if they were the only ones who had to deal with crime in the city.

10:20:49 P.M.
Caller: Could you send some police over here to 7979 Rockwell Avenue? About 50 kids are busting up cars.

Dispatcher: What are they doing?
Caller: Busting up the cars, windows and everything.
Dispatcher: About how many is there?
Caller: About 50.
Dispatcher: All righty.

10:37:15 P.M.
Caller: They got clubs out there. There's a kid out there.
Dispatcher: All right.
Caller: Did you get that?
Dispatcher: Yeah, a kid is hurt outside, and there's a fight. Right? That was it?
Caller: Yeah, that's it! Send a police car to seven—
Dispatcher: Wait a minute. Wait a minute. Wait a minute. You asked me, and I'm asking you. I have the information, you can hang up now.

10:38:25 P.M.
Caller: There's about 20 kids outside fighting.
Dispatcher: We'll send somebody around.

10:41:01 P.M.
Caller: There's about 50 teenagers, baseball bats. A gang fight—
Dispatcher: We'll get somebody right over there.

10:42:32 P.M.
Caller: We've been calling. Everybody in the damn neighborhood's been calling. I call the district, they tell me to call 911. What are we supposed to do here? There's cars. There's a whole damn convoy of cars coming up here. You got a damn riot goin' up here.
Dispatcher: Police will be there.

10:44:13 P.M.
Caller: This is one of the sisters at St. Cecilia's Convent on Rhawn Street. There's a bunch of kids out in the parking lot, and it looks like they are beating up one kid.
Dispatcher: We'll send someone out.

10:44:23 P.M.

Caller: They are beating the hell out of people with baseball bats up here. When are you going to send somebody?

Dispatcher: Who's got a bat, sir?

Caller: Who got a bat? Some gorilla. What the hell do you mean?

Dispatcher: Wait a minute! Wait a minute! Don't talk to me like that. I asked you a question.

10:46:22 P.M.

Caller: We're having a problem outside our house here.

Dispatcher: What's the address there?

Caller: OK. 525 Rhawn.

Dispatcher: 525 Rhawn?

Caller: Right.

Dispatcher: Is it R—

Caller: R-H-A-W-N! We've got kids being beat up. And no one wants to help us!

Dispatcher: I'm trying to help you, ma'am. I have to first understand you.

Caller: Rhawn. R as in robot. *H as in* health. *A as in* apple. . . . *Does that help?*

Dispatcher: Immensely. Now, can you continue? What's the problem there?

Caller: We've been calling for 20 minutes now to get the cops up here, and no one's come.

Dispatcher: We'll send the police, ma'am.

Caller: Pardon me?

Dispatcher: We will send the police.

Caller: Send them now, not in 10 minutes, but now.

Dispatcher: We will send the police, ma'am.

At least thirty-three calls were made to 911 by people in the neighborhood of Fox Chase who were frantic about what was happening. From the time of the first call it took forty minutes for a police car to be dispatched, and when the police finally did arrive, it was too late anyway. The boy that some of the callers had been so desperate and upset about, sixteen-year-old Edward Polec, had been beaten so severely with baseball bats by an angry mob that he had seven skull fractures. Bent on revenge for what turned out to be a bogus claim of rape, a group of teenagers had tripped up Polec and then beaten him to death near the church where he had once been an altar boy. He died the next day.

In the first days after the incident, news of the conduct of the 911 operators, but not the contents of the tapes, started making its way into print. Then, on the day before Thanksgiving, the tapes themselves were released to the media, and what was a personnel and procedural problem with 911 became an unmitigated disaster. The transcriptions were shocking enough, but the audio took listeners to the very limits of belief, for it revealed an almost surreal give-and-take between callers who were in hysterics and begging for help and 911 operators who were rude, arrogant, and disdainful. The story of the tapes led the Thanksgiving Day broadcast of the ABC nightly news, which from Rendell's perspective meant he now had a national story on his hands. He was in North Carolina, vacationing with his wife's relatives, and so was temporarily insulated from reporters and questions, but Cohen knew the situation was "white hot." Reporters were staking out the mayor's house, and talk of the tapes was everywhere, and media requests from all over the country were piling up, and almost the second the mayor returned, Cohen told him he had to do something and do it quickly.

Rendell listened to the tapes, found the conduct of the 911 operators appalling, and publicly announced that three operators would be fired and three suspended. It was a decisive action, motivated by genuine outrage, and it produced a remarkable but all too predictable result.

The mayor was accused of racism because all six of those disciplined were black. It was a ridiculous and spurious charge prompted by black politicians who were obviously trying to shore up their strength within their own constituencies and by those who were obviously hoping to induce Dwight Evans to challenge the mayor for reelection in the Democratic primary. Almost ironically, Rendell first heard of the charge minutes before a private meeting with several powerful black ministers in the city in which he planned to ask for their political endorsement so as to shove Evans further out of the race. When the meeting began, he told the ministers he had had no idea that all the disciplined operators were black, and given Rendell's personal and political views, this was an assertion that rang true. The Rendell administration had paid copious attention to every decision that even remotely involved race, and it seemed ridiculous to think that Rendell would have disregarded the issue now, particularly if doing so meant flinging the door open to a black challenger.

Sitting at the round table in his office, he pointed out his efforts on behalf of the city's black community. He pointed out the number of blacks who had been hired by the city. He pointed out that the city had both a black police commissioner and a black fire commissioner thanks to his appointments. Most important of all perhaps, he pointed out how debilitating it would be for him to engage in a bitterly contested campaign, particularly when so many obstacles were still facing the city. "I need to be able to spend one hundred percent of my time on these issues. I cannot be campaigning six hours a day. I cannot worry about having to raise money."

He didn't try to bully those around him at the table. He didn't promise them the sun, and he didn't suggest that there was some specific quid pro quo for their support. He spoke without venality or secret motive. He did not want a challenger not merely for his own sake but for the sake of a city that needed him not sixteen hours a day or eighteen hours a day but every single hour if the city was still to have a chance.

"The last thing we need in this city is a black-white election," he said with a sense of sorrow, well aware of what such an election would be like—bitter, divisive, fueled by spoken and unspoken hatred.

He asked for their support, and the ministers, while cordial, gave no commitment one way or another. In the succeeding days, the drumbeats protesting the mayor's behavior only intensified, spreading the gospel of a mayor who not only had turned his back on the city's neighborhoods but also was a racist. Speculation about Dwight Evans heightened—with everything to gain and nothing to lose, he would jump in.

Rendell needed something to diminish the chorus that he was a downtown mayor driven by the edifice complex—a desire to build monuments, just as a little boy stacks wooden blocks one upon the other. Then, toward the end of December, came a momentous announcement.

The federal government had determined the winners of the intense competition for the six urban empowerment zones. Each zone carried with it a $100-million grant in antipoverty aid to be used to create jobs, improve education, and fix up housing. As an added incentive to create jobs, each zone would also be able to offer businesses lucrative federal tax breaks. Given his close relationship with both the president and Cisneros, many had thought the city would be an automatic winner, in particular since it had filed a joint application with Camden, New Jersey. The legislation for the empowerment zones had been written by New Jersey senator Bill Bradley, and he had inserted a provision that at least one zone consist of an urban area covering two states. Bradley readily acknowledged that the language was meant to favor Philadelphia and Camden, and only two other areas filed applications under the bistate criteria. But if Rendell had learned anything in his political life, it was that there are no guarantees. In the passing of a single second, one man's supposed fortune could turn to misfortune, and so the city's application was exhaustive.

Empowerment zones were at the center of Clinton's urban policy, and for well over a year, Rendell had been plotting a strategy to obtain one. The most direct competition came from the area of Kansas City, covering both Missouri and Kansas. It wasn't the quality of that area's application that worried Rendell. When it came to need, there simply was no contest, and Philadelphia's application was a harrowing reminder of how deeply entrenched the problems were: an income gap between rich and poor that had gone up 14 percent between 1984 and 1990; a ranking of second among cities in the country in the number of people age sixteen or older not working; a number of vacant homes that was greater than that of Detroit and St. Louis combined; a mortality rate among "Philadelphians of color" that was worse than that of Panama, Romania, Jamaica, and Bulgaria. But Rendell also knew that whereas need sometimes counted in politics, more often it did not, and he feared that the president might want to offer a zone to Kansas City as a showing of goodwill toward a U.S. senator from Kansas who was thinking of seeking higher office.

Atlanta won an empowerment zone. So did Baltimore. So did Chicago. So did Detroit. So did New York. And so did the joint application submitted by Philadelphia and Camden. The formal announcement, elaborately coordinated by the White House, had both the president and the vice president on conference-call hookups with seventeen places. Since everybody could hear everybody else, Rendell instinctively realized what was happening—a veritable "oink fest," as he described it, in which everyone, *everyone,* would want to say something to the president and offer effusions of praise and thanks that would make the Academy Awards seem like an admirable model of restraint. He hoped against hope that it would not happen, and things were OK for a while, but once Zell Miller, the governor of Georgia, got the ball rolling, he knew the cause was lost, and when his turn finally came, he took advantage of it. "We want to say thanks to you and the vice president for not losing faith in American cities," said Rendell.

Almost at the very second after the empowerment-zone awards were announced, Dwight Evans's name slithered first into a whisper and then into silence altogether. And without Evans in the race, there would be no race regardless of who decided to run.

As far as Rendell was concerned, the truest measure of his rebound wasn't in any poll but was in the cornucopia of Christmas gifts on the table in his office—canisters of Baileys liqueur, towering fruit baskets, pistachios in burlap sacks, Godiva chocolates, bottles of wine, custom-designed T-shirts. Rendell knew what these gifts were about. He called them "suck" gifts, and the way they spilled all over one another on the table was a better sign than any scientific poll.

"If I was wounded," he said as he eyed the bounty, "there wouldn't be this level."

Visibly relieved, Rendell could sense the restoration of a political image that had been bruised not only by the possibility of a primary challenge but also by the 911 débâcle. In the difficult days following it, the White House chief of staff, Leon E. Panetta, had called and wondered if he might like to become the head of the Democratic National Committee. Rendell turned the offer down.

He still very much wanted to be mayor. He also knew that if he left in the middle of the term, council president Street would succeed him as mayor under the city charter. Despite his personal fondness and loyalty to Street, he realized this would be untenable. The city council president had changed, but in politics, change had no chance against perception. During focus group sessions with voters that the Rendell campaign had secretly conducted the previous August, the response to Street had been hair-raising.

"John Street is extremely unpopular among white voters," the Hickman-Brown polling firm concluded. "Of all the personalities we discussed, no person generated so much hostility in the three groups of white voters as John Street. . . . The participants tried to outdo each other in saying critical things about him." Street was described as a "pit bull," "full of rage," having a "big mouth, a big African rotten mouth," "always screaming about something," and those actually were the nicest things said about him. Their comments revealed a toxic combination of racism and the reputation of a man who seemed forever defined by whites for his histrionics and his outbursts, regardless of the fact that he had tempered such public conduct in recent years. Many of those in the focus groups acknowledged that Street and Rendell did have a good working relationship, and that Street had done a good job of presiding over the city council. But they still loathed him, a political reality that wasn't lost on the mayor.

"Can you imagine if I had resigned and appointed John Street as mayor?" he said the day after the empowerment zones were announced. "Can you imagine how unpopular I would be?"

IV

As good a courtroom verbalist as he was, Mike McGovern could produce no argument to counter that of his wife, who was ready to leave for the suburbs as soon as he gave the go-ahead. When reasons to stay and reasons to go were put on paper, the result was like trying to represent a client who had videotaped a murder he committed and then sent the tape to the police with his name and address on a return envelope. The location of the McGoverns' home in the city, in the farthest reaches of the northeast, a block away from the Bucks County line, made them a little bit like potential refugees, dissidents who knew that if things got really, really grim, they could walk to freedom. "Do I run for it?" he had asked once.

But there was something about the city that stirred in the blood of Mike McGovern, a lingering chemical. Much of it was based on his memory of Port Richmond when he was a child and a teenager and a young man—the kinetic energy and texture of it, the way everyone was forced to interact with everyone else, the way everyone learned when it was time to cheer together and when it was time to fight, the little things and the nuances you could learn nowhere else and stood by you as you got older. He could not say that Rendell had made it any easier for a middle-class family such as his to stay in the city, but he did think that the mayor had produced an enormous spiritual change. In 1992, six months after Rendell had taken office, McGovern thought the city was dying. He kept thinking about a song by Randy Newman about the death of a city, and he also thought about the movie *Avalon,* in which an immigrant family bit by bit loses its roots and its sense of place in a city that has changed and splintered.

But now he felt differently. He felt something about the city that he hadn't felt in years. He felt pride. He did have loyalty to the city, and what drew him to the place were emotional values—the city's heart, the city's unique soul and character, the city's humor and passion—values that could not be easily measured against lousy schools and spotty snow removal. He knew that his wife would leave tomorrow if given the chance, but he couldn't bring himself to do that. He didn't want to be a commuter from Yardley or New Hope or Warrington. He didn't want to run for cover in Bucks County. He had aspirations of becoming a judge someday, and because of that he needed to maintain a residence in the city. But this was not the only thing that compelled him to stay.

He wanted to be a Philadelphian, a city dweller, because it meant something special to him and gave him a certain identity that the suburbs could never supply regardless of all the presumed advantages. "I have always defined myself as a Port Richmond guy first and primarily a Philadelphian," said McGovern one night as he was driving into Center City. "I don't want to lose that, because I like being a Philadelphian. Once you leave Philadelphia, you lose your standing to care and complain about it."

The elevated road curved into the sinew of the city. The sun was trickling down beneath the horizon, and the light fell on the buildings in such a way that they seemed both enormous and vulnerable, strong and delicate, not a place of alienation and remoteness but a place of power and possibility.

"Look at it!" said McGovern, still captured by something he had seen a thousand times before. "It's just super!" The look on his face was a mixture of pride and wonderment. His soul could be found in the dappled light of those buildings, and it became clear that whatever reasons there were to leave, they would not matter. He was born a city dweller, and he would remain one.

V

The mugging at the train station in Chestnut Hill in broad daylight had been a breaking point, but in December 1994, at just about the same time the city was being awarded an empowerment zone, there was one final slap in the face for Linda and Jon Morrison. As Jon left the house to go to work, he found the Volvo station wagon parked outside on the street, right where it had been parked the night before, but with one variation: the car was up on bricks, and all four tires were gone. If nothing else, the thieves had been maniacally courteous, piling all the nuts in a neat pile, in case the Morrisons wanted to use them again.

In January of 1995, at about the time Rendell made his official announcement of his candidacy for reelection, the Morrisons bought a home in Newtown in Bucks County. It had aluminum siding and a two-car

garage and vinyl flooring. It had none of the amenities Linda had wanted
in a home, none of the charm of the Queen Village colonial or the Chestnut Hill gingerbread. "This looks like a *Father Knows Best* kind of home,"
she said as she sheepishly pulled out a real estate brochure about it. The
day she looked at it, she breezed through in about ten minutes and felt no
emotional attachment whatsoever. But Linda did not want emotional attachment anymore. She wanted only the freedom to feel safe and walk the
dog at night and not look over her shoulder, the freedom not to shut her
windows tight in ninety-degree heat, and the house in Newtown, regardless of its appearance, provided that assurance.

Originally she had felt angry about moving out of the city, convinced
that she and her family were being driven away by a series of factors that
could have been controlled. "I don't think they believe in anything, really,"
she had finally come to conclude of the Rendell administration. "They believe in efficiency, whatever that is." She thought that the mayor, as well
intended as he might have been, had never been a visionary, and she also
thought that Cohen, suffering from the insulation of an office that had become his cage, had no idea of what it truly meant to live in the city and
grapple with the problems that she and tens of thousands of others grappled with every day.

"David Cohen needs to be mugged," said Linda.

But the closer the time came to move, the more the feelings of anger
gave way to other emotions. At the beginning of June 1995, two weeks before the movers were to come, Linda took the commuter train from Chestnut Hill and returned to the old neighborhood of Queen Village to wander
around one final time before leaving the city altogether.

In a horrible space of two years, between 1990 and 1992, Linda's
mother and two of her brothers had died of cancer. And staring out the window of the train now as it lurched its way through the desert of North Philadelphia on its way downtown, she experienced a similar sense of helpless
loss. "It reminds me of that cancer eating away," she said quietly, continuing to stare out the window into the deadness of the desert where nothing moved. "I feel sad in the same way."

The train passed by Wister Station and entered an area of weeds and tree
limbs as wild as uncut hair, and it reminded Linda of an ancient city she
had once read about that had become extinct after a period of thriving.
"The jungle overgrows it, both vegetative and living," she said as she
stared out the window. The train pulled into Wayne Junction, with its rub

of graffiti on the station walls, and then continued on past a tableau of boarded-up stone houses and empty factories.

"Aren't they beautiful?" said Linda wistfully of the houses. And she was right. At a certain time and in a certain place, they had been beautiful, not symbols of despair at the end of the century but symbols of sturdiness at the beginning of it. "And these factories," she said as she continued to stare out the window. "That's what I think are the very saddest. They represented progress and productivity and the production of wealth. They were an asset instead of a liability."

The train stopped again, and Linda got off and walked back to those streets and crevices where she and her husband and tiny baby had lived before they fled in the summer of 1992. She went back to the playground where she had taken her son, Ian, to play. She went back to the colonial on Queen Street where they had lived, and she pointed to the bedroom that had been her son's. She pointed to the white marble steps that had been splattered with blood after the young woman had been stabbed. She went back to the sliver of Kauffman Street, where the Section 8 apartment complex was, and the sight of it again filled her with rage. "I hate them. I hate everyone who lives there," she said.

All the horror came back, the constant din of chaos, but all the wonderful moments came back as well. She remembered how she and Jon, after work, would sit on the marble steps sipping from glasses of wine. She remembered how much she liked her neighbors and the sense of community she felt, a feeling of togetherness and of being a part of something. Her thirst for the city was unquenchable this day, every crevice taken in as if she had never laid eyes on any of it before, not a stagnant or a hopeless place at all but a place, even within the small circumference of where she walked, filled with variation. It seemed impossible that anyone with an affinity for cities such as Linda had could actually be leaving, just as it seemed impossible that anyone who had been through what she and her family had been through could stay. The ambivalence in her was abundant, and the more she wandered and remembered, the quieter she became.

"I am really grieving," she said. "I feel like when my family died. I feel the same way."

Eventually she got back on the commuter train. She went through the desert of North Philadelphia and back into Chestnut Hill, the oasis of city life that had turned out to be no oasis at all.

She and her husband closed on the *Father Knows Best* house in Newtown in Bucks County in the middle of June 1995. Seven days later the movers came, and the Morrisons were gone.

Six months and seven days from that moment, on the very first day of 1996, Ed Rendell would finish the incredible journey of his four-year term as mayor. In the absence of some catastrophe, he would begin another term. He would stand with both hands placed firmly on the edges of the podium and give an inauguration speech, just as he had before. He would make promises and offer challenges, just as he had before. He would state his best of intentions, just as he had before.

Linda Morrison might listen to what he said on that day, or she might not, because other than as a matter of curiosity, it would have no bearing on her at all.

She wept when she left the perfect house on Benezet Street in Chestnut Hill, just as she had mourned three years earlier when she had said good-bye to Queen Village. But the feelings were different. When she left Queen Village and moved to the suburbs, she also knew that she would return to the city, give it one more chance.

In saying good-bye now, she knew that the chance had come and gone, and there would not, could not, be another one.

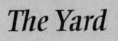

The Yard

EIGHTEEN

A Prayer for the City

I

The mayor sat in his customary spot at the table in the Cabinet Room, surrounded by a clump of executives judiciously dressed in innocuous shades of blue and gray and beige. The executives seemed as mousy and nonthreatening as their wardrobes, but the mayor knew exactly what was going on, how this was little more than a setup and how, once you cut through the obsequious slick of legalese and corporate-speak, he was basically being asked to lie.

The more he listened on this August day in 1995, the more his face turned ashen, and it wasn't just the disingenuousness of what he was hearing that was troubling him. It was the realization that his city, and all cities like it that had once been the definition of American industrial might and strength, were on the verge of a certain kind of extinction.

The subject at hand in the Cabinet Room was a plant closure, and the number of jobs at stake was so small as to seem irrelevant: 240. But in the realm of the mayor and the city, where every job counted and was fought over, the loss was significant. Beyond the actual number, there were the deeper reverberations of the psychic loss. The jobs were at the Breyers Ice Cream factory. They were the jobs that had helped lay the foundation of the city, and Breyers, beyond being the maker of the country's top-selling ice cream, was a hallowed name in the industrial arc of Philadelphia. It was here that Breyers was founded in 1866, when William A. Breyer used a hand-operated freezer to produce his ice cream and then sold the delicacy from a wagon. His "pledge of purity" caught on quickly, and in 1924 a then massive plant was built in West Philadelphia, adorned by a huge neon sign in distinctive script that could be seen from miles away on one of the city's expressways, a stable beacon keeping an eye over the quilt of working-class row houses that spread beneath it. But Breyers, like so many other companies in the 1990s, was undergoing corporate restructuring. And although the explanation for such restructuring could be debated by economists from now until the end of the century—how to some degree corporate shedding is the natural reaction of capitalism when new jobs requiring new skills inevitably take the place of old ones—the set of victims seemed forever constant: the city and those who lived and worked within it.

In a six-minute meeting at the end of August, the company that now owned Breyers, Unilever, a multinational conglomerate, had told its workers that the plant was closing. Several days later Rendell met with representatives of Unilever and Breyers to see if anything could be done to keep the plant open. Given his innate optimism, he refused to believe that any situation was hopeless. But his hands were clasped together instead of conducting their concerto, and this wasn't a gesture of prayer but more a gesture of weary acceptance. He offered to modernize the existing plant or help Unilever, with its more than $2 billion in assets, build a new one. "We think we can compete," he said softly, sounding like a parent begging a school to give his problem child one more chance. "We think we can do a better bottom line. I don't want to waste our time, but we think we can compete." Loans, cheap land, tax benefits—they were all available just as long as Unilever did not close the Breyers plant. "It's got a strong identification with the city of Philadelphia," Rendell said, hoping that might count for something.

And then he sat there quietly as Jerry Phelan, a senior vice president for manufacturing, explained the rationale of Unilever in maintaining its competitive edge in the ice-cream business. "I hate to use the word, but we did computer modeling studies," said Phelan somewhat sheepishly. Those models, which took every need into account except the human ones, made it clear that the only way to keep pace with the competition was through purchase and consolidation and plant closures. First it was at Good Humor, where the studies said that four plants, all of them in industrial cities, needed to be closed. Then it was at Gold Bond Ice Cream, where, as Phelan put it, they "took out" three of six plants, as if they were enemy machine-gun nests. Then it was through an investment at Klondike, where the computer studies said that two of the three existing plants had to go. Then Unilever purchased Breyers from Kraft, and the computer modeling studies said there were nine manufacturing plants, and that was too many, and there was an overcapacity problem, and some of these plants had to be taken out as well.

"We have a great workforce here," said Phelan, trying to be complimentary but not realizing the tragedy of what he was saying. "It has nothing to do with labor. It has nothing to do with gas rates. It's a question of capacity, where do we take it? It is really that simple. . . . We have a capacity issue that we have to address if we want to be competitive, and we want to be competitive."

The computer modeling study gave Unilever a choice of plants to close—the one in Philadelphia or the one in the Boston suburb of Framingham. The Framingham plant was built in 1964, when the suburbanization of industry was exploding. It was all on one level, and its former owners had poured a significant amount of money into it in 1991. The Philadelphia plant was sixty-eight years old and awkwardly laid out in terms of the modern requirements of mass production—too many levels, too much useless square footage. Millions could be spent to modernize it, but other than pleasing the mayor and the workers who earned their livelihood there, what was the point? "If you do that," said Phelan, sitting close to the mayor, on his left, "you still end up with a seventy-year plant."

In the 1930s, the Breyers plant in Philadelphia was the largest and the most modern ice-cream manufacturing plant in the world, capable of producing seventy thousand gallons of ice cream a day and replete with its own laboratory and a staff of chemists to ensure the "pledge of purity." Public tours were proudly conducted. But in the ceaseless wave of technology that made things bigger and better and faster than anyone had ever dreamed was possible, with less labor than anyone had ever dreamed was possible, it was now obsolete. Even if its workers churned out oceans of ice cream twenty-four hours a day, 365 days a year, it could not compete. The plant, built in the density of a once-bustling city because that is where the workers were, was now an unwanted orphan. And the closing of the plant wasn't some startling new trend but further evidence of an unrelenting one in which the number of workers employed in manufacturing nationwide had dropped from 33 percent of the workforce in the 1950s to 17 percent. In the 1960s alone, the number of blue-collar jobs lost in the country's four largest cities—New York, Chicago, Detroit, and Philadelphia—had been more than one million.

Rendell listened to Phelan's recitation of plant closures and consolidations and computer modeling studies, his hand now pressed against his jaw. The more Phelan spoke in his tone of sheepish apology, as if the mayor should somehow feel sorry for the company and understand its predicament, the more the expression on the mayor's face showed traces of exasperation. On countless occasions over the past four years, he had sat at his place at that table in the Cabinet Room and with charm and guile had convinced people not to make the decision they were about to make. Dozens of times he had turned what he didn't want to hear into something that he did want to hear. In virtually every situation, he had found the filament of hope and seized upon it to the exclusion of everything else, as if pulling a family heirloom from a fire.

He listened to Phelan lay out the competitive rigors of the ice-cream business, *the ice-cream business,* and explain how the only way to respond to those rigors was to close one plant after another. He asked what it would cost for the city to build a brand-new state-of-the-art plant, and he didn't blanch at the figure that was given, $60 million, until he heard what such an investment would yield: fifty jobs.

When it was his turn to speak, he initially looked as if he might burst. He grimaced slightly, as if neither Phelan nor the other nervous and pursed-lipped executives around him grasped the true impact of what had just been articulated. What he said wasn't angry; it was mournful.

"Everything you laid out—it would make a textbook study in business school, but it is a horror story to hear for the future of our country. What is going to happen to our people between technology and competition and everything else? The older a city is—it's harder for us to compete. What are we going to do for cities? I'll be a two-term mayor, and I'll get out before the carnage really starts, but what's going to happen to our country? What are cities going to do? Our cities are going to be horrible places."

"I agree with you," said Phelan. "The cities are in big trouble." As a show of commiseration with the mayor, he noted that he was from New York, although, of course, he didn't live in New York anymore but in that urban metropolis of Green Bay, Wisconsin. "We don't like closing plants," he continued, even though, by his own recital, Unilever had closed nine of them and was about to close a tenth. "We don't like taking people from their jobs."

But Rendell wasn't particularly interested in Phelan's expressions of guilt. As the meeting progressed, it became clear to him that the company's major preoccupation was spin: it was hoping to convince the reporters waiting outside that what was occurring behind the closed doors with the mayor was a valiant, last-gasp effort to save the plant. Company representatives were clearly hoping to cast the meeting as some noble attempt to see whether anything could be done to avoid the closing.

But the mayor himself knew that was ridiculous. "We were dead in the water before you came down here," he said. "There's no way we can compete. Why are we talking in ifs?"

"You might have put an if on the table," said a company lawyer whose beige suit fit much too snugly.

"How?" Rendell asked incredulously, noting that the plant would not have been saved even if the workers had worked for free.

"What do I say [to the reporters]," asked Rendell. "Do I go out there and lie? I don't know what to say. If I was inclined to lie, I don't know what to say."

"Our willingness to meet with you was to see if there was a glimmer—" said the lawyer.

"There was never a glimmer," answered the mayor.

"I think it would be fair to characterize it as an effort of the city and the company to do something about this," said the company lawyer.

"That would not be fair," answered the mayor. "I think you should not comment because everything you say would be a lie."

So Rendell went outside to meet with the reporters. Refusing to lie, he characterized the meeting as fruitless because a decision to close the plant had been made before the meeting. And the four corporate representatives, like prison escapees, quietly snuck out a side entrance. They went back to their jobs, while the 240 workers at the Breyers plant learned for certain

that they were losing theirs. The mayor gave his impromptu press conference, then trudged the hundred feet back to his office. In the cocoon of privacy, his mood was still somber. He moved to the round table and peered
at his schedule to see what was next, because there was always something
next. But then he looked up, and the dispassion with which he suddenly
spoke seemed far more frightening in its own way than any of his eruptions
of the past four years.

"We have clearly stopped and delayed the death of the city of Philadelphia through relatively heroic measures. Will the disease kill this patient?
Meetings like this make me feel if I was the most competent public official
in the history of the United States and was here for the rest of my life, I
don't think I could save it."

But like all the mayor's moods, this feeling was momentary. In the wake
of the closing of Breyers, with barely four months left before his term as
mayor ended, came the opportunity of something magnificent not just for
the city but for the entire country, something beyond anyone's wildest
imagination.

It all depended on what happened down at the yard.

II

Bernard Meyer was from a small seaport town in northern Germany, and
initially at least he knew little about the machinations that had taken place
in regard to the yard during the past four years. He wasn't familiar with any
of the workers who had earned a living there. But he did know that the
navy was shutting the yard down in the middle of September of 1995, and
he also knew that he had an idea for it that not only made sense but also reflected a faith in and a respect for the industrial heritage of the city that virtually no one in the city shared.

He wanted to build ships there, just as he did in his little seaport town in
northern Germany. Given the moribund condition of the commercial shipbuilding industry in the United States, not to mention the foggy perception
of him here as a stranger from across the Atlantic, there may have been
something fanciful about that desire. A commercial cruise ship hadn't been
built in the United States since 1952, when Eisenhower took office, and
who was this Bernard Meyer anyway? What did he know about the dynamics of the U.S. economy, particularly as they applied to the struggling
industrial city? He came from a town called Papenburg that was so tiny it

wasn't on most maps. And the company he ran, a two-hundred-year-old family concern called Meyer Werft, had no name recognition whatsoever in the United States.

Bernard Meyer himself was forty-seven and had inherited the company from his father, and far from being flamboyant or aggressive, he was the very opposite. He took pride in describing himself to a reporter as a tea drinker, and when problems arose at the yard in Papenburg, they were often settled over tea in his office. But he knew about ships, and his company had established itself as one of the world's leading builders of them, controlling 25 percent of the world's orders for new cruise liners and sophisticated tankers for transporting liquefied natural gas and chemicals. He also knew what it was like to amass an almost fanatically loyal workforce. The average length of employment for the nearly two thousand workers at Meyer Werft was fifteen years, and a staff of instructors was on hand to teach the theory and practices of modern shipbuilding, since Bernard Meyer insisted on lifetime training.

Bernard Meyer knew that there was a potential boom in the cruise market, with Disney about to place an order for two ships and North America itself accounting for 85 percent of the passenger traffic. He knew that he was looking to gain a toehold in the United States, but he also knew the prohibitive cost of building a shipyard from scratch. When he got his first glimpse of those dry docks down at the yard, he was giddy. Looking like a tourist, with a cap on his head and a camera around his neck, he took hundreds of pictures the day he visited. He seemed to not quite believe what he had found, remarking over and over how stunning it was that these irreplaceable dry docks, so perfect for building ships, were going to be abandoned and left to corrode on the shores of America. Ironically, it was he, a foreigner, who saw glorious potential, not loss.

"There is tremendous potential in Philadelphia," Bernard Meyer wrote in a letter to the mayor. "The physical assets being transferred by the U.S. Navy are virtually irreplaceable. The skills of the workforce are world competitive. The enterprise that will be created from the merger of physical assets, skilled workforce, Meyer Werft management and technology will revitalize this once proud Philadelphia industry and provide a model for global partnership that will be envied around the world."

He spoke boldly, with infectious optimism, and in that respect, regardless of language barriers and ocean barriers and the different customs of the two countries, he bore a remarkable resemblance to a man who lived in Philadelphia and also happened to be the city's mayor.

A deal like this, if it was to come together, required the cooperation of everyone at every political level all the way up to the president of the United States. Land mines lay everywhere, and each one had to be handled deftly. Meyer Werft was an industrial business, and like other industrial businesses, such as automobile manufacturers, it expected public assistance. The subsidy involved, reaching into the hundreds of millions of dollars, required enormous faith in the notion that commercial shipbuilding could be resurrected in the city and would not disintegrate into some economic boondoggle. The economic onus on both the state of Pennsylvania and its newly elected governor, Tom Ridge, was enormous. Bernard Meyer, for his part, had to negotiate volatile political waters in his native Germany, including a labor force that was nervous about losing jobs overseas and a government that might well be loath to let coveted shipbuilding technology wind up in the United States. But with as many as eight thousand potential jobs on the line, the kind of high-paying industrial jobs that every politician dreamed of but so few could produce, the deal was also worth every single cent of risk. "There will be extraordinary obstacles to overcome," Meyer had written. "And many complex issues to resolve. Will the rewards be worth the effort?

"I think so. . . ."

Ed Rendell had become mayor just after turning forty-eight and would end his first term four days short of turning fifty-two. He had inherited a city that was reeling in no particular direction, and he had nursed it back to a semblance of health. He had infused hope from seemingly bottomless canisters, and he had understood the power of bread and circuses. He had taken on the unions. He had restored the budget. He had restored the faith of Wall Street in a place that had been a laughingstock. He had opened a convention center with a shower of confetti. He had assumed responsibility for the poor by assuming control of the housing authority. He had engineered a $100-million empowerment zone for the neighborhoods. The downtown never looked better, and certain pockets of the city still gleamed with the purest extract of what made it great and irreplaceable.

By any measure, he had done so much.

By any measure, he had done so little.

Between 1990 and 1994, the city had lost sixty-one thousand people in spite of the almost universal admission that Rendell had been its best mayor in nearly thirty years and perhaps the best ever. The city was still losing jobs by the thousands, nearly one hundred thousand since 1988 and close to forty thousand since Rendell took office. The city was still increasingly becoming a repository for those in need and those in poverty, with nearly 30 percent of its population on the brink, as opposed to 20 percent when Rendell became mayor. The vise was catastrophic, an inverted downsizing. If a major corporation had done this kind of cutting, getting rid of its most productive employees and keeping only those with the greatest need, the result would have been a swift death. But a city does not have the luxury to choose who should stay and who should leave, nor should it.

From a political perspective, the future of the yard had little impact on Rendell. With his term in office nearly complete, he was by any measure invincible. Three months from now, on the first Tuesday in November of 1995, he would run for reelection against a Republican challenger whose name, Joe Rocks, did little justice to the essence of his mediocrity. But the future of the yard went beyond politics. From the very beginning, in 1992, and dozens of times after that, Rendell had said over and over again that the key to the city's health lay in its ability to maintain and create jobs. Saving the shipyard had become the defining moment not of his political future, which seemed brighter than ever, but of something far more important and awesome.

Could the city ever be truly saved, or would it always be vainly struggling on some form of life support? As his four-year term in office counted down to its final breaths and the fate of the yard moved to a point of finality one way or another, death or rebirth, there would be a clear answer.

He had made his mistakes over the past four years, the most egregious of them born of his impulsiveness and his disregard for standards of behavior. He was the embodiment of a public man, utterly defined by his place in the public eye and the way the public reacted to him, and the private acts that usually define a life—family, friendships, religious faith— seemed of little sustaining moment to him. Whatever it was, wherever it was, he hated being outside the center of the circle. But in the elusive definition of what it means to be a public servant, no one else came closer to the ideals that the concept represents. He gave of himself tirelessly, and his motive wasn't pure self-aggrandizement or strokes of the ego, nor was it mere obligation. He was hardly a student of urban history and urban planning. He had no grand theory that could be explained on paper. But he understood exactly what a city was about—sounds and sights and smells, all the different senses, held together by the spontaneity of choreography, each day, each hour, each minute different from the previous one.

And whatever else could be said about Ed Rendell, this much was true: whenever he had fixed in his mind where he needed to go and what he needed to do, he had never let anything get in his way. He did what all heroes do regardless of their flaws and contradictions. He refused to fail.

III

Bill Keller knew better than anyone else how much was at stake.

He was a state representative whose legislative district contained the yard. He was also a former longshoreman with a rough and meaty face that looked a little bit like a pitted road in need of repair and a gruff voice like that of a harried short-order cook. He wasn't smooth or particularly sophisticated. But he relied on judgment, the judgment that came from knowing dozens of shipyard workers who were scared to death of losing their jobs and from seeing dozens of high school kids hanging on street corners day after day without a speck of faith in the future.

He watched Bernard Meyer that fall day in 1994 as the German businessman first set foot in the yard. He saw him run up and down the steps of the dry docks as if he had just made a remarkable archaeological discovery. He watched him take picture after picture. And he realized that this man, regardless of where he was from, was on to something powerful. Keller knew that nothing could be done to prevent the navy from closing down the yard. But he was convinced that an incredible amount could be done to get Bernard Meyer and his company to come to this city and build ships every bit as grand and as awesome as the ones that had been built there for nearly two centuries. As Keller drove down Emily and Moyamensing Streets in South Philadelphia in the shadow of the yard, as he passed by Bunny Cleaners and Pennsport Caterers and Avenue Pizza, he fretted over those high school kids hanging on the corner who never seemed to have anything to do. He also fretted over those shipyard workers who were wondering what it would be like to switch careers in midlife and become truck drivers or medical technicians, if such jobs were even available, and he knew that this was an opportunity that could not be squandered.

Keller believed wholly in Bernard Meyer after that tour. Using his hooks that reached deep into the city's labyrinthine corridors of labor, he contacted union leaders. Meetings were set up, and a memorandum of understanding was quickly hammered out between Meyer Werft and the various unions that represented employees at the yard. Initially some two thousand jobs would be phased in at the yard once it was in the hands of Meyer Werft. There were estimates that an additional six thousand jobs might indirectly be created. In terms of eventual tax benefits to the city and to the state of Pennsylvania, the estimates went as high as $30 million.

In March of 1995, a contingent of local labor leaders met in Washington with Labor Secretary Robert Reich. Keller was there, and so was Phil Rowan, the charismatic business manager of Local 902 of the International Brotherhood of Electrical Workers, who had the word *love* tattooed on one set of knuckles and the word *hate* on the other, just in case his mood changed. They had no audiovisuals or fancy briefing books. In some ways, they were not very well prepared, except that they had spent a lifetime building things and making things and knew exactly what it was like to live in city neighborhoods that depend on such strength for their sustenance. In local and state taxes alone, the impact of the closure of the yard was $113 million, according to one estimate. But it was the potential human loss that was the most devastating.

"The workers are going to go out, and they'll never reenter the workforce," Keller told Reich. "They'll have side jobs as bartenders and plumbers and carpenters, and they'll send their wives to work. Is that the kind of economy you want?"

Extremely impressed, Reich quickly embraced the Meyer Werft proposal because of its unprecedented potential to save and create jobs and seemed willing to free up tens of millions of dollars for worker retraining.

Reich's support was a valuable piece of the puzzle, but only one piece. The city needed to be on board. So did the newly elected governors of two states: Ridge of Pennsylvania and Whitman of New Jersey. So did the local business community. And every piece had to fit perfectly, particularly because of the intricacies of financing such a huge project.

In Papenburg, Meyer Werft had built the largest covered building dock in the world so that ship construction could go on year-round. It wanted to replicate this facility at the yard. The cost of this and other modernization projects was estimated at $388 million. The company, in a proposal it issued in May, sought a public investment of $167 million: $96 million from the state of Pennsylvania; $29 million from New Jersey, where a third of the workers lived; $20 million from the city of Philadelphia; and $22 million from the regional port authority.

Bit by bit this puzzle of a myriad of pieces began to fall into place. After an initially begrudging reaction, Rendell became a believer in the project and began to support it actively. In the push and pull of the city, this was the most incredible opportunity that had come his way during his four years as mayor. There was something historic about it, about the idea of the dying industrial city proving every negativist and every naysayer wrong and bringing back the very thing that everyone in America had become convinced could not be brought back: industry.

IV

If Tom Ridge was remarkable for anything, it was an earnestness that he had put to political use, a self-effacement that the voters of Pennsylvania ultimately found attractive. At one point during his campaign for governor, he called himself the "guy no one's ever heard of from the city no one's ever been to," and he was right on both counts, a six-term Republican congressman from Erie with a mixed voting record that made him impossible to peg politically. What was most impressive about him was his background—the son of humble Slovak-Irish Catholic parents who won a scholarship to Harvard, was drafted into the army after graduation, won a Bronze Star in Vietnam, and had suffered a severe loss of hearing that required him to wear a hearing aid. *Decent* was the word most used by people to describe him, and it was that quality that had catapulted him into the governor's chair at the beginning of 1995.

In Erie, where he had been a congressman for twelve years, a big economic-development project might require a public subsidy of a million dollars, not the hundreds of millions that were being sought here to build a new shipyard. Ridge had little direct experience in putting such deals together. He had basically run on a platform of deregulation and lowering taxes, and to some economists the Meyer Werft deal was a typical example of "smokestack chasing," in which the public subsidy of heavy industry would never be offset by the return. It was also unrealistic to think that Ridge and his staff, within weeks of moving into the state capital, would embrace such a project without questioning every single aspect of it. "[They] didn't know where the bathrooms were, and they were being asked to do the biggest deal in the history of the state" was the way one observer put it. And they seemed overwhelmed by the sheer expense of the proposal and by the ratio of public money to private money that was being sought.

Rendell was not discouraged. He saw Ridge as solid and decent. He was thoroughly convinced that the governor, once he got over the shock of how much money the state needed to invest, would embrace the Meyer Werft proposal as something irresistible and indispensable for the future of the city and the state—the creation of a whole new industry. But Bill Keller, working within the trenches of the state capital in Harrisburg, did not share Rendell's faith.

Right from the beginning, he didn't feel right about the state's attitude. State deadlines for responding to Meyer Werft's proposal were being missed, and all Keller kept hearing was that the amount being sought from the state was "too much money, too much money, too much money." Instead of focusing on ways to get the project done and bridge the significant gaps that did exist, Ridge's staff seemed far more preoccupied with the spin the governor was getting in the media.

"Don't you understand there are three thousand people losing their jobs?" Keller said in desperation to David Fuscus, the governor's deputy chief of staff for economic development.

"Well, we're looking into it," was the response.

At a meeting at the end of August 1995, Keller said Fuscus accused him of "ginning" up shipyard workers by getting them to send negative faxes to the governor.

"Don't say we have to gin anyone up," replied Keller.

But Fuscus apparently refused to leave it alone, as if he were testing Keller, almost goading him.

"I told you not to say that," said Keller, and he took several steps toward Fuscus before others intervened.

Several days later it was relayed to Keller that the governor and his people were livid with him: a local television news crew had suddenly shown up to ask pointed questions about the status of the Meyer Werft proposal, and they were convinced it was Keller who had put the crew up to it. "If it's you, and you continue to do this, you will seriously jeopardize this project" was the substance of the message that was relayed to Keller.

"Yeah, it was me," said Keller, and he too had a message for the governor: "Tell him to kiss my fucking ass."

Bill Keller knew there was potential harm in being so emotional, but he had grown up in the shadow of the yard, and his whole life had been informed by the availability of work on the waterfront. In the summer of 1968, when he was still in high school, he got up early each morning and stood under the foot of the Walt Whitman Bridge to see whether he could help unload the ships carrying cocoa beans and other imported products.

The boss would hire the union men first, then the kids like him, known as clean heads because they had yet to experience the joy of the dirt that fell from the pallets of cargo. The job paid well, and Keller eventually became a full-fledged member of Local 1291 of the International Longshoremen's Association. There were roughly two thousand men in the local when he joined. In the fall of 1995, there were about four hundred, and it wasn't just the sixteen- and seventeen-year-old kids on the corner with nothing to do that got to him but the way they mingled with twenty-two- and twenty-three-year-olds who had nothing to do either. He also knew what it was like to lose a job, to somehow struggle with the horrible doubt that you might not be able to provide for your family anymore.

He thought that if he could somehow convey these feelings and images to the thirty-something members of the governor's staff, most of whom had spent their adult lives in the rarefied air of the nation's capital rubbing shoulders with other thirty-somethings, he could make them understand why the Meyer Werft project was so crucial.

"Did you ever lose a job?" Keller at one point said he asked Fuscus. "Do you know what it's like? There's a feeling in the pit of your stomach."

Fuscus barely responded, and the creeping fear that Keller had felt about the project from the very beginning only intensified. "You can't even say [the governor and his staff] were ignoring these people or casting them away," he said. "They don't see them."

V

After a long summer of frustration, there were finally some indications of hope.

On September 7, Ridge met with labor leaders and said he would personally get involved in the deal and try to make it happen. It was a positive sign, and many of those who were at the meeting walked out feeling buoyant for the first time.

Four days later the waiting was over. The state issued its written response to Meyer Werft's proposal, and no one could have possibly predicted the substance of it.

The money the state was offering, $45 million, was roughly half what the company had originally sought. That was disappointing perhaps, but not necessarily surprising, given that this was ostensibly the first round of negotiations in what everyone acknowledged was a large and complicated economic-development project. What stunned everyone was the structure the state proposed: A basic fifty-fifty split in profits between the private and public partners as well as state representation on the board of directors of the local subsidiary that would run the new shipyard. The state also was asking Meyer Werft to put up an additional $40 million in equity and assume $229 million in debt and lines of credit. Accountants analyzing the state's proposal determined that Meyer Werft's internal rate of return would be 4.8 percent. By any business standard, that was unacceptably low.

Up until this moment, Rendell had been little more than a cheerleader for the project. He had sensed that Ridge, although outwardly cordial, considered him a future political threat. Rendell had absolutely no intention of challenging Ridge for reelection three years from then, but the dynamic put Rendell into the kind of absurd situation that only politics can generate: the more he leaned on Ridge to do the Meyer Werft deal because it would be great for the city, the more the governor might be inclined not to do it on the very basis that what would be great for the city would be great for Ed Rendell and therefore antithetical to his own political interests.

Ridge believed the offer made by the state was extremely generous under the circumstances. He felt Meyer Werft's equity position was totally insufficient given the magnitude of the project. He was also disturbed that the shipbuilder had refused to commit any of its orders for new cruise ships to construction at the yard. But from his vantage point, the state's proposal was not final. Instead, it was the opening offer in what he assumed would be negotiations between the state and the shipbuilder. He believed he had unequivocally communicated that to the head of Meyer Werft's Philadelphia subsidiary, Michael Schwarz. But Schwarz, based on his conversations with state officials, had a completely different interpretation of the state's proposal: there was virtually *no* room for negotiation.

Whatever the interpretation, communications between the state and Meyer Werft had totally broken down. It was also clear that Rendell could no longer sit by and hope that it would all somehow work itself out. Bernard Meyer's already delicate position in Germany had been made even more precarious because of the state's proposal—certification that he was foolishly risking millions of the company's money and its revolutionary technology on something five thousand miles away, across the Atlantic, that wasn't even wanted. On September 14, Meyer spoke with the mayor by phone, and he called the state's offer ridiculous and insulting. He seemed poised at that moment to pull out. But Rendell talked him out of it.

He agreed with Meyer that the offer made by the state was an "insult," and he promised to use his political artistry to rectify it and bring the warring parties back to the table.

The next day, September 15, the Philadelphia Naval Shipyard officially closed after 194 years of service to the country, and an estimated nineteen hundred workers walked out of the yard for the last time, with little fanfare.

The final rites at the yard, far from being nostalgic and tinged by bitter-sweet emotion, were lugubrious and almost robotic. Yard officials tried to portray the workers as heroic to the bitter end, dedicating themselves self-lessly to the overhaul of the final ship, the aircraft carrier *Kennedy,* before it pushed back out to sea. But as far as Jim Mangan could tell, the aura of depression had sunk in to the point where everyone was pretty much going through the motions. The work got done, but it got done joylessly and without any particular sense of pride. An emotional flatness seemed to overarch everything, and Mangan himself did little more than deliver the interoffice mail, drive a forklift with welding equipment over to the ship, and play pinochle over in the 94 Building. If he welded, it was only to make a little overtime. The days got long, and Mangan found himself with plenty of time in which to pity himself, too much time, and he couldn't wait for it to end, the uncertainty of losing a job in many ways worse than the finality of knowing it was over.

As in previous instances where some breathless pronouncement had been made about the yard's future, Mangan fought any remote impulse to get excited about the Meyer Werft proposal. His basic rule of thumb hadn't changed: the more politicians talked about the possibility of something happening, the more he became convinced of the very impossibility of it ever happening. But he also knew that the talk of Meyer Werft had flooded the yard. It raised hope and kept people going a little bit, giving them something to cling to in a time and at a moment that was unimaginably bleak, and Mangan himself hoped that his native pessimism was wrong. He had heard the stories as everyone had heard the stories, men with years of work at the yard, skilled artisans at the peak of their craft, now standing in front of sorting machines over at the post office so they could at least get their twenty-five years in and make their federal pension, doing jobs that, as Mangan ruefully put it, "chimpanzees could do."

"The American dream got yanked from them," he said. "They had eigh-teen to twenty years in a job that no longer exists for them." If he could help it, and he didn't think he could, he wouldn't work at the post office or drive a tractor trailer into the hellhole of New York or get a real estate license or, God forbid, go into sales. He may not have loved welding, but it was something he had labored over and learned, a craft and not a rote reaction. He had performed it well enough to build ships, and out there on the sheen of the ocean was palpable proof of the work he had done. To acknowledge the obsolescence of that skill may have been the most painful cut of all, the thing that hurt the most. And if by some miracle the Meyer Werft deal came together, if the geopolitical forces of the mayor and two governors and the president of the United States and the labor secretary and the European Union somehow reconciled their differences, he knew what he would do, as any man or woman would do who had spent a lifetime perfecting a certain craft: he would jump at the chance to continue.

Shortly before the yard closed, Mangan and his fellow workers lined up at one of the piers and walked into a building of makeshift corrugated metal to get their exit papers. Mangan got a package about his pension and how to continue his life insurance, and then he got something else. It was a little plaque with a circular emblem engraved with the words PHILADELPHIA NAVAL SHIPYARD and the illustration of a ship. Underneath was a smaller engraving that said MAINSTAY OF THE FLEET 1801–1995.

Given the future that was facing him, it was just one more personal effect to throw into a clear plastic bag and carry out of the yard, not a memento at all, but a tombstone.

On the morning of the final day, Mangan got to work at 7:30 A.M. He and his fellow workers milled about, trading phone numbers, half heartedly promising to stay in touch. The *Kennedy* had already sailed out, and three hours later, with nothing left to do, he went home to Haworth Street for good.

In the succeeding days, he tried to find relief in the six-month cushion that severance and unemployment provided. As he perused the want ads and began to pay for his health care because he didn't have a job that took care of it anymore, he began to joke that maybe the best thing to do was get on the interstate near his house and drive in the wrong direction so his family could collect on the $200,000 of life insurance that he still had in force.

"That thought has entered my mind in my more morose moments— 'Jesus Christ, what am I going to do for the six kids?' At least I could give them that before they take that away from me." But then he thought better of it.

"With my luck, I'd probably survive. I would survive the collision and

be a cripple the rest of my life and be more of a burden to my family than
I already am."

VI

By the early afternoon of September 15, the rumors were rife that the
Meyer Werft deal was dead. Relations between the state and the shipbuilder had totally deteriorated, with both sides privately sniping at each
other in letters. But so far at least, there had been no public pronouncement
from anyone, and Rendell desperately wanted to keep it that way. He believed that the deal could still be resurrected, but he also knew that any official statement about the obvious differences that did exist would only
make it that much harder. Meyer Werft kept quiet. So did the city. An almost providential break came when it was discovered that Henry Holcomb, the reporter for the *Inquirer* who had intensively covered the story,
was out of town attending to his ailing mother. Bit by bit, as the afternoon
wore on, there was a feeling shared by Rendell and Cohen that if they
could get through the day without any public comment that the deal was
in tatters, they could then quietly go about the business of patching it up.
Two P.M. became 3:00 P.M became 4:00 P.M. There were sighs of relief,
even amazement that a situation so volatile had been kept quiet.

Then, at 4:53 P.M., a press release from the governor's office in Harrisburg started inching from a fax machine.

It was called a press release, and it certainly looked like one. But what it
amounted to was a vicious attack clearly designed to belittle and humiliate
Meyer Werft, and no one who had ever been involved in sensitive negotiations could recall ever before seeing anything remotely resembling it.
"Have you ever seen a government attack a potential client that was entering negotiations?" said Cohen later. "It was unprecedented. It was the most
disgusting press release I have ever seen." Sam Katz, who was serving as
a financial adviser to Bernard Meyer, described it in a letter to him as the
kind of "attack" release that candidates trade during a particularly nasty
campaign. Given the vitriol and the passion of it, Katz concluded that the
governor's staff had spent far more time crafting the incendiary release
than they ever had in crafting the financial particulars of their proposal.

"Nothing could have prepared me for the arrogance, parochialism and foolishness of the Ridge team's performance," Katz wrote in his letter to Bernard Meyer.

It was all about spin because it always seemed to be about spin, and the spin the governor was taking was that the breakdown in negotiations had all been Meyer Werft's fault. The company was portrayed as cheap, unco-operative, greedy, manipulative, and most incredible of all, somehow responsible for the plight of the workers at the yard. "Meyer walked away from this project because they weren't willing to put forward the substantial and necessary financial commitment to make this project workable," Pennsylvania commerce secretary Thomas Hagen was quoted as saying in the release. "At a time when the economic future of so many shipyard workers hangs in the balance, it is unfortunate that a shipbuilding firm such as Meyer—with such tremendous financial assets—would not be willing to invest enough in this viable project." The release then hammered away, over and over, at ways in which Meyer Werft had been unwilling to put up virtually any private funds.

The words of the press release stung Bernard Meyer deeply. He had never spoken publicly of his frustration with the governor. The idea of respect was supremely important to him, and now he had been humiliated, not just privately but publicly and on a grand scale.

Commercial shipbuilding, an art the city had once mastered and revolutionized, was surely dead in Philadelphia. There was no way that Bernard Meyer could proceed now, and there was a grave sense of loss, a sense that a golden opportunity for the city to reclaim itself as the Workshop of the World was irrevocably lost, a sense that another ominous death rattle had sounded in the slow and halting push toward true revival. It was a message that was understood by virtually everybody, the inevitable pathology of the city.

Except for the mayor of the city and his chief of staff. And the more people said that this deal was dead and couldn't be done, the more they got that glint of anticipation in their eyes.

Quietly over the weekend, David Cohen came up with a plan. And while he later called it an insane one, it was also ingenious, a plan for financing the shipyard free of the one entity that had posed the greatest obstacle, the state of Pennsylvania. If Bernard Meyer and his company were to come back, Cohen knew that this was the only possible way they would do it, with the assurance that Governor Ridge didn't even exist.

Basically Cohen's plan called for floating a bond issue through the agency that promoted port activity in the region, the Delaware River Port Authority. The financing was complicated, but navigating the politics was even more treacherous because the makeup of the authority involved not one state but two. And yet almost overnight a myriad of politicians, some Republican and some Democratic, some from New Jersey and some from Pennsylvania, many of whom in ordinary times had difficulty sitting next to one another without clawing and spitting, came together. Almost overnight they agreed to put up $110 million in the proceeds of a new bond issue that would finance the Meyer Werft deal, a true testament to what government can indeed accomplish when it has the will. With the city increasing its share to $30 million, the shipbuilder could get the public funding necessary to do the deal without a single nickel from the state of Pennsylvania.

But the situation was still fragile and volatile. Bernard Meyer needed a massive signal of reassurance that the shipyard could be operated without interference from the governor. Someone of unprecedented authority had to provide the message. So Rendell and Cohen, reaching as far as they possibly could into their bag of political tricks, made a bid for the only person they knew who could offer that type of reassurance: the president of the United States.

On the morning of September 18, Cohen called Marcia Hale at the White House and asked whether the president might be willing to contact Bernard Meyer personally at some point. It was an unprecedented request. Cohen was aware of the political ramifications of a president of the United States making in effect a sales call to a German industrialist to request his business, and he promised that no one would ever know about it. "We would never say anything publicly unless it worked," he told Hale.

She gave no immediate answer, but by the afternoon a deal that three days earlier had been dead had been stitched back together with remarkable skill. The momentum and the anticipation continued to build, the eyes of Rendell and Cohen getting ever more feverish, each piece in the totally reconstructed puzzle laid out with exquisite precision, everybody behaving and playing the part he or she needed to play.

Then back came the governor.

Bloodied and pummeled in the local media for his and his staff's cartoonish efforts, Governor Ridge held a press conference that afternoon in an apparent effort to send out a message that he still very much wanted Meyer

Werft to come to the city. Ironically, Ridge did see the worth of Meyer Werft. He was extremely cautious, but he also understood what the project represented: not just another new employer coming into the state but a new employer offering an approach to shipbuilding unlike anything in the United States. He also had a personal affinity for what the workers at the yard were going through. His own father, a traveling salesman for Armour who toiled seventy hours a week, had lost his job. He had gotten all of two weeks' notice after twenty-eight years with the company, and it had taken him more than a year to recover from the shock of what happened. It wasn't just the fear of not finding another job that affected him, the governor remembered, but the sense of helplessness, of saying to himself after all those years and all that loyalty, "Hey, wait a minute. What did I do?"

But the governor seemed incapable of expressing how he truly felt. In trying to reverse the damage of the press release and other slights, he only confirmed the increasing criticisms of those who said he had no idea of what he was doing and was the epitome of the small-time congressman from a small-time town whose decency had become an effective mask for his utter lack of tact and instinct. In front of a chorus of reporters and television cameras, he held up a dollar in one hand and two lonely pennies in the other.

The dollar, said Ridge, signified the investment of the state. The two pennies signified the investment of Meyer Werft.

It was a stunning visual image that made its away across the Atlantic— a jingoistic American politician going out of his way to belittle and embarrass a respected businessman who months earlier had been personally hailed by German chancellor Helmut Kohl. Coming on the heels of the press release, it did nothing but reinforce every fear that Bernard Meyer already felt.

Rendell and Cohen tried to ignore the incalculable damage that the governor had wreaked, now for a second time in four days. They made sure that Schwarz, the Meyer Werft negotiator, was invited to a fund-raiser that was being held that night for the president in Philadelphia. Rendell talked Clinton into spending a few moments with Schwarz, and arrangements were made for the two of them to have their picture taken together.

"We're shameless," Cohen later admitted. "We'll play every card."

But the next day, when Schwarz appeared unannounced in Cohen's office at 3:10 P.M. and made clear that the mayor might want to be there to listen to what he had to say, there were no smiles.

Rendell walked around the corner in his familiar waddle, his feet trudging purposely over the weathered linoleum. He had that bemused look on his face, as if there always had been something fanciful about being mayor anyway, a bizarre and wonderful way to spend a few years. But as he neared Cohen's office, he knew what was on the line.

"The real long-term battle of the cities is this stuff. If this stuff doesn't work, we're dead."

"It was a privilege for me to be there last night," Schwarz began, referring to the opportunity to meet the president. "It was fascinating. And I wasn't suffering. I'm suffering now. I spent the night on the phone with Bernard Meyer and part of the morning. I'm informing you—nobody knows—it's fresh out of my fax. Bernard Meyer has decided to withdraw. Whether you served us well at this particular moment, it will not be enough in the next crisis. He feels he has been used by Ridge for a political game. I regret, gentlemen. What can I say? What can I do?"

With that, he delivered two copies of Bernard Meyer's letter, one for the mayor and one for Cohen. Addressed to Rendell, the letter was heartfelt and emotional, an expression of the reluctance with which Bernard Meyer was giving up his dream. As a courtesy, the letter had been written to the mayor in English, and the imperfect language made it all the more poignant.

> I was very shocked when Michael Schwarz told me first about the press release and then about the press conference of Governor Ridge, when he, instead of presenting the actual facts of our proposal, he put out a dollar note and 2 pennies to show what the Government is doing and what Meyer Werft is doing. This was the last sign for me to stop in order not to lose face and the name of a shipyard and a family who [has been] in business [for] 200 years. To start up with a brand-new shipbuilding facility in Philadelphia, to create innovative high-tech shipbuilding, to turn around the negative trend of shipbuilding in the U.S. . . . must not only be supported by some subsidies but much more by the will and the emotional support of all parties and political resources.
>
> I realized this weekend that despite the fact that I was supported in a fantastic and brilliant way by so many friends including the President, Mr. Clinton, I will never get this support from all parties which are essential to realize such a difficult but futuristic project.

Therefore please understand my final decision to terminate our activities in your Philadelphia, a town I fell in love with; but emotions are one thing. Facts have to guide us now.

Rendell paused after reading the letter. He had five seconds to figure out what to do next. He rubbed his face with his hands and took a breath, as if steadying himself before the final assault on the mountain. And then he spoke as if the message so unequivocally communicated to him without a hint of hope, that the dream was over, had never been delivered. The tone in his voice didn't betray ruefulness or regret, but something strange and spellbinding. Optimism.

He and Cohen shared with Schwarz the outlines of the new financing package, in which there would be no involvement by the state whatsoever. They promised they were not interested in a seat on the board of directors. They vowed a rate of return on the investment that would be profitable. "We will blow away any impediments that you have," said the mayor with that rat-a-tat-tat of surety and familial warmth. "The state will not have anything to do with it. The structure will be yours."

"We will ask Meyer Werft on behalf of the city of Philadelphia and the United States of America to come back," added Cohen.

"You may get this deal as early as tomorrow," said the mayor.

"All this is in play already," said Cohen.

They were not bluffing.

"I will relay this message," said Schwarz. "What kind of effort you are making."

As for Bernard Meyer's official letter of withdrawal, Rendell handed his copy to Cohen. "We're gonna deep-freeze this letter," he said.

The next day, September 20, Bernard Meyer met with his board of directors and issued a statement to the German press announcing his withdrawal from the project. "I think it's vague enough so that it's not too much of a disaster," said Cohen to a colleague over the phone. But it only made the possibility of the deal even more remote. "We have a patient where the heart has stopped beating," he acknowledged. "The brain waves are still going, but people are beginning to disconnect the life-support systems."

Cohen paced the office. As if it were an act of Providence, this was the first time in nearly four years that a phone wasn't ringing or the infernal beeper wasn't screeching during the heat of the day. He was proud of what he had done—taken an audacious idea for financing and navigated it through a hive of politics and gotten it to the point of being inches from completion. Somehow, in some way, Bernard Meyer had to be brought back to the table for the sake of the city and for Cohen's own vain sense of himself as the miracle maker. All he needed was an opening, a sliver of space, a way to show Bernard Meyer just how good he was, the ultimate urban gunfighter in a blue suit who always fixed what others messed up. And then, as usual, the wheels began to click and whir . . .

Five hours later, at 5:00 P.M., the siren of an unmarked black sedan cleared away the crawl of rush-hour traffic so David Cohen could get to his house in Chestnut Hill. The car, driven with usual aplomb by Sergeant Buchanico, squeezed in between lanes of the expressway, narrowly avoiding one chrome fender after another. But Cohen, on the portable phone in the front passenger seat, was oblivious to what was happening outside anyway. He got home in record time. His two boys were there, and he explained to them what was happening, and although they were certainly young enough to need baby-sitters, they were certainly old enough to know their father had really gone over the rational edge this time.

"I don't want you to go to Germany," said Benjamin. "You don't even know how to speak German."

"Who do you know in Germany?" asked Josh.

"Maybe no one," their father admitted, particularly when he was going to Germany unannounced, without even an invitation, to see a man who might decide not to see him at all.

He went upstairs to his bedroom and packed quickly and carefully, layering shirts, socks, several ties, and a copy of *Midnight in the Garden of Good and Evil* into a black bag with the lettering TEAM PHILADELPHIA. He went back outside, where Sergeant Buchanico was waiting. He was driven helter-skelter back to his office, where, like a spy, he received his final batch of secret documents—a letter from Ridge to Bernard Meyer pledging his support, a printout outlining the financing. He was driven to the airport just in time to make a 7:20 P.M. flight on British Airways. He settled into seat A10 and hurtled through the night to a place he had never been to before, to convince a man from another land with another culture who didn't even know he was coming to do a deal that seemed dead.

Cohen arrived at Heathrow in London the following day, September 21, at 7:25 A.M., and had enough of a layover that he could go to a Thomas Cook lounge and shave, shower, and put on a clean shirt and tie. At 10:55 A.M., he flew Lufthansa flight 4035 to Bremen, about an hour's drive from Papenburg. When he got to the airport at Bremen a little after 1:00 P.M., he was paged. It was the mayor calling. The good news was that Bernard Meyer had been contacted and now knew he was coming (the plan had always been not to contact Meyer until Cohen was in the air, on the assumption that he would not refuse a meeting if he knew Cohen had already traveled several thousand miles in the middle of the night). The bad news was that Bernard Meyer was out of town.

Cohen walked over to the Hertz office at the Bremen airport, where the clerk did not speak any English, and he, true to the words of his son Benjamin, did not know a stitch of German. He was given a makeshift map and set off on his way to the Maritim Hotel in Bremen, known for its wonderful view of the city's Burgerpark. It was now rush hour, and Cohen discovered that the map was basically useless. None of the streets was straight. Some of them changed names without notice. Others had no names at all, and those that did were of course in German. The drive took an hour and a half instead of a half hour. And once he got to his hotel room, he was faced with a situation that he hadn't faced in at least twenty years. He had nothing to do. And he had to do it in Bremen.

Back in the mayor's office in Philadelphia, Ed Rendell worked feverishly to keep the deal intact. In the city, there was a remarkable surge of momentum, particularly once word leaked out that Cohen was in Germany. His reputation as someone who always got what he pursued only reinforced the belief that Meyer Werft would return to negotiations and added to the fervor. But in Germany, the signals continued to be clouded. In Philadelphia, the mayor sat at his desk, his face tilted downward and his eyes downcast.

"Maybe none of this stuff can work," he said quietly.

"The problem is Bernard has gone just too far," said Cohen when he spoke with the mayor by phone later that afternoon. "He's informed his labor employees [of the withdrawal]. He's informed his banks. He's informed the German equivalent of the SEC. He's informed the press."

Rendell told Cohen of his idea to lead a huge delegation of congressmen and other elected officials to Papenburg and explain to various German interests involved that what happened to Bernard Meyer wasn't a show of disrespect but the nature of American politics, in which rudeness and gratuitous potshots were common features of the sport. The great pomp of such a delegation flooding the pristine atmosphere of Papenburg, Rendell hoped, would give Meyer the cover he needed to come back into the deal. "Tell [Meyer] I can suck up as good as anyone on earth," said Rendell over the phone. "That may be the best thing we've learned in my years on the job."

Several hours later, he spoke to Cohen again, this time to convey the news that Meyer had agreed to a meeting the next day in Papenburg. "At least he's not irritated by your visit. Keep your fingers crossed."

An hour afterward, the Delaware River Port Authority officially approved the bond package that would supply $110 million of public financing to Meyer Werft. Six days after the governor's disastrous press release and three days after his even more disastrous press conference, everything was in place—the public money, the structure, the rate of return, the support of every politician imaginable. Even President Clinton was playing an active role, agreeing to call Bernard Meyer if the deal seemed on the cusp of closure and needed one final push.

Now all eyes focused on Cohen, still stuck in a hotel room in Bremen with its view of the Burgerpark.

"It's not so easy to make phone calls from here," he ruminated to the mayor at one point, although he was certainly trying.

"David in a hotel room in Bremen?" Rendell mused after he hung up. "He must be going through call withdrawal."

VII

At noon the next day, Rendell, looking for any hope across the Atlantic, took it as a positive signal that he had not yet heard from Cohen. The meeting between the chief of staff and Bernard Meyer had begun at 8:00 A.M. Philadelphia time, and if Meyer had dispatched Cohen quickly, sent him off in a rowboat on the North Sea, the mayor assumed he would have heard something. Ever maneuvering, he seized upon yet another line of attack: using his leverage with the White House and Commerce Secretary Ron Brown to try to get Disney to move its order for two cruise ships from an Italian shipbuilder to the new Meyer Werft shipyard in Philadelphia.

At 2:15 P.M. the phone rang in the mayor's office.

It was Cohen calling from Papenburg, where it was 8:15 P.M.

"I don't know where we are. We started at a definite no. I don't know if we're still there or not."

Cohen said that Bernard Meyer had been "blown away" by the particulars of the new financing package and liked the idea of a huge delegation coming to Papenburg to provide him with cover to come back to the table. "You could tell that this had appeal to him, but he's sort of stuck on—he's told everyone [he's not coming], and wishy-washiness is really criticized over here."

Rendell told Cohen of his idea to get Secretary Brown to intervene with Disney. He said he also thought he could get the State Department to ease the German government's fears of losing shipbuilding technology to the United States.

"I don't know if business concerns [matter] to him at this point," said Cohen. "I think you should say you still haven't heard from me. Since we have no idea where this is heading, I think you shouldn't say anything."

Of all the requests made to the mayor, that was always the hardest. But he seemed eager to do his best to comply.

"Whatever you say. I will say you guys are now dining."

Three and a half hours later, when Rendell had not heard from Cohen again, he felt almost giddy. It must mean they were having dinner, a long and glorious dinner at which all the issues were somehow being resolved. It must mean that Cohen had worn Bernard Meyer down and convinced him that this was too good a deal to pass up. "This has to be a good sign," he said as he paced about the office. "You have to believe that they're doing some good. I mean it's a four-hour dinner." Too excited to work, he opened the most recent batch of gifts he had received. Turning some of the items on their sides to make sure he understood them from every possible perspective, he came to a swift conclusion.

"I get the most useless junk," he said.

A little bit after 6:00 P.M. the phone rang in the mayor's office.

It was Cohen.

David Cohen had never worked harder in his entire life to make something happen, and the qualities that had made him such a sensation in his own country had transported themselves across the Atlantic. Cohen's greatest gift may have been knowing just how to serve powerful men in a way that made them think his ideas had really been theirs all along—an appealing combination of obsequiousness and quiet strength, ego sublimation and steady faith in his convictions.

He could tell that Bernard Meyer's original plan was to be polite but dismissive, get him in and out as quickly as possible and give the dream of a new shipyard that would be the envy of the industrial world a final burial. But a rapport was established, and there was a plain simplicity to Cohen that made him hard to say no to—still in the same suit he had worn on the plane, with that boyish face untouched by the slightest whiff of a hard edge, appearing uninvited on the doorstep of Meyer Werft like a wayward puppy, remarkably buoyant despite jet lag and lack of sleep.

Bit by bit as the afternoon progressed, Cohen had sensed that he was making headway, whittling away with dogged patience. As he went over the idyllic terms of the financing and put forth letters of support from Governor Ridge and President Clinton, he could feel the war that Bernard Meyer was waging within himself, torn between his heart and his own professional code of not going back on his word. Cohen himself had been almost overcome by the magnificence of the massive Papenburg shipyard, easily capable of working on two cruise ships at once yet so precise in its modern technology as to be somehow delicate. It made the idea that such an opportunity might fall through the fingers of the city not just frustrating or regretful but almost cruel.

He met with Meyer for several hours that afternoon. The two men, along with several others, had a dinner that lasted nearly three hours. And then they met again for another forty-five minutes. Cohen returned to his hotel room around 1:00 A.M. German time, the emotional residue of a day unlike any other in his life still very much with him. And then he called the mayor.

"I don't think it's good," he said.

One could almost hear the mayor deflating.

"He is obviously anguished," Cohen continued. "This is a dream he's had, and with our proposal this is a dream that he could have had." But Meyer had also told him that he had "built a prison" for himself over the past week by announcing he was pulling out, and he did not know how to get out of it without losing all face and credibility, particularly after being so terribly humiliated by Governor Ridge. When the shipbuilder had announced his decision to his workforce, he received a five-minute standing ovation. So overcome with gratitude, the workers in turn promised a 20 percent increase in productivity. Various European labor leaders had also spoken positively of the decision and said it was good not only for Germany but for the entire European Union.

"He's a wonderful man," said Cohen, speaking of Bernard Meyer with an emotion that he rarely expressed about anyone. "It was very frustrating. If it makes you feel any better, it was very frustrating for him."

"It doesn't make me feel any better," said the mayor.

Rendell trudged around the corner to the Reception Room to hold a press briefing. Withdrawn and somber, he reported that Meyer Werft would not be coming to the city. He was well aware of the degree to which Governor Ridge's actions had destroyed that dream, but he refused to place any blame publicly. "What happened, happened," he said with a shrug. "We'll see where we go from here."

The reporters, satisfied with his answers, drifted away to file their stories and make their obligatory deadlines, and Rendell returned to his office. It was dark outside, and a church bell pealed seven times like the distant sound of a buoy. He sat at the round table he had sat at a thousand times and there in the silence, with the light of a lamp in the corner of the room spreading its light, took out several clean pieces of paper. The silence gave way to the scratch of Rendell's pen and then to the quiet mouthing of words as he composed what he wanted to write. He looked like a boy back in grade school, and there by himself in the softness of that light, he wrote out a letter to Bernard Meyer, one final chance, one final hope. He did not have anyone to read it to make sure the spin was right. He did not use a fancy word-processing program or a spelling checker. He relied on the one place that had always served him well when he allowed it to, the spontaneous dictates of his own heart.

> It is heartbreaking to think that this incredible idea will be sunk because of timing and some indefensible comments made over here. It is too important to you, your dream, and to us for it not to happen.

The ostensible culmination of Ed Rendell's four years in office would come shortly, in the general election, when voters would approve or reject him. But despite the typical worries and fears of overconfidence, he knew he was too far ahead in the polls and enjoyed too much popularity in the city to lose. The real fight for the future *had* come here, and the fading away of the dream of a new shipyard, the fading away of the sounds that once defined the very marrow of the city, only reinforced for him a truth that he fought as much as possible to reject.

He had stopped the bleeding of the patient he had inherited on that faraway January day four years earlier. But he could not stop the creep of cancer. Because no one could.

Sitting at that table in the light, surrounded by a misshapen pile of papers and the plastic wrap from a sandwich, he continued to write his letter. At times such as this, he understood the wrenching futility of it all. But he would never stop trying. Because he was the mayor, and this was his city.

"Good luck to you," he wrote to Bernard Meyer on the last line. "I hope our paths will cross again."

As Jim Mangan sat at home on Haworth Street, struggling to figure out what to do with his life, one thing was now certain: he would never go back to work in the yard.

After 194 years of service and honor, it was another artifact in the city.

The *Pennsylvania* and the *Relief.* The *Antietam* and the *Omaha.* The *Philadelphia* and the *Wichita.* The *New Jersey* and the *Wisconsin.* The *Los Angeles* and the *Chicago.*

These and all the other ships that had been spawned by strong and steady hands from year to year and decade to decade and century to century in the first American city had become a roll call of the dead.

Epilogue

David Cohen's office was as empty and eerie as it had been five years earlier on that Sunday morning in January 1992 when he had started out in
gray jeans and a plaid work shirt with so little to rely on besides faith in
himself and the man who was about to become mayor.

The picture of Judge Lord was gone. So were the life-size pictures of his
children. So was the little box with the calculator inside and the inscription
on the front that read BILLING KING. Other mementos that he had amassed
during the reign had been removed as well: the letter of thanks from Clinton, the framed reprints of the glowing articles in the *Inquirer* and *Daily
News* and *Philadelphia Magazine* that snaked up the length of a wall like
mounted trophies.

An opportunity had come, and he figured that if he didn't seize it now, he would not get another chance for ten or fifteen years. So it was some-time in the fall of 1996 that he had gone to Rendell to discuss something that didn't seem possible given how inseparable they had become. But it was time to leave.

The chairman at Cohen's former law firm, Ballard Spahr, was planning to retire at the end of 1997 and Cohen was being seriously wooed as a suc-cessor to the position. Rendell, like everyone else, believed that Cohen would never leave his post as chief of staff. "It's going to be harder for David to walk away from this than me," he had said at one point. Of course Cohen ruminated about his job from time to time, and of course he ex-pressed requisite remorse over his children growing up without him, but he still worked with singular fixation. If Cohen did leave, Rendell figured it would be to go off and run a major corporation somewhere, make the mil-lions upon millions that he could no doubt make. But Cohen himself had always said that he would one day return to the practice of law. When he talked about his children now, pointing out that Benjamin would be fifteen and Josh eleven if he stayed until the end of Rendell's second term in the year 2000, there was a genuine sense that he could not afford to miss any more of their lives. Becoming chairman of the city's best law firm was a major undertaking, but it was nothing compared to what greeted him each morning as chief of staff.

Rendell did not try to dissuade him from leaving, because he knew he had no standing. Between the mayoral campaign days of 1990 and 1991 and his service to the city once the administration had started, Cohen had dedicated more than seven years of his life to Rendell on a twenty-four-hour-a-day basis. If he decided that it was his destiny to return to the prac-tice of law, he would have the mayor's blessing, regardless of how hard it would be and the void that would be created. In describing their relation-ship, Rendell said there were times that Cohen felt like his younger brother. There were also times Cohen had emerged as a father figure be-cause of the way he sometimes scolded the mayor for so rarely consider-ing the concept of discretion, much less employing it even when he did consider it. But regardless of the situation, Rendell thought of Cohen in a way that he so rarely felt with anyone else, a connection that went beyond companionship as just another pile of junk food to be eaten and forgotten. "At all times," said the mayor, "he is my friend."

Cohen's last day in the service of the city was April 4, 1997, and by the standards with which he had started one thousand nine hundred and fifteen days earlier, the time went by quietly. There had been a huge good-bye party the previous night at the Palestra gymnasium on the Penn campus, so the number of well-wishers on this last day was little more than a handful. He stood at his desk cleaning out the last remaining items: bar association cards, the round little buttons that the Secret Service had issued for the various visits of the president and vice president so those who hovered around would be recognized as sanctioned sycophants and wouldn't be ousted, an old manual for a portable phone that he didn't own anymore. As he rummaged with his usual meticulousness, he talked aloud about some of the high points that he had been through: the night of the Number when the computer had spit out a budget deficit of $1.246 billion and F. John White had said "holy shit" because there wasn't anything else to say; the night Rendell had announced his five-year plan for the economic resurrection of the city out of near-bankruptcy; positive fund balances in the city budget for five consecutive years.

His greatest regret, he said, was the contentiousness of the labor negotiations, an indication of the degree to which Cohen loathed confrontation despite the fact that it had been the administration's finest hour. As for the failed dream of a new shipyard that would have been built by the German company Meyer Werft, he largely waved any memory of it away with his hands, as if the only way to deal with it was just to minimize it. Regardless of his gesture, the tragedy of that failure had been incalculable. And yet the city had gone on with gritty and admirable resilience, and so had those who lived within it.

The boundaries of the suburbs didn't seem to entice Mike McGovern very much any more and he had undertaken his new profession as defense attorney with the same zeal that had marked his life in the district attorney's office. After the partnership with the two former prosecutors had dissolved, McGovern had gone to work for the firm of Monteverde, McAlee, Fitzpatrick, Tanker & Hurd. In December 1996, he represented Edward A. Greene, one of four former Philadelphia police officers charged with shaking down patrons at an illegal cockfight and robbing them of nearly $30,000. The case was highly publicized, and when it was over, all four had been acquitted. The feeling afterward was so very different from what McGovern had been used to as an assistant district attorney, but it was every bit as sweet, and in that moment, he knew he had made the moral leap from prosecutor to criminal lawyer.

His wife, Mary Pat, would be getting her teaching degree from Temple University in January 1998, and given her own personal experience with the Philadelphia school system as a parent, it seemed to be the last place on earth where she would want to work once she got her certification. But on the basis of some classroom work she had done at a local school and the students and teachers she had met there, she was now considering it.

The McGoverns' oldest daughter, Bridget, had also been imbued with the fever of the city, even if it happened to be a different city. A brilliant student, she had decided to attend New York University in the fall. She wanted to be a writer, and she could think of no better place to pursue the craft than in the realities of Washington Square and Greenwich Village. Her father could think of no worse place for an eighteen-year-old to be than in the realities of Washington Square and Greenwich Village. But he was terribly proud of her, and she had received $25,000 in scholarships.

Jim Mangan's road after the closing of the navy yard had not been seamless. Around Thanksgiving of 1995, he went to work as a welder for a company called DeVal. He was there only about two months before he was laid off again. He handled it with typical stoicism, the price of working-class life in the city, but the layoff also convinced him that the craft of welding, despite the fifteen years he had put into it, had no future use. Utilizing retraining money made available to workers who had been at the yard, he went to school and got his commercial driver's license. He was hired in July 1996 by a moving company called Ware's. The work wasn't easy, subject to the vagaries of when people wanted to move—holidays, the high heat of the summer. The base pay of twelve dollars an hour was substantially less than the sixteen dollars and fifty cents that he had made at the yard. But with opportunities for overtime during the summer, and a willingness to work sixteen and seventeen hour days, he was able to make what he described as a "livable wage." Money at times was "tight as hell," but he was supporting his family. He was providing as he always had.

Fifi Mazzccua continued as always, undaunted, unflappable, somehow able to cope. In March 1996, one of the great-grands, Kalih, was hit by a car when he rushed across Germantown Avenue without looking. He went into a coma and was in St. Christopher's Hospital for Children for a week. He came out with double vision, and then his behavior at home deteriorated to the point where Fifi, with great sorrow and reluctance, had no choice but to have him placed in a residential school. Fifi called him every day and visited him every week, but they missed each other madly. "I love it, grandma," Kalih, now seven, told her of the school, "but I want to come home." He returned on Easter Sunday in 1997, and when he arrived at the house on Huntingdon Street, he walked up the stairway to the second floor and kissed his door and his dresser as if he had just found Mecca. His hair hadn't been trimmed for two months so the family got him a haircut. He played with his friends with joyous abandon and ripped his shirt. When the eight hours were up and it was time for him to return to school, Fifi burst into tears and could not bear to make the trip back with him.

Her church, Cookman United, was beset by a series of arson fires in 1996, and there were financial problems that threatened closure. But the congregation fought back and the church righted itself. In her own neighborhood the drug trade had slackened, and hard as it was with Kalih, she knew she was doing the right thing. "Today is Monday," said Fifi as she puttered about the apartment where she worked, laughing and making mirth as if it were already Christmas. "The sun is shining. God is in her heaven. The kids are all right. I feel good enough to come home and drink a cold beer."

As Fifi pushed forward, so did the mayor. He did not stumble over the ashes of Meyer Werft in those waning days of the first term, but reached out yet again, in total secret, in the beginning of 1996. Cohen was sent to Miami for a meeting with Bernard Meyer that was never revealed to the media for fear, as one internal document put it, "that if any of this became public everyone could look crazy." The mayor didn't want the city to be rebuffed again publicly, so instead it happened in private.

But neither he, nor Governor Ridge, gave up pursuit. Another international shipbuilder, Kvaerner ASA, expressed serious interest in the navy yard. By April of 1997, a deal was being methodically negotiated that would create one thousand jobs at the yard and guarantee the construction of three container ships. The governor clearly recognized the importance of such jobs to the city. But in also trying to overcome memories of his ineptitude with Meyer Werft, he now seemed willing to give everything away. Even though the Kvaerner proposal offered a thousand jobs less than the Meyer Werft proposal, the state was contemplating offering the Norwegian shipbuilder a grant of around $180 million—or four times more than what had been originally offered to Meyer Werft. In effect, Ridge's bungling of Meyer Werft not only cost him politically; it also potentially could cost taxpayers millions upon millions of dollars. Kvaerner was a quality shipbuilder, and its presence at the yard would be an inspiration for the city. But Meyer Werft would have provided a similar uplift at far less a taxpayer price.

As Rendell crossed his fingers for the revival of shipbuilding, he also seized on the concept of the city as tourist destination and audience pool and suburban diversion with greater tenacity than ever.

A new luxury hotel was slated to be built across the street from City Hall. Several blocks down on Market Street, the old PSFS building, heralded as the country's first modern-style skyscraper when it was built in 1932, was becoming a 600-room Loews Hotel. Several other hotel deals were in the works, which would give the city an additional 2,300 hotel rooms if they came to closure. A Hard Rock Cafe was coming, and so perhaps was a Planet Hollywood. In addition, a formal agreement for a $130-million entertainment center on the waterfront was about to be entered into as well. The developer, the Simon DeBartolo Group, Inc., the nation's largest publicly held real estate developer, had as its pièce de résistance the $600-million Mall of America in suburban Minneapolis-St. Paul, and it clearly had seized on the American city as the next frontier for a similarly self-contained and climate-controlled experience. The project in Philadelphia called for an array of features: a 24-to-30-screen "megaplex" movie theater, a virtual reality game world, an entertainment extravaganza called the American Experience (in apparent answer to the boring stasis of Independence Hall, which didn't offer anything interactive or cyberspaced besides the authenticity of its history). In the economic development business, such projects were becoming the newest rage for cities and had an actual label. They were called Urban Entertainment Centers, and the implication was obvious that cities themselves, solely on the basis of providing the intoxicating and spontaneous clash of different sights and sounds and textures, were clearly not entertaining enough anymore, at least for those with disposable dollars to spend. Instead, if a city wanted to be an Urban Entertainment Center, it would have to find a developer to build one.

All these deals were announced with fanfare. They did generate jobs and they did further the revival of the downtown as a tourist destination. There was little question that at least some of them would not have happened without the inexhaustible ability of the mayor to market the city. But many of the jobs they threw off were of both low skill and low self-esteem, nowhere near what might have been generated by the birth of a new shipyard using state-of-the-art technology. These were the jobs that so desperately needed to be created, for Jim Mangan and the other men and women of the navy yard, for the city of Philadelphia, for an entire nation.

Between 1973 and the mid-1990s, three-fifths of the American workforce had actually lost ground in terms of real family income. At the same time, income increased by a third for the wealthiest 5 percent of the nation and doubled for the top 1 percent. Twenty years ago, the chief executive officer of a corporation earned roughly forty times the salary of an average worker. By 1995 that ratio had multiplied to one hundred and ninety.

The trend of tourism raised the specter of a city workplace increasingly made up of waiters, ushers, tour guides, busboys, bellboys, sales clerks, and interactive cyberhelpers, an image that seemed bitterly ironic given the city's historic place as the best embodiment of American work. But to Rendell, mourning the loss of the industrial city was little more than distracting and nostalgic self-pity. Like his brethren across the country, he was working to rebuild and reinvent a wholly new place, and with slight variation they all shared the same vision: City as place to frolic for a few days on a convention, City as Six Flags for suburbanites looking for a weekend break from the monotony but able to cling to enough sanitized icons and links to the walking paths of the shopping mall to feel familiar, City as Disney extravaganza with floats lit up by a thousand points of light, City increasingly fashioned and designed not for those who lived within it but for those who never would.

Regardless of the ultimate merits of the strategy, Rendell and Cohen had a right to feel a sense of satisfaction. In 1996, for the first time in seven years, the city actually posted a gain of jobs. It came to precisely one hundred, .001 percent of the 104,000 that had been lost in the previous decade, but it did suggest a change in the trend. Further proof of that came in the first three months of 1997 when the number of jobs in the city increased by 3,300.

"I feel amazingly fulfilled," said Cohen, poring over the contents of his desk. "We have succeeded beyond any reasonable expectation." But he also knew that the city, like all American cities, was still on a tightrope. The infinitesimal growth of jobs had occurred in the midst of a national economy that some described as the strongest since World War II, and Cohen knew what would happen if that resurgence suddenly veered in a different direction. "One little downturn in the economy and we're back to two percent job loss a year," he said. "We have fought so hard and the best we can say is that we're right on the edge. The city is poised for greatness and it is also poised to spiral down—taxes, jobs, and people."

In fact, despite the optimism that Cohen expressed, the city was still continuing to spiral down in many ways, the cancer still creeping. On the basis of new census data, the city's population loss between 1990 and 1996 had totaled roughly 105,000, or 6.8 percent, and various projections pointed toward continued decline through the end of the decade. There were some who argued that population loss was actually good for the city, enabling it to retool and scale down and provide new housing more in keeping with the suburban trends that had come to define the desires and habits of so many millions. But those leaving the city were the very ones the city desperately needed to keep. As a story in the *Inquirer* pointed out, aggregate tax returns for the years 1992, 1993, and 1994 showed that $1.6 billion in income had moved out of Philadelphia to the surrounding suburbs while the amount the city took in from the suburbs totaled $680 million.

New census data made available in 1997 only further underscored the alarming increase in the city's poverty rate. The new figures showed that it had risen to a minimum of 23 percent and perhaps went as high as 31 percent, meaning that nearly a third of the entire city, *a third,* might be below the poverty line. For children the figures were far more distressing, anywhere between 29 percent and 52 percent. And none of this was unique to Philadelphia, but right in line with increases that had occurred in Brooklyn and the Bronx and Detroit and Chicago and Los Angeles.

There was no mystery as to why people were leaving the city. Regardless of what Rendell had accomplished, the city's pull was still almost purely an emotional one. Those who stayed did so on the basis of loyalty, or because of a job, or because the qualities that had turned so many away from cities were the very qualities that enticed them—difference, diversity, diversion. By any economic basis, the basis on which most people made decisions, the city was still noncompetitive with its surrounding suburbs to the point of impotence. Taxes were still far too high. The perception of crime, far more corrosive than actual crime figures themselves, had not been ameliorated. The school system continued to flop and flounder and had the trust of no one, in large part because of endemic problems, but also because the mayor, cowed by the politics, had never brought to the schools anywhere near the intensity that he had given to the union negotiations, or the budget, or economic development. Those who went to a public school in the city had little faith. Those who did not were forced to pay the burden of the city's greatest hidden tax—private and parochial schools—until they could no longer afford it, or got tired of affording it, and moved across the boundary.

Every bit as corrosive for the city were the man-made acts of venality and selfishness. The racial politics that had been displayed during the first term made easy decisions difficult and fractious. The extortionate threats of every self-interest group imaginable, vowing to heap embarrassment and woe on the mayor if he didn't do exactly what they wanted, had a similar impact, to the point where the public interest often seemed irrelevant. The pettiness of politics, the insecurity and spite that can develop from jealousy and over-the-shoulder looks to the next election, had never been more evident than in the lost opportunity for a new shipyard. For corporate America, the city had become a potential source of opportunity, not because they believed in the city, but because they knew exactly the chain of desperation that would be set off in the mayor's office the very second a threat was made to leave. Then there were the chilling effects of state and federal policy.

The state and federal governments were easy villains almost to the point of cliché, and Rendell himself, at the very beginning of his first term, realized that the city had absolutely no standing to ask for help unless it cleaned up its own fiscal mess. The city had done that, and coupled with the boom in the national economy, some sort of sustained job growth did seem possible. The mayor had spent enough time in the state capital and the nation's capital to know that any kind of massive help was as fine a dream as his growing hair, so he had adopted a minimalist philosophy: if you're not going to help us, then please just leave us alone.

But in the summer of 1996 came the funnel cloud of welfare reform, fueled by that terrifying force known as a presidential election year, and there were estimates that the city would have to create 28,000 jobs to handle the cutoff in benefits that was being proposed. Such job creation might be possible in places where there was a combination of a prosperous economy and innovative welfare policy on the state level, but as a report from an organization called Public/Private Ventures noted, "Philadelphia benefits from neither."

The city had an overall unemployment rate of 7 percent, but the unemployment rate for low-skilled workers was 16 percent and for laborers 21 percent, and the effects of welfare reform might increase the citywide rate to 11 percent. Such a projection might well be subject to the calculus of self-serving doomsday catastrophe, but there was no debate that welfare reform would have a devastating impact on the city. Given the inchlike progress that had been made after the mayor himself had spent hundreds of hours on economic development, the idea of the city now being told to go out and find tens of thousands of jobs was sadistic. There was also the damaging psychological impact, the image of a city with a faint and tenuous toehold on the hill not falling back on its own but of being kicked to the bottom.

Rendell's optimism had been more than just a trait of personality. It had changed the entire feel of the city, to the point where the perpetual focus wasn't on the litany of problems, but on what just maybe, *maybe,* could be done. It was always a precarious perch, but Rendell had managed to sustain the momentum, as if by constantly talking about all that might be coming and planning for it as if it were already here, it somehow *was* already here. In a way he wasn't America's Mayor but America's first publicly elected cult leader, winning the hearts and minds of hundreds of thousands on the basis of what Mike McGovern described as "blind faith."

"Realistically, I feel that the heart of the problem still exists," said McGovern in summing up his feelings about the city. "The infrastructure, the flight of the middle class, the breakdown of the neighborhoods, the loss of jobs, the lack of a decent educational system. But as contradictory as it sounds, I still have a lot of hope and optimism. There *is* an infectious, contagious optimism about the town. A lot of it is attributable to Ed's relentless cheerleading." The effect of welfare reform—or welfare repeal as some more accurately described it—could undo all the energy of that hope, and in the summer of 1996, with the legislation still pending, Rendell had appealed to the president in a letter:

> The legislation before Congress demands work but does not produce jobs. In Philadelphia, we are already struggling to find work for dislocated workers, people with extensive and recent work experience. For example, with your help, we are desperately struggling with the task of finding meaningful new jobs for over eight thousand dislocated workers from the Philadelphia Naval Shipyard. In the face of the demands that those on welfare in our city go to work or face an abrupt cutoff of benefits, we must therefore ask: "Where are the jobs?"

"We have not been hit that hard yet," said Cohen of the impact of welfare reform, which had now become actual law and ended the federal guarantee of aid to the poor. "I have no doubt it's coming, and it's coming in a serious way." But he still described himself as relentlessly optimistic, not simply because of the new hotel and restaurant deals that were blossoming and unfolding, but because he was convinced of the very sanctity of the

American city, confident that it had a place in the nation's landscape too valuable to sacrifice. "I know a region cannot survive without its core city," he said. "If the city goes down, the region goes down." The immediate effect of such a total implosion, he said, would be a 25 percent drop in the property values of the surrounding areas, and no suburbanite, however far he had fled to the western edge of the metroplex, would ever stand for that. But he also knew it was a speculative prediction, and what he said next was as disturbing as it was chilling: that the only way to prove the worth of the American city would be through the complete collapse of one.

Then, and only then, as those property values plummeted and suburbanites who thought they were safe were not safe at all, would politicians and voters see why cities must be preserved, not out of moral obligation but out of necessity. "What scares me is, I'm not sure that a major city [isn't] going to have to implode to prove the point, and you sure as hell don't want it to be your city." In the painful race that American cities had been running for the past half-century, up and down, hot and not, on the edge and barely above the surface even in the most bountiful of times, he saw Washington, D.C., as the most likely candidate for obliteration. Given his doomsday theory, he actually considered that good news. To a certain degree, it was always comforting to know that there was someplace out there in even worse shape than you were in. More important, he hoped that the dysfunctional condition of the nation's capital would finally force those whose influence went far beyond its borders to enact real change nationwide and give cities the footing they needed to be economically competitive.

There were innumerable shifts that could be made without havoc or wasteful billions. The creation of the suburban era in American life wasn't accidental or the result of social inevitability. People left the city for the suburbs because they were given the economic wherewithal by the federal government through the creation of the modern mortgage and the home tax deduction. They left because they could afford it, because there was government-engineered incentive to leave, and cities could be sustained and rebuilt in the very same way.

At the specific request of the White House, Rendell spent months working on a document called the New Urban Agenda that he unveiled at the National Press Club in Washington in April 1994. He suggested a host of practical ideas that didn't involve money, but changes in federal policy that, as he wrote, "can help cities without having a significant impact on [the federal] budget." Among the suggestions: an agreement that 15 percent of all federal procurement be purchased from firms located in urban empowerment zones; the elimination of unfunded mandates that in the case of the American Disabilities Act, for example, would cost the city $140 million in curb cuts and ramps; streamlining policy to help cities rid themselves of the environmental nightmares of its abandoned factories; restoration of the tax credit for historic rehabilitation.

The proposal giving distressed urban areas a preference in federal procurement was acted upon. Steps were also being taken to ease the red tape for clearing abandoned factories and for reducing unfunded mandates. But the historic rehabilitation tax credit had not been revived. Nor had another initiative Rendell had suggested, the creation of a federal capital budget to rebuild the urban infrastructure. Nor had simple changes in the tax code to further spur private investment and the creation of jobs. "The New Urban Agenda is no panacea, nor is it guaranteed to make cities succeed," Rendell had written. "What is certain, however, is that without it or some other significant help, cities will surely fail."

They were honest words, spoken from the vantage point of someone who had seen the sorrow over and over—the homeless man wrapped in rags on the rim of the perfectly sculpted fountain; the son in the relentless light of the hospital waiting room who wanted to know why, *why,* his father had been killed in the line of duty, the little girl who had taken his hand on the shabby block of Stella and asked for a swimming pool. The statistics alone—a city that in twenty-five years had lost over a quarter-million jobs, a city that in twenty-five years had lost 30 percent of its tax base—described a place that had already lost one of its limbs to cancer. But still his words to some degree were seen as exaggeration, another mayor just crying wolf.

Cohen himself, expanding upon a model that was being considered for Washington, D.C., had a tantalizing suggestion: a federal tax credit of 10 percent for *all* residents of cities that were officially deemed to be distressed on the basis of such established criteria as mortality, poverty rates, and unemployment. Such a credit would immediately offset the taxes that so many cities levied on residents and businesses to remain solvent. Just as important, it would encourage those of means to return to the city not on the basis of emotion or culture or entertainment but on the basis that had the only real chance of working in America—a direct appeal to the pocketbook. It could potentially bring to cities what they needed the most, not just changes in the tax code or job-creation money or federal procurement, but the infectious and electric surge of human capital that is the first step in all turnarounds and miracles.

It was an idea, an intriguing idea, but in the tenor of the country, it seemed likely to remain exactly that. Soccer moms and soccer dads were the latest political obsession, and it was their needs that set the agenda. Given the reconstituted downtown of the American city, streets paved with the newest standard of health—Disney and Niketown and Hard Rock Cafe and Planet Hollywood and Starbucks and megaplex movie theaters with enough screens to entertain an entire neighborhood for two hours—there was a perception that cities had turned the corner into good times anyway.

There were positive signs. Reported major crimes dropped 3 percent nationwide in 1996, including 14 percent in New York and 12 percent in Los Angeles. Beyond crime, community development groups, proving the miracle of persistence, had built new housing in areas of cities around the country that seemed beyond hope. But these changes were blips, not sustained trends. The idea that cities had come close to reversing themselves was dangerously misleading, ignorant of poverty rates; ignorant of the timeline of decline that occurred not just for five years but for nearly fifty; ignorant of social and racial stratification; ignorant of the types of jobs that the audience economy threw off; ignorant of what would happen in the next recession when the disposable dollars of tourists and suburbanites were no longer disposable. There was also the danger that what lay behind the fancy wrap of the downtown, the gray areas of abandoned factories and worn-out neighborhoods, had been rendered invisible, the Bermuda Triangle of American life.

The movers came at 1:30 P.M., and an hour later had carted out Cohen's desk, bookcase, round table, and pictures. It left him in the awkward position of working in an office that now had nothing in it except for a golf putter, a rolled-up Oriental carpet, a stale-looking couch, and a hard-backed wooden chair. Undeterred, Cohen stood at the credenza by the window and continued to work. He fielded a call about the school board, and he described to a well-wisher how he was now standing in an office that had virtually no furniture in it. At 4:15 P.M., he gave up his six-shooter, his beeper, and noted, almost like recalling the first words of his children, that it was the mayor who had made the final beep. There was something fitting about that, a perfect beginning-and-end symmetry in their working relationship. Cohen was moving only several blocks away, and he would continue to serve in a highly active role as an advisor. He still had the keys to City Hall, and given his loyalty to Rendell, he would always be on call.

But Cohen would have a different object of obsession now, the law firm of Ballard Spahr. Inevitably ethical conflicts would arise that would make it impossible for Cohen to dispense advice even if he wanted to. The mayor, as hard as he tried to convince himself that Cohen really wasn't going very far, knew how different it would be. During the course of a given day in the second floor right angle of City Hall where they had toiled, they had actually seen quite little of each other. But the presence of Cohen, willing to work forty-eight hours a day if only Congress would pass the necessary legislation, provided a comfort as steady as a light-house. In a literal sense the light of Cohen's office had always been on, the one precious square of dependability in the architectural cuckoo's nest of City Hall. In a city that had spent so much of its modern history in varying degrees of chaos and conflict, the uplift of that was immeasurable. Or as the mayor himself put it, "The best thing about David was that he was al-ways there."

Rendell had no choice but to carry on. The intensity of his mission had not diminished, but there were inevitable questions about what he would do with his own future once his second term expired. By city charter he could not seek reelection as mayor. Running for statewide office was a possibility, governor or senator, but Rendell himself wasn't sure if he had the burning desire to mount another massive campaign. He talked about maybe heading a foundation, or going into business with his son. He even mused about becoming baseball commissioner, and his name had already been touted in the press. Given his encyclopedic knowledge of sports and his unique ability to massage egos, it was a job that suited him perfectly. But it seemed unimaginable for Rendell to leave his natural habitat of poli-tics. However he had come by it, wherever he had gained it, he had the rare gift of public leadership, and it was far too essential to be sacrificed to a ball and a bat.

When Cohen was asked how he felt about Rendell, it wasn't at all sur-prising that he used almost exactly the same words as the mayor had used about him. "We are best friends, but we are also like brothers. He's like my father. I'm like his father." It was around 5:00 P.M., and he sat in a chair in the corner of his empty office, the walls adorned with dozens of jutting hooks where the pictures had once been. It had all the pleasantry of a mini-malist stage set for some avant-garde play about hell and the deprivation of the bureaucrat, but he didn't seem to mind. He still had a phone. He still had a credenza on which to read the final trickle of memos and letters. If that's all that had been afforded to him at the beginning, it wouldn't have mattered. It was only when he was asked if he had grown to love the mayor that he became uncomfortable, a slight pause and squirm as if the question didn't seem to make the slightest sense, an emotion that had no place in the pragmatist's repeated journey from point A to point B. "I love my family," he said.

But in the world of politics and power, a world that almost inevitably turned affection into hate and regard into scorn, it was more than just loyalty that had made him so indefatigable on behalf of Ed Rendell. He might not be able to express it, and his pragmatist's religion would never allow him the liberation of saying it, but it was abundantly clear that he did love the mayor, just as it was abundantly clear that the mayor loved him. In the endless war for the survival of the city, they had pulled off perhaps the greatest miracle of all. They had remained true to each other. They had remained intact. "We have been to hell and back," said Cohen as he sat in that chair. "There's an intensity of what we have been through that is unique."

At about 7:00 P.M., after one final meeting, it was time to go. He was having dinner with his family and his best friend, Arthur Makadon, at a Chinese restaurant and there was no point in being late, particularly since everything had come to a standstill. But the phone rang, and it was the mayor on the line asking him about a letter. Cohen of course knew exactly what he was referring to and said he would bring it right over. He went with his usual purpose to his secretary's desk in the outer office, but he had gotten confused and the letter on the desk wasn't the one that the mayor wanted. He searched the empty corners of his own office, then went to a series of clunky beige cabinets, then to an accordion file, and he could not find it.

He went over to the mayor and said it wasn't there, and the mayor told him not to worry about it, and then he went back to his office and searched the very same places again. A police officer had come to put his remaining possessions into his car, and now he was running late for dinner, and he finally seemed poised to leave and turn the lights out for good. But then he went back to the accordion file and looked all over again, combing through the same crevices he had just combed through moments ago, but still, *still,* he could not find it. And then the strangest thing happened, and David L. Cohen did something he had never before done until the very last minute of his very last day. He left without finding it, descending the curved stairway of City Hall with the familiar echo of scuffed sole against stone that he had made a thousand times before, but with the unfamiliar step of someone who no longer served the city.

Acknowledgments

A book such as this is truly a collaborative effort, and there are dozens who helped. Michael Carlisle, my agent at the William Morris Agency, played so many roles in this book that I finally lost track—cheerleader, editor, therapist, slayer of panic attacks. His care and compassion were just unique. Jon Karp, my editor at Random House, was wonderful. He worked inexhaustibly, with an invigorating meticulousness that kept me on my toes at all times. He both listened and gave criticism in proper measure, and was wise far beyond his years. Jon's bosses, Harold Evans and Ann Godoff, were at all times supportive and enthusiastic.

Within the Random House team, there were so many who went out of their way to make this book special: Sean Abbott, Deborah Aiges, Dennis Ambrose, Gabrielle Bordwin, Bridget Marmion, Tanya Pérez-Rock, and Robbin Schiff. Special mention must go to Abigail Winograd for making me realize that copyediting truly can be an art form, particularly with writers who clearly ignored their grammar lessons in school. Sorry, Abigail.

Within the labyrinth of the mayor's office, there were many who graciously put up with me for four years. I have never seen a trio work with better cheer than Marge Staton, Donna Cisowski, and Annie Karl. The mayor had a variety of schedulers, three of whom deserve Purple Hearts for ultimate grace under pressure: Eden Kratchman, Karen Lewis, and the saintly Susan Segal. Robin Schatz, who headed constituent services for the mayor, had a gift for compassion that was inspirational. Within David Cohen's office, Ginnie Lehoe and Yvonne Reed could not have been nicer.

I am indebted to Anthony Buchanico for getting me to the thick of the action time and time again. I would also like to thank some of the other police officers who, in addition to their daily duties protecting the mayor, made my life incredibly pleasant: Joe Adams, Rudy Braxton, Jr., Ron Clemins, Mike Gulkis, Ernie Kiefer, Tony Pino, Jimmy Previti, Joe Rimato, Deborah Sheeron, and Reggie Wilkins.

Among others who worked for the city, special thanks should go to Ted

Beitchman for his spirited opinions on government, the media, baseball, and bars; Joe Torsella for his engaging ideas on how to energize cities; and Greg Rost for being both kind and wise.

I simply could not have written this book without the help of three other people who were connected to the city. One is Kevin Feeley, who not only put up with every pain-in-the-neck request I made but also became a valued friend. The other two are David Cohen and Ed Rendell.

David Cohen and I basically shared an office for four years, to the point where I put up a little picture of my children in his bookcase as a way of claiming turf. I utterly invaded his personal space, and he didn't protest once. As for the mayor, what can I say? The pressures on him at all times were relentless, but he never took them out on me. By year two of my presence, I would have understood completely if he had pulled me from the little leather couch where I sat and tossed me into the City Hall courtyard. Instead he went out of his way to give me the best, most unfettered view possible into the heart of the city.

I also could not have written this book without the incredible cooperation of four individuals who gave of their time tirelessly—Mike McGovern, Jim Mangan, Fifi Mazzccua, and Linda Morrison. They truly are heroes, not only because of their passion for the city, but also for putting up with me.

On a personal note, I would like to thank Matt Purdy for reading the manuscript in its most bloated form and offering smart suggestions. I would like to thank Rick Hole for keeping me both sane and properly medicated when it didn't ever seem like this book would get written. I would like to thank E. Ann Wilcox, then the librarian at the Maritime Museum, for her help in locating crucial documents about the navy yard. I would also like to thank Ian Keith. I had intended to make Ian, a schoolteacher in Philadelphia at the time, one of the voices in the book. He had a rich and resonant story, but I was never able to find the right home for it. We spent hundreds of hours together, and I made frequent demands on his time. I do not believe the time was wasted, because it was in the process of our encounters that we developed a friendship and respect far more lasting than any book.

I would like to thank my children, Gerry, Zachary, and Caleb, for their patience and understanding during the five and a half years it took me to do this. "We should say thank you to God for printing such a heavy book," remarked Caleb, who is five, and truer words have never been spoken.

I would also like to give thanks and love to the incomparable Kim. She came into my life at the right time, she listened to my rants of self-doubt with remarkable attentiveness, and for some reason that must have to do with miracles, she is still here.

A Note About Sources

In writing about the events of City Hall, I based almost 90 percent of this book on personal observation. In instances where I was not present, I relied in most cases on reconstructions provided either by the mayor himself or David Cohen. Because of the nature of the research, I spent thousands of hours with each of them over the course of four years. I was also given permission to view thousands of pages of documents, many of them confidential.

I had dozens of encounters with Michael McGovern, Jim Mangan, Fifi Mazzccua, and Linda Morrison in researching and writing about each of them.

Because so much of the book is based on firsthand accounts, interviews for the purposes of reconstruction were not necessary in many instances. During the course of research, however, lengthy interviews were conducted with the following individuals: Ted Beitchman, Anthony Buchanico, Mark Carter, Larry Ceisler, Richard Chlan, Rhonda Cohen, Jack Collins, Alan Davis, Father Edward Deliman, Michael DiBerardinis, Posquale Dudley, Isadore Epstein, Dwight Evans, Kevin Feeley, Terry Gillen, Gaynell Gillespie, Mayor W. Wilson Goode, William Hankowsky, Peter Hearn, Ronald Henry, Rev. Clarence Hester, Robin Hynicka, Ken Jarin, Barbara Kaplan, Sam Katz, Ian Keith, Bill Keller, Alan Kessler, Hank Klibanoff, Carol Koren, Bennett Levin, Ted McKee, Mary Pat McGovern, Daniel McElhatton, Arthur Makadon, Tony Mazzccua, Peter Moor, Jon Morrison, Neil Oxman, Samira Pitts, Bill Reil, Kathy Reilly, Midge Rendell, Nellie Reynolds, Governor Tom Ridge, Phil Rowan, Len Rubin, Sarah Rubin, Jonathan Saidel, Robin Schatz, Michael Smerconish, Joseph Torsella, Fred Voigt, F. John White, and Ed Zubrow.

In the course of my research, I read numerous books on cities in general and Philadelphia in particular. There were several that were particularly helpful: *The Philadelphia Negro* by W.E.B. Du Bois; *A Nation of Cities* by Mark I. Gelfand; *Crabgrass Frontier* by Kenneth T. Jackson; *American Apartheid* by Douglas S. Massey and Nancy A. Denton; *The Private City* by Sam

Bass Warner, Jr.; and *The Declining Significance of Race* by William Julius Wilson.

Prologue

I accompanied the mayor from Philadelphia to Washington on June 3, 1992, when he testified before the Senate Finance Committee, and was with him both before and after his testimony. The quote about how "everything that goes on is a power struggle between black politicians and white politicians" was said in my presence on June 5, 1992, in a telephone conversation with a member of the governor's office.

I was personally present at both Lankenau and Hahnemann University hospitals the night of November 16, 1993, when the mayor responded to the shootings of three police officers in different parts of the city. Information about the U.S. Conference of Mayors' emergency meeting on violent crime on November 15, 1993, came largely from a memo about the meeting that was sent to the mayor by a participant.

Information on the shootings of police officers Robert Hayes and John Marynowitz on June 16, 1993, was compiled from interviews with Mayor Rendell, David Cohen, and Anthony Buchanico as well as from accounts of the incident in *The Philadelphia Inquirer* and *Philadelphia Daily News*. The speech the mayor gave to the Red Cross the morning after the shootings was viewed on tape.

Chapter One: Ego and Id

The account of David Cohen on January 5, 1992, the day before the inauguration, came from personal observation. Background on Cohen as a law student and young lawyer came from interviews with Cohen, Rhonda Cohen, Arthur Makadon, and others who knew him during this period. Background on Rendell came from interviews with the mayor and Midge Rendell. I also drew on an excellent profile of him, "Acting on Impulse" by Marc Duvoisin, that appeared in the *Inquirer Magazine* on January 12, 1992. Rendell's description of the reaction to his speech before the Democratic National Convention when he was the city's district attorney was related in an interview on July 10, 1992. The account of Rendell after his loss in the 1987 Democratic mayoral primary came from interviews with the mayor, Alan Kessler, Arthur Makadon, Neil Oxman, and Midge Rendell, as well as personal observation, since I was a reporter at the time for the *Inquirer*.

The account of Rendell's campaigning for mayor in 1991 was based on personal observation. The account of the *Inquirer* delving into Rendell's personal life for possible acts of sexual harrassment was based on a telephone interview with Cohen on December 11, 1991. All the details concerning the mayor's in-auguration on January 6, 1992, were based on personal observation. The memo from Neil Oxman at the end of the chapter was personally viewed.

Chapter Two: The Number

The account of the night at the beginning of 1992 when the city discovered it had a budget deficit of $1.246 billion came from interviews with David Cohen and F. John White. The account of the night of February 19, 1992, when the five-year plan was finished, came from personal observation, as did the entire account of the following day when Rendell met with labor leaders and gave his televised speech about the budget.

I was personally present at dozens of private meetings in which the city's budget was discussed. Other information about the budget and the city's financial and social conditions came from the *City of Philadelphia: Five-Year Financial Plan* and numerous stories that appeared in the *Inquirer* and *Daily News*. A particularly good account of the city's dire financial straits was written by *Inquirer* reporter Matthew Purdy for the 1994 regional almanac that was published by the newspaper. The list of firsts for the city was based on information that appeared in *Philadelphia Architecture: A Guide to the City*.

Statistics about the state of the cities from the 1950s to the present came most heavily from *A Nation of Cities* by Mark I. Gelfand, *Cities Without Suburbs* by David Rusk, and a reprint of the testimony before the Senate Subcommittee on Reorganization and International Organizations on July 24, 1959. That is where Professor Raymond Vernon of Harvard uttered his memorable quote about cities, but he wasn't the only one to issue dire warnings. At least a dozen public officials issued similar pleas for help. The testimony in general provided shocking proof of how deeply entrenched the problems of America's cities were forty years ago and how little corrective action was taken. The testimony also shows that the concept of regionalism, which some academics and public officials embrace as a novel concept, is hardly new at all.

The events of April 1, 1992, when the mayor debated whether to appear with Mickey Mouse, were all personally observed. So were the events of the next day.

Chapter Three: The Yard

Much of the historical information about the yard came from the library of the Maritime Museum (it is now called the Independence Seaport Museum). The library contained rare documents about the yard and transcribed interviews with workers who were once employed there. The library's interview with Pat

D'Amico was the basis for the material that was used about her in this chapter. Other sources of information about the yard included the yard's own files as well as clippings in the *Inquirer* and *Daily News*. The mayor's comments about the futility of the suit that was filed to block closure were made in my presence on several occasions during 1992 and 1993.

Information about Sovereign Oil came from private memos, clippings in the *Inquirer,* and personal observation of events that took place on May 14 and 16, 1992. The account of the visit by a delegation of Japanese officials to Philadelphia came from the book *Diary of the Japanese Visit to Philadelphia in 1872* by Henry B. Ashmead.

Chapter Four: The Racial Trifecta

The account of the twenty-four-hour period on July 19, 1992, in which Robbie Burns was killed and the neighborhood reaction, came from press accounts in the *Inquirer* and *Daily News* as well as confidential memos from the police department. I was present when the mayor called the cardinal by phone on July 20, 1992. I rode with the mayor that night to the gymnasium in Kensington and personally observed all the events described in the chapter. The history of Kensington came from a variety of written sources, the two best of which were *Whitetown, U.S.A.* by Peter Binzen and *Voices of Kensington* by Jean Seder. The mayor's comment about Passover was made in my presence on April 6, 1993.

I was present at the private meeting on July 21, 1992, in which Latino leaders claimed they were being treated unfairly. I was also present at the private meeting between the mayor and black ministers on July 22, 1992, that resulted in the walkout. I was present on December 14, 1992, when the publisher of the *Philadelphia Gay News* asked the mayor about underrepresentation of lesbians in the administration. I was present on August 21, 1992, when Italian-American leaders threatened to march in protest unless the head of the city's art commission was fired. I was also present on January 15, 1993, when State Senator Hardy Williams claimed a conspiracy in the failure of a police officer to get a promotion. Information on the police department's internal review of the officer's record was supplied eleven days later by the mayor.

Chapter Five: "Watch Out"

The account of the trial of *Commonwealth v. William Taylor* came from personal observation of the trial on August 20 and 21, 1992, interviews with Michael McGovern, court and police records, and press accounts. I was present on August 21, 1992, when the mayor held the press conference announcing that the Miss International U.S. Beauty Pageant had been salvaged.

Chapter Six: "Fast Eddie, We Are Ready"

David Cohen's "vacation memorandum," written in August 1992, was personally viewed. I was present on March 20, 1992, when Cohen decided who should get tickets to the NCAA basketball playoffs in Philadelphia. The account of the city councilperson asking Cohen to do something about the homeless people beneath his window was related to me by Cohen on April 7, 1992. I was present on June 17, 1992, when Cohen assured a city councilperson over the phone that a friend would be getting legal work. I was present on June 16, 1992, when he called the police commissioner about a stolen car that belonged to a friend of the mayor's. The memo from Cohen about bathroom locations in City Hall, written on October 27, 1993, was personally viewed.

The account of the union negotiations in general during the spring and summer of 1992 was based on being present at dozens of private meetings held by the mayor, Cohen, and various members of the city's negotiating team. Hundreds of pages of confidential documents describing in detail the city's strategy were also given to me. During the negotiations in the spring and summer of 1992, I attempted to gain insight into the strategy of the unions, in particular District Council 33, but efforts to interview union head James Sutton and lawyer Deborah Willig were rebuffed.

The contents of the "strike contingency plans" notebook were personally viewed. The account of negotiations with the unions during the middle of June 1992 in which Thomas Paine Cronin screamed at city negotiators came from interviews with several of the latter. I was present at the meeting on May 30, 1992, when city negotiators discussed strategy, including the leak of the "Crazy Work Rules" memo. The memo was subsequently supplied to me. I was also present on June 25, 1992, at the meeting in the mayor's home when strategy was further discussed, including the injection of race by playing one union off against the other, the use of layoff notices, and the possible contracting out of sanitation. The unions' rally on June 29, 1992, was personally observed, as was the mayor's reaction to it.

Chapter Seven: Crisis of Faith

The account of the mayor at one point promising wage increases of 4 and 6 percent to the unions during the Democratic National Convention in July 1992, as well as the mayor and David Cohen meeting privately with national union head Gerald McEntee, came from an extensive two-hour interview with chief city negotiator Alan Davis. The interview took place on October 13, 1992, a week after the dispute was settled, when events were still fresh in his mind. Davis brought up the mayor's crisis of faith on his own initiative. Notes of the meeting with McEntee, which took place on July 28, 1992, were supplied by Cohen. The account of the conversation between Willig and Davis at the end of July 1992 was based on the interview with Davis. I was present at the meeting on August 6, 1992, between Rendell and national union leaders. The mayor's comment about being pregnant all the time if he were a woman was made in my presence on September 21, 1993.

Chapter Eight: Profiles in Courage

I was in the mayor's car when he traveled to the viewing for slain officer Charles Knox on September 3, 1992. I was present on September 16, 1992, when David Cohen told the mayor that the state supreme court had ruled in favor of the city on the issue of fact-finding. The account of the city's decision to file an appeal with the state supreme court came from being present at numerous discussions. The account of a black politician circulating a letter with the implied threat of violence was based on an interview with Cohen.

The interior of John Street's office was personally observed on several occasions. The account of a city official receiving a call from Street's office about a parking space was based on a memo that was written on February 11, 1992, and personally viewed. Cohen's response was in his own handwriting at the bottom of the memo. The account of Street's request for tickets to a sporting event was based on a phone call that the mayor made to an official of the Philadelphia Phillies on December 15, 1992. The account of Street's meeting with editors of the *Daily News* was given to me by a participant. The memo from *Daily News* editor Richard Aregood, describing Street's behavior, was written on July 1, 1992, and personally viewed.

The events of September 23, 1992, in which the city elected to implement its last and best offer, were all personally observed. The account of the mayor and Street going through the elaborate choreography of giving up on two outstanding issues was described to me by the mayor. I was present on September 25, 1992, when Cohen discussed the idea of former Labor Secretary Ray Marshall coming to Philadelphia to proclaim the contract a fair one. I was present at the meeting later that day when the mayor, Cohen, and Street discussed the status of negotiations.

The account of negotiations at the Holiday Inn Midtown was based upon interviews with several city negotiators who were there. I was present for all but one of the events that took place on October 5 and 6, 1992, when settlement was reached. I was not present when the mayor, Cohen, and Sutton met in the mayor's private office in the early morning hours of October 6. I was in an office next door, however, and was able to hear what was being said. The letter that was written by the mayor to Street promising that sanitation would not be contracted out was personally viewed.

Chapter Nine: Tidbits of Urban Wisdom

Extensive interviews with Linda Morrison formed the basis of most of this chapter. Her memo about the Southwark Plaza housing project, which she gave to me, was written on December 21, 1992. Other information about Southwark came from press accounts in the *Inquirer* and *Daily News*. The history of public housing in the United States came from a variety of sources, including the essay "Distressed Public Housing: Where Do We Go from Here?" by Michael Shill, a professor of law and real estate at the University of Pennsylvania. Information on the status of families at the Philadelphia Housing Authority in 1959 was contained in a master's thesis by James C. Webb that is on file at the main library of the University of Pennsylvania. The quote from President Roosevelt on the dangers of becoming dependent on governmental relief came from the book *The End of Equality* by Mickey Kaus.

Chapter Ten: Getting Paid

The account of *Commonwealth v. Carlton Bennett and Giovanni Reed* was based on personal observation of the trial between January 21 and 27, 1993, interviews with McGovern, and court and police records.

The account of the Philadelphia Housing Authority in general was based on dozens of meetings with the mayor and other officials at which I was present. As with the union negotiations, I was also made privy to hundreds of pages of documents, many of them confidential. I also benefited from excellent coverage of the authority by Matthew Purdy of the *Inquirer*. I was present on January 25, 1993, when Michael Smerconish, then the regional administrator for the federal Department of Housing and Urban Development, engaged in a screaming match with Lucien Blackwell, then a local congressman. I was present at the meeting on January 29, 1993, in which Smerconish and the mayor discussed the two finalists for the post of executive director of the housing authority. I was present for several discussions at the beginning of February 1993 when Rendell, after expressing initial enthusiasm for finalist David Gilmore, began to waver. I was also present on May 6, 1992, when Rendell said that the housing authority was being driven primarily by the issues of patronage and race.

HUD's draft audit of the authority was made available to me. Gaynell Gillespie's account of the burning of her infant son by a radiator in a public housing high-rise was based on an interview with her on December 22, 1992. The letter from John Paone to the mayor describing the inner workings of the authority, written on February 8, 1993, was personally viewed.

Chapter Eleven: Urban Sacrifice

David Cohen's reaction to the visit of President Clinton on May 28, 1993, was personally observed. The account of the mayor's testimony before the Base Closure and Realignment Commission on May 9, 1993, and his reaction on June 27, 1993, when thousands of defense jobs in the city were saved, were based on clippings in the *Inquirer*.

I was present on March 15, 1993, when the mayor made his comment about "giving bread and circuses to the people." I was present on the tarmac of Philadelphia International Airport on May 28, 1993, when the president arrived. The account of the mayor's limousine ride to City Hall with the president was supplied by the mayor.

There have been numerous books written about the impact of federal policy on the American city, but three were invaluable in the writing of this section: *Crabgrass Frontier* by Kenneth T. Jackson, *A Nation of Cities* by Mark I. Gelfand, and *The Contested City* by John H. Mollenkopf. Other sources included *History and Policies of the Home Owners' Loan Corporation* by C. Lowell Harriss, the essay "Housing the Underclass" by David W. Bartelt, which appeared in the book *The Underclass Debate,* and the research report *Metropolitan Disparities and Economic Growth,* published by the National League of Cities in March 1992. I personally viewed at the National Archives in Washington all the maps and neighborhood surveys by the Home Owners' Loan Corporation for the city of Philadelphia. I am indebted to Kenneth Jackson for making me aware of the existence of such records in the archives.

In determining the nation's attitude toward cities, *The Intellectual Versus the City* by Morton and Lucia White and *The Culture of Cities* by Lewis Mumford were both quite helpful. So was the essay "City Lights" by Lewis H. Lapham that appeared in *Harper's Magazine* in July 1992.

Roosevelt's quote about the American city came from Gelfand's *A Nation of Cities,* as did the quote by Henry Ford. Mayor Richardson Dilworth's dire and prescient predictions about the American city were made before the same senate subcommittee that also heard the testimony of Professor Vernon. Professor Robert T. Wood's speech about American attitudes toward cities was part of a series of lectures in 1959 and 1960 sponsored by the Fels Institute at the University of Pennsylvania.

William Schneider's essay "The Suburban Century Begins," in the July 1992 issue of *The Atlantic Monthly,* was a penetrating analysis of the significance of the 1992 presidential election. All the events of May 15, 1992, when the mayor went to Washington for a series of private meetings about the plight of the cities in the aftermath of the Los Angeles riots, were personally observed.

Chapter Twelve: The Last Sermon

I was present on June 26, 1993, for the opening of the city's new convention center. The account of the opening of the Centennial Exhibition in the city on May 10, 1876, was based primarily on the book *The Illustrated History of the Centennial Exhibition* by James D. McCabe. A book published in 1876 called *What Ben Beverly Saw at the Great Exposition* was also helpful.

I was present on June 27, 1993, when Robin Hynicka gave his last sermon at Cookman United Methodist Church. Extensive interviews with Fifi Mazzccua and Robin Hynicka were relied upon for the rest of this chapter.

Chapter Thirteen: Hot Dog Day

The events of July 23, 1993, when the mayor proclaimed "Hot Dog Day" were all personally observed. I was present on May 10, 1993, when Rendell made his comment about Sidney Kimmel and building a new orchestra hall in the city. I was also present on May 7, 1993, when Rendell called potential campaign contributors over the phone. I was present on December 8, 1992, when Cohen created his plan to trace the source of leaks to the press. The mayor's strategy in sending people over to see David Cohen was observed on several occasions. I was present on February 22, 1994, when Cohen told the mayor they should no longer pay a campaign worker. I was also present on February 25, 1994, when Rendell talked with the worker and said he was going to assist him in finding a job.

The account of the city and HUD entering into a partnership for the operation of the housing authority in August 1993 was based on personal observations at meetings and extensive interviews with the mayor and Cohen. In relating his strategy for dealing with HUD, Cohen supplied me with both the draft he sent to HUD officials and the markup of that draft by HUD officials so that I could see the changes. The president's congratulating Rendell on becoming chairman of the board of the housing authority took place on September 9, 1993, and was related to me by the mayor.

Cohen expressed his feelings about his son Benjamin in an interview on November 12, 1993. The depiction of Rendell in the aftermath of the two election losses in 1986 and 1987 was based on an extensive interview with his wife on October 9, 1996. I was present on October 11, 1993, when the mayor and Cohen had differing reactions to the Phillies' win in the fifth game of the National League Championship Series.

Chapter Fourteen: "We Hardly Knew Ye"

I was with McGovern during his last two days in the district attorney's office on September 9 and 10, 1993. The account of the McGoverns' experience with the Philadelphia public schools was based on an interview with Mary Pat McGovern on March 6, 1995.

I was present with the mayor on September 14, 1993, when he went by helicopter to the USS *John F. Kennedy* as it was sailing into the navy yard. The quotes of various politicians about their expectations for the yard came from clippings in the *Inquirer*.

The experiences of Jim Mangan's children in the public school system were based on interviews with Mangan and two of his daughters, Cheryl and Michelle.

Chapter Fifteen: Vision for the City

The account of Linda Morrison's mugging at a commuter train station on December 7, 1993, was based on several interviews with Morrison and was also supplemented by a detailed memo of the incident that she wrote to David Cohen on December 21, 1993. Background on the Chestnut Hill neighborhood came from *Suburb in the City* by David R. Contosta, as well as my own personal experience of living there during Rendell's first term as mayor. Morrison's account of her decision to leave the city's employ in the spring of 1994 was based on extensive interviews with her. That account was also supplemented by nearly a dozen memos that Morrison wrote to Cohen. Cohen's memo about parking authority garages, written on February 23, 1994, was personally viewed, as was his memo of May 4, 1994, stating that too much emphasis was being placed on contracting out.

The account of the administration's reaction to the *Inquirer*'s coverage of the Stinson-Marks race for the state senate at the end of 1993 was based on being present for numerous discussions in which the issue was discussed. The letters that Rendell sent to major fund-raisers on October 20, 1993, were personally viewed. I was present on December 6, 1993, when former city controller Thomas Leonard suggested to Cohen the formation of a blue-ribbon panel to help the *Inquirer* win a Pulitzer. Rendell's comment about not caring if the paper won a Pulitzer was made in my presence at the beginning of 1994. The mayor's comments to Democratic National Committee chairman David Wilhelm and White House staffer Marcia Hale about the city dying were made in my presence on December 12, 1993. Cohen's comment about rewarding Legg Mason for donating to the fund for the city's Christmas display was made in my presence on December 7, 1993.

I was present on March 22, 1994, when Rendell and Cohen traveled to Washington for a private meeting with HUD Secretary Henry Cisneros, and was also present for the meeting. James Carville's quote about Pennsylvania was repeated to me nearly a dozen times in the four years I was with the mayor.

I was present for virtually all the comments that were made on March 22 and 23, 1994, in regards to the profile of the mayor by Lisa DePaulo of *Philadelphia Magazine.* I was not present when the mayor spoke to DePaulo on the Metroliner from Washington to Philadelphia, but the contents of the conversation were later related to me.

Chapter Sixteen: "Inappropriate Conduct"

Rendell's intent to give Street $10,000 for a political fund-raiser as "some assuagement" was made in my presence on April 11, 1994. The mayor's suggestion of a $1 million UDAG grant to the wife of Street's law partner was made in my presence on July 15, 1993. (The grant was never awarded.) I was present at the meeting on December 14, 1992, in which the mayor and Street met with Willie Mays. The mayor's assurances to hotel-casino operators that whoever built a large convention hotel would get a casino franchise were made in my presence on January 11, and March 24, 1994. The account of the city demolishing twenty-five structures a week was based on an *Inquirer* story by Vernon Loeb on May 16, 1994.

The account of politicians' efforts to use the navy yard to turn Russian ships into scrap metal was based on clippings in the *Inquirer.* I was present on July 15, 1994, when Rendell said he had been asked to revise the findings of a consultant who was negative about the idea. The mayor's comment that he should quit and run for governor was made to me on February 22, 1994.

Rendell's grabbing of *Inquirer* reporter Amy Rosenberg on May 18, 1994, was personally observed. The letter of *Inquirer* city editor David Tucker on May 19, 1994, about the incident, was personally viewed as was the mayor's written response on May 24, 1994. The *Daily News*'s questioning of its coverage of the mayor was based on a source intimately familiar with the situation.

The account of the fatal shooting of six-year-old Michelle Cutner on June 29, 1994, was based on clippings in the *Inquirer* and *Daily News.* I was present at the neighborhood meeting the next night, and I know that Rendell was aware of it because I asked him if he was going to attend. The reaction of Neil Oxman to the mayor's absence at the meeting was made during an interview on September 22, 1994. David Cohen's memo analyzing the mayor's schedule, written on July 15, 1994, was personally viewed.

The account of Tony Mazzccua's life sentence for murder was based on a three-hour taped interview that took place on February 20, 1996, as well as a complete review of the court proceedings against him. I was also present on several occasions when Fifi Mazzccua visited her son in prison. The account of the death of Kim Armstrong on August 12, 1994, was based on clippings in the *Inquirer* and *Daily News.* I was present at the community meeting on August 26, 1994, in which Armstrong's death was discussed.

Chapter Seventeen: Don't Mess with Ed

David Cohen's account of his conversation with Dwight Evans in Harrisburg was based on an interview with Cohen on August 4, 1994. The events of July 11, 1994, when the Philadelphia Plan was announced, were all personally observed. The mayor's assessment of the plan as a "drop in the bucket" was made on July 22, 1994. The account of the city's competition with Camden for twelve hundred jobs at PNC Bank was based primarily on letters and other internal correspondence made available to me. The amount of business that the bank did with the city came from memos prepared by the city treasurer's office. Rendell's comment to PNC Bank chairman Thomas O'Brien was contained in a note he wrote on August 24, 1995.

The account of the mayor's behavior with photographer Sharon Wohlmuth at a party to celebrate the publication of the book *Sisters* on October 20, 1994, was based primarily on an interview with Wohlmuth. At least five other individuals familiar with the details of the incident were also interviewed. I was present when Wohlmuth's collaborator on *Sisters,* Carol Saline, told a member of the mayor's office that the incident had been kept out of the press because Wohlmuth had refused to talk about it.

I was present on February 28, 1994, when members of the black clergy presented the mayor with a list of written demands. The letter from *Philadelphia Tribune* publisher Robert W. Bogle thanking Cohen for his help in getting additional parking spaces was written on August 16, 1994, and personally viewed.

The recitation of calls made to 911 operators the night Edward Polec died, on November 11, 1994, came from a police transcription of the calls. I was present on November 29, 1994, when Rendell sought endorsement for reelection from various members of the black clergy. I was also present at the press conference on December 21, 1994, in which the winners of the empowerment zones were officially announced by President Clinton.

The comments by focus-group voters about Street were contained in a January 1995 report by the Hickman-Brown polling firm that was personally viewed. Rendell's comment about the public never forgiving him if he resigned as mayor was made in my presence on December 22, 1994.

I was present with McGovern on July 28, 1994, when he rode into Center City. I was also present with Morrison on June 10, 1995, when she returned by commuter train to Queen Village shortly before leaving the city.

Chapter Eighteen: A Prayer for the City

I was present at the meeting between the mayor and officials representing Breyers on August 23, 1995, when it became evident that the parent company, Unilever, was going to close the Breyers manufacturing plant in the city.

The account of the city's efforts to bring Meyer Werft into the shipyard in the fall of 1995 was primarily based on being present at dozens of private discussions and meetings. I was also made privy to hundreds of pages of internal documents, and also benefited from comprehensive coverage in the *Inquirer* by Henry Holcomb. The portrait of Bernard Meyer was drawn from coverage by Holcomb and interviews with several people who met and corresponded with him, including David Cohen, financial advisor Samuel Katz, attorney Peter Hearn, and state representative Bill Keller. The account of Keller's experiences with state officials was based on a three-hour interview with Keller on October 19, 1996. Jim Mangan's account of his final days at the yard was based on an interview on September 29, 1995. Governor Ridge's view of the negotiations was given in an interview on February 12, 1997.

I was present on September 18, 1995, when Cohen spoke to Hale, of the White House, and asked if the president might be willing to call Bernard Meyer. I was not physically present in Cohen's office on September 19, 1995, when Michael Schwarz privately communicated to the mayor and Cohen that Meyer was withdrawing the project, but the mayor positioned me outside the door so that I could listen to what was being said. The letter that Schwarz delivered to the mayor during the meeting was personally viewed. I accompanied Cohen to his house on September 20, 1995, when he packed to go to Germany to see Bernard Meyer. Cohen's subsequent experiences in Germany were related to me in interviews that took place on September 23 and October 2, 1995.

The mayor allowed me to listen in when Cohen called from Germany on September 21 and 22, 1995, with various updates. I was present on September 22, 1995, when Rendell wrote his letter to Bernard Meyer.

Epilogue

I was present for Cohen's last day of work on April 4, 1977. Rendell's quote questioning whether Cohen would leave as chief of staff, as well as predictions the mayor made about his own political future, came from an interview that was conducted on July 24, 1996. Cohen's visit to Miami to see Bernard Meyer at the begining of 1996 was based on memos indicating such a visit. Information on the whereabouts of McGovern, Mangan, and Mazzccua in the spring of 1997 came from interviews with each of them. Information on various new economic-development deals for the city came from press accounts in the *Inquirer* and an interview on April 17, 1997, with William Hankowsky, the president of the Philadelphia Industrial Development Corporation. Census data for the city came from an article in the *Daily News* on March 21, 1997, and one in the *Inquirer* on April 6, 1997. Information on city and state negotiations with Norwegian shipbuilder Kvaerner ASA was primarily based on internal documents that were personally viewed during the spring of 1997.

The report on the future impact of welfare reform was prepared by Public/Private Ventures on March 28, 1997. Statistics on unemployment rates for the city came from that report. Rendell's letter to President Clinton, written on July 23, 1996, was personally viewed. The mayor's plan to help American cities was primarily based on a copy of his urban agenda, which was released on April 15, 1994. Additional ideas came from a letter Rendell wrote to the president on August 8, 1996. Data on the disparity in wages were contained in a speech that was given to the Center for National Policy by Massachusetts senator Edward M. Kennedy on February 8, 1996. The detailed plan for federal tax breaks for Washington, D.C., was spelled out in an article in *The Washington Post* on June 9, 1997.

Selected Bibliography

Adams, Carolyn, David Bartelt, David Elesh, Ira Goldstein, Nancy Kleniewski, and William Yancey. *Philadelphia: Neighborhoods, Division, and Conflict in a Postindustrial City.* Philadelphia: Temple University Press, 1991.

Alotta, Robert I. *Mermaids, Monasteries, Cherokees and Custer.* Chicago: Bonus Books, 1990.

Baltzell, E. Digby. *Philadelphia Gentlemen.* 1958. New Brunswick, N.J.: Transaction Publishers, 1992.

Banfield, Edward C. *The Unheavenly City.* Boston and Toronto: Little, Brown and Company, 1968.

Bartelt, David W. "Housing the Underclass," in *The Underclass Debate,* ed. Michael B. Katz. Princeton: Princeton University Press, 1993. 118–57.

Beers, Paul B. *Pennsylvania Politics Today and Yesterday.* University Park and London: The Pennsylvania State University Press, 1980.

Binzen, Peter. *Whitetown, U.S.A.* New York: Random House, 1970.

Blodget, Lorin, and Edwin T. Freedley. *Philadelphia and Its Industries.* Philadelphia: Gelwicks and Story, 1885.

Bradbury, Katharine L., Anthony Downs, and Kenneth A. Small. *Urban Decline and the Future of American Cities.* Washington, D.C.: The Brookings Institution, 1982.

Chubb, John E., and Terry M. Moe. *Politics, Markets & America's Schools.* Washington, D.C.: The Brookings Institution, 1990.

Clark, Dennis. *The Irish in Philadelphia.* Philadelphia: Temple University Press, 1973.

Contosta, David R. *Suburb in the City.* Columbus: Ohio State University Press, 1992.

Cotter, John L., Daniel G. Roberts, and Michael Parrington. *The Buried Past: An Archaeological History of Philadelphia.* Philadelphia: University of Pennsylvania Press, 1992.

Dale, John Thomas. *What Ben Beverly Saw at the Great Exposition.* Chicago: Centennial Publishing Co., 1876.

Daughen, Joseph R., and Peter Binzen. *The Cop Who Would Be King.* Boston and Toronto: Little, Brown and Company, 1977.

Du Bois, W.E.B. *The Autobiography of W.E.B. Du Bois.* New York: International Publishers, 1968.

———. *The Philadelphia Negro.* 1989. Millwood, N.Y.: Kraus-Thomson Organization Limited, 1973.

———, ed. *The Negro American Family.* Atlanta: Atlanta University Press, 1908.

Freedley, Edwin T. *Philadelphia and Its Manufactures: A Hand-book of the Great Manufactories and Representative Mercantile Houses of Philadelphia, in 1867.* Philadelphia: Edward Young & Co.

Gallery, John Andrew, ed. *Philadelphia Architecture.* Cambridge and London: The MIT Press, 1984.

Gelfand, Mark I. *A Nation of Cities.* New York: Oxford University Press, 1975.

Girouard, Mark. *Cities & People.* New Haven and London: Yale University Press, 1985.

Guinther, John. *The Direction of Cities.* New York: Viking, 1996.

Hall, Peter. *Cities of Tomorrow.* Oxford and Cambridge: Basil Blackwell Ltd., 1988.

Harriss, C. Lowell. *History and Policies of the Home Owners' Loan Corporation.* New York: National Bureau of Economic Research, 1951.

Jackson, Kenneth T. *Crabgrass Frontier.* New York: Oxford University Press, 1987.

Jacobs, Jane. *The Death and Life of Great American Cities.* 1961. New York: Vintage Books, 1992.

———. *The Economy of Cities.* New York: Random House, 1969.

Kaus, Mickey. *The End of Equality.* New York: HarperCollins Publishers, 1992.

Lane, Roger. *Roots of Violence in Black Philadelphia, 1860–1900.* Cambridge and London: Harvard University Press, 1986.

———. *William Dorsey's Philadelphia & Ours.* New York and Oxford: Oxford University Press, 1991.

Lemann, Nicholas. *The Promised Land.* New York: Knopf, 1991.

Looney, Robert F. *Old Philadelphia in Early Photographs, 1839–1914.* New York: Dover Publications, 1976.

McCabe, James D. *The Illustrated History of the Centennial Exhibition.* Philadelphia: National Publishing Co., 1975.

MacFarlane, John J. *Manufacturing in Philadelphia, 1683–1912.* Philadelphia: Philadelphia Commercial Museum, 1912.

Madden, Janice Fanning, and William J. Stull. *Work, Wages and Poverty.* Philadelphia: University of Pennsylvania Press, 1991.

Manufactories and Manufacturers of Pennsylvania of the Nineteenth Century. Philadelphia: Galaxy Publishing Company, 1875.

Massey, Douglas S., and Nancy A. Denton. *American Apartheid.* Cambridge and London: Harvard University Press, 1993.

Miller, Fredric M., Morris J. Vogel, and Allen F. Davis. *Still Philadelphia.* Philadelphia: Temple University Press, 1983.

Mollenkopf, John H. *The Contested City.* Princeton: Princeton University Press, 1983.

Mumford, Lewis. *The City in History.* San Diego and New York: Harcourt Brace Jovanovich, 1961.

———. *The Culture of Cities.* 1938. Orlando: Harcourt Brace Jovanovich, 1970.

Murray, Charles. *Losing Ground.* 1984. New York: HarperCollins Publishers, 1994.

Osborne, David, and Ted Gaebler. *Reinventing Government.* Reading, Mass.: Addison-Wesley Publishing Company, Inc., 1992.

Philadelphia and Its Environs. Philadelphia: J. B. Lippincott and Co., 1876.

Resnik, Henry S. *Turning on the System.* New York: Pantheon Books, 1970.

Rifkin, Jeremy. *The End of Work.* 1995. New York: G. P. Putnam's Sons, 1996.

Rusk, David. *Cities Without Suburbs.* Baltimore: Johns Hopkins University Press, 1993.

Scranton, Philip, and Walter Licht. *Worksights: Industrial Philadelphia, 1890–1950.* Philadelphia: Temple University Press, 1986.

Seder, Jean. *Voices of Kensington.* McLean, Va.: EPM Publications, 1990.

Silcox, Harry. *A Place to Live and Work.* University Park: Pennsylvania State University Press, 1994.

Smith, Billy G. *The "Lower" Sort: Philadelphia's Laboring People, 1750–1800.* Ithaca, N.Y.: Cornell University Press, 1990.

———, ed. *Life in Early Philadelphia.* University Park: Pennsylvania State University Press, 1995.

Teaford, Jon C. *City and Suburb.* Baltimore and London: The Johns Hopkins University Press, 1979.

———. *The Rough Road to Renaissance.* Baltimore and London: The Johns Hopkins University Press, 1990.

United States National Advisory Commission on Civil Disorders. *Report of the National Advisory Commission on Civil Disorders.* New York: Bantam Books, 1968.

United States Congressional Senate Subcommittee on Reorganization and International Organizations of the Committee on Government Operations. *Hearing on a Bill to Provide for the Establishment of a Commission on Metropolitan Problems and to Provide for the Establishment of a Department of Urbiculture.* 86th Cong., 1st Sess., S 1431, S 2397. Washington: GPO, 1959.

United States House Subcommittee of the Committee on Government Operations. *Hearings on a Bill to Establish a Department of Urban Affairs and Housing and for Other Purposes.* 87th Cong., 1st Sess., HR 6433. Washington: GPO, 1961.

Wainwright, Nicholas B., ed. *Diary of Sidney George Fisher, 1834–1871.* Philadelphia: Historical Society of Pennsylvania, 1967.

Warner, Sam Bass, Jr. *The Private City.* 1968. Philadelphia: University of Pennsylvania Press, 1975.

———. *The Urban Wilderness.* New York: Harper and Row, 1972.

Weber, Max. *The City.* New York: Macmillan Publishing Co., 1958.

Weigley, Russell F., ed. *Philadelphia: A 300-Year History.* New York and London: W. W. Norton & Company, 1982.

What Is the Centennial? And How to See It. Philadelphia: Press of Thomas S. Dando, 1876.

White, Lucia, and Morton White. *The Intellectual Versus the City.* New York: New American Library, 1962.

Wilson, William Julius. *The Declining Significance of Race.* Chicago: The University of Chicago Press, 1980.

Workshop of the World. Wallingford, Pa.: The Oliver Evans Press, 1990.

WPA Guide to Philadelphia. Philadelphia: University of Pennsylvania Press, 1988. Reprint of *Philadelphia: A Guide to the Nation's Birthplace,* 1937.

Zulker, William Allen. *John Wanamaker.* Wayne, Pa.: Eaglecrest Press, 1993.

Photo Captions

Title Page: Panorama of the city, with Girard College in center, taken from a building in North Philadelphia.

Prologue: Ed Rendell at the Liberty Medal ceremonies with recipient Shimon Peres.

Chapter One: The lights of Boathouse Row.

Chapter Two: David Cohen in his office.

Chapter Three: Jim Mangan and his family, taken outside their home.

Chapter Four: Abandoned factory in the neighborhood of Kensington.

Chapter Five: Mike McGovern in a City Hall courtroom.

Chapter Six: Walnut Street taken from Rittenhouse Square.

Chapter Seven: City Hall.

Chapter Eight: Ed Rendell announcing candidacy for reelection in 1995.

Chapter Nine: Linda Morrison with Independence Hall in background.

Chapter Ten: Southwark Plaza public housing project at night.

Chapter Eleven: Man walking across empty lot in North Philadelphia with mural of former NBA basketball great Julius Erving in background.

Chapter Twelve: Fifi Mazzccua and the four great-grandchildren who live with her, before Sunday church.

Chapter Thirteen: View of the city along Girard Avenue. The hanging of sneakers is a Philadelphia tradition.

Chapter Fourteen: Jim Mangan flanked by mothballed ships at the navy yard.

Chapter Fifteen: Homeless person on Sansom Street in Center City.

Chapter Sixteen: Tony Mazzccua at Graterford Prison.

Chapter Seventeen: Ed Rendell in his office.

Chapter Eighteen: Empty dry dock at navy yard.

Epilogue: Ed Rendell at his second inauguration, flanked by City Council President John Street.

Index

About the Author

BUZZ BISSINGER spent five and a half years writing this book, during which time he had exclusive access to Mayor Ed Rendell's administration. From 1981 to 1988 he was a reporter at *The Philadelphia Inquirer,* where he won a Pulitzer Prize for investigative reporting, and later the *Chicago Tribune.* He was a Nieman Fellow at Harvard University in 1985–86 and is a contributing editor to *Vanity Fair.* He is the author of the acclaimed bestseller *Friday Night Lights.*

About the Type

This book was set in Times Roman, designed by Stanley Morison specifically for *The Times* of London. The typeface was introduced in the newspaper in 1932. Times Roman had its greatest success in the United States as a book and commercial typeface, rather than one used in newspapers.